MILTON STUDIES
# VII

# MILTON STUDIES
*James D. Simmonds, Editor*

# MILTON STUDIES VII

## *"Eyes Fast Fixt"*

### Current Perspectives in Milton Methodology

*Albert C. Labriola*

*Michael Lieb*

**Guest Editors**

UNIVERSITY OF PITTSBURGH PRESS

# MILTON STUDIES

is published annually by the University of Pittsburgh Press as a forum for Milton scholarship and criticism. Articles submitted for publication may be biographical; they may interpret some aspect of Milton's writings; or they may define literary, intellectual, or historical contexts—by studying the work of his contemporaries, the traditions which affected his thought and art, contemporary political and religious movements, his influence on other writers, or the history of critical response to his work.

Manuscripts should be upwards of 3,000 words in length and should conform to the *MLA Style Sheet*. They will be returned only if sufficient postage is enclosed (overseas contributors enclose international reply coupons). Manuscripts and editorial correspondence should be addressed to James D. Simmonds, Department of English, University of Pittsburgh, Pittsburgh, Pa. 15260.

*Milton Studies* does not review books.

Within the United States, *Milton Studies* may be ordered from the University of Pittsburgh Press, Pittsburgh, Pa. 15260.

Overseas orders should be addressed to Feffer and Simons, Inc., 100 Park Avenue, New York, N.Y. 10017, U.S.A.

Library of Congress Catalog Card Number 69-12335

ISBN 0-8229-3174-5 (Volume I) (out of print)

ISBN 0-8229-3194-x (Volume II)

ISBN 0-8229-3218-0 (Volume III)

ISBN 0-8229-3244-x (Volume IV)

ISBN 0-8229-3272-5 (Volume V)

ISBN 0-8229-3288-1 (Volume VI)

ISBN 0-8229-3305-5 (Volume VII)

US ISSN 0076-8820

Copyright © 1975, University of Pittsburgh Press

Feffer and Simons, Inc., London

Manufactured in the United States of America

# CONTENTS

vi                          *Contents*

# PREFACE

A COLLECTION OF original essays on the poetry of John Milton, this volume brings together the work of American, Canadian, and European scholars whose contributions represent a tribute not only to Milton as a writer but to the variety of approaches that his writings have elicited. As such, the volume performs a dual function: it offers commentary on a wide spectrum of Milton's writings, and it embodies within that commentary some of the more significant methodological perspectives that characterize the current field of Milton scholarship.

From the first point of view, the essays range in their concerns from the elegies, the Nativity poem, the twin poems, and the Ludlow masque to the three major poems. Within this range of concerns, greatest attention is accorded *Paradise Lost*, which becomes a focal point of critical exegesis. At the same time, in its coverage of Milton's other writings, the collection attempts to maintain that sense of balance appropriate to a volume as interested in diversity as it is in uniformity.

From the second point of view, the collection has a singularly important aim. Unifying all the essays that compose the volume, that aim is to suggest what directions critical methodology is currently taking in the study of Milton's works. In this sense, the volume is as much a model of critical approaches as it is a collection of essays on various subjects bearing upon Milton. Within this larger context, each essay is important not only in its own right but in what it says about the nature of Milton scholarship.

In an era of intense scholarly activity on all fronts, this volume provides an opportunity for Milton scholarship to take stock of what it is up to. Precisely what Milton scholarship is up to, as the present collection attempts to suggest, is what criticism itself has always been up to: if the volume embodies current perspectives in Milton methodology, those perspectives are the prevailing ones with which criticism has been universally concerned. Thus, the volume should assume an importance not only for Milton studies but for criticism in general. Why such is the case will become clear in the following exposition of the volume's plan and of how the essays in the collection accord with it.

The plan of the volume is to make available in one collection the kinds of approaches that Milton's writings have elicited in recent years. Each essay is designed to embody one of those approaches. Accordingly, the essays range in their methodological concerns from thematic and dramaturgical to mythic and iconographical. This spectrum of concerns manifests the various perspectives that constitute the volume as a whole. Theme, dramaturgy, affect, style, psychobiography, genre, concept, typology, myth, iconography: these form the bases of the various approaches embodied in the respective essays. Every essay thereby establishes a way of seeing unique to the perspective it embodies but complementary to the perspectives it shares with the essays that surround it. If a particular essay embodies the typological approach, for example, it may well be expected to address itself to the same theological concerns to which an essay embodying the mythical or iconographical approach addresses itself. Or, if a particular essay embodies a thematic approach, it may well be expected to address itself to the same structural concerns to which an essay embodying the affective or stylistic approach addresses itself. In this way, essays maintain their identity according to the perspective they embody while concurrently suggesting their relationships with corresponding approaches.

We offer the foregoing examples, of course, from the vantage point of what actually happens in the present collection. In so doing, we wish to suggest that the classifications we have assigned to these essays are not meant to be exclusionary. They simply provide a way of coming to terms with what may be called the prevailing outlook of each essay. They do not exclude complementary perspectives to which that outlook may directly or indirectly give rise. As a result, a particular essay may (and should) invite additional classifications that call to mind not only the perspectives that constitute this volume but those with which the volume does not profess immediate concern. In this sense, the scope of the volume is both self-contained and open-ended. It embraces perspectives that it feels are of utmost importance to Milton scholarship and suggests others that it assumes are also of importance but cannot be included because of the limitations of space.

From that point of view, the volume offers a viable means of becoming acquainted with some of the more significant aspects of Milton methodology. Precisely what that "methodology" is may be found in the methodological overview that Dr. Steadman's essay provides. We suggest here only some of its larger ramifications in conjunction with our prefatory comments on the volume as a whole.

As part of the balance that is so crucial to the volume, the essays largely make use of two methodologies, fundamental not only to Milton criticism but to criticism in general. Those methodologies may be classified as textural and historical, the one characterized by what Dr. Steadman calls "internal evidence," the other by what he calls "external evidence"; the first deriving its proof from "patterns" intrinsic to the text, the second from "relationships" extrinsic to the text. Commonplace, the distinction hardly needs elaboration here. We call attention to it only to suggest its appropriateness to Milton studies, if for no other reason than that it is one upon which Milton himself expatiates in his *Logic*. There, he distinguishes between arguments that are either "artificial" or "inartificial," the first supported by what is "innate" to it (*"insitum"*), the second by what is "external" to it (*"assumptum"*).[1] Pervading his entire stance as logician, this outlook culminates in his chapter on "Method" (Bk. II, chap. 17), an implicit celebration of method *"in omni vita."*[2] Such an outlook would go far to corroborate Dr. Steadman's observation that Milton was the product of an age "preoccupied with methodology." In one sense, this volume is a fitting tribute to that methodology.

Introduced by Dr. Steadman's methodological overview, the collection is represented by five essays that employ textural methodology and five that employ historical methodology, although there are, to be sure, elements of both methodologies in each of the ten essays.

These methodologies, in turn, assume the various perspectives that compose the volume as a whole. Preparing for such perspectives in his methodological overview, Dr. Steadman lays the groundwork for what is to come. His essay is important not only for the focus it provides in its discourse on methodology but because of the scrutiny it encourages us to engage in concerning the entire question of methodology. Dealing with "the limitations as well as the capabilities of methodology in literary studies," Dr. Steadman is after "the skeptical methodologist," one who is not guilty of an overreliance on methodology but who is capable of determining how applicable a methodology

is to the subject he is treating. It is from this point of view, Dr. Steadman suggests, that we should read the essays that follow.

Opening with a discourse on the various approaches available
to the critic, Professor Rajan reinforces that point of view by demon-
strating how well Milton's works lend themselves to a thematic perspective. Within this context, Professor Rajan explores Milton's use
of parody or "parodic structures" as a thematic device that allows
us to appreciate the "connective life" of his works. Understanding
that, we can see how the use of "parodic structures" becomes "part
of an education in the nature of vision." Precisely that kind of education,
in turn, may be said to underlie Professor Grose's dramaturgical analysis
of *Samson Agonistes*. Examining Milton's dramatic techniques in the
portrayal of character, Professor Grose demonstrates the way in which
the process of discovery transforms not only Samson (particularly in
his relationship with the Chorus) but the reader (particularly in his
understanding of that relationship).

If Professor Rajan's emphasis is thematic and Professor Grose's
dramaturgical, Professor Fish's is affective. Like Professors Rajan and
Grose, Professor Fish is interested in the advantages of "an education
in the nature of vision." From the perspective of the reader's response
to Milton's poetry, the kind of vision to which Professor Fish addresses
himself emerges from an analysis of *L'Allegro* and *Il Penseroso*. Paying
close attention to what goes on in the text of both poems, he paradoxically establishes what might be called an antitextural approach, one
that advises us to "turn our attention from the text to the experience
it gives," that is, to "the nature of the activities" that the text requires
of its readers. In contrast to Professor Fish, Dr. Häublein "returns"
to the text (specifically, *Paradise Lost*) to perform a detailed, even
methodical, analysis of Milton's stylistic and paraphrastic techniques
in Book VII. With its use of charts, numerical tabulations, and painstaking exegeses of a few, select passages, the essay becomes a model
of at least one kind of textural analysis.

In its own way, Professor Shawcross' essay is likewise a model
of a certain kind of textural analysis, that which explores "the psychodynamic propensities" of figurative and allusive discourse. Ranging
over those works that have a bearing upon Milton's relationship with
Diodati, Professor Shawcross engages in a form of textural exegesis
that is certain to indoctrinate us all into what "an education in the

nature of vision" truly signifies. The essay thereby challenges us to reevaluate our understanding of both poetic language and the personality that emerges from that language. As the fifth grouped under the heading of textural methodology, Professor Shawcross' essay has an extrinsic interest as well, since its concern is not only with matters of text but with matters of fact. Although the thrust of the essay is textural, its significance is biographical. Its import is therefore transitional: it leads us into the following five essays that fall under the heading of historical methodology. Professor Rollinson's essay is the first in that group because it consciously employs the historical method in order to illuminate a subject that has direct ties with textural concerns. In this sense, it too is of obvious extrinsic interest as a transitional essay. Although its thrust is historical, its significance is generic. From this perspective, it relates Milton's Nativity poem to the tradition of the "literary hymn" in antiquity and in Renaissance Europe, thereby establishing the connection between the "literary" and the "liturgical" hymn.

Establishing that connection, Professor Rollinson's essay anticipates the concerns of Professor Chambers' essay. In his exploration of Milton's handling of "religious time" in *Paradise Regained*, Professor Chambers distinguishes between Christian time (*kairos*) and liturgical time (*chronos*). As such, his essay embodies a conceptual approach that manifests itself both schematically and historically in order to illuminate the theme, action, and structure of *Paradise Regained*. The essay is therefore significant not only for what it says but for the way in which it recalls the other essays in the volume. If that is the case, its equally significant concern with typology anticipates Professor Rosenblatt's essay, which establishes a typological milieu for the figure of Moses in *Paradise Lost*, first by attending to the Hebraic or Platonic tradition surrounding Moses and then by exploring the Christian tradition that views Moses as a type of Christ. Doing so illuminates not only the Mosaic traditions that Milton inherited but the application of those traditions in *Paradise Lost*.

Drawing upon the foregoing perspectives, the last two essays that fall under the heading of historical methodology establish a mythic and an iconographic perspective respectively. In his essay on the mythic implications of the Genesis prohibition not to eat of the forbidden fruit, Professor Lieb is concerned first to demonstrate the Renaissance association of that prohibition with the taboo and second to suggest the cultic ramifications of this association in religious thought. In that way, he attempts to provide a historical basis for understanding the function of the prohibition in *Paradise Lost*. That historical outlook is similarly reflected in Professor Labriola's essay, which brings to bear upon the imagery of Milton's epic the wealth of iconographic representation generated by the Middle Ages and the Renaissance. In doing so, it offers a panoramic view of the landscape of *Paradise Lost*, made possible by the perspective it establishes.

Such, in brief, are the plan and layout of the present volume, which seeks to offer a coherent account of the "current perspectives in Milton methodology" as a tribute both to Milton and to the variety of approaches his writings have inspired.

A. C. L. and M. L.
November 18, 1974


### NOTES

1. See, in particular, chapters 2 and 32–33 of the first book, in *The Works of John Milton*, ed. Frank Allen Patterson, 18 vols. in 21 (New York, 1931–38), vol. XI, pp. 27, 279-93.

2. Ibid., vol. XI, p. 471.

MILTON STUDIES
# VII

# THE EPIC AS PSEUDOMORPH: METHODOLOGY IN MILTON STUDIES

## *John M. Steadman*

The range and variety of contemporary critical approaches to Milton's poetry are a healthy corrective to the simplistic readings and stereotyped interpretations that often result from a strictly unilateral approach and too narrow or too rigid a methodology. Although each of these approaches must necessarily be limited by the kind of evidence it can evaluate and organize with authority and probability, they complement one another and thus facilitate a multifaceted, comprehensive vision of Milton's major epic and its total meaning—even though the total meaning is accessible to none of these methods individually and necessarily achieves its fullest expression in and through the poem itself. Inherent in most of these approaches, moreover, is an inevitable (and ultimately unresolvable) tension between subjective and objective factors— between the demand for solid, demonstrable evidence and the pressures of the aesthetic imperative. Overemphasizing the former may desiccate aesthetic experience; overstressing the latter may do violence to the original meaning and value-content of the poem. For such substitute creations ("pseudomorphs") the historical method, in its various forms (history of genres, history of ideas, history of verbal and visual imagery, etc.), may be a useful corrective. It cannot guarantee absolute accuracy, however; and it must function as a complement, not as a substitute, for aesthetic intuition.

THE ESSAYS in this volume center on problems of method in Milton scholarship and criticism. Written by diverse hands and differing in orientation and approach, they significantly complement one another. In their range and variety they are not only a tribute to the complexity of Milton's poetry—in its matter, form, and expression, in its fusion of classical, biblical, and Renaissance traditions, and in its innovations in all three—but also a reflection of the critical preoccupations of our own time. By examining the same poetic object under the various lights of a critical spectrum comprehending literary and intellectual history, iconography and mythography, psychology and anthropology, one may hope to detect shades and structures of meaning that might otherwise pass unnoticed.[1]

That such a collection should center on Milton is poetic justice. He was keenly aware of problems of method as schoolmaster and theologian, as logician and rhetorician, and as historian and poet. Milton lived in a century preoccupied with methodology. In one form or another—poetry or logic, mathematics or ethics, natural history or the arts of discourse—the desire for a valid and infallible method seems to have been a ruling passion of the age, a chronic obsession like the search for the Northwest Passage, a key to the Apocalypse, or the recovery of the philosophers' stone.

In a sense the seventeenth-century preoccupation with method is still with us, though we are likely to direct our methodologies less toward the isolation of clear and distinct ideas or the discovery of universal laws than to the recognition of ambiguities. For the play of shadows is a potential object of knowledge, no less than is the play of light. Philology, like theology, possesses its *via negativa,* where unknowing may itself become a mode of cognition.

Like other tertiary industries, Milton scholarship has been accused of inflationary spirals, the consequences of overproduction and under-capitalization. I shall not discuss these charges except to point out that it is, after all, a cooperative enterprise; its producers are usually its principal consumers. Since the days of Masson, it has exhibited few signs of becoming a monopoly. Moreover, as in the case of the Cyprus mines, modern techniques have succeeded in extracting highly marketable ores from what had hitherto seemed a long-exhausted vein. We need not apologize, therefore, for the Milton "industry," even though its profits and delights may belong rather to the Horatian than to the Keynesian scale of values.

Even its sternest critics have never accused it of *under*production, however. To do justice to a single year's work in Milton studies would be difficult, and to compress a half-century's research into a single chapter would be embarrassing. The renascence of seventeenth-century studies (or should we call it a "baroque revival"?) within the last quarter-century has given a fresh stimulus to Milton scholarship, accelerating and diversifying its development. Specialized researches on apparently tangential topics—emblem literature, devotional treatises, metaphysical verse, dictionaries and reference manuals, the reformation of prose style—have illuminated Milton's art and thought. Along with more general studies of the intellectual and political background of his age, they have helped to place his work in a more exact, though also more complex, perspective. The combination of conventional and experimental techniques, old and new methods of analysis, has enriched Milton scholarship with a more variegated critical vocabulary and more flexible methodological assumptions, rephrasing old and unsolved problems and formulating new ones. We are not only increasingly aware of the internal complexity of his major work— its ambiguities and paradoxes, its intellectual and artistic tensions, and its suggestion (at times) of deeper and unresolved spiritual conflicts. We are also aware that no single methodology can cope adequately with them. A unilateral approach can yield only a partial view.[2] From a fixed angle of vision we can observe an object steadily, but we cannot see it whole.

Hence, instead of essaying a comprehensive survey of Milton criticism, I shall devote the greater part of this paper to a more general problem: the limitations as well as the capabilities of methodology in literary studies. What kind of knowledge can we legitimately hope to achieve through a particular critical approach, and what modes of experience lie beyond its special competence? What types of insight are within its focal range or beyond its field of vision? Is a certain technique likely to aid or obstruct our understanding of Milton's poetry? I do not expect to answer these questions, or even to explore them exhaustively. This is not a "Critique of Pure (or Practical) Methodology" or even a Prolegomenon. It is merely a preliminary and tentative reconnaissance before, in the end, we return to *Paradise Lost*.

In discussing methods of interpretation, moreover, I shall not consider bibliography or (in the narrower sense) philology. Let us assume that the text has already been established (though this is indeed a major assumption!) and that the reader is already familiar with the literal sense of the author's vocabulary, including proper names. What remains is the problem of exploring the meaning of the poem in all its complexity: the internal relationships between theme and structure, character and fable, thought and language, image and idea; the external relationships to sources and models and to literary and intellectual tradition; and finally, the complex relations temporarily linking poet, poem, and reader—a *catena aurea* between the value structures of discrete but momentarily interlocking worlds.

## I

To begin with, we should not overestimate the potentialities of any critical technique. Literary interpretation is not an exact science. It is really an art of divination like haruspicy or necromancy—dissecting a work and examining its entrails in order to verify not the future but the past; cross-examining the reluctant ghosts of the ancients and extorting answers to questions they had rarely dreamed of raising. No critical method can be an infallible guide, nor can any secondary technique of interpretation acquire the immediacy and conviction of primary insight. It is equally useful and equally authoritative, perhaps; but its authority and functions belong to a different order of truth and a different level of evidence.

Still less should we place implicit faith in its scope, its relevance, or its certitude. We should accept its aid as we would accept the hospitality of Circe or Procrustes—constantly bearing in mind the likelihood of betrayal. Since no literary methodology possesses apodictic certainty, since no technique of interpretation is universally valid, there is little point in extolling certain methods as orthodox and condemning others as heretical, defining fallacies and heterodoxies as though one were a logician or a grand inquisitor.

A recognition of the limits of methodology is no less essential for the literary scholar than for the natural scientist. Just as Boyle praised the "skeptical chemist" for his doubts about the pretensions of alchemy, we may applaud the misgivings of the philological Pyrrhonist—the critic who distrusts an overreliance on discipline no less than a neglect of discipline; the scholar who is equally skeptical of the extremes of subjective and objective judgment, the vagueness of impressionistic criticism and the rigidity of formal method.

Between the attitudes of the skeptical methodologist (as we shall call him) and the credulous reader there would appear to be a world of difference, but in actuality the disparity is less striking than it seems. In different contexts the same reader can (and should) display radically divergent attitudes toward the same work: critical doubt no less than poetic faith, a conscious suspension of belief as well as a willing suspension of disbelief. To a precritical experience of the poem that is largely personal, subjective, and synthetic, he must add a critical reexamination that is (as far as possible) impersonal, objective, and analytic. Aesthetic experience (sometimes ignored by the professional scholar) and painstaking analysis (often neglected by the dilettante) must complement each other, serving as mutual checks against idiosyncrasies of personality on the one hand and those of method on the other. By weighing his immediate personal reactions against the results of dispassionate analysis, by comparing his own impressions with those of other readers, and by examining the underlying assumptions of several critical techniques, including his own, the reader-critic-scholar (if he is lucky) may arrive at a comprehensive and balanced view of the poem as a whole—a view that is not only faithful to his immediate "intuition" of the work but also capable of rational and objective proof.

For a responsible view must surely take account of both extremes, however difficult this may seem to be. A generation ago, critics would probably have expressed this difficulty in terms of a tension between affective and cognitive values. A generation still earlier would possibly have visualized it as a conflict between the opposed authorities of reason and emotion, the rival certitudes of logic and imagination. A popular music-drama, for instance, dramatizes precisely such a conflict through a dialogue between a judge with a juridical respect for objective evidence and an Arcadian shepherd as firmly committed to the subjective testimony of emotion:

LORD CH[ANCELLOR]. Now, sir, what excuse have you to offer for having disobeyed an order of the Court of Chancery?

STREPH[ON]. My Lord, I know no Courts of Chancery; I go by Nature's Acts of Parliament. The bees—the breeze—the seas—the rooks—the brooks—the gales—the fountains and the mountains cry, "You love this maiden—take her, we command you!" 'Tis writ in heaven by the bright barbèd dart that leaps forth into lurid light from each grim thundercloud. The very rain pours forth her sad and sodden sympathy! When chorused Nature bids me take my love, shall I reply, "Nay, but a certain Chancellor forbids it"? Sir, you are England's Lord High Chancellor, but are you Chancellor of birds and trees, King of the winds and Prince of thunderclouds?

LORD CH. No. It's a nice point. I don't know that I ever met it before. But my difficulty is that at present there's no evidence before the Court that chorused Nature has interested herself in the matter.

STREPH. No evidence! You have my word for it. I tell you that she bade me take my love.

LORD CH.  Ah! but, my good sir, you mustn't tell us what she told you—it's not evidence. Now an affidavit from a thunderstorm, or a few words on oath from a heavy shower, would meet with all the attention they deserve.

STREPH.  And have you the heart to apply the prosaic rules of evidence to a case which bubbles over with poetical emotion?

LORD CH.  Distinctly. I have always kept my duty strictly before my eyes, and it is to that fact that I owe my advancement to my present distinguished position.[3]

It is unfortunate that Strephon did not possess the legal and literary tact to plead his case before some medieval Court of Nature instead of a Victorian court of chancery. Nevertheless, the terms of the conflict, as he presents them, are real; and perhaps they may dramatize the problem of the literary methodologist, who must achieve a working compromise between the subjective claims of Strephon's "poetical emotion" and the objective authority of the Chancellor's "rules of evidence." Neither disputant is entirely in the right, and the balanced view that we require of our skeptical methodologist should comprehend the testimony of both.

Methodology alone cannot assure certainty or even probability. Tactlessly applied, it can become a parody of scholarship, resulting in a reading that is virtually a caricature of the original. In his pursuit of a novel or revolutionary interpretation, the scholar's learning and mental agility may actually work against him. Imagination runs away with the evidence, and invention outsoars judgment. In the analysis of Renaissance poetry such critical distortions are especially hard to avoid. Few authors of the period were indifferent to the rhetoric of obscurity. Most of them found as keen delight in turns on words or plays on meaning as in the mordents, turns, and trills of a court musician. Almost any trope—whether metaphor, allegory, irony, or the like—involves a conscious or unconscious distortion of meaning, an artificial discrepancy between word and thing or between literal and referential sense. In the interpretation of figurative discourse, the modern scholar, like many a Renaissance reader, possesses a virtually inexhaustible field for exercising his own imagination, correlating and classifying images in order to discover new patterns of meaning, inverting ironic and literal statement, sporting with allegories and types. Almost every symbol is potentially polysemous; rarely confined to a single referent, it may accommodate as many meanings and levels of meaning as the point of a scholastic needle, trampled by Dionysian hierarchies. Add to these the Renaissance poet's delight in paronomasia and other forms of word play, his obsession with enigmas and hieroglyphs, his belief in cosmic correspondences, and the semantic possibilities of even the simplest poem will apparently approach infinity.

To exercise responsible control, to strike a judicious balance between internal and external evidence, the scholar has to rely, in the long run, not on methodology alone or on aesthetic intuition simply, but on a combination of the two. In many instances (one suspects) his own personal judgment is the deciding factor—his sense that a method which has worked admirably elsewhere is not really pertinent for this particular poet or this particular poem, his uneasy conviction that a plausibly argued interpretation nevertheless seems to "go against the grain" of the text. In such cases the real grounds of his decision are subjective experience rather than objective analysis, relative rather than absolute criteria of judgment, and empirical rather than logical proofs. Though he may seem to be impartial in weighing his evidence, we may suspect the covert pressure of the miller's thumb.

No scholar can entirely escape his own subjectivity, and it is far from desirable that he should. Though he may aim at objectivity, a completely objective view of a poem is as unattainable as the Kantian thing-in-itself. At best he can essay a kind of intersubjectivity; and this (one assumes) is why he subscribes to learned journals in his field. At its best, literary scholarship can be neither strictly personal nor rigidly impersonal, but loosely interpersonal. Far from being fixed and static, the meaning and values of a poem may vary for the poet himself in different moods and even at different stages of composition. Rhetorical colors, gaudy as they often are, may acquire different tones and shadings under different light. The text of an epic or drama has, in fact, something of the quality of a fresco in a badly lit church, visited at various hours of the day by tourists of unreliable vision— near-sighted or far-sighted or astigmatic—yet occasionally gifted with twenty-twenty vision.

The critic's method may become, at times, essentially a form of rhetoric, a technique of delivery rather than discovery. It may seem less a method of interpretation than a method of rendering a particular interpretation plausible and convincing to other scholars, and perhaps to the critic himself. In such cases the interpretation precedes the application of method; the scholar's methodology serves primarily to substantiate and validate a prior and more or less intuitive insight, an insight that may turn out to be merely a chimera.

Though close attention to the text and an equally scrupulous regard for historical context may curb a few of the excesses of critical imagination, they cannot in themselves assure a valid and reliable interpretation. Literary scholarship is not, on the whole, a scientific discipline; and perhaps we may thank the illogical gods that it is not. Unlike the physical sciences, it possesses neither the accuracy of mathematical demonstrations nor the precision of controlled laboratory experiments. Its philological and historical approaches are not, for the most part, a legacy of the "new science" (though it was once fashionable to insist on their scientific and inductive character). Instead they derive, in large part, from the techniques of Renaissance humanism. We are the residual heirs, the decadent descendants, not of Bacon and Galileo but of Sturmius and Vittorino da Feltre.

Although the historical method has sometimes been regarded as a panacea for all kinds of procedural errors and fallacies, it cannot guarantee certainty, and its effectiveness is often curtailed by the very diversity of its materials. Reduced to its essentials, it amounts to little more than the demand that a given work be interpreted in the light of its historical context—that the scholar's interpretation be consistent with what he has ascertained about the intellectual and literary background of the author and his age. This is a sensible precaution, but hardly a very abstruse principle, and it leaves just as much room for scholarly aberrations as for insights. The methods of Homeric criticism or the techniques of Shakespearean research will not be equally effective for the interpretation of Milton; the historical methods we apply to Kalmuck heroic poetry and to French neoclassical epic will be as different as the presuppositions an art historian will bring to the interpretation of a Melanesian mask and a sculpture by Pigalle. The effectiveness of the historical method is relative to particular cultures and (even more narrowly) to particular works. Its validity is contingent and conditional, and it may easily be misapplied.

Moreover, the historical approach is not so much a single, clearly definable methodology as a variety of methods—an assortment as heterogeneous as the contents of Pandora's box. It can (and often does) comprehend numerology and iconography as well as biography; literary history and art history as well as the history of ideas; the rhetoric and poetics of a period as well as its ethics and politics. Historical methodology may comprise elements so diverse as lexicography and natural science, epistemology and scriptural commentary, biblical typology and pagan myth, Ramist logic and Hermetic magic, humanistic pedagogy and gnostic abecedemancy. The validity of the critic's interpretation depends not on the absolute superiority of one method to another, but on the relevance of his chosen technique to a specific passage in a specific poem, its relation to a certain author in a given society at a particular moment. The crucial problem is not so much the application of the method as the determination of its genuine applicability. And this, in many cases, may lie well beyond the scope of the methodologist.

As the problems of interpretation may vary widely with different genres and periods, it is difficult to make categorical statements about the validity of any particular methodology. An effective method must be tailored to the individual poem. For the same reason, it is unwise to place a discussion of methodology on too abstract a level. Attempts to base it on epistemological or aesthetic theory, on ontological questions like "the mode of existence of a work of art," or on particular psychological schools rarely do justice to all types of poetry. They tend at times to become rigid and monolithic. It is not without reason, for instance, that critics have sometimes objected to a literary methodology closely based on Crocean aesthetics as misleading. In the opinion of one Italian scholar, the Crocean method of interpretation tends to distort rather than clarify the sense of a work like the *Commedia*. Shattering the unity of the poem or diverting attention from unity to multiplicity, it favors (he suggests) a fragmentary, "estheticizing" mode of reading which relies entirely on taste and is weak in historical and philological understanding.[4]

In some instances a combination of methods may prove fruitful, whereas a unilateral approach may lead to distortion. In other cases a successful technique of interpretation may result in absurdity if pressed too zealously or too far. A method appropriate to one period or genre may produce ludicrous results when applied to another. The same techniques of interpretation are not always applicable to different authors of the same period or even to various works by the same writer. As the value of a particular method varies with the nature of the work, a technique that illuminates one poem may darken another. Literary scholarship possesses no single and universally applicable methodology, equally valid for all authors and genres and uniformly guaranteeing infallible results. In so uncertain, so various, and so indefinable a discipline as ours, there is little point in singling out a few methods as orthodox and excoriating the rest as heretical—anathematizing the "personal heresy" and condemning a catalogue of fallacies: autobiographical, affective, intentional. In certain contexts even these allegedly "fallacious" approaches may yield valuable insights into a particular work. The attempt to distinguish categorically between "valid" and "invalid" methods sometimes results in dogmatism, fostering an exaggerated reliance on certain techniques and an implicit faith in their universal applicability. At best, their value is relative and limited; and by ignoring their limitations, we obscure their actual field of competence. Such attempts to discriminate categorically between literary orthodoxy and heresy rest (it would appear) on the tacit but erroneous assumption that literary scholarship can be an exact science —that its principles are inevitably and universally effective, applicable to all sorts and conditions of poetry, just as the rules of logic are applicable to all kinds of propositions, or the laws of nature to all sorts and conditions of men.

## II

The abuses of methodology are more dangerous than its neglect. By slighting method, the scholar merely runs the usual risks of impressionistic criticism—the agreeable peril of taking his own subjective reading of the work as the definitive interpretation, seeing only the one "Sordello"—but Sordello and *his* Sordello. Yet at least this sort of impressionism is honest; it does not masquerade as literary science. It does not pretend to be more than the reflection of an individual and personal view, and it is content with merely relative and tentative authority. If wrong, it is unpretentiously wrong; it does not compound its errors of misinterpretation by grounding them on sophistical proofs.

An error in methodology, on the other hand, may be more insidious, inasmuch as it pretends to objectivity and impersonality. A simple misreading of the text—overreading a metaphor or underreading an allegory; detecting ambiguities where none were intended or missing a subtle pun; mistaking undercutting for open assertion and straight assertion for irony—this kind of mistake does less harm than a misinterpretation deceptively grounded on an irrelevant or unreliable method, on an exaggerated dependence upon one technique at the expense of others, or on the failure to realize the limits as well as the capabilities of the particular approach one is following. To err by the book, to court madness by method, is to be systematically wrong. The rationalization of error, in the long run, does far more harm than a naive blunder or an unsophisticated mistake.

Like the neglect of method, an overreliance on methodology may radically transform the very work it professes to interpret, superimposing formal patterns or patterns of meaning never intended by the author on a content projected by the critic himself. The poem or painting then becomes (as recent critics have justly observed) a sort of glorified Rorschach card.[5]

In some cases, differences in critical procedures and terminology may result in the application of anachronistic categories of genre and style or the intrusion of poetic and rhetorical standards alien to the poet's age. In such instances the form and texture of the original work may be obscured by secondary patterns projected by the twentieth-century critic. In other cases the formal design may remain fairly intact, but its conceptual and emotional content, the inherent patterns of meanings and the intrinsic hierarchies of ideas, may be radically altered. A love lyric may be transformed into a discourse on alchemy or a meditation on the beatific vision; conversely, an allegorical poem on these subjects may be mistaken for a simple serenade. A saga of gory freebootery and heroic rapine may be rationalized into a lecture on physics or moralized as a psychological struggle between reason and passion or nature and grace. By a sort of critical atavism the process of literary development may be reversed, and the genres turned back toward their social and psychological origins. History may be reconverted into myth, and epithalamion into *hieros gamos*. Comedy and tragedy and tragicomedy may be reabsorbed into rituals of sacrifice and atonement and regeneration. The epic itself may become a metrical cryptogram, a riddle to be deciphered by mythical and allegorical codes or by mathematical analysis.

Even though the poem may retain its form more or less intact, its meaning has been profoundly altered. Even though patterns of incident, verbal patterns, and patterns of imagery may remain superficially unaltered, their reference and significance have been changed. Particular images, episodes, and personages have been enriched or impoverished, complicated or simplified, through the addition or loss of secondary meanings. The original intellectual content has quietly vanished, and a new pattern of meaning has taken its place. Even though the outer form remains largely unaffected, the matter and argument have changed. The poet's meaning and intent have been displaced by those of the commentator. The critic's analysis has become a kind of vicarious poesis; the scholar's exegesis has resulted in a substitute creation. Like the cuckoo, the scholiast has quietly deposited his wind-eggs in the skylark's nest. When these mature, acquiring the distinctive plumage and cries of their own species, they may indeed outsing and outsoar their rivals. Small wonder that we unskilled ornithologists should sometimes confuse the critic's fledglings with the poet's own brood, mistaking the "wandering voice" of the commentator for the bard's authentic song.

### III

This technique of semantic displacement may be better illustrated, however, by an image drawn not from ornithology but from geology. Pseudomorphs (we are reliably informed) are crystals that retain only the "external form of the mineral of which they originally consisted." Inside, they possess the "internal structure and composition of the mineral that has replaced it." Some are formed by the substitution of one mineral for another, like galena for pyromorphite. Some are produced by gradual changes in composition through the addition or loss of some particular ingredient. Some result from a process of incrustation and infiltration. Whatever "crystalline substance happens to fill the hollow left in a geological layer by [the] crystals that have disintegrated" will be "forced by the mold to take on a crystal form not [properly] its own." Without chemical analysis the pseudomorph may easily "mislead the observer into taking it for a crystal of the original kind."[6]

Berchorius, as we know, discovered moral allegories in the natural history of Bartholomew the Englishman. Perhaps this extract from mineralogical lore—allegorically interpreted—may serve equally well as an exemplum for exegetes or a fable for critics. For literary scholarship has been at times astonishingly rich in pseudomorphs. Crystalline structures of undeniable beauty and value, they occur with greatest frequency in broken or inverted strata, usually in association with chronological displacement and methodological anachronisms. Most of the varieties of geological pseudomorphosis, moreover, can be paralleled in literary interpretation. Having effectively infiltrated the text, by gradual seepage or by more violent forms of intrusion, the exegete quietly displaces its original material, altering texture and substance and substituting his own intention for the author's intent. Into a work whose primary significance has been lost through historical change or obscured by the incrustations of glossators, he inserts a new and alien core of meaning. Leaving the external form of the epic or drama intact but infusing a different conceptual content, he replaces the poet's invention by his own device.

This metaphor, drawn from mineralogy, has served the cultural historian so well that it would be unfair to deny it to the literary historian. Spengler appropriated it to describe the hybridized and syncretic culture and architecture of late classical antiquity. In the basilica he perceived not only the characteristic "architectural type" of "the Late Classical 'Pseudomorphosis'" but also an "inversion of the Classical temple." "It employs the means of the Classical," he suggested, "to express the opposite thereof, and is unable to free itself from these means." Or again, in the words of a later historian of the period, "disintegrating Greek thought is the older crystal of the simile, Eastern thought the new substance forced into its mold."[7]

In literature, as in social history, pseudomorphism can mediate between different cultures or epochs, interpreting the patterns and motifs of one society in terms of the values and ideas of another culture, superimposing new and vital secondary meanings on the obsolescent forms and conventions of an earlier literature. It was, in fact, largely through a process of pseudomorphosis—a substitution of inner content and meaning—that many of the principal writers of antiquity were rendered doctrinally acceptable to the Middle Ages and morally intelligible to the Renaissance. The reinterpretation of classical poetry in terms of natural history, moral philosophy, or Christian theology resulted in inner semantic changes just as fundamental as the geological process of incrustation and infiltration. Overladen by commentaries and permeated by allegorical readings, classical poetry acquired meanings unintended by its authors and unsuspected by its original audience. Moralized—and in some instances Christianized—the classical forms served as the medium of radically different values, the vehicle of a very different social and intellectual content. The hermeneutical techniques whereby Virgil and Ovid were adapted to the needs of medieval and Renaissance society were scarcely less striking than the iconographical errors of identity that led to the veneration of a pagan comedian as a Christian saint and the confusion of Marcus Aurelius with the Emperor Constantine.

The Renaissance Homer and Virgil were (it would seem) pseudomorphs. That *Paradise Lost,* in turn, should suffer a similar fate is hardly surprising. No methodology can enable us to see a poem precisely as its author intended it, and in the course of three hundred years of critical interpretation—neoclassical, romantic, Victorian, and modern—Milton's epic has undergone a series of chemical changes. Fortunately, it is an exceptionally large crystal, capable of resisting a complete transmutation. Moreover, the critical infiltrations and scholarly substitutions have tended to displace one another.

If the inadequacies of our own methodology cause us dismay, it is heartening to reflect that the real *Paradise Lost*—Milton's *Paradise Lost*—was itself a pseudomorph. It was, in a sense, an "inversion" of the classical epic, just as Spengler's late classical pseudomorph was an "inversion of the Classical" temple. And perhaps it too employs "the means of the Classical to express the opposite thereof."[8] Indeed, the history of the European literary epic appears to have been, in large part, a continuing pseudomorphosis, a reiterated adaptation of traditional forms and styles to the cultural demands of a new age or a different society. In some cases the poem becomes a true pseudomorph: the older form persists with only minor variations, while the content is radically altered. In other instances, there is metamorphosis as well: hybridization of formal traditions, experiments with epic structure, greater variety in external form, and a more notable continuity in subject matter. Yet even these imperfect pseudomorphs usually reflect a genuine awareness of operating within an inherited genre and a conscious effort to accommodate its formal conventions to the ethical, political, or religious values of the poet's own society.

We have overworked our metaphor, and perhaps (as Lewis Carroll suggested) we should pay it extra for overtime. At this point we shall leave it, with only a final glance at its implicit distinction between matter and form. In theory, if not always in practice, Renaissance methods of poetic composition are sometimes significantly different from our own. Though we should not permit our own methodology to be dominated by their theories (which frequently relied all too heavily on misunderstood classical sources, and in practice often tended to become authoritarian and inflexible), we can hardly afford to ignore them. In seeking a valid method of interpretation, we must surely take into account the Renaissance poet's own views on the nature of poetry and its methods of composition.

IV

In contrast to romantic theories of organic form, critics of the late sixteenth and early seventeenth centuries usually stressed the classical distinction between form and matter and the principle of ideal imitation. Distinguishing the formal, final, and material causes of a genre, they urged the heroic poet to select an argument capable of receiving the perfect idea of an epic and to exhibit in the protagonist himself the perfect norms of heroic virtue. Inasmuch as the plot was the form or "soul" of the poem, it was through the disposition of incidents that the poet was to impose the ideal form of epic or tragedy upon his unformed subject matter. The delineation of heroic character was partly contingent, therefore, on the requirements of the fable. Even when the plot itself centered on an act of *proairesis*, the poet must accommodate this act of moral decision to the demands of narrative or dramatic structure, the imperatives of epic or tragic form. Other structures—patterns of imagery and idea, metrical and prosodic patterns, syntactical and stylistic patterns, symbolic forms—were normally regarded as secondary: extrinsic ornament or symbolic superstructures to the primary structure of the narrative itself. They were the textures and colors, the skin and garments, superimposed on the skeletal structure and musculature of the plot.

The poet's method was thus conceived (theoretically) in terms of the imposition of an ideal and determinate form on a variable and indeterminate subject matter. The act of composition was rather like minting a coin in gold or copper or silver. The pattern stamped by the die gave the work its essential form, its generic identity as heroic poem. Yet its value would be partly contingent on its material. According to the nature of its content, the epic would be divine or secular, heroic or counterheroic, gold or bronze or lead.

Despite its inadequacies by twentieth-century standards, this theory of composition, oversimplified and overrationalized as it was, constituted an essential part of the historical background of *Paradise Lost;* and as such it is important for the contemporary scholar as a frame of reference for interpreting both the formal craftsmanship of the poem and its intellectual content. It is not surprising, therefore, that recent scholarship has frequently approached Milton's epic from one or both of these angles, exploring its relationship to both literary and intellectual history, to the epic tradition on the one hand and the history of ideas on the other. As we shall not, unfortunately, be able to examine these approaches in detail or to discuss the contributions of individual scholars and critics, we shall note only a few of the problems that these angles of approach may present to the methodologist.

V

Interpreting a work in its historical context is not precisely the same thing as writing literary history. As the literary relationships they involve are not altogether the same, the questions they raise must sometimes be formulated in rather different ways. The critic who attempts to examine the relationship of *Paradise Lost* to the epic tradition must attempt to see the tradition not as it appears to a twentieth-century scholar but as it appeared to men of the seventeenth century. He must approach the earlier heroic poets and epic theorists, as far as possible, through the eyes of Milton's contemporaries, bearing in mind the diversity of Renaissance interpretations of classical writers and the major divergences between seventeenth-century and twentieth-century interpretations of their works. From a methodological standpoint this approach possesses inevitable limitations: the variety of the epic tradition; the inconsistency of critical opinion on major as well as minor points; the fragmentary nature of Milton's own remarks on the epic; his stated preference (in at least one instance) for the actual practice of the ancient poets as a better rule and guide than abstract theory; his tendency on several occasions to subvert the rules of art, deliberately undercutting or inverting the conventions of rhetoric and poetic.

Nevertheless, despite its limitations, this approach may serve as a corrective to errors in interpretation. Closer attention to the critical theory and practice of Milton's own age might have prevented several recent misinterpretations based on a confusion between the logical and poetic senses of "argument," a misconstruction of the real "subject" of the poem, and a tendency to blur the distinction between history and fiction. Tactfully applied, without exaggerating its capabilities, this approach might cast further light on the function of the heroic image in Milton's epic, on the primary significance of plot for the disposition of the poem, and on the interrelationship among character, passion, and thought in structuring the fable. It might clarify to some extent the controversial problem of the correlation of style with subject matter and of imagery with concept. Finally, it might leave a clearer recognition of the poet's conscious artistry in ordering his material in accordance with his own ideals of epic form, in investing his characters with consistency and verisimilitude, and in feigning "probable"— if not "necessary"—circumstances to conduct his action, plausibly and justly, to its foreseen end.

Like literary history, the history of ideas may easily become an end in itself, and legitimately so. As an instrument of Milton criticism, however, it must be clearly reoriented toward the function of a particular idea in a particular context in a particular poem. Just as the study of form will center upon the pattern of incidents and the motives behind them, the study of the poem's intellectual content will focus on the pattern of ideas. It will take into account the relationship between formal and conceptual patterns, the junction or disjunction of narrative and doctrinal designs, the correlation of plot and purpose, image and idea. Finally, over and beyond these intrinsic patterns, it will examine the external relationships of this doctrinal content to the poet's intellectual background, analyzing his exploitation of traditional themes and his conscious innovations on tradition.

This approach would be less necessary if we possessed a fuller knowledge of the seventeenth-century background—if we were psychologically attuned to its modes of thought and feeling, if we shared its outlook and education, if we were fully aware of the varieties of meaning and the diversity of connotations inherent in an apparently simple "idea." Preferably the writer ought to be able to speak for himself, without the obsequious intervention of a commentator to paraphrase his words, explain what he really meant, and alternately flatter and discredit him. For a seventeenth-century audience, fit though few, the mediation of the scholiast would probably have seemed obtrusive. For the twentieth-century reader, on the other hand, it is a regrettable necessity. Thrusting our own values and ideas on the poet, imposing our own interpretations on the poem, projecting our own sensibilities and attitudes into seventeenth-century verse, we may experience difficulty in isolating a particular concept and preserving its original meaning and intention. We may likewise fail to recognize a seventeenth-century commonplace as a commonplace until it has been pointed out to us.

This is the primary justification for the vast corpus of scholarly researches on Milton's intellectual background, for detailed comparisons between the doctrinal content of his epic and that of his prose treatises, for invoking the aid of the whole encyclopedia of arts and sciences (ethics and theology, biblical commentary and metaphysics, natural history and political theory) and a variety of pseudosciences as well.

The history-of-ideas approach is also significant for the reexamination of Milton's rhetorical exploitation of the commonplaces of invention, the use or abuse of logic and rhetoric by his characters, the probable and "logical" unfolding of the plot, and the conscious juxtaposition of correlative or antithetical concepts in the structure of his epic. We are all familiar with the vital importance of certain ideas or clusters of ideas for the dramatic action, as well as the doctrinal content, of *Paradise Lost:* nature and grace, justice and mercy, force and fraud; obedience and disobedience, innocence and guilt; hierarchy and the scale of being, order and disorder, creation and destruction, corruption and regeneration; heroic virtue and brutishness, felicity and the highest good, the loss and restoration of the divine image, the fortunate fall. Without recognizing these and many other concepts explicit or implicit in Milton's epic, without perceiving their identity as clear and distinct ideas, and without following their complex interplay and relationships throughout the work, we shall not only miss much of the dialectical element in *Paradise Lost;* we shall obscure the formal outlines of the plot. Similarly, if we overlook the *topos* of Adam's fall in Renaissance meditations on the misery and dignity of the *condition humaine,* we may miss one of the essential factors in Milton's choice of argument—its implications for self-knowledge.

All the same, this approach possesses several inevitable drawbacks. With a few notable exceptions (such as the *De Doctrina Christiana, The Doctrine and Discipline of Divorce,* etc.), Milton's prose works rarely provide a systematic and comprehensive statement of personal doctrine and belief. He employs ethical arguments, but evolves no ethical system. He writes treatises on important political and ecclesiastical issues, but no exhaustive survey of the art of government. He alludes to scientific and metaphysical doctrines, but composes no books on natural history or on metaphysics. And, of course, we would hardly expect him to; his education, like his major interests and professional competence, was essentially literary and humanistic.

For a systematic exposition of these and many other provinces of seventeenth-century learning, the scholar must go outside Milton's own writings and seek elucidation from other authors. The accidental result, unfortunately, is to encourage an exaggerated and hypothetical estimate of Milton's reading. Though we can identify many of the authors whose works he knew in part, the greater part of his reading remains hidden from us. We can only guess at its nature and extent, as we reconstruct the image of Hercules from a marble foot. Taking our awareness of Milton's colossal erudition as our point of departure, we are compelled to gloss his text with allusions to a wide scattering of authors, without positive evidence that he knew them. (As most of us who have tried it are aware, source-hunting is a wasteful and expensive sport. Like other inaccurate marksmen, the source hunter must disperse his shot in the hope of winging an unexpected analogue.)

Even in his own works, moreover, Milton's presentation of his ideas was often strongly molded by literary context; and we risk distorting his views if we attempt to detach them from their original matrix, or to treat them consistently as actual beliefs. Sometimes they are little more than convenient arguments or literary conventions. In his prose treatises he employed the rhetorical techniques he had mastered at school and university, utilizing the method of composition through commonplaces, selecting the arguments and *topoi* most convenient for constructing a probable and plausible case. In his poetry, his deployment of ideas was relative not only to the character, situation, and rhetorical tactics of his dramatic persons, but also to the shifting boundaries between truth and fiction conventional in epic poetry and in Renaissance theories of composition. Even in the case of a historical subject, the epic poet was licensed to expand and reorganize his material through the addition of fictional details and episodes. Frequently these were his own inventions; sometimes they were borrowings from one or more other poets. (No reader, of course, would literally interpret the etiological myth concerning the constellation Libra as astronomical or cosmological doctrine.) There is ample room for doubt as to how far he believed in the Ptolemaic cosmos, so conveniently adapted to an epic of moral and cosmic order; and we may likewise question his belief in other scientific or pseudoscientific doctrines that occur in his poetry. In his verse as in his prose, his ideas have often been altered by their context (or by purely literary factors such as requirements of genre, imitation of classical models, rhetorical intent); and in attempting to elucidate them through comparison, we may actually be comparing variables rather than constants.

Although analysis of formal structure and analysis of intellectual content are merely two of many contemporary approaches to *Paradise Lost*, they may indicate the necessary interdependence of methodologies. Both approaches are inevitably complementary, for the objects of their study are linked. In analyzing Milton's epic against the background of the history of ideas, the scholar must also consider the impact of Renaissance critical theory and the influence of classical or contemporary models. He cannot adequately interpret the intellectual content of the poem without also considering the demands of epic form, nor can he study its formal characteristics without taking into account its doctrinal and historical subject matter. Formal and material causes have been reciprocally influenced and mutually conditioned; and a responsible interpretation of the poem must accord equal emphasis to both. An awareness of their interrelationship is as essential for the twentieth-century scholar as for the seventeenth-century poet.

An attempt to place problems of form and content in Milton's poetry firmly within a Renaissance intellectual and aesthetic context is, however, merely a useful expedient rather than an imperative. If carried to extremes, it may, in fact, sacrifice the interests of the twentieth-century reader to those of his seventeenth-century ancestors, overstressing the links between artist and artifact and underemphasizing the more vital bonds between epic and audience. It is more dangerous to remove the poem from the intuitive experience of the reader than to detach it from the intentionality of its author. By neglecting the author's cultural milieu, we may distort its meaning; by neglecting our own milieu, we may destroy its vitality. Several of the most valuable contributions to recent Milton criticism have centered, accordingly, on the intentional relationships between reader and poem, on neosymbolist conceptions of form as content and structure itself as meaning. Though at times their methods tend to overshadow the poem itself, they are important not only for their insights into Milton's works, but also for their positive contributions to aesthetic theory. Drawing heavily on Cassirer's theory of symbolic form but synthesizing recent developments in a variety of disciplines (anthropology and depth psychology, iconology and linguistics, phenomenology and gestalt theory), they are, in large part, unrecognized prolegomena to a new theory of aesthetic cognition, a tentative (and still unsystematized) epistemology of art. At the same time, the range of the historical method has been extended by approaching Milton's oeuvre from angles that have elucidated the poetry and prose of his near-contemporaries —neo-Aristotelian poetics, Ciceronian and anti-Ciceronian rhetoric, Ramist logic, Ripa's iconology and Conti's mythography, emblem literature, Hermetic correspondences, relationships between literal and allegorical levels or between *verba* and *res*, and the principles of neo-classical and baroque art. Like Bacon's rhetoric, Milton scholarship has added reason to imagination, seeking a judicious compromise between the historical approach and modern critical methods. Its diversity and its occasional inconsistency are the inevitable consequence of the critical endeavor to see *Paradise Lost* simultaneously in its original literary milieu and in our own time, to view it both as a seventeenth-century artifact and as a twentieth-century experience, to consider its relation to its present as well as its original audience, to be honest both to the poet's intent and to the reader's response. Confronted by the alternative dangers of historicism and psychologism, Milton criticism cannot be more or less than a continuous dialogue between the poet's art and the reader's projection. We should regard it as little more than a tentative treaty between author and audience, constantly renegotiating the claims and redefining the rights and responsibilities of each. It is a study (never perfectly achieved) of the "subjective" correlative as well as a redefinition of the "correlative object."[9]

One must not overlook the historical context of Milton's poetry— its relation to literary history, the history of ideas, the history of critical theory, the history of art, social, political, and ecclesiastical history, or the history of his own life and development of his art and thought; but one cannot afford to confuse the provinces of history and immediate experience. One must interpret his poem in the light of history rather than on the basis of history or in historical terms. A work of fiction cannot be satisfactorily explained by a methodology based on fact, or a work of the imagination entirely comprehended by reason. Though literary scholarship may legitimately aspire, albeit with difficulty, to quasi-scientific objectivity and universal validity, literary experience must inevitably remain subjective, relative, and personal—valid (in the last analysis) only for the individual observer. The inalienable characteristic of much seventeenth-century poetry was that it was addressed to the individual imagination, designed to elicit a personal and necessarily subjective emotional response. Insofar as it endeavored to instruct, it aspired to universality (or at least to the intersubjectivity of a fit audience, though few), but the doctrinal pattern must, in each case, be an individual discovery; and instruction was by no means the only end or function of poetry. In reading a seventeenth-century work, a man of our century can and should attempt to achieve a certain intersubjectivity with a seventeenth-century audience, but he cannot detach himself altogether from the values and attitudes of his own society without doing violence to his own sensibility and (indirectly) to the efficacy of the poem. It would be less than an amusing paradox if the reader's quest for the "historical Milton" were to result in greater understanding of *Paradise Lost* as a document of intellectual or literary history but in diminished personal or social relevance, and diluted emotional value, for ourselves.

## VI

A completely satisfactory interpretation of *Paradise Lost* must seem, accordingly, to be a constantly receding goal, and Milton scholarship itself a sort of infinite regress. Like the style, form, and content of the poet's epic, the scholar's techniques of interpretation are necessarily interrelated and complementary. If he is to employ any one of these approaches accurately, he must be conscious of precisely what it can and cannot do, and of how far and in what ways it should dovetail with other methods. With a clear recognition of the limitations of his method, the reader may approach the poem, perhaps, in the spirit of a seventeenth-century bowler—conscious of a bias and pursuing direction by indirection. Without such awareness, confident of no limitations on a direct approach, he may find himself engaged in a characteristically Gilbertian game of billiards, playing on "a cloth untrue with a twisted cue / And elliptical billiard balls."

No methodology will quite reach the core of Milton's epic, and a single method single-mindedly followed may go very far awry. His poem will always promise ambiguities defying the ingenuity of Oedipus or the Sphinx, archetypal patterns above the myths of Olympus and neo-Platonic forms, and depths well beyond the diving range of the Freudian "psychobathysphere."

Having led our skeptical methodologist to the edge of an abyss whose depths no methodology is likely to measure, we may safely abandon him there, at the precipitous brink of the poem. Midway between an "O altitudo" and a "vast abrupt" he will encounter (one feels) little danger, not even Geryon in the shape of another critic. His method, sagaciously followed, will keep him securely on the well-trodden periphery of *Paradise Lost*. It will not encourage him to pursue Milton's "adventurous song" into the unreasonable altitudes of Shelley's "intense inane," but it will scarcely tempt him to risk his neck in exploring the poem's hidden depths. It will permit him to follow (with critical caution) a level and occasionally thorny path, without experiencing the normal symptoms of altitude sickness. Without dizziness or cardiac murmurs, without nausea or shortness of breath, he will be as safe on the brink of critical uncertainty as on the lecture platform of his own classroom. At a respectful distance he will admire and applaud the hermeneutic feats of more intrepid researchers—explorers who may never uncover the author's full intent but may, in consequence, have discovered themselves.

If there is a heroism of the mind (as Milton believed), it is to be achieved, surely, not through consistent caution, but through occasional risk.

The Henry E. Huntington Library

## NOTES

Portions of this study were presented orally on December 28, 1971, in a conference on "Methods of Interpretation" (English Section I) under the chairmanship of Professor William A. Ringler, Jr., at the annual meeting of the Modern Language Association of America. I am grateful to Professor Ringler for his kind invitation to participate in the conference and to my friends and colleagues at the Huntington Library—Professors Hallett Smith, John Loftis, Alice Scoufos, Paul Zall, D. D. Hale, James Riddell, Mrs. Winifred Freese, and Miss Mary Isabel Fry—for helpful criticism of the original version of this paper.

1. Among recent studies of methodology in Milton scholarship, see George A. Gullette, "Methodology in Milton's Source Studies" (dissertation, University of Michigan, 1945); idem, "Some Inadequacies of Method in the Study of Milton's Sources," *Papers of the Michigan Academy*, XXXII (1945), 447–56; James Holly Hanford and James G. Taaffe, *A Milton Handbook*, 5th ed. (New York, 1970), pp. 288–93; Douglas Bush, *Paradise Lost in Our Time: Some Comments* (Ithaca, 1945); Douglas Bush, "The Critical Significance of Biographical Evidence; John Milton," *English Institute Essays, 1946* (New York, 1947), pp. 5–19; A. J. A. Waldock, *Paradise Lost and Its Critics* (Cambridge, Eng., 1947); Robert M. Adams, *Ikon: John Milton and the Modern Critics* (Ithaca, 1955); James E. Thorpe, Jr., ed., *Milton Criticism: Selections from Four Centuries* (New York, 1950); John Milton, *Complete Poems and Major Prose*, ed. Merritt Y. Hughes (New York, 1957). For the critical problems arising from the relationship of Milton's epic to its audience and from the difference between the expectations of

the seventeenth-century and the twentieth-century reader, see Stanley E. Fish, *Surprised by Sin: The Reader in Paradise Lost* (New York, 1967); Balachandra Rajan, *Paradise Lost and the Seventeenth-Century Reader* (London, 1947); Michael Lieb, *"Paradise Lost* and the Twentieth Century Reader," *Cithara*, IX (1969), 27–42; Lawrence W. Hyman, "Milton's Samson and the Modern Reader," *CE*, XXVIII (1966), 39–43.

2. For a valuable critique of bibliographical methods and of attempts to treat textual analysis as a positivistic and "scientific" discipline, see James Thorpe, *Principles of Textual Criticism* (San Marino, Calif., 1972), especially pp. 3–49. Among recent studies of methodology in literary studies, see E. D. Hirsch, Jr., *Validity in Interpretation* (New Haven, 1967). See also Natalino Sapegno's discussion of methodology in the foreword to his edition of Dante's *Commedia* (Florence, 1967), vol. I, pp. vii–x. Implicitly censuring the Crocean approach to problems of literary criticism, Sapegno maintains that the editor or expositor of the *Divine Comedy* "should not neglect any of those cultural references which would help the reader to take into account the complex historical and cultural matter that the poet's imagination has reworked in new and original ways. His consent to the writer's great art and humanity is not satisfied by an impressionistic and dilettante admiration, but finds its justification in a real and full understanding of a poetry that derives light and meaning from a peculiar and remote (from us) historical condition." Sapegno entirely renounces "the method of so-called 'esthetic' illustration in use today," which consists in underlining particular beauties and beauties of episode and in distinguishing "poetry" from "nonpoetry." In his opinion, this is a method not for understanding but rather for distorting the sense of a work like the *Commedia*, conceived with so rigorous a conceptual and imaginative unity. Such a method is harmful (he argues) insofar as it "breaks the unity" of the poem or diverts attention from it, favoring a mode of reading that is fragmentary and estheticizing, that relies entirely on taste and that is poor in the historical and philological sense.

3. *Iolanthe; or, The Peer and the Peri*, in *The Plays of Gilbert and Sullivan* (New York, 1941), pp. 214–15.

4. See Sapegno, foreword to Dante's *Commedia*.

5. See E. H. Gombrich, *Art and Illusion*, 2nd ed., rev. (Princeton, 1969), pp. 181–202; Stanley Stewart, "Thomas Wilson's *Christian Dictionary* and the 'Idea' of Marvell's Garden,'" in *New Aspects of Lexicography*, ed. Howard D. Weinbrot (Carbondale and Edwardsville, Ill., 1972), pp. 36–57.

6. *Encyclopaedia Britannica*, 9th ed., s.v. "Geology," "Mineralogy." Cf. Hans Jonas, *The Gnostic Religion*, 2nd ed., rev. (Boston, 1963), pp. 36–37: "If a different crystalline substance happens to fill the hollow left in a geological layer by crystals that have disintegrated, it is forced by the mold to take on a crystal form not its own and without chemical analysis will mislead the observer into taking it for a crystal of the original kind."

7. Oswald Spengler, *The Decline of the West*, trans. Charles Francis Atkinson (New York, 1927), pp. 209–10; Jonas, *Gnostic Religion*, p. 37. Cf. Erwin Panofsky, Father Time," in *Studies in Iconology: Humanistic Themes in the Art of the Renaissance* (New York, 1972), pp. 70–71, for the adaptation of the term *pseudomorphosis* to art history. Through the survival of medieval traditional attributes, Panofsky observes, "certain Renaissance figures became invested with a meaning which, for all their classicizing appearance, had not been present in their classical prototypes."

8. Cf. Spengler, *Decline of the West*, pp. 209–10; Jonas, *Gnostic Religion*, p. 37.

9. Cf. Cedric H. Whitman, *Homer and the Heroic Tradition* (New York, 1965):

It is not always easy to trace the involuted and interwoven meanings—if indeed they should even be called meanings—of ancient poetic symbols. Jungian analysis finds their significance in the "collective unconscious" of humanity, or of a culture, at large; but this is too general for our purpose. We are not in pursuit of a primeval archetype, but of the specific intentions of a specific poem. Our object is not the collective significance of myth, though this may play a part. Our object is Homer's meaning in using such material. (p. 13)

The unity of meaning and form, a truism in modern criticism, is nowhere more pertinent than in the critique of Homer, for whom form, intention, subject matter, diction, and versification were no more separable than the gases of the earth's atmosphere. Today, criticism and philosophy alike have turned toward a new approach, an approach to poetic creativity whole, as if its various aspects belonged together. The tendency is, in fact, to form a descriptive phenomenology of poetic experience which can take account of the interplay of the subjective and objective particulars of reality. (p. viii)

# THE CUNNING RESEMBLANCE

## B. Rajan

This paper seeks to assess the importance of parody as a continuing element in the structure of Milton's poems. It considers first the extended oppositions marshaled around the area of decision in *Comus*. Parodic dispositions play a crucial part in defining these oppositions and in relating them to the central act of choice. The masque form allows a preliminary rehearsal in which the didactic kernel of the oeuvre can be elegantly choreographed. In *Paradise Lost* we see the massive and intricate structural elaboration of the principles expounded in the masque. The structures thus established enclose a human journey. *Paradise Regained* and *Samson Agonistes* are the poems of this journey, with the emphasis, previously distributed more or less equally between the envelopment and the agents, now falling more heavily on the agents. The continuing and prominent presence of parody in Milton's structures and the decisive part it plays in setting those structures in motion indicate that Milton's use of parody amounts to more than a poetic technique or literary strategy. In Milton's work the structure is the issue and parody part of an education in the nature of understanding.

THE STRUCTURAL approach to Milton's poetry has been gaining in importance in recent years. This may be because other approaches have had their turn, but it can also be argued that the manner in which they made use of their turn has enhanced the possibilities of the structural approach so that it becomes what is called for and not merely what remains. Thus, the approach to the poem through the history of ideas has made evident the shaping power of certain key ideas, particularly when they constitute themselves in what can be described as a world picture or world vision. Yet while ideas may be structurally present in a Milton poem, the poem's structure is clearly more than a structure of ideas. At the other extreme, the mythic approach can argue that all works of the imagination issue from certain primary matrices which stand apart from history however much they may be subject to historical adaptation or displacement. Yet to argue this is only to raise the question of the more intricate totalities these primary patterns must enter to achieve the transformation of archetypes into art. Language, and even the interplay between the structures of myth and the structures of language, do not wholly account for the difference between the path of literature and the highway of cliché. The generic approach, sometimes evolved from a mythic foundation, can take us through the history of the form, defining its nature through its usage, up to the point where the inheritance encounters the individual talent. At that point of revolutionary fulfillment, we are asked to witness within the frame of precedent the new life of the unprecedented. Though the unique has its structure, it is a structure we can only discover, not predict; and the generic approach, like others that we have outlined, must find its fulfillment, or at least its complement, in another means of entering the poem. Finally, close criticism, with its felicities of the microscope, its intent examination of the poem's local life, may seem to promise a way away from structures. But in its fastidious attentiveness to details, it can only make us more aware of the manner in which these details are placed and joined, by relationships which are in the end not less than the entire poem in its connective life.

The above paragraph has not been written to suggest that all roads lead to a promised prospect from which the poem can be definitively viewed and therefore forgotten. Milton's poems will maintain our interest by also defeating the structural approach; but since criticism progresses, we can expect to profit from the defeat.

The word "structure" has been freely and perhaps wantonly used, but there is no convenient word which can stand for a poem's togetherness, for what we have earlier characterized as its connective life, and for what might more abstractly be called its principles of cohesion. As we speak of structure in this sense, we do not need to set aside altogether the sense of something constructed; but we also need to think of a world in motion as much as of an edifice, of a field of force as much as of a pattern. We need, in addition, to remain aware of a vital relationship between structure and movement. The poem writes out a pattern. But the pattern, in something like its wholeness, surrounds its own disclosure in the poem from the beginning. We can watch this feat being achieved in the opening lines of *Paradise Lost*, where the strenuously marshaled postponements of the syntax enable the theme to stand forth suspended in its stillness before the predicate launches the sentence into motion. Yet it is only in microcosm that the relationship can be a matter of syntactic maneuvering. On a larger scale it becomes possible not simply because the fable is not new, but because the poet, in his allusive reach, draws upon expectation in drawing upon history. There are consequently frames of understanding which can be invoked before they are expounded and before they are brought into full relationship with the onward movement of the poem's life. Because the poem mounts its own distinctive pattern of cohesiveness upon the familiar patterns which it invokes and absorbs, it is able to maintain surprise while confirming the mind in aftersight and foresight. The individuality of the poem potentiates the communality of the inheritance.

As we consider the principles of cohesion of poems and particularly of major poems by Milton, it becomes apparent that these principles are reflected in more than one structure. Some of the approaches already mentioned encompass prominent structural elements sometimes insisted on by their proponents as necessary or even primary forms of understanding. The attempt to ascertain the poem's character through its disposition of poetic resources can lead to further observations, also significant, on metaphoric structure and on narrative interplay, on the relation of plot to counterplot, and on the relation of the tragic to the providential outcome.[1] A poem as fully designed as *Paradise Lost* also invites reflection upon its spatial form, its dialectical engagement of opposites, and on the relationship of pattern to process not simply in the poem's own becoming, but in the larger world of which that becoming is a mimesis. Other structural manifestations, architectural and numerological, can be expounded.[2] It might simplify the task of understanding slightly if some of these manifestations were shown not to exist, but those that remain are numerous enough and varied enough to testify both to the scale of the problem and to the reconciling range of the poem's integrity. It becomes evident that if we are to be answerable to the poem's identity as well as to its rootedness, we must move our inquiry behind its particular structures to the structure of relationship between those structures, the entire complex of connective life which the poem succeeds in bringing into being.

An undertaking so amply defined cannot be carried forward adequately in a single paper and is perhaps offered less as an ideal than as a means of curbing irrelevance. To adumbrate a poem's principles of cohesion in this way also has a further advantage; it leads to the consequence that these principles are most likely to be found within the poem itself. To say that a poem characterizes itself by crucial relationships which are distinctive to itself is not, one hopes, to say anything remarkable, but the observation apparently brings us to the edge of the formalist peril. We are saved from immersion by the further observation that the poem as a self-sustaining (not to mention self-consuming) artifact evidently sustains considerably more than itself. *Paradise Lost,* Book VII, line 242, has something to offer the literary theorist if we think of the poem as the self-balanced earth. Structures are significant not simply in their unattached elegance but because of their affinity with other structures and with the inescapable concerns and responses which these structures have been able to embody and to vivify. This may be why a poem which puts several structures into movements of relationship seems able to attain and to substantiate a more telling understanding of the nature of meaning and mind.

A large context has been indicated so that a note might be written toward what might be considered in such a context. The purpose of this paper is to consider briefly Milton's uses of parody or, to put it more stridently, the place occupied by parody in his stylizations of understanding. The point is not to examine a strategy in the abstract, but to reach back through its repeated deployments to the recognitions which engendered the strategy. With Milton the structure is the issue, and what the poem is saying is a function of how it coheres.

*Comus* is the first of Milton's poems in which the deployments of parody are prominent. The question of whether *Comus* is a masque is an academic ritual in which the present author has already made his gestures.[3] It will suffice that the relation between masque and anti-masque, the true dance of order versus the false rout of misrule, sets in motion an appropriate context for parody. Moreover, the mythological "hinge" of the poem turns on the possibility of a downward metamorphosis, balanced by the possibility of an upward spiritualization. The poem thus locates itself upon the scale of nature and around man's amphibious position on that scale. This central contrast, which the poem animates by its choice of fable, is linked to a series of extended oppositions—light versus darkness, truth versus error, spirit versus flesh, chastity versus lust, and temperance versus indulgence. These oppositions are not meant to collapse into each other but rather to comment upon each other; their collective presence in the poem means that to cite one of them is to invoke and expand this commentary. Because the parallel formations on either side of the area of decision in the dark wood are extended, the range of involvement at the center is maximized. We also have laid before us in structural terms the ultimate clarity behind that local confusion of which the dark wood is the carefully chosen symbol.

Ontology may be clear, but existence is unclear. Final oppositions can be unmistakable because the difference between their terms is maximized. Human choices involve the sense of loss, the pull of the contrary principle, the plausible cases for mistaken causes. Even in Milton's monumentally choreographed dramas of freedom, the central entanglements are not to be ignored. If the principles of creativeness and destructiveness are elaborated and engaged in the dialectic of contraries, the parodic dispositions within that dialectic suggest resemblances as well as oppositions. Between the contrasting extremes we can expect to see developed a connecting spectrum of discriminations and affinities. In this way the world surrounding the act of choice seems designed not only to extend and frame the anatomy of the act but to endow it with something of the range and permanence of the cosmic patterns it is made to involve.

Despite the occasional criticism of its weightiness, *Comus* is a poem unshaken by the weight of woe. Its contraries are figures in a dance rather than embattled armies. But if we do not exclude from our horizon the poems which are to come, if we look at the work within the shapings of the macrowork, we can see how the parallel ranks of opposition, the disputed center, the repeated marking of the way up and the way down, the enmeshing of consequences in the immediate imperatives of a decision from which one cannot abstain, point to the poems that have yet to be written and initiate structures that have still to achieve their full weight. Comus is not Satan, and his habitat is not a "universe of death" (*PL* II, 622)[4] but the nocturnal side of the natural world. The philosophical ballet in which he is a participant is meant to be danced out rather than struggled through. But the difference from what follows remains one of degree. The confrontations have only to gather their due presence in the imagination for the later poems to spring into life between them.

Within a range of polarization restricted to what the form can reasonably bear, Comus clearly represents the principle of destructiveness. He is the false guide in contrast to the true guide, the Attendant Spirit. The heavenly Trinity is not parodied, and darkness is not congealed into the extremity of darkness visible, but night and day stand in the kind of opposition which the representations of a masque might be expected to strengthen. Comus' first speech puts this to us and, more important, suggests that where he stands may be less important than the direction in which he looks. But Comus' "Tipsy dance, and jollity" (the mutation of *L'Allegro*, 26, is interesting) is not merely a rite honoring Cotytto, touched (115–19) by that delusive elfin music to which Milton also refers in *Paradise Lost* (I, 781–88). Though consecrated to darkness, the dance is also an imitation of that mystical dance of the "starry quire" which Adam invokes and which Raphael suggests as a figure of things celestial (*PL* III, 579–81; V, 175–79, 619–27). Comus is not wholly erroneous in claiming to be "of purer fire" than strict age, sour severity, rigor, and advice. But his is the fire of destructiveness "self-fed and self consum'd," rather than the fire which refines away the dross of earthly things.

"As he our darkness, cannot we his light / Imitate when we please?" is Mammon's twisted query (*PL* II, 269–70). Comus can mock the light with his "Orient liquor in a crystal glass," offering a false dawn and a false transparency. The imagery is renewed in lines 671–72, and the poem provides us with no lack of opportunities for meditating on the difference between fires and on the difference between the dance and the orgy. It is less in these mockeries than in improving on his mother, Circe, that Comus begins to reveal his talents as a parodist. Nothing is changed in the downward degradation except the human countenance, the "express resemblance of the gods" and reason's mintage "charactered in the face" (68–77, 525–29). All else remains as it was, and the imitation of light is intact except for the one vital commitment that dedicates the totality to darkness.

The noise of Comus' revels is heard from afar by the Lady as the "swilled insolence" of "late wassailers." The transformed, boasting themselves "more comely than before," are seen in their reality as "ugly-headed monsters." Comus' "cordial julep . . . with spirits of balm, and fragrant syrups mixed" is described as a liquorish bait "fit to ensnare a brute" (177–78, 75, 694, 671–73, 699). At these points we are adequately advised on how to identify the misrepresentations before us. There are other occasions when understanding is left to the intelligence. Some parodies need vigilance to be discerned as parodies, and in a fallen world they may well seem more plausible than the realities they displace. When Comus appears before the Lady as a false shepherd, a pseudo–Attendant Spirit guiding us down the wrong route, it is appropriate that the Lady should respond with remarks on courtesy in humble places. Uriel will later be similarly deceived by Satan. It is left to Christ to do better when "an aged man in rural weeds" (*PR* I, 314) accosts him in one of those pastoral disguises in which evil finds pleasure in camouflaging itself. The parody should warn us that a greater misrepresentation is in the making; but the cunning resemblance Comus offers is apparently cunning enough to mislead an adequate number of critics.

We have suggested that the confrontations of the masque form, the structure of contrasts into which the form is extended, the intermediate ground of parody between the oppositions, the repeated orientations upward and downward, and the mandatory decision at the center, indicate that the crisis of choice will turn on the confusion between true and false understandings. Is the right response to the abundance of nature the eager exploration of its bounty and the seizing of the day as it offers itself? How are youth and joy to find fulfillment in a creative relationship with the physical world? It is not obvious, though it is finally true, that the answer is in discipline, in the purer fire and the higher music, in a deepening sense of the structure of reality, in the body consecrated as the unpolluted temple of the mind, not denied its nature but equally not abandoned to that nature. When the Lady makes her choice or, more correctly, refuses to be diverted from a choice already made, her rescue by Sabrina (a force of nature as much as a means of grace) and the birth of youth and joy from the unspotted side of Psyche indicate, and not without underlining, the direction in which we are to look for a fulfilling relationship between mind and the physical world. The other path is laid out not only to seem attractive but to appeal to the intelligence when it is insufficiently alert. To those standing at the threshold it is the broad way and the green which seem to promise the flowering of one's capabilities. Yet another lady in the prime of earliest youth will wisely shun it (*Sonnet 9*).

When Comus (681) accuses the Lady of inverting the covenants of her trust with nature, we ought to suspect that the "philosophy" he offers her is merely the result of such an inversion and is to be distinguished from that "divine philosophy" (475) to which the soul is wedded in creativeness. Indeed it might be said that all the acts of choice which unfold before us in the crises of Milton's poetry are basically challenges to resist inversion. Inversion is not always parody, but it is the condition of both parody and negation. It is therefore structurally just that inversion should repeatedly occupy the central positions it holds in Milton's work. When it is surrounded, as in *Comus* and elsewhere, with structures of parody and opposition that both bear upon it and are supported by it, the whole is put together in the way we have learned to expect.

With *Areopagitica* we pass to a different phase of the encounter with error and to a different aspect of the legend of Cupid and Psyche:

Good and evill we know in the field of this World grow up together almost inseparably; and the knowledge of good is so involv'd and interwoven with the knowledge of evill, and in so many cunning resemblances hardly to be discern'd, that those confused seeds which were impos'd on *Psyche* as an incessant labour to cull out, and sort asunder, were not more intermixt. It was from out the rinde of one apple tasted, that the knowledge of good and evill as two twins cleaving together leapt forth into the World. And perhaps this is that doom which *Adam* fell into of knowing good and evill, that is to say of knowing good by evill.[5]

Expounding structures ought not to disqualify the critic from pausing to observe the facts of local life. We can note how the artfully judged deferments of the syntax dramatize the caution with which the rind of that apple is punctured and how the tentative tasting is juxtaposed explosively with the energy with which the two twins leap into the world. The contrast between the single apple and the double result is also nicely deliberate, intensifying the force of "cleaving together." Because the maneuvering of the sentence puts the act before us in the order of its unfolding, we are made almost kinetically aware of the hand on the trigger and the unleashed consequence. There were boundaries from the beginning to Comus' curious tasting (713). Over the paragraph as a whole, we are led from the classical to the Christian and from the type to the truth. Yet the progression is not explicitly put before us. It is there potently, in the drama of the rhetoric.

*Areopagitica* is dominated by images of labor and progress in the reconstituting of truth—the temple built collectively from many timbers, the bringing together of the torn body of Osiris-Orpheus, the separation of the wheat from the tares, and the confused seeds which Psyche must sort asunder. We live in a world dominated by contending and opposite principles, but their shadows mix in a confusion which demands our vigilance in detecting the right outline. Good is known only in its involvement with evil; but our commitment to it can grow in confidence and solidity as the interwoven strands are isolated and disengaged. The thought is partially taken up in *Paradise Lost* (XI, 84–89) and is in the end a reminder that man runs his course between extremities within which he must shape the meaning of his existence. The structures which Milton has been building therefore have a profound justification both in reality and in the doctrinal and exemplary force of its mimesis. We can say without being excessively fanciful that the movement of the poem is the bringing together of the pieces of the torn body. To cull out the seeds, whether in life or in art, is to come to understand and to respond creatively to the dialectic of contraries which underlies the confusions of existence. What the poem through its enactments progressively ·remembers and finally establishes is the homogeneous and proportional body of truth, the unity of being which is its pattern.[6]

The two twins cleave together with intent to deceive. Parody refined into the cunning resemblance is the *modus operandi* of temptation. Yet it is not to be assumed that the darkness imitates the light only when it pleases and always by design. Lost happiness remains a model for lasting hell which simulates in parody the world from which it is cast out. The need for this simulation becomes more evident when we allow ourselves the suggestion that if good and evil were fully independent principles they would express this fact in independent aesthetics. One does not wish to go so far as to imply that a Manichean cosmos is incapable of parody; the point is that when evil is thought of as the ultimate perversion of the good, it follows that the perverting energy will seek to declare itself in parodic utterance. Parody is then not only the natural, but to some extent the compulsive, mode of the demonic; but it is so only given a certain view of the manner in which the demonic came into being. In other words, the Fall is the prior condition of what might be termed necessitated and unilateral parody. In a poem such as *Paradise Lost*, parodic structures are a continuing and powerful reminder of how lasting hell is to be apprehended as the maximum possible distortion of lost happiness.

As we approach the vast design of *Paradise Lost*, we should remain aware that many lesser designs are constellated within it and related dynamically to each other by the planetary wheelings of the poem. To consider parodic structures in such a world is to chart only a single route through that world. The resultant simplifications can be kept under control only to the extent that what we witness is brought back to the poem's intricate integrity. It becomes apparent, not far from the outset, that a theater for parody is being established by a massing of contraries far more systematic than that which surrounds the journey through the dark wood in *Comus*. Moreover, these contraries are displayed in an ontological space which they are instrumental in shaping. Milton's unusual location of Hell, whatever its sanctions, contributes to this spatial disposition, just as his unusual chronology for the celestial cycle creates an alternation between the forces of creativeness and destructiveness that is the counterpart in time of the spatial pattern.[7] The result is a "self-interfering" structure of the kind envisaged by Buckminster Fuller in which form is reinforced by energy and in which cohesion is achieved through tension. Mr. Fuller's celebrated knot is the model of this structure, the point being that the shape of the knot is made clearer and its binding strength increased by the contrary forces that flow through its intertwinings.[8]

As the mobilized contraries confront each other in the poem across the maximum possible distance of alienation, the self-balanced earth between them is apprehended as the middle ground and battle ground, and man himself, poised between his own internal contraries, reflects in his nature both the cosmos that envelops him and the garden he inhabits.[9] The enormous exploratory thrust of Satan's journey (the archetype and parody of every subsequent quest) is an outreaching of destructive energy cutting through the cosmos to its central concern. Attention has been drawn elsewhere to the sedulous building up of pressures that converge relentlessly on the fragile peace of paradise and to the explosion of consequences from the apparently infinitesimal act to the infinite theater which has been made to surround it.[10] The hinge of the poem is man's freedom; but if freedom is the recognition of necessity, we must learn to reach out and to reach back to the limits of awareness before the structures of necessity are known. This is one way of putting it to ourselves that a center of concern is not quite the same thing as a center of significance. The powerful homocentric dispositions of Milton's universe direct our attention effectively to the main area of crisis; but other dispositions are needed to tell us not only what the crisis means but in what context meaning is to be anchored.

It is possible for the critic to write his own poem within the commodious frame of *Paradise Lost* and even to write it in the words of the epic. Our confidence that we are contemplating Milton's design rather than our own inventiveness is increased when we consider the measures Milton took to strengthen that design and the possibilities he excluded in order to achieve it. His chronology and his location of hell have already been mentioned. To these decisions we should now add the carefully built relationships that cause Christ and Satan to emerge as dramatic antagonists, reinforcing the array of antagonisms which the poem is continually in the process of marshaling.[11] The most celebrated of these relationships is that between the heavenly and the infernal Trinity. The risks Milton takes in his presentation of Sin and Death and the highly advanced exercise in black comedy he brings off[12] surely indicate the importance he attaches to the war of contraries and to parody as a means of understanding. The detailed contrasts between the celestial and infernal councils (strengthened by their juxtaposition in the reading sequence) also point strongly in the same direction; but the price paid is a presentation of the heavenly with which readers have always had their difficulties. It would be naive to assume that Milton was unaware of the price. The more prudent hypothesis is that he thought the delineation of the great contentions that shape man's nature and his destiny important enough to warrant the price being paid.

As the massed contraries point to and define the gulf of alienation between them, gestures of simulation can be made, which, far from establishing reconnection, serve only to widen the gulf by their deforming and inverting force. We can think of Pandemonium versus the Creation, the causeway to hell versus the golden chain by which the earth hangs suspended from heaven, the address to the Sun in the fourth book versus the invocation to light in the third, Satan's destructive versus Christ's redemptive journey, the word made flesh versus the antiword made serpent. "Evil be thou my good" (IV, 110), with its development into Book IX, lines 477–79, and the counterprovidence which insistently seeks "out of good still to find means of evil" (I, 165) provide us with the principles of inversion; but once again it is the Sin-Death episode which provides the ghoulish anatomy of these principles. Incest and cannibalism are an advanced statement of the Elder Brother's characterization of evil as "self-fed, and self-consum'd" (596). The intent is to make clear that the difference between good and evil and between the two armies of mobilized oppositions into

which good and evil are constellated is the difference between self-
centeredness and God-centeredness. If we have one development out
of *Comus* we also have the other: the "unpolluted temple of the mind"
(460) has become the temple of "the upright heart and pure" (I, 18).
We should realize from the beginning that the mind cannot be its
own place if it seeks to retain its character as mind.

The distinction between two forms of centeredness has to be
made with force and even with that monstrous force with which Milton
endows the diabolic alternative. As we approach the human condition,
the forces that penetrate that condition will not remain evident in
their ontological purity. Nevertheless, the structures that surround the
central issues, the alienations and the parodic subversions, instruct
us on how those issues are to be apprehended, on how we are to
detect the simulations of a cosmic and pervading intent to deceive.
The relations between true and false, between icon and idol (to use
Professor Steadman's distinction),[13] between metaphoric understanding and parodic misstatement, grow out of the poem's basic structures
and therefore progressively educate us in the application and meaning
of those structures. We need this education not only because the seeds
are confused, but because as we advance in the ironies of understanding,
we must learn to reject the seed that seems likely to flower. The
green way is not the way of growth. We rise by agreeing to fall and
fall by seeking to rise. Satan "unmoved" (II, 429), as he undertakes
his mission, is trapped in "eternal restless change" (*Comus*, 595). Christ,
visibly moved by divine compassion (III, 141), is the constancy and
stillness within the pulsation of things. Identity is not found in the
heroic cry of independence but in the rootedness of creative dependence. Courage in Satan, statesmanship in Beelzebub, loyalty and "firm
concord" in the fallen angels can only be destructive in their consequences if the "express resemblance of the gods" that ought to inform
these qualities is replaced by a contrary commitment. All other parts
may remain as they were, but the student of finalities will not be
confused. Whether the body is the temple or the dungeon of the
soul, whether earth is the shadow of heaven or the circuit of darkness,
whether "virtues" are to achieve or to extinguish their potential, can
be determined only in relation to the center by which the elements
of being are consecrated or defiled. If a cunning resemblance of heroism
is set before us, it is to teach us to disengage the better fortitude.

The distinctions made apply most clearly to the fallen angels,
who have no way to take but that of purification into the final perversity.

When the virtues corroded from within are human virtues, their presence in more than human measures can initially be impressive; but the humanizing also means that the case histories become more potent indications of how we are to act in the uncertain area of our freedom. Reason is but choice, and we are shown how the cumulative consequences of choice take over the indeterminate middle ground of the cosmos, evolving it inexorably toward either cosmic polarity. The two ways stand before us not simply in the didactic teaching of *Comus*, the dialectic of contraries in *Paradise Lost*, the golden chain and the causeway in the spatial architecture of the poem, or the transformations of mazy error and wantonness as we move from innocent to ruined landscapes, but also in Adam and Eve as they simulate in human experience, rather than in cosmic design, the demonic motion of rising in order to fall and the celestial motion of falling in order to rise.[14] Adam and Eve can feel "Divinity within them breeding wings" (IX, 1010), and Adam can compare himself to Jupiter (IX, 1029-41) on another occasion when duty is forgotten. The "glorious trial of exceeding love" (IX, 961) can parody another glorious trial already set before us in the third book. (The link between Book IX, lines 938 ff., and Book III, lines 150 ff., is specific, and it can be argued that Book IX, lines 973-76, mocks the *felix culpa*.) But in the end the storm of passions in the minds of Adam and Eve (IX, 1121 ff.) anticipates the winds that are to be let loose over the earth; the "vain contest" between them (IX, 1189) anticipates the onset of war in the animal kingdom; and the tyranny established within themselves comes to be writ large in the character of history. The end of the downward movement is that embodying and imbruting (*Comus*, 467) which in the tenth book is the symbolic fate of Satan and his followers. We are made witness to the end in its ferocious and ultimate clarity so that we can be made more strongly aware of the meaningfulness of the contrary movement in its minute beginnings: Adam's soliloquy in its studied contrasts to Satan's soliloquy in Book IV, the reharmonizing of his relationship with Eve and the falling in order to rise as the pair, prostrate in "humiliation meek," nevertheless stand repentant in their "lowliest plight" (X, 1099-1104; XI, 1). As Adam progresses from parody to paradigm we too should come to understand the difference between the creative simulation and the destructive resemblance.

The brief allusions made here to the structure of *Paradise Lost* can do no more than hint at their variety and at the degree of their interpenetration. In the remarks made about Milton's use of parody, the effort has not been to provide an inventory of parodic occurrences but rather to suggest the place of parody in the poem's cohesiveness. The point is that parody is not to be regarded as a poetic device, a literary strategy, or even as a notable characteristic of the poem's architecture or dynamics. It is part of an education in the nature of vision.

There is an unfolding momentum in the logic of Milton's oeuvre. In *Comus* we have the didactic kernel, elegantly choreographed. In *Paradise Lost* we have the massive and intricate structural elaboration of the principles expounded in the masque. The structures enclose a human journey. *Paradise Regained* and *Samson Agonistes* are the poems of that journey. Here too we can go back to the beginning, seeing these poems as the fuller exploration of that initial progress through the dark wood.

Milton's final poems are not without patterns of contrast, but it cannot be said that these patterns are insistently proclaimed. The macrowork has reached a point in its development at which the reader can be deemed to be sufficiently educated in structures of understanding already asserted with energy and intricacy. The emphasis, previously distributed more or less equally between the agents and the envelopment, now falls more heavily on the agents. We are concerned with the mind's search for order and, even more important, with its search for the principle of its rootedness, rather than with the presentation of a frame of order within which the movements of relationship and rebellion can be worked out and understood.

To say that *Paradise Regained* is built around a quest for identity is not an entirely felicitous characterization. The image suggested by the phrase is that of a territory progressively occupied by the protagonist's discovery of himself. It might be more satisfactory to suggest that Christ makes himself in attaining himself, that what he is is inseparable from how he acts. The poem is more than a series of retreating refusals, because each retreat helps to define more fastidiously the narrow and inviolable ground of man's being. It is also more than an advance into heroic knowledge, because concurrent with each step in the advance, we witness a preparation for action and the progressive taking on of a destiny.

Barbara Lewalski has shown how the choice in *Paradise Regained* is between true and false roles and how Satan offers to Christ the cunning resemblance of prophet, priest, and king.[15] It is possible to state the terms of misrepresentation in ways that complement Professor Lewalski's. We can argue, for example, that each of Christ's refusals is an affirming of god-centeredness, beginning with the statement that man does not live by bread alone (I, 349–50), dismissing the banquet because of a deeper hunger of which Satan can know nothing (II, 389), declining the kingdoms of the world in the name of sovereignty over the mind, rejecting even the kingdom of the mind in the name of dependence on a higher principle, and, in the final temptation, standing and affirming the nature of full being upon the perilous and creative ground of that dependence. The paradox is that a destiny which takes in the world must be achieved without recourse to the resources of the world; and this can only be done if the true self is defined on another level, or by a different coordinate. The false self takes the raiment for the reality, and for that self destiny depends on amassing the right instruments, on taking opportunity at the flood, and on seizing the day of politics. In its simulations it can offer everything but the one crucial element, the express resemblance of the gods. The true self, in achieving its nature, disengages and progressively affirms the creative power of that element, refusing the opulence in the name of the essence. To dominate the day, one does not seize it. The true self is able to stand and wait, having heard the strict measure in the pace of things (*Sonnet 7*, *Sonnet 16*).

Another way of grasping the principles that shape this duel between the two selves is to make use of A. S. P. Woodhouse's favorite distinction, which seems to apply more directly to *Paradise Regained* than to *Comus*.[16] It can be said that what Christ is doing more and more strongly as the poem proceeds is affirming his citizenship of the world of grace, while Satan's function in the evolving logic is to affirm his imprisonment within the dimensions of nature—an imprisonment not less conclusive because Satan rules over and is therefore able to "offer" the resources of the world in which he is trapped. As we move from the senses (the banquet), to the passions (the traditional kingdoms), and thence to the understanding (Athens), it becomes apparent that the temptation of learning is necessary, almost by consent between the antagonists, as the highest offer the natural world can make. It is here surely that the false likeness is at its closest to the express resemblance of the gods. When Christ rejects Athens he takes the last and most intellectually difficult step in establishing the true ground of man's being. Nothing remains now but to stand upon that ground against the full application of the power he has already refused. Without the higher citizenship, any use of nature is the wrong use and the covenants of our trust are once again being inverted. Through that citizenship, the world of nature, wrenched away into a self-destructive autonomy, is reintegrated into the structure on which its fulfillment depends.

Because, according to theological convention, Christ suffers the temptations in his human nature, the way forward is the way back, the remaking of an identity laid aside. His progress therefore is a paradigm of that journey, individually in life and collectively in history, to the lost paradise, the buried self, the neo-Platonic Ithaca, the remembered image of a higher belonging which it is the effort of man to recognize and restore. In that seeking which is also a making, it is no accident that Eden is "raised" in the "waste wilderness" (I, 7), as the heavens and earth rise out of chaos, and pandemonium rises parodically out of a "dismal situation waste and wild" (*PL* I, 9–10, 710–11, 60).

In *Samson Agonistes* the true and the false are given overall representation in the God of Israel and the God of the Philistines. Dagon, "upward man and downward fish" (*PL* I, 462–63), is reminiscent of Sin, "woman to the waist" and serpent below (II, 650–53). Samson, blind but endowed with "inward eyes" at the end (*SA*, 1687–89), falls in order to rise. The Philistines, blind at noonday, as Samson once saw himself, rise in order to fall. Recognition, reversal, the strong sense of hubris in the catastrophe, and the Chorus' use of the wheel of fortune image (167–69) play their part in strengthening these movements. It is evident that the text Donne set before himself—"Therefore that he may raise the Lord throws down"—was one of which Milton was also firmly conscious.[17]

Within these familiar curvatures, Samson's blindness stands in contrast to Christ's vision, the mill of Gaza to the hill of the kingdoms, the stumbling, partly passionate movement forward to the calm clarity of the perfect man's advance. The distance between the two protagonists reinforces our understanding that where we begin and what we begin with are less important than where or how we proceed. Samson's fallible gropings draw us into the structures that frame and enlarge decisions more effectively than the acts of any previous agent. In our involvement with him and our contemplation of him, we learn to recognize the human blindness and to see the possibility of disengagement from its servitude.

To achieve his true nature, Samson must assert himself against the bondage of his past and show that he is able not to succumb to his own previous travesty of his destiny. He has reduced heroism to self-glorifying feats of strength, the "tedious havoc" which Milton elsewhere castigates (*PL* IX, 30). In his dealings with Delilah he has frivolously inverted the covenants of his trust. "Admired of all and dreaded," he has walked on hostile ground "Fearless of danger, like a petty god" (529–31), as if his election made him a center of significance instead of the instrument of the power that elected him.

Before Samson can defend himself against the reenactment of his past he must respond suitably to Manoa's testing. To the reader enlightened by Christianity (whether or not he subscribes to this particular view of the Atonement), it will be apparent that only God can pay Samson's ransom and that Manoa's endeavors are parodic in this sense (*PL* III, 221; *SA*, 483). But within the Old Testament dispositions of the poem, the mockery lies in replacing a covenant with God with an agreement with Dagon and in further suggestions (*SA*, 516–18) that the "deliverance" thus secured may be divinely authorized. That God will not abandon his creation (581 ff.) is a conviction which Christ has affirmed and which Adam has parodied; but to keep alive that possibility Samson must cling to the thread of connection represented by a covenant which, though betrayed, is not repudiated. "Ease after pain" may not seem unreasonable, but we must remember that it is the solution which Comus (686) offers the Lady.

Delilah's entrance is more sumptuously parodic as she floats on stage a Quinquireme of Nineveh, carrying the rich freight of Samson's woe. Against the true reconciliation of Adam and Eve, the reconciliation she proposes can be measured and found to be mockery. It also mocks that higher reconciliation with the divine will by which lower harmonizations are held in place and sanctified. It is in short a proposal for inversion, for the wrong dependence, and for the parodic displacement of God-centeredness. The "resemblance" she offers requires no great intellectual acumen to identify; but to resist it successfully is to demonstrate that the blindness of a past self is no longer in control.

In rejecting wrong roles, Samson prepares for the right one, not simply by elimination, but by restoring the subverted self through the choices he makes and the understandings he must find in order to make them. It is nevertheless true that his rejections are passionate rather than untroubled and not wholly emancipated from the weaknesses they reject. Perhaps it is this very impurity which makes him our representative among those cosmic structures with their remote protagonists which the previous poems have so elaborately brought into being. Samson now comes to a more difficult test. Having shown that he is able to pass through the snare of his sensuality, he must free himself next from a specification of heroism of which he was himself a notably forceful example. Unfortunately, while Harapha's nearly comic discomfiture effectively discredits a style of heroism which was once respectable to the extent of being "classical" but which we are now invited to consider as parodic, Samson's encounter with him is not rich in opportunities for displaying the better fortitude. However, Samson does ringingly affirm his trust in the living God, and the Chorus does meditate on patience as the exercise of saints. If at this point the heftier rather than the higher heroism seems triumphant, the true test of commitment is to come. Inward promptings are not excessively difficult to follow when they guide one to interesting marriages. Rousing motions which call for the humiliation of a newly regenerated strength require the admission that the strength is dependent on a higher principle and must be placed without reservation at the disposal of that principle. It should not by now be structurally unexpected that the capitulation before the herald by which Samson demonstrates his readiness to observe God's providence "and on him sole depend" (PL XII, 563-64), is the act by which he falls in order to rise. The two-handed engine will strike in a new version, and the design of things will be discovered in the close.

This brief survey has sought not so much to outline the uses of parody in Milton's poetry as to indicate the insufficiency of a word such as "uses." The persisting presence of parody in the oeuvre and the variety and nuances of that presence will be evident. It should also be evident that the parodic deployments take place within characteristic structures and rhythms of relationship, bearing witness thereby to an integrity of awareness which seems present from the beginning in Comus and which the logic of the oeuvre seems to unfold. The capacity of these structures to comment on each other, and the shaping power they generate between them, sustain a world deeply significant and sweepingly inclusive. The structures as we consider them are more than an "approach" to this world. They are the force of its being and the style of its affirmation.

University of Western Ontario

### NOTES

1. A. E. Barker, "Structural Pattern in *Paradise Lost*," in *Milton: Modern Essays in Criticism*, ed. idem. (New York, 1965), pp. 142-55. The term "counterplot" is taken from Geoffrey Hartman's "Milton's Counterplot," also reprinted in Barker, pp. 386-96.

2. The literature on structures in Milton's work is voluminous, and there are few books recently published on the poetry which do not have something to say on the subject. The bibliography appended to Barker, "Structural Pattern in *Paradise Lost*," is a convenient starting point. One might add E. M. W. Tillyard's "The Causeway from Hell to the World in the Tenth Book of *Paradise Lost*," *SP*, XXXVIII (1941), 266-70; Maurice Kelley, *This Great Argument* (Princeton, 1941), p. 193; and Jackson I. Cope, *The Metaphoric Structure of "Paradise Lost"* (Baltimore, 1962). The dialectic of contraries, explored by the present author in conjunction with other structures in *"Paradise Lost" and the Seventeenth Century Reader* (London, 1947), pp. 42-57, is treated at book length by Michael Lieb, *The Dialectics of Creation* (Amherst, Mass., 1970); Roy Daniells, in *Milton Mannerism and Baroque* (Toronto, 1963), comments stimulatingly on Milton's architecture of space. Gunnar Qvarnström's *The Enchanted Palace* (Stockholm, 1967) is concerned with numerological structures in *Paradise Lost*. John T. Shawcross' "The Balanced Structure of *Paradise Lost*" expounds a structure based on the numerological center in the ten-book version (*SP*, LXII [1965], 696-718). The present author's "*Paradise Lost* and the Balance of Structures," *UTQ*, XLI (1972), 219-26, considers possibilities in the twelve-book version. In *The Lofty Rhyme* (London, 1970), I attempt to comment on the structure of Milton's oeuvre or macrowork and the place which the individual poems occupy in that structure. In *The Heavenly Muse* (Toronto, 1973), pp. 176-207 and elsewhere, A. S. P. Woodhouse discusses the relationship of Milton's structural patterns to classical models. Burton J. Weber, in *The Construction of "Paradise Lost"* (Carbondale, Ill., 1971) discards most of the evidence the above authors thought they were providing in favor of a view of his own.

3. Rajan, *Lofty Rhyme*, pp. 24-27.

4. Milton's poetry is quoted from *The Poems of John Milton*, ed. John Carey and Alastair Fowler (London, 1968).

5. *Complete Prose Works*, ed. D. M. Wolfe (New Haven, 1953-), vol. II, p. 514.

6. Yeats' favorite phrase, "Unity of Being," and his repeated exemplification of that unity in a perfectly proportioned human body have an evident affinity with Milton's homogeneous and proportional body of truth.

7. Rajan, *Lofty Rhyme*, pp. 57-60.

8. Hugh Kenner, *The Pound Era* (Berkeley, 1971), pp. 165-67.

9. For the relationship between Adam and the garden, see Barbara Lewalski, "Innocence and Experience in Milton's Eden," *New Essays on "Paradise Lost,"* ed. Thomas Kranidas (Berkeley, 1969), pp. 90–95.

10. Rajan, *"Paradise Lost* and the Balance of Structures," pp. 224–25.

11. Rajan, *Lofty Rhyme*, pp. 60–61.

12. Joseph Summers, in *The Muse's Method* (London, 1960), pp. 46–70, discusses the satiric element in this episode.

13. *Milton and the Renaissance Hero* (Oxford, 1967). Professor Steadman's documentation of Milton's persistent contrasting of the true and false is important for an understanding of the cunning resemblance. The relationship between true and false is also taken up by Dennis Burden in *The Logical Epic* (London, 1967). In *The Christian Poet in "Paradise Lost"* (Berkeley, 1972), William Riggs sees the poet in the poem as vulnerable to the Satanic parody in the very process of seeking to affirm the celestial truth.

14. A further parodic refinement of these rhythms is suggested by A. E. Barker in "The Relevance of Regeneration," in *"Paradise Lost": A Tercentenary Tribute*, ed. B. Rajan (Toronto, 1969), pp. 56–57.

15. *Milton's Brief Epic* (Providence, 1966).

16. *Heavenly Muse*, p. 5, pp. 63ff., p. 178, and elsewhere.

17. Hymne to God my God, in my Sicknesse," *The Divine Poems*, ed. Helen Gardner (Oxford, 1952), p. 50. The editor's commentary on the poem notes that the "text of Donne's sermon to his own soul is not apparently Scriptural" (p. 109).

# "HIS UNCONTROLLABLE INTENT": DISCOVERY AS ACTION IN *SAMSON AGONISTES*

## *Christopher Grose*

As suggested in *An Apology* and *Paradise Lost*, the conception of a "virtuous wisdom" uniting word with "event" provides the model for a Miltonic action that rejoins the two plots of *Samson Agonistes*. Milton's protagonist gains his identity during the work, through careful listening, dramatic imitation, and finally in the scrupulous substitution of a proper for an improper choral position on his assisting the Dagonalia. Where his countrymen refuse to articulate what the logic of this situation requires, Samson discovers the ability to complete the system of scruple binding them, and thence to frame, and act upon, the theory of a "dispensing" agency in death itself. He thus frees himself from the Chorus' "thoughts" and "vain reasonings," and so reverses a process that began when he "thought it lawful" to marry Dalila. The Messenger's confused report is faithful to his experience, and points squarely at the way providence works in the pre-Christian era. The work refuses to distinguish among the separate terms for divine guidance in lines 1545–48. Milton gives virtually the same name ("motions") to what turned Samson toward the woman at Timna, to what gets Samson offstage, and to what brings the Messenger on.

## I

To JUDGE from recent work, readers of *Samson Agonistes* are having increasing difficulty with the fact that Samson's recovery, however it is defined, issues in the *power* of his virtue. If the regeneration of the protagonist becomes the middle Dr. Johnson thought was missing, what are we to make of Samson's final act, and the poem's climactic moment, the destruction of Dagon's temple? To be sure, there are disagreements among the proponents of what E. W. Tayler has described as "the standard interpretation of the play"; disagree-

ments, for example, as to whether Samson's victory is spiritual or
active in nature, or how we are to respond to the physical emphasis
never quite abandoned by the Chorus or Manoa.[1] But even the advo-
cates of a paradoxical or ironic reading for the play—and this has
been the most helpful of recent approaches—have been reluctant to
ascribe full importance to what happens onstage in this drama, with
the result that we still may think of the Messenger's report as somehow
providing us with the poem's crucial moment.[2] The most acute of
the play's recent readings, indeed, builds from the claim that in *Samson
Agonistes* we have two plots, incapable of connection by any causal
formula; and that, as a result, "*As far as we know,* the intersection
of God's plan—foretold by the angel—and Samson's victory over himself, is accidental."[3]

Nevertheless, certain features in *Samson Agonistes*, as well as analogous situations elsewhere in Milton's prose and verse, provide us
with a notion of an "act" that needs further exploration. They may
even be said to provide the poem with a characteristically Miltonic
"action." If it is not the kind of middle Dr. Johnson would have recognized as such, that is perhaps because of the way in which Milton
yokes virtue with power, action with discourse. Samson's recovery
results, we might say, in the kind of action that throughout Milton's
work extends "virtuous words" into an "event" or outcome at least
vaguely apocalyptic in its nature. This kind of action is familiar enough
in the major poems, even where (as in the published version of *A
Mask*) a sacred vehemence is only threatened. Its essential nature is
perhaps most clearly framed, however, in a prose incident of the
antiprelatical period; an incident in which Milton, writing as the anonymous Apologist, describes an ideal discursive situation. In an elaborate
compliment to the early actions of the Long Parliament (including
the Bishops' Exclusion Bill, Laud's impeachment, the execution of Straf-
ford, and most recently the "miraculous and lossless" suppression of
the Irish Rebellion), Milton attributed their initial success to "the force
of so much united excellence meeting in one globe of brightnesse
and efficacy." Unlike the ancient worthies, the Parliament had expelled
the oppressors of "the inward persuasion" without mere force. In the
case of the rebellion, "while two armies in the field stood gazing on,"
they had killed one of the shapes of tyranny with a magical combination
of wisdom and power:

With such a majesty had their wisdome begirt it selfe, that whereas others had levied warre to subdue a nation that sought for peace, they sitting here in peace could so many miles extend the force of their single words as to overawe the dissolute stoutnesse of an armed power secretly stirr'd up and almost hir'd against them.[4]

It is not my purpose here to show how pervasive this imagery was in Milton's discussion of education or of his own early career. It may suffice to recall the survey of poetry's powers in *Ad Patrem*, Milton's early reluctance to enter the priesthood as an "unweapon'd creature in the word," and (in *Of Education*) the frequent reviews to be undertaken by Milton's scholars, to unify "the whole body of their perfected knowledge, like the last embattelling of a Romane legion."[5] Instead, I wish to view this retrospective account of the Long Parliament's "virtuous words" as a convenient epitome of a Miltonic discursive "scene," whether in a historical or literary context, and to define Miltonic tragedy as involving one kind of collapse in this scene: the removal, specifically, of the kind of "correspondence," at once social and metaphysical, that made of Orpheus and Amphion the types of poetic efficacy, and in some minds brought England to the verge of being a nation of prophets.

Some such collapse is evident in the way the Apologist attempts to defend an earlier contribution to the pamphlet controversy on the ground that, with Luther, he could not write a dull style, "as being *of an ardent spirit*."[6] Milton had prayed for the arrival of the Son in a "vehement" manner his antagonist Joseph Hall had attacked. Milton's reply illustrates nicely the instability of the scene enjoyed by the Long Parliament. First, he now wishes us to view the work of 1641 as a decorous satire, and proceeds to defend it on stylistic grounds, according to its aims ("to astound and astonish the guilty Prelats"), and he offers precedents both secular and divine. "Neither was it a prayer so much as a hymne in prose frequent both in the Prophets, and in humane authors; therefore the stile was greater than for an ordinary prayer."[7] But more important, he turns on the "diabolical slanderer of prayers" with a defense of the "unpremeditated" manner, and of what he calls "the gift of free conceptions":

Certainly Readers, the worship of God singly in it selfe, the very act of prayer and thanksgiving with those free and unimpos'd expressions which from a sincere heart unbidden come into the outward gesture, is the greatest decency that can be imagin'd.[8]

Clearly enough, Milton cannot have it both ways. But what matters most here, for our purposes, is that in attempting to absorb prayer into the spheres of literary convention or the Apologist's own psychology, Milton necessarily distracts us from the less convenient elements in the acts of the prophetic poet or speaker. His theatrical metaphor in *An Apology* includes only the "gestures" of the actor, and they are viewed somewhat narrowly, as the "sincere" expressions of the soul. In effect, Milton thus isolates the figure of the actor-sage from his "scene": the prophet has become a spectacle (as the Chorus finds Samson at the outset, and as we experience his final act offstage), the scene or act diminishing until it is confined to his "outward gesture." By sharp contrast, what Milton hopes to recover, in urging the nation's resumption of "zeal," is precisely the rest of the scene as he now imagines it to have been during 1641: a "virtuous wisdom" in the original sense of the word, by which Parliament is said to have "extended so many miles the force of their single words."

In this prose incident, the alternate objects of tragic imitation—"the changes of that which is called fortune from without, or the wily subtleties and refluxes of man's thoughts from within"—were correspondent, even made identical, as they are not at the moment he is writing. The same is true, or seems true, to Adam and Eve at the outset of their anticipatory regeneration in *Paradise Lost*. Formally, this originates in Adam's lament, a speech within which we can hear the characteristic voices of the Father, the Son, and Satan. Speaking to himself, Adam descends into the maze of hypothetical rationalization. The complaint is then quoted in the retort of an imagined disobedient son (762); Adam is pursued by reason—and by doubt (782)—to the point of his "conviction," and the inverted pride, of the following:

> Him after all Disputes
> Forc't I absolve: all my evasions vain
> And reasonings, though through Mazes, lead me still
> But to my own conviction: first and last
> On mee, mee only, as the source and spring
> Of all corruption, all the blame lights due;
> So might the wrath.                                    (X, 828–34)[9]

To this the reply comes immediately, from within: "Fond wish!" This reply, however, is simply and suspiciously antifeminist, and it attempts to reassert the false analogy between man and the fallen angels: Adam's speech "concludes thee miserable / Beyond all past example and future, / To *Satan* only like both crime and doom" (X, 839-41). As most readers recognize, Adam is virtually quoting the great soliloquy of Satan on Mount Niphates ("Mee miserable . . . "). And the arrival of Eve, with quite the same "fond wish," gives Adam opportunity to respond, in effect, to his own despair. Once again, monologue itself contains "dramatic" exchange and seems to actuate a dramatic narrative.

To view *Samson Agonistes* in this way, I believe, is to recover— and necessarily to redefine—the connections, "invisible" and "secret" only to the Danite Chorus, between Samson's final act and the drama we hear; connections that recent criticism has disregarded and even denied. At the outset of Milton's tragedy too, the moral and intellectual refluxes seem divorced from fate, the divine narrative; and Milton explores the "very act of prayer" turned in upon itself, worship become ostensible soliloquy. Many details in the tragedy, taken together with the Argument, suggest that as a whole it is a displaced lament, that its action preempts Samson's initial purpose, to "sit a while and bemoan his condition." Unlike the Adam of Book X, who is temporarily enclosed in "gloomiest shade," Samson has sought to find some ease at the bank, a setting that "hath choice of Sun or shade," and a place where he can "feel amends, / The breath of Heav'n fresh-blowing, pure and sweet, / With day-spring born" (9-11). But even here, he is prey to a kind of thought that is, so to speak, "unbodied," and that turns out to be an actual dramatic adversary, however disguised. He finds

> Ease to the body some, none to the mind
> From restless thoughts, that like a deadly swarm
> Of Hornets arm'd, no sooner found alone,
> But rush upon me thronging, and present
> Times past, what once I was, and what am now.          (18-22)

Almost everyone in the play offers such "thoughts," and for the most part they intensify Samson's sense of loss. They also point to one dominant mode of the poem as memorial, with Samson an active participant as well as "critical" opponent, in depicting his own fame. Nor is the body exempt from the effects of these thoughts, despite the initial hopes of finding some ease onstage:

> Thoughts my Tormentors arm'd with deadly stings
> Mangle my apprehensive tenderest parts,

Exasperate, exulcerate, and raise
Dire inflammation which no cooling herb
Or med'cinal liquor can assuage,
Nor breath of Vernal Air from snowy *Alp*.
Sleep hath forsook and giv'n me o'er
To death's benumbing Opium as my only cure.
Thence faintings, swoonings of despair,
And sense of Heav'n's desertion.                        (623–32)[10]

The commentators seem generally agreed that this is Samson's low
point in the play. His long speech ends in a wish for "speedy death,
/ The close of all my miseries, and the balm" (650–51). At this point
in the play, Manoa has theorized that the drooping of his son's spirits
proceeds from "anguish of the mind and humors black, / That mingle
with thy fancy" (600–01). Samson's response to this amateur psychology
is a speech of simultaneous discovery and explanation. With an emphasis somewhat different from that of the opening monologue, Milton
resorts to the syntax he seems always to use in forging continuities
from ordinary disparates. And he piles on words insistently and shock-
ingly physical to describe the effects of Samson's griefs. Having found
passage to the inmost mind, Samson reports, his torment must there
"exercise all his fierce accidents, / And on her purest spirits prey,
/ As on entrails, joints, and limbs, / With answerable pains, but more
intense, / Though void of corporal sense" (612–16).

Samson's name for the result is "black mortification," a word which
Milton considered was wrongly, or in any case too vaguely, linked
with the process of regeneration.[11] In *Christian Doctrine*, he criticized
those writers who divided regeneration arbitrarily into mortification
of the flesh and quickening of the spirit, and he concluded that mortification "cannot be a constituent part of regeneration, inasmuch as
it partly precedes it (that is to say, as corruption precedes generation)
and partly follows it; in which latter capacity it belongs rather to
repentance."[12] The context of the passage in *Samson Agonistes*, though
—its immediate engagement with the departure of Manoa—makes
it clear that "torment" here means "thought" or any "talk"; and this
in no hidden, inner, or otherwise "offstage" sense. Samson is not just
talking about something he feels, here or anywhere else in the poem.
In specific, even parodic, fashion he is referring to and using the
speeches of the play, in particular his own first monologue. If thoughts
"return" to torment Samson, as they do to both Adam and Satan

in *Paradise Lost,* they do so more in the manner of Book X than of the soliloquy on Mt. Niphates: they do so in person, in order to "awaken" an inward grief, to adopt the phrasing with which Milton introduces Manoa's own entrance.[13] One might almost say that the first monologue *creates* the cast of characters, the voices if not the *personae* of the drama, and that they then materialize onstage in their own persons, to "awaken" griefs by attaching them to specific, external ownership. In Samson's opening monologue, Milton has thus initiated a restorative process of a kind partly similar to the last section of *Paradise Lost,* but with qualifications that are specifically appropriate to tragedy.

What I wish to emphasize in the following pages is the self-consciousness with which these tormenting "thoughts" are framed as such, and the formal accessibility of this process. "Thoughts" in this poem are *sayings:* "Many are the sayings of the wise"; and we can distinguish the manner of proverbial wisdom—the vocabulary and syntactical habits shared by all the characters, up to the final choruses—from the locus of Samson's special kind of knowledge, that openness to what in this poem's vocabulary is called "intimate impulse." Even Manoa can be regarded as a kind of Stoic tempter, inviting Samson to a "fixed mind" completely abstracted from "corporal sense," somewhat in the fashion of Shakespeare's John of Gaunt in his exchange with the exiled Bolingbroke.[14] But it is the Chorus that we associate most closely with the "thoughts" to which we have referred, and which provides Samson with the first instance of speakers outside himself, to continue a process that begins in soliloquy. When the Chorus first enters, we may recall, Milton seems to detach speech from dramatic gesture, to the point of comic mechanization. According to Samson, the Chorus' first speech (a particularly ironic form of commentary describing his postures and moralizing his plight as a "mirror of our fickle state") reaches his ears "disjointed," surviving its journey only as a "sound of words." (Consistently, what happens at the bank is careful *listening.*) Almost immediately the Chorus comments on its own function; if successful, it can accomplish tragic effects, providing Samson—here considered as spectator, rather than protagonist—with "counsel or consolation."[15] Clearly it is less the air than the extravagance of the Chorus' claim (that "apt words" can soothe body and mind alike) that dissolves the distinction between these very different words.

Samson's response ignores this claim, however, to make a "critic's" distinction that is lost on the Chorus, here and elsewhere. It reads almost like an attack on what the Chorus is most interested in, the chatty moralizing of well-meaning friends. What revives him is the gesture itself, as distinct from what they say they are; their *coming* may provide him with a lesson "of my own experience." The ostensible role of the Chorus, possibly as members of a specific nation or tribe as well as an onstage audience, becomes a "superscription"; Samson will learn about friendship "not by talk." Indeed, Samson greets his countrymen with a generalization (itself a "thought") that questions their intent and proposes an "uncontrollable" effect of their mission onstage, in terms with which we are by now familiar:

> Your coming, Friends, revives me, for I learn
> Now of my own experience, not by talk,
> How counterfeit a coin they are who friends
> Bear in their Superscription (of the most
> I would be understood); in prosperous days
> They swarm, but in adverse withdraw thir head
> Not to be found, though sought.                    (187–93)

For their own part, the men of Dan seem remarkably self-conscious, in the extent to which they comment on their own contribution, in the way their outlook is framed specifically as "thoughts." The expression of their collective despair is a particularly paralyzing *form* of consolation, and it can hardly be called counsel; ultimately it poses Samson's severest temptation. Paralyzed by the case, it would seem, the Danites cannot even perform their function until they have set it off as useless, inapplicable:

> Many are the sayings of the wise
> In ancient and in modern books enroll'd,
> Extolling Patience as the truest fortitude,
> And to the bearing well of all calamities,
> All chances incident to man's frail life
> Consolatories writ
> With studied argument, and much persuasion sought
> Lenient of grief and anxious thought,
> But with th'afflicted in his pangs thir sound
> Little prevails, or rather seems a tune,
> Harsh, and of dissonant mood from his complaint,
> Unless he feel within
> Some source of consolation from above;

> Secret refreshings, that repair his strength,
> And fainting spirits uphold. (652–66)

Located just after Samson's prayer for "speedy death," this speech marks a low point in the choric notion of what it can accomplish, and it brings to a head the poem's critique of reason—or at least vain reasonings.

The play's self-consciousness about thought and "thoughts" also serves as the basis for its explanation of the action's background. Early in the poem, Samson at one point describes his alienation from God rather specifically as a recourse to thought. Recalling the first direct collision between his kind of knowing—in apparent conspiracy with physical desire—and parental authority, Samson claims that

> what I motion'd was of God; I knew
> From intimate impulse, and therefore urg'd
> The Marriage on; that by occasion hence
> I might begin *Israel's* Deliverance,
> The work to which I was divinely call'd. (222–26)

With Dalila, it seems, he did not "know"; he merely "thought it lawful from my former act, / And the same end, still watching to oppress / *Israel's* oppressors" (231–33). It is obviously a crucial speech: he no longer thinks it lawful, he was simply wrong—a claim that the work as a whole may question.[16] The basis of his "thought," we may notice, was his own experience, his former act. What matters most here—even more than the reference, presumably to Samson's first marriage—is the sense of continuity, now seemingly lost, between God, impulse, act, and thought. Samson now lacks the radical integrity of personality and psyche, conceived in dramatistic terms, in which Milton was so interested from his early writing onward.

The pattern is reiterated within the play itself, as we might expect. In the opening speech, particularly, we can see Samson move into sententious forms of thought, forms that we associate too cleanly and after the fact with a choric "character." But Milton's epithet for Samson is a reminder that we should not confuse the pattern with the overall action of the play, which reverses the direction Samson describes above. The intimate impulse, or the "rousing motions" which Samson claims to feel during his final exchange with the Chorus, also has a local residence within the work, in the way we hear the entire exchange between the protagonist and his onstage spectators, an exchange that

actually begins within the opening monologue.[17] I am speaking of
the kind of ironic imagination of hostile positions that can easily be
mistaken for sarcasm or the fear of public ridicule—mistaken, that
is, for a function of character rather than a constituent of action. When
the swaggering Harapha accuses Samson of being a "Revolter," Samson does not so much "descend to Harapha's level" as provide the
substance of his epithet:

> My Nation was subjected to your Lords.
> It was the force of Conquest; force with force
> Is well ejected when the Conquer'd can.
> But I a private person, whom my Country
> As a league-breaker gave up bound, presum'd
> Single Rebellion and did Hostile Acts.
> I was no private but a person rais'd
> With strength sufficient and command from Heav'n
> To free my Country.                                    (1205–13)

Harapha is hardly capable of understanding the distinction anticipated
in lines 1208–10; but the abrupt reversal can be achieved only when
"Revolter," like the earlier "Friends," becomes a superscription dramatically embraced, and so understood.

The dramatizing of the rousing motions seems most clearly marked
from the point where Samson can assume the part of the Chorus
or Manoa; and where, in doing so, he bypasses the block their wisdom
represents, even to the point of silencing them. Following Harapha's
angry departure, the Chorus fears further affliction at the hands of
the offended Lords. Samson's response indicates his own clear sense
of the challenge he has just been posed; but it also imagines a harmony
between Philistine self-interest and his own unwished-for survival,
and—beyond that—the glimpse of a hate (on their part) that could
be self-destructive as well as prove "friendly"—"to me":

> Much more affliction than already felt
> They cannot well impose, nor I sustain;
> If they intend advantage of my labors,
> The work of many hands, which earns my keeping
> With no small profit daily to my owners.
> But come what will, my deadliest foe will prove
> My speediest friend, by death to rid me hence,
> The worst that he can give, to me the best.
> Yet so it may fall out, because thir end

Is hate, not help to me, it may with mine
Draw thir own ruin who attempt the deed.          (1257-67)

The movement here, signaled with some care, is from imaginatively
entertained economic pragmatism—why the Philistines are unlikely
to indulge Harapha's wounded pride—to an acceptance of paradoxical
values; and thence to a discovery barely beginning to crystallize. This
too is "practical" in its nature; Samson has triumphed over the Chorus
specifically in his knowledge of the world.

The Chorus seems to mistake this crucial moment for mere venge-
fulness. To judge from the way it now recommends patience as "more
oft the exercise / Of Saints," at least, it cannot yet understand the
notion of a delivery that is partial and involves real responsibility
or cost. It is comely and reviving when God works through "plain
Heroic magnitude of mind," but the Chorus puts this simply as one
of the alternatives in the never-ending course of history, as part of
a balance we have just seen Samson transcend (precisely by imagining
the Philistine viewpoint) in a fashion patently dialectical. In comment-
ing the way a chorus usually does, this nation is in effect proving
Samson's point at the very moment the "rousing motions" are discernible to us: the point, namely, that "their servile minds / Me thir Deliverer sent would not receive" (1213–14). (One may legitimately wonder
whether they ever do, or would, receive him.)[18]

Here as earlier, the choric role and style cannot be distinguished
from a vision of history. In general, we might say, the Chorus consistently finds in Samson *not* a Nazarite but in effect another Adam,
an epitome rather than hero of mankind. He is a "mirror of our fickle
state" (164); his strength, which "might have subdu'd the Earth," provided only that it was attended with "virtue" (173–74), has served
only to prove the hackneyed wisdom of the ages. What the Chorus
offers, in somewhat Polonian form, is an outlook that is both "classical"
and Augustinian. Closer to the disillusioned historical views of Eccle-
siastes than to the prophetic "Chiliasm" of Milton's early pamphlets,
this is also the traditional substance of *de casibus* tragedy. This is
a world of immutable laws, if it is not quite fortune's world. In it,
the elect themselves are thrown "lower than thou didst exalt them
high" (689); and Samson merely fell farther than other men, and from
a different *kind* of high estate, possessed of strength and (for a time)
of virtue, not "long descent of birth" (171), or luck. "In fine, / Just

or unjust, alike seem miserable, / For oft alike, both come to evil end" (702–04). With their unmistakable echo of the way in which Satan "must" perceive God's beneficence in *Paradise Lost*, these summary lines strongly suggest their most characteristic gesture, the accusation or "appointment" of the governing deity. In the choric account, as in Manoa's (at times the two seem indistinguishable as outlooks), God not only permits evil; it is the divine obsession. God's providence is essentially tragic, in an old-fashioned way, and he can have dealt *already* with Samson in bringing him low. The dispensation they consistently assume to this point in the play is champion-centered, not quite theocentric; and their Samson seems almost a kind of Satan *manqué*.

What seems so striking about this passage, I think, is its distance on heroic martyrdom; the tone expresses not so much the anguish of real oppression as the wish for amusement of the audience at an entertainment. We might almost say of the Danites, indeed, that their willingness to accept only a total and instantaneous delivery—and a messianic Deliverer—is the measure of their inability, at this point, to understand tragedy, as they come to define it later. Eventually the Chorus recognizes the partiality of God's human imagery, that there can only be ministers; to quote from *An Apology*'s description of human talent, ordinary men contain only in part "what was all" in Christ.[19] As it turns out, this is a world in which men can be "thy glorious Champion" at one moment and in some single way. But at this point the Chorus is reduced to prayer for an exception, for yet another exception to the old rule: "So deal not with this once thy glorious Champion, / The Image of thy strength, and mighty minister" (705–06). Patience itself here must have the kind of magic that recalls the promised effects of Stoic resolution in Milton's hell. Here it makes "each his own Deliverer, / And Victor over all / That tyranny or fortune can inflict" (1289–91). And ultimately they ask, with Manoa and Dalila, for peace—or, more specifically, a "peaceful end" to Samson's labors. Like Manoa, the Chorus seeks to bring him back "home to thy country and to his sacred house" (518), at one level a regression singularly inappropriate to any true descendant of Abraham.[20] It seems fair to say on the whole that their quietism, which should not be confused with the inner paradise promised by Michael, is responsible for the conditional way in which Manoa defines Samson's legacy at lines 1714–17.

If this seems extreme as an account of the choric "character," I submit, it is because the men of Dan never sound quite this way again. When we hear the choric voice subsequently, it is from Samson; initially removable from what Samson has called its "superscription," it is now actually detached and can be recognized as an overlay of his own attitude, a more and more conscious assumption of the choric mask. "Masters' commands come with a power resistless / To such as owe them absolute subjection; / And for a life who will not change his purpose? / (So mutable are all the ways of men)" (1404-07). The speech is literally duplicitous and seems addressed to at least two audiences; but it may be viewed as a remarkably vivid extension, and not necessarily the origin, of Samson's "act." Nor is Samson the only one changing parts here. When the Philistine Officer leaves, the Chorus actually continues his arguments; the Danites are answered only by their own former arguments, now posed by Samson on their behalf, and in their voice—to himself. From what Samson has already learned in the exchange thus far (and also from the debilitating "Besides" of the passage below) it is clear, for example, that Samson poses these questions as it were *in review:*

> Shall I abuse this Consecrated gift
> Of strength, again returning with my hair
> After my great transgression, so requite
> Favor renew'd, and add a greater sin
> By prostituting holy things to Idols;
> A *Nazarite* in place abominable
> Vaunting my strength in honor to thir *Dagon?*
> Besides, how vile, contemptible, ridiculous,
> What act more execrably unclean, profane?          (1354-62)

The position of the Chorus and Manoa is being rejected as it is being logically "extenuated." It does not seem too much to say, in fact, that reason itself is being (or has been) rejected at the moment Samson seems most dexterous in supplying "reasons."

The articulation of the choric wisdom by a more and more conscious (or "awakened") Samson takes on the character of rhetorical combat in the stichomythic exchange that follows, where the Chorus seems to attain the extent of its "reach." These parries and thrusts repeat points already gained: for example, the distinction clarified during the exchange with Harapha between religious and civil spheres, a distinction the Chorus misses at lines 1363-64. Indeed, it would

seem that the lack of progression here is a function of wilting choric
reason; Samson must provide the choric response requisite to this stage
of the argument and so *replace* its evasive suggestion that he employ
"mental reservation":

> *Chorus.* Yet with this strength thou serv'st the *Philistines*
>         Idolatrous, uncircumcis'd, unclean.
> *Samson.* Not in thir Idol-Worship, but by labor
>         Honest and lawful to deserve my food
>         Of those who have me in thir civil power.
> *Chorus.* Where the heart joins not, outward acts defile not.
> *Samson.* Where outward force constrains, the sentence holds.
>
>                                                    (1363–69)

Samson follows up, in the Chorus' own terms, with a distinction that
directly confronts the "reason" governing this situation: the reason
he may *not* obey the Philistine (or choric?) strictures except "where
outward force constrains." The gesture, once again, serves not merely
to embarrass the Chorus with its responsibilities; he presents the choric
consciousness, complete with what it cannot bring itself to articulate,
to himself. And as earlier, the effect of his doing so is to discover
the paradox of a special "dispensation," one that spreads the heroic
potential in Israel to "thee." Signaled as earlier by "yet," the reversal
is devastating, given especially Samson's scrupulous entertainment of
what the Chorus *should* be saying at this point:

>                            If I obey them,
>     I do it freely; venturing to displease
>     God for the fear of Man, and Man prefer,
>     Set God behind: which in his jealousy
>     Shall never, unrepented, find forgiveness.
>     Yet that he may dispense with me or thee
>     Present in Temples at Idolatrous Rites
>     For some important cause, thou needst not doubt.        (1372–79)

Discovery here is born of the self-conscious *completion* of the choric
position, and it constitutes the repentance of which he speaks; he
has actually heard what the Chorus could not bring itself to say. The
tone of the final lines is extraordinarily difficult to capture, in part
because of the way "dispense" compresses the speaker's own sense
of uselessness (even reprobation?) with the discovery of a providential
agency even in his own death. Surely these lines contain the "presage
in the mind" to which Samson refers eight lines later; are they not also
the "rousing motions" that he can only report he now begins to feel,

the motions that "dispose / To something extraordinary my thoughts" (1382-83)? Samson here is not so much reassuring the Chorus (which wonders "how thou wilt here come off" [1380]) as he is describing what we have experienced with him during this·work, and so replacing the Chorus with "Thee"—a more fully conscious and heroic audience, in effect that potential one to which Manoa refers at line 1715.

I am saying, in other words, that the real victory of this poem takes place onstage, and that it consists in the extinction of the choric part and its replacement by a dramatically more flexible, *freer*, Samson. To put it more bluntly, I am arguing that in effect the obligatory victory of Samson over the Philistines has been displaced in Milton's tragedy and is rendered as a victory over himself and his own nation, a group of hearers for which we might adopt Erik Erikson's term "pseudo-species."[21] We have, then, the situation of the Psalms that Milton versified early in the 1650s, the banding together of "the Nations" to resist God's "uncontrollable intent," as possessed by "just men." The extinction of the choric part seems all but complete in the farewell that now ensues, in the way Samson gives its truisms the kind of double reference which S. F. Johnson has seen in Hamlet's exchanges with Osric.[22] Speaking now for the Hebrew community to the Officer, who returns with some of Milton's lamest iambics, he pretends once again to fear the indignity of being trailed through the streets. Now he insists on scruple only to the extent of refusing to comply with anything "Scandalous or forbidden in our Law"—a scruple he has previously decided to defy "for some important cause," having articulated and "extenuated" it for the Chorus (1409, 1379). Turning to his countrymen just after the Officer's departure, he offers the somewhat greater complexity of the following lines:

> Happ'n what may, of me expect to hear
> Nothing dishonorable, impure, unworthy
> Our God, our Law, my Nation, or myself;
> The last of me or no I cannot warrant.          (1423-26)

Unless we accept a more limited Samson than most readers have discovered at this point—an "overconfident" Samson under the illusion that he will manage the kind of unblemished victory that the Chorus fondly projects in its recommendation of Patience—I think we do well to think of Samson here as reassuring his countrymen now more distantly, from the standpoint of his discovery. The reassurance, we may notice, forms a countermovement within this speech and makes

the last in a series of three such countermovements at the end of
Samson's final speeches: (1) at line 1265, beginning at "Yet so it may
fall out"; (2) "Yet that he may dispense with me or thee" (1377);
(3) "Happ'n what may, of me expect to hear / Nothing dishonorable,
impure, unworthy / Our God, our Law, my Nation, or my Self; /
The last of me or no I cannot warrant." What this member in the
series seems to add is a greater sense of harmony among the discrepant
elements of line 1425: "Our God, our Law, my Nation, or my Self."
Given especially Samson's recent definitition of that self ("my con-
science and internal peace"), we are likely to sense the tragic vision
behind the line, the discontinuities so uneasily contained in the outward
balance both within line 1425 and between lines 1425 and 1426: God
. . . Law . . . Nation . . . my Self / . . . me. As the ego is dismissed, the
self here has become in its place the radical source of all value, and
in this sense "messianic"; its actions, further, will affect other levels.
While pretending to speak to and for the community, Samson also
speaks *from within*, and speaks both to and for *us*.[23]

## II

Such a thesis clearly puts great pressure on the way in which
Milton renders Samson's "actual" destruction of the Philistine temple,
in what Arnold Stein calls the poem's "big scene," and by extension
on the entire conclusion.[24] To argue that Samson's obligatory victory
over the Philistine nation is rendered here as a victory over himself
and his *own* nation, of course, is to claim the virtual identity of what
have recently been considered the poem's two plots. The play itself,
in fact, seems almost systematically to blur the distinction between
that obligatory victory and its own onstage dialectical procedure, if
not actually to merge the two victories. It has not been sufficiently
emphasized to what extent the poem makes a scrupulous and even
somewhat labored attempt to define what "really" happens offstage,
following the departure of the resolved Samson. The reader in search
of hard facts—at least if he assumes that they would differ from the
"secret presage" or the cataclysmic "noise"—might well concur with
Manoa's complaint that "The accident was loud, and here before thee
/ With rueful cry, yet *what it was* we hear not" (1552–53; italics added).
Despite its remarkable omissions (Dalila and Harapha are included
only as "other persons," and the final chorus is not even mentioned),

the Argument does dwell at some length on the conclusion and specifies both the placement and style of the Messenger's narration. Like the arrival of Samson's "friends and equals," his story is an interruption: "in the midst of which discourse [Manoa's] an Ebrew comes in haste; confusedly at first; and afterwards more distinctly relating the Catastrophe, what Samson had done to the Philistines, and by accident to himself; wherewith the Tragedy ends." The poem's presentation of Samson's final act, then, is highly mediated. At worst it is little more than the combination of memory and fame, the constructions, respectively, of the Messenger and the Chorus. Like earlier stage entrances—notably those of the words, then the persons of the Chorus—it is carefully introduced, appearing first as an ambiguous noise, at length to be revealed in its true light, "at nearer view."

Milton seems deliberately to emphasize the mode of narration, in the Messenger's account; and he does so in language that connects this segment of the poem with the "unpremeditatedness" of *Paradise Lost*. The story *itself* "would burst forth, but I recover breath / And sense distract, to know well what I utter" (1555–56). The point of this is lost on Manoa, whose next request (for the "sum," then the circumstance) seems to assume the possibility of an accurate description apart from its effects, and even the comfort of an orthodox moral. At the very least, we might say that Manoa seems to assume a correspondence between an "argument" and what in *Paradise Lost* is called "process of speech." His comments and stylistic demands can be taken as an attempt to read certain crucial assumptions into an account that is confused almost to the core. In fact, the Messenger's narration seems to deny the implicit distinction between form and matter or, in Manoa's terms, the "sum" and the "circumstance." Manoa senses, or rather he wishes to discover, a conversion to joy, a rather simple form of *felix culpa*. But the "sum" he receives is most unsatisfying. To the question about the cause for self-violence among his foes, he receives the answer "inevitable cause, / At once to destroy and be destroy'd" (1586–87). In this, Manoa can find only ignominious death, according to the principle "death to life is crown or shame" (1578); his concluding apostrophe is "lastly over-strong against thyself!" (1590). Still, he is impressed with the *excess* of moral material, even as he assumes that the pieces will fit: "More than enough we know; but while things yet / Are in confusion, give us . . . / Relation more particular and distinct" (1592–95). We are clearly dealing with the essential and tragic confusion at the heart of the poem's world. Manoa's "yet" here points not so much to any future moment in Gaza as to a different dispensation hereafter. He knows "more than enough" precisely *because* "things yet / Are in confusion." And they remain so, for onstage observers, up to the final ambivalence of his "*Samson* hath quit himself / Like *Samson*" and the choric "All is best, though we oft doubt" (1709–10; 1745). We should recall that at the very point where the Messenger is reporting most directly as an eyewitness, Samson is seen "immixt" with the Philistine lords and priests, and that the Messenger stresses once again the inevitability of his fate. Does not the spectacle of such promiscuity point to the operation of evil temporarily mixing with good, in advance of its "redundance"—that ultimate segregation in a post-Samson world, when evil "on itself shall back recoil, / And mix no more with goodness, when at last / Gather'd like scum, and settl'd to itself, / It shall be in eternal restless change / Self-fed and self-consum'd" (*A Mask*, 593–97)? The plight of Gaza seems to image the essential nature of the pre-Christian world, which in *Samson Agonistes* we experience in its closing phase.

The final choruses seek, among other things, to define the nature of Samson's act. In doing so, they necessarily perform a function that we have viewed as a kind of prime strategy in the poem as a whole; by explicating the account of the Messenger, so frugal particularly with regard to Samson's experience, they necessarily reduce it to a "just measure"—an action that is at once appropriate to tragedy and, perhaps, a distortion due to human "thought." The moral they draw, like the final choruses of Euripides, seems in its diffuseness to cover almost any conceivable phenomenon; like the choric philosophy throughout, it seems a kind of lowest common denominator of tragic wisdom, the only lesson that could resolve the preceding semichoruses. These may be viewed without hopeless distortion as the ambivalent appreciation of Dalila's "fame."

The misunderstandings of the semichoruses relate to two areas in which we have rather full information; one of the work as a whole, the other a report.[25] Manoa has recently told us, for example, of the various motives of the Philistines he visited in his efforts to procure ransom for his son; and the account is remarkably particular and civil:

> Some much averse I found and wondrous harsh,
> Contemptuous, proud, set on revenge and spite;

That part most reverenc'd *Dagon* and his Priests:
Others more moderate seeming, but thir aim
Private reward, for which both God and State
They easily would set to sale: a third
More generous far and civil, who confess'd
They had enough reveng'd, having reduc't
Thir foe to misery beneath thir fears,
The rest was magnanimity to remit,
If some convenient ransom were propos'd.     (1461–71)

In contrast, much of what the first semichorus says about the Philistines both echoes and considerably extends Samson's "uninformed" description in his farewell speech to the brethren, a speech that generates the sense of approaching fulfillment: the completion of the enemy. "Lords are lordliest in thir wine; / And the well-feasted Priest then soonest fir'd / With zeal, if aught Religion seem concérn'd" (1418–20). Here, as in the dismissal of Samson, Milton seems to encourage the view of a *convergence* of nations, of what I have called the work's "pseudo-species." Earlier, in the way the Chorus seems to absorb the Officer's arguments, it is difficult to escape the sense at least of a collective "deafness" in Officer and Chorus alike, a deafness from which the work's own echoes of itself seem designed to release us. At lines 1408–09, the chorus seems almost unconcerned; the main point of Samson's "resolution" seems gained, and no one sane *could* mean the rest of what he says. Similarly, the Officer's praise in line 1410— engaging with what we know is a deceptive posture and not Samson's act—could easily be the Chorus' own: at this point everyone onstage seems to be sighing with relief. Here at the conclusion, almost everything the Chorus says about the Philistines can be applied to the Danites and even to Samson. In pointing to an unconscious suicidal impulse of the Philistines, the gloating semichorus omits the parallels: the welcome destroyer was a rejected deliverer; the Hebrews as an onstage nation resemble the offstage Philistines; Samson is, or was, like both.[26] This is to force the correspondences, to be sure. But Samson's clear "recapitulation" of the mortal men on *both* sides seems almost inescapable in the final words of this semichorus, which ascribe the suicide *too totally*, not to Samson, but to mortal man's being "insensate left, or to sense reprobate, / And with blindness internal struck" (1685–86). The attempt to define the victory, to make pat and pious distinctions, serves only to telescope more clearly the victors and the vanquished; no less than Samson, the Philistines who "Unwittingly importun'd /

Thir own destruction to come speedy upon them" (1680–81) are entangled in the fold of dire necessity.

The second semichorus is limited in the way it argues from the experience of the hero to the reflourishing of true "virtue," after denouncing the fallibility of fame and reputation. Here it is helpful to recall how clearly Samson's experience was acknowledged to surmount the reach of the Chorus at line 1380, for this speech frames Samson's victory specifically as an act of virtue. But the second semichorus makes the hero's "virtual extinction" into a matter of simple mistake, reducing it almost to an elementary question of appearance versus reality and ascribing that mistake, as in the first semichorus, exclusively to the Philistines:

> But he though blind of sight,
> Despis'd and thought extinguish't quite,
> With inward eyes illuminated
> His fiery virtue rous'd
> From under ashes into sudden flame,
> And as an ev'ning Dragon came,
> Assailant on the perched roosts,
> And nests in order rang'd
> Of tame villatic Fowl; but as an Eagle
> His cloudless thunder bolted on thir heads.
> So virtue giv'n for lost,
> Deprest, and overthrown, as seem'd,
> Like that self-begott'n bird
> In the *Arabian* woods embost,
> That no second knows nor third,
> And lay erewhile a Holocaust,
> From out her ashy womb now teem'd,
> Revives, reflourishes, then vigorous most
> When most unactive deem'd,
> And though her body die, her fame survives,
> A secular bird ages of lives.        (1687–1707)

For all the gains of this semichorus, we need to ask whether this revival could have occurred without what seem to strike them as the "outward" conditions. We are told that Samson was illuminated "with inward eyes," that he roused his "fiery virtue" "from under ashes into sudden flame." But it seems reasonable to object that Samson's virtue, as a matter of "intimate impulse," *is* a bodily thing, that their initial concessive clause, "though blind of sight," involves the very taproot of Samson's special *kind* of virtue. Given for lost by whom?

"Deprest, and overthrown, as seem'd" to whom? The fullest answer here involves the recognition that the second semichorus spiritualizes the story, abstracts Samson the bodily man from his "virtue," in a way that absolves themselves from the kind of participation, and dispensation, to which Samson alone is open.

In this connection, we may notice the detail of the phoenix, a final extended flight in a poem remarkably free of lyric indulgences. The second semichorus makes some difficult distinctions in saying what Samson did, how he "came." He did so "as an ev'ning Dragon . . . / Assailant on the perched roosts, / And nests in order rang'd / Of tame villatic Fowl." But this was "cloudless thunder," and they compare it to an eagle before their ultimate figure for "virtue giv'n for lost," the self-begotten bird "embost" in the Arabian woods. What this emblematic creature signifies seems clearest in line 1706: her *fame* survives "though her body die." Milton cannot eliminate conventional associations by fiat here; instead he forces us to confront the isolation that comes with human virtue.[27] From the summary lines, "And though her body die, her fame survives, / A secular bird ages of lives," the bird itself has disappeared; she endures only as fame, if she has not perished outright with her body. Possession is made indistinguishable from self. Milton's phoenix, then, does not know it will reflourish; and virtue itself, like the phoenix, is a *"secular* bird ages *of lives."* Heroic virtue is circumscribed physically; though self-begotten, it (she?) "no second knows nor third." If these lines hint at typological significance, the bird's uniqueness is still the measure of its limitation in time, if not of its imprisonment.

The final chorus seems definitive even formally; its discussion of heroic experience and tragic effects is strikingly similar to the normative stanzas we are now accustomed to discover in seventeenth-century poems employing "hieroglyphic form." The quintessential choric act, it projects formally the "just measure" to which the tragic passions of "pity and fear, or terror" have, within the work itself, been reduced. More than Manoa's attempt to harmonize the picture, the final fourteen lines connect, but do not merge, the public and private experience of the poem. Indeed the Chorus here seems uncharacteristically scrupulous in its hesitation to make Manoa's kind of assertion. Instead it formulates the conditions requisite to an assertion of eternal providence, from the standpoint of the "evil days" mentioned in the invocation

to Book VII of *Paradise Lost*. More clearly than Manoa's response
to the semichoruses, this is the definitive and not just the national
or "tribal" response; and we can tell partly from the "unexclusive"
way it parcels the truth so as to distinguish it from "true experience"
or history. Uncharacteristically, too, this Chorus does not build on
antithesis. The divine wisdom hides his face, or rather seems to do
so. He returns ("really"), and has in fact just borne witness to his
faithful Champion "gloriously." On *all* this depends the consequence
of Gaza's mourning, as well as the larger, psalmlike claim that such
is shared somehow by "all that band them to resist / His uncontrollable
intent" (1753–54).

   Like Milton's theology and so much of his poetry, then, the final
chorus emphasizes the problem of knowing and worshiping God, here
in the specific pre-Christian context of the Jewish Captivity. In such
a setting—and in human affairs when tragically viewed, Milton seems
to imply—we experience the curious mixture of history and cyclic
recurrence that is revealed in the verbs of these lines.[28] Like so many
of Euripides' final choruses (and Milton was quoting the sense of them
as early as 1637 in explaining his own philosophical quest to Charles
Diodati), it emphasizes the disparity between human doubt and the
"unsearchable dispose / Of highest wisdom." But it is remarkable
to what extent the final chorus asserts what that wisdom "brings about,"
and—the same thing, it seems—how it is "found" in human affairs:

> All is best, though we oft doubt,
> What th'unsearchable dispose
> Of highest wisdom brings about,
> And ever best found in the close.
> Oft he seems to hide his face,
> But unexpectedly returns
> And to his faithful Champion hath in place
> Bore witness gloriously; whence *Gaza* mourns
> And all that band them to resist
> His uncontrollable intent;
> His servants he with new acquist
> Of true experience from this great event
> With peace and consolation hath dismist,
> And calm of mind, all passion spent.          (1745–58)

This is close to the tragic theory of Milton's preface. But we should
notice the Chorus' suggestion that the servants are *already* dismissed,
possessed of that tragic effect, "calm of mind." The phrasing serves

to distinguish them, perhaps, from any lingering ("deaf"?) audience. This is a consolidating chorus in that it focuses on the experience at once of the community and of the faithful champion; the ultimate access of wisdom is best found—or has been here—by both. If the *deus absconditus*, the "sense of Heav'n's desertion," is a Hebrew experience shared by Samson personally, the unexpected return applies alike to his faithful champion and to "us"—or at least to that generalized "Thee" with whom God can "dispense" under certain circumstances, along with the hero. What amalgamates the experience of Samson and audience, though, is a "close," a "great event" that involves the loss of Samson himself. The merging of chorus and hero is clearest if we compare the vestigial lament of Manoa's maidens, visiting his tomb on "feastful days," with the Chorus' description of *how* the highest wisdom is best found. This happens, the Chorus suggests, "in the close," a phrase in which Milton involves a metaphor of musical resolution with "event" or merely "ending." (Samson's final deed, we may recall from his reported speech in the Temple, is something "of my own accord.") But the sense of "ending" here by no means dominates our impression of this final chorus. Instead, it is absorbed into a context of human wisdom, here the wisdom that urges, as it imitates, "calm of mind." As for what *has* happened, we may turn to the Chorus' phrase for the manner of the witness we have been viewing: it happened, we are told, "in place." The phrase surely implies a sense of limit in the experience of the hero and even, perhaps, a recognition of the kind recorded in Sonnet 7: "It shall be still in strictest measure ev'n / To that same lot." It is a sense of placement, moreover, that is unshared by the phoenix (that "no second knows, nor third"), or for that matter by Satan in *Paradise Lost*. As a whole, the final chorus can be read as a tragically modified version of "All is . . . as ever in my great Task-Master's eye."

Unlike the celebration that forms the actual conclusion to Milton's tragedy, then, the catastrophe to *Samson Agonistes* would seem to function like the narrative "validation" of a gradually discovered heroic wisdom. But it is important to stress that the destruction of Dagon's temple is an offstage narrative *equivalent*, so to speak, and not really an incident of this work. To adapt the words of *An Apology*, it is a miraculous though not lossless guarantee, removed from mortal sight, of the victory we *have* observed and joined in celebrating. This is

by no means to say, of course, that we are left without glimpses
of the entire narrative "system," or signs of that correspondence which
for Samson marked the early phase of his career. In Milton's verse
from the Nativity ode onward, we are rarely left quite deserted. If
what God wills is fate—as He claims in Book III of *Paradise Lost*—
then Miltonic poetry, somewhat in the manner of *Hamlet*, projects
the world of a will correct to Heaven. In *Paradise Lost*, Milton provides
us with a fictional equivalent to the Long Parliament's "majestic" words,
in several quite different ways: in the ordinary discursive experience
of prelapsarian Eden, for example; or in the Bard's own attempt to
pursue his "great Argument," imaged especially in the articulation
of epic invocation with a confirming or "answerable" narrative wonder.
Or consider such moments of fallen experience as these:

> He spake: and to confirm his words, out-flew
> Millions of flaming swords, drawn from the thighs
> Of mighty Cherubim; the sudden blaze
> Far round illumin'd hell.                        (I, 663–66)

> [Satan] sought them both, but wish'd his hap might find
> *Eve* separate, he wish'd, but not with hope
> Of what so seldom chanc'd, when to his wish,
> Beyond his hope, *Eve* separate he spies,
> Veil'd in a Cloud of Fragrance.            (IX, 421–25)

>                  see the Morn,
> All unconcern'd with our unrest, begins
> Her rosy progress smiling . . .
>    .    .    .    .    .    .    .
> What can be toilsome in these pleasant Walks?
> Here let us live, though in fall'n state, content.
>   So spake, so wish'd much humbl'd *Eve*, but Fate
> Subscrib'd not; Nature first gave Signs, imprest
> On Bird, Beast, Air, Air suddenly eclips'd
> After short blush of Morn.                (XI, 173–84)

No writer ever quite escapes this artful management of circumstance.
But it is remarkable to what extent this engagement of narrative with
wish, or drama, works as a kind of radical form in Milton's poetic
practice. To take an earlier and more complex example, *Lycidas* seems
to involve the generation of both drama and narrative from the interior
monologue of the uncouth swain; the visit of rustic mourners, and
the exterior landscape in some way answerable to his song, are features
that somehow appear to *emerge* during the poem, which as monologue
(or "false surmise") in fact denies them in advance.[29]

In the case of a dramatic work proclaiming itself as never intended for the stage, it seems even more evident that we should not confine the search for authorial presence to the final pronouncements of any character, even should this be a final choral "stanza." Like other poems, *Samson Agonistes* everywhere reveals its author's business, most remarkably perhaps in its vestiges of narrative; those moments when Milton pushes his actors onstage, or has them "blown," almost willy-nilly. Throughout the drama, the nature of Milton's world is revealed as the tension, or the potential collusion, of wisdom with the "true experience" constituted by the arrangement of incidents, with what in tragedy is supposed to just *happen:* the wily subtleties and refluxes of man's mind with whatever hath passion or admiration in the changes of that which is called fortune from without. "I know your friendly minds and—O what noise!" (1508) cries Manoa, interrupted by the dismal accident. Again, both Manoa and the Chorus anticipate the meaning of the poem's final arrival without recognizing that it fulfills simultaneously a "thought" or principle and their *wish:* "Evil news rides post, while good news baits. / And to our wish I see one hither speeding, / An *Ebrew,* as I guess, and of our Tribe" (1538–40). But it is in the Messenger's account of how he arrived that Milton hints most suggestively at the kind of world we have in this poem. Like the initial words of the Chorus, the Messenger's account itself "enters" almost in the manner of a character; on it is based the entire final celebration. But the initial confusion assigned by the Argument to his narrative also applies to the matter of getting him onstage, in what must be one of dramatic literature's least plausible entrances. What brought him here—and what he presumes will deliver him from the "dire imagination" that pursues him or (what is the same thing) from the actual "sight" of this so horrid spectacle—is "providence or instinct of nature":

> But providence or instinct of nature seems,
> Or reason though disturb'd, and scarce consulted,
> To have guided me aright, I know not how
> To thee.                                                        (1545–48)

More than the Chorus, it is surely the Messenger in his confusion who is Milton's spokesman for the truth about what governs the narrative scene in this play. His lines seem to fuse radical alternatives in the poem, the quietistic faith of the Chorus and Manoa, and the "antinomian" part of Samson's outlook. But they do so in a way that specifically recalls what led Samson to the woman at Timna, as well as what got him offstage and to the Temple of Dagon. Thus the Messenger's evident indecision as to which of his conductors was at work points up the fact that in *Samson Agonistes* these are (or seem to be for *our* purposes) replaceable components. The self-generated "problem" of his presence onstage is thereby solved in a way that describes the scene, and hints at the action, of the entire drama.

University of California, Los Angeles

### NOTES

1. "Milton's *Samson:* The Form of Christian Tragedy," *English Literary Renaissance*, III (1973), 306; for Samson's inner victory, see William O. Harris, "Despair and 'Patience and the Truest Fortitude' in *Samson Agonistes*," *ELH*, XXX (1963), 107–20, and the "activist" views of Paul Baumgartner ("Milton and Patience," *Studies in Philology*, LX [1963], 209–10) and John Huntley ("A Revaluation of the Chorus' Role in Milton's *Samson Agonistes*," LXIV [1966], 141–45). Franklin R. Baruch argues that in *Samson Agonistes* the physical world, the "preoccupation" of Manoa and Chorus alike, is left behind only in Samson's "essentially spiritual moment of confrontation" ("Time, Body, and Spirit at the Close of *Samson Agonistes*," *ELH*, XXXVI [1969], 327). Although I agree with Huntley and Baumgartner that Milton's tragic action involves a return to the world and to actions that express faith, I cannot find that lines 1636–39 provide Samson with anything he lacked when he left the stage, or that his keenest insight was "the result of one overt act (going with the Officer because of his 'rousing motions')" (Huntley, "A Revaluation," p. 141n.). For an account of "action" to which I am indebted see Paul R. Sellin, "Milton's Epithet Agonistes," *SEL*, IV (1964), 137–62.

2. See, for example, Joseph H. Summers, "The Movements of the Drama," in *The Lyric and Dramatic Milton*, ed. Joseph H. Summers (New York, 1965), 153–75, and Anthony Low, "Action and Suffering in *Samson Agonistes*," *PMLA*, LXXXIV (1969), 514–19, as well as Tayler, "Milton's *Samson.*"

3. Stanley Fish, "Question and Answer in *Samson Agonistes*," *Critical Quarterly*, XI (1969), 260.

4. *An Apology Against a Pamphlet*, in *Complete Prose Works of John Milton*, ed. Don M. Wolfe et al. (New Haven, 1953–), vol. I, pp. 925–26; hereafter cited as *YP*.

5. In "Letter to a Friend" (1633), *YP*, I, 319; the editors have emended to "world." *Of Education* (To Master Samuel Hartlib), *YP*, II, 407.

6. *An Apology*, *YP*, I, 901.

7. Ibid., p. 930.

8. Ibid., pp. 941–42.

9. All references to Milton's poetry are from the text of Merritt Y. Hughes, *John Milton: Complete Poems and Major Prose* (New York, 1957).

10. Compare the Chorus' punctuation of Dalila's exit: "She's gone, a manifest Serpent by her sting / Discover'd in the end; till now conceal'd" (997–98).

11. Milton records the common metaphors for renovation (hearing, or hearkening, and tasting) in *De Doctrina Christiana*, I, 17, in *The Works of John Milton*, ed. F. A. Patterson et al. (New York, 1931–38), vol. XV, p. 355, hereafter cited as *CM*. Dalila calls Samson "more deaf / To prayers, than winds and seas" (960-61); Samson remarks to Harapha, "The way to know were not to see but taste" (1091). For a full study of the parallels between *Samson Agonistes* and the regenerative process, see John M. Steadman, "'Faithful Champion': The Theological Basis of Milton's Hero of Faith," *Anglia*, LXXVII (1959), 12-28; and French Fogle, "The Action of *Samson Agonistes*," in *Essays in American and English Literature*, ed. Max F. Schulz (Athens, Ohio, 1967), pp. 177-96.

12. *CM*, XV, 373.

13. "Ay me, another inward grief awak't, / With mention of that name renews th'assault" (330-31).

14. *Richard II*, act one, scene three.

15. Compare Harapha's greeting: "I come not, *Samson*, to condole thy chance, / As these perhaps, yet wish it had not been, / Though for no friendly intent. I am of *Gath*" (1076-78).

16. But see Huntley, "A Revaluation," p. 135; and Tayler, "Milton's *Samson*," p. 312.

17. For the view that Samson's decision to accompany the Officer is a sharp reversal of earlier decisions, see G. A. Wilkes, "The Interpretation of *Samson Agonistes*," *Huntington Library Quarterly*, XXVI (1963), 377-78, and the response of Tayler, "Milton's *Samson*," p. 307.

18. See especially Huntley, "A Revaluation," and Baruch, "Time, Body, and Spirit," for full studies of the Chorus.

19. *YP*, I, 900.

20. In *Paradise Lost*, Book XII, Abraham is the "one faithful man" from whom will descend the "one peculiar Nation" of divine favor, following the aversion of God's "holy Eyes" from Canaan. Abraham is called from his father's house "by Vision":

> He straight obeys,
> Not knowing to what Land, yet firm believes:
> .     .     .     .     .     .     .
> He leaves his Gods, his Friends, and native Soil
> Trusting all his wealth
> With God, who call'd him, in a land unknown.          (XII, 126-34)

And Michael instructs Adam to ponder

> that all Nations of the Earth
> Shall in his Seed be blessed; by that Seed
> Is meant thy great deliverer, who shall bruise
> The Serpent's head.          (XII, 148-51)

For complementary views of the Chorus' mission and the nature of its misunderstanding, see Huntley, "A Revaluation," p. 143; and Baruch, "Time, Body, and Spirit," pp. 320-26.

21. Erik H. Erikson, "Insight and Freedom" (Ninth T. B. Davie Memorial Lecture, University of Capetown, 1968); see also idem, *Gandhi's Truth: On the Origins of Militant Nonviolence* (New York, 1969), pp. 431-33.

22. S. F. Johnson, "The Regeneration of Hamlet," *Shakespeare Quarterly*, III (1952), 187-207.

23. The Chorus' dismissal of Samson seems to involve his special kind of pragmatism; they will countenance *whatever* may "serve his glory best, and spread his name / Great among the Heathen round." But even here they fulfill the function of Samson's "thoughts" by presenting "What once I was," this final time by repeating Samson's own account of his birth (23–29). In each version, the marvel of the angelic visitation dominates the "frame" of its syntactic context. In Samson's version, the presence of the marvel blunts the force of the question ("O wherefore was my birth from Heav'n foretold") (23). As they dismiss Samson, the Chorus seems willing to accept the prophecy as already fulfilled: its Samson seems already to be receding into history as it prays for his protection:

> Send thee the Angel of thy Birth, to stand
> Fast by thy side, who from thy Father's field
> Rode up in flames after his message told
> Of thy conception, and be now a shield
> Of fire; that Spirit that first rusht on thee
> In the camp of *Dan*
> Be efficacious in thee now at need.
> For never was from Heaven imparted
> Measure of strength so great to mortal seed,
> As in thy wondrous actions hath been seen.                    (1431–40)

This is hardly the object of their final praise, either in definition or in the extent of qualification. But see Huntley, "A Revaluation," p. 142.

24. *Heroic Knowledge* (Minneapolis, 1957), p. 193.

25. For an account of this report that is close to the one developed below, see Fish, "Question and Answer," pp. 257–60.

26. Anthony Low develops a similar point in "Action and Suffering."

27. Sandys' comment: "By this narration of the Phoenix in Ovid's *Metamorphosis* XV, the ancient fathers, Tertullian, Epiphanius, and Ambrose, goe about to illustrate the immortality of the soule, and resurrection of the body. These are said to be such who excell in piety and vertue; rare, if any, and renewed but once in five hundred yeares with the Phoenix: Indifferent things are common; but the excellent are valued for their rarity" (*Ovid's Metamorphosis Englished, Mythologized, and Represented in Figures by George Sandys*, ed. Karl K. Hulley and Stanley T. Vandersall [Lincoln, Nebr., 1970], p. 707). On the phoenix, see also Huntley, "A Revaluation," p. 144; Baruch, "Time, Body, and Spirit," pp. 328, 332, 334; and, at greater length, Albert R. Cirillo, "The Design of *Samson Agonistes:* Time, Light, and the Phoenix," in *Calm of Mind: Essays on Paradise Regained and Samson Agonistes*, ed. Joseph Anthony Wittreich (Cleveland, 1971), pp. 209–33.

28. Compare the discussion of Baruch, "Time, Body, and Spirit," p. 335.

29. The nineteenth sonnet is similarly helpful in describing the situation of Miltonic lament. Like Herbert's "The Collar," this sonnet frames the speaker's "murmur" in such a way that the narrative program ("When I consider . . . ") is overwhelmed by complaint, which builds toward the bitter succinctness of the question, "Doth God exact day-labor, light denied?" Patience replies "soon"; but she arrives, or was already there, "to prevent / That murmur" (8–9). For a more extensive treatment of this matter in *Lycidas* and *Paradise Lost*, see my "Lucky Words: Process of Speech in *Lycidas*," *JEGP*, LXX (1971), 383–403; and my *Milton's Epic Process: Paradise Lost and Its Miltonic Background* (New Haven, 1973).

# WHAT IT'S LIKE TO READ
# *L'ALLEGRO* AND *IL PENSEROSO*

## Stanley E. Fish

Rosemond Tuve has written that the pleasures enumerated in
*L'Allegro* all have "the flat absence of any relationship to responsibility which we sometimes call innocence." This paper argues
that the experience of reading the poem is itself such a pleasure,
involving just that absence. *L'Allegro* is so structured that at no
point is the reader held responsible for an action or an image or a
unit of thought beyond the moment of its fleeting appearance in a
line or couplet. Rather than compelling attention, the verse operates to diffuse attention, and, as a result, we move from linguistic
event to linguistic event with almost no hostages from our previous
experiences and therefore with no obligation to relate what we are
reading to what we have read. In the act of reading the poem, we
experience as a gift (from Milton) the care-less freedom which is
its subject. In contrast, the activities required of us in the act of
reading *Il Penseroso* are consistently and self-consciously strenuous.
Rather than permitting us to move from one discrete unit to
another, the verse of the second poem binds us to the cares of consecutive thought—the care of attending to implications, the care of
carrying into one line or couplet the syntax or sense of previous
lines and couplets, the care of rendering judgments and drawing
conclusions. Here, then, is a new answer to an old question: who
or what are L'Allegro and Il Penseroso? L'Allegro and Il Penseroso
are the reader: that is, they stand for modes of being which the
reader realizes in his response to the poems bearing their names.
This analysis can be supported by the previous criticism if it is
regarded as a disguised report of what readers have all the while
been doing as they negotiate these poems.

### I

I HAVE only one point to make and everything else follows from it:
*L'Allegro* is easier to read than *Il Penseroso*. This I assume is hardly

news, but if one were a subscriber to the *Times Literary Supplement* in 1934, the matter might seem to be shrouded in considerable doubt, for on October 18 of that year J. P. Curgenven initiated a remarkable correspondence by asking and answering the question, "Who comes to the window in *L'Allegro*, line 46?" Curgenven is disturbed by those who construe "come" (45) as dependent on "hear" (41), which thus, he says, "gives the crude rendering: 'to hear the lark . . . to come, in spite of sorrow, and at my window bid good morrow!'" "Surely," he exclaims, "'come' is dependent on 'admit' (38) and parallel to 'live' (39) and 'hear' (41), and thus it is L'Allegro who comes to his own window and bids good morrow" (p. 715). Curgenven attributes the alternative mistaken reading to two causes: "the expectation of finding inaccuracies in Milton's descriptions of natural phenomena" and the presence in earlier poetry of "some striking references to birds singing their good morrows" and among these, some larks. He duly cites these references, admitting in passing that Milton had no doubt read the poems in question. It is only the first of many curiosities in this exchange that Curgenven spends so much time marshaling evidence in support of the position he opposes.

One week later (October 25) the question is taken up again by T. Sturge Moore, who finds Curgenven's reading "unnatural." "Yet," he goes on, "I agree . . . that to make the lark come is absurd" (p. 735). Moore, it seems, has another candidate. "Surely [a word that appears often in this correspondence, but with a diminishing force], it is *Mirth* [who] is begged to come to the window. The poet has asked to be admitted of her crew . . . and runs on to enumerate advantages he hopes to gain . . . breaking off he resumes his petition: *Then*, as lark and sun rise, is the moment for the Goddess to come and bid him good morrow." A third week (November 1) finds Professor Grierson joining the fray to argue for the one reading that both Moore and Curgenven dismiss out of hand. It *is* the lark who comes, not in nature, but in the mind of the speaker who might well think, in spite of the natural error, that he was being wakened by the bird. A poet, Grierson reminds us, "is not a scientist, . . . he tells truth in his own way" (p. 755). On November 8, B. A. Wright becomes the first of several fence straddlers. He agrees with Curgenven that the syntax and the pronunciation of lines 39–48 are "perfectly clear" (a statement belied by the existence of his letter) and that the poet is himself the subject of the infinitive "come" as he is of the infinitives "live" and "hear." Noting, however, that Mr. Moore understands Mirth to be the subject of "come," Wright admits that this makes good sense and is grammatically typical of Milton. "Either of these interpretations," he concludes, "seems to me possible" (p. 775), although he "cannot with Professor Grierson imagine Milton imagining the lark first 'at his watch towre in the skies' and then still singing at his own bedroom window." (Notice that this assumes what is by no means certain, that it is the lark, not "dull night," who is "startled.") Grierson for his part continues to defend the lark (on November 15) but concedes that "if we are to judge by strict grammar then the most defensible meaning is that it is the cheerful man who comes to the window" (p. 795). "If I am in error," he continues, "I should prefer to take 'Then to come' as a boldly elliptical construction which leaves it quite indefinite who it is that comes." This retreat of course is more strategical than sincere, but it points toward the only conclusion the exchange will finally allow.

In the weeks that follow, old positions are restated and new ones put forward. Tillyard appears (November 15) to support Wright and the cheerful man by alluding, as he often did, to the *First Prolusion*. Joan Sargeaunt offers to remind us "of Bishop Copleston's sly dig at the literal seriousness of critics" (p. 795); presumably (although I am not sure) *she* intends some sly dig at the length and heat of the present correspondence and agrees with Grierson when he declares, "It is vain to argue these questions" (p. 795). Wright, however, will have none of that. It is a matter, he insists, of "Milton's poetic honour. Professor Grierson would seem to imply that any reader is entitled to his own interpretation of the lines," but no one, Wright thunders, is entitled to an interpretation which "makes Milton talk nonsense" (p. 840). Grierson's reading of the lines, he continues, is possible only "when they are isolated from their context." Grierson rather wearily replies "I am afraid Mr. Wright is growing indignant with me which is a sign I should stop" (p. 855). He goes on long enough, however, to insist that "there remain some difficulties" (an understatement, I think) and to declare that where there is doubt, "surely [that word again] one may allow some freedom of interpretation." And indeed the limits of freedom had already been extended by B. R. Rowbottom, who on November 22 had proposed still another interpretation.

"Neither 'Mirth' nor 'The Lark' nor 'The Cheerful Man' is 'then' to come and bid good-morrow at the window through the Sweet-Briar, or the Vine, or the twisted Eglantine, in spite of sorrow, but the 'Dawn' . . . while the Cock scatters the rear of darkness thin" (p. 840).

The controversy ends on November 29 with a letter from W. A. Jones, The County School, Cardiganshire, who reports that his classes of school children "invariably and without noticing any difficulty understand the lines" (p. 856). Whether or not the editors took this as a comment on the entire affair is a matter of conjecture, but at any rate they append a footnote to Jones' letter: "We cannot continue this correspondence."

The point, of course, is that this correspondence could have been continued indefinitely, but even in its abbreviated form, it allows us to make some observations.

1. The proponent of each reading makes concessions, usually by acknowledging that there *is* evidence for the readings he opposes.

2. Each critic is able to point to details which do in fact support his position.

3. But in order fully to support his respective position every one of the critics is moved to make *sense* of the lines by supplying connections more firm and delimiting than the connections available in the text.

4. This making of sense always involves an attempt to arrange the images and events of the passage into a sequence of logical action.

Thus V. B. Halpert, a latecomer to the controversy in 1963, argues for the lark on the basis of the temporal adverb "then," which, she says, signals a break from the simple infinitive construction of "to live" and "to hear" and therefore indicates the beginning of a new action with a new agent—the lark, who "after startling the dull night will then leave its watch tower and come to the poet's window."[1] "In other words," Halpert concludes, "the word *then* signifies a sequence of events." Perhaps so, but it is a sequence which Edith Riggs, who is also committed to making the lines "make perfect sense," finds "unhappy" and "dangerously close to *non*-sense."[2] She proposes a new sequence, one that puts "night" rather than the lark in the watchtower: "The lark, the first of day's forces, startles the enemy from his watch tower in the sky . . . Night is routed and forced to flee." Whether or not the routed night also stops at the poet's window to bid him good-morrow, Miss Riggs does not say (although nothing I can think of would debar her from saying it); she simply concludes on a note of triumph I find impossible to share: "The new reading thus rids the poem of a jarring image and replaces it by one . . . more meaningful within the total context of the passage."

What are we to make of all this? I find myself at least partly in Grierson's camp, and finally in the camp of Jones' children; for if the entire exchange proves anything, it is that Milton does not wish to bind us to any one of these interpretations. I do not mean (as Grierson seems to) that he left us free to choose whatever interpretation we might prefer, but that he left us free *not* to choose, or more simply, that he left us free. As Brooks and Hardy observe, the reader of these lines "is hurried through a series of infinitives . . . the last of which is completely ambiguous in its subject."[3] I would only add that the ambiguity is *so* complete that unless someone asks us to, we do not worry about it, and we do not worry about it (or even notice it) because while no subject is specified for "come," any number of subjects—lark, poet, Mirth, Dawn, Night—are available. What is *not* available is the connecting word or sustained syntactical unit which would pressure us to decide between them, and in the absence of that pressure, we are not obliged to decide. Nor are we obliged to decide between the different (and plausible) sequences which choosing any one of these subjects would generate:

1. If it is the lark who comes to the window, he does so while the cock "with lively din" scatters the rear of darkness thin, and the two birds thus perform complementary actions.

2. If it is the dawn that comes to the window, she does so while the cock with lively din scatters the rear of darkness thin and is thus faithful to our understanding of the relationship between cock's crowing and dawn.

3. If it is the poet (L'Allegro) who comes to the window, he does so in response to lark, cock, and dawn; that is, while they are performing their related functions.

4. And if it is Mirth who comes to the window, the action allies her with lark, cock, and dawn in the awakening of L'Allegro.

All of these readings hang on the word "while" in line 49, but since "while" is less time-specific than other temporal adverbs, it does not firmly call for any one of these and, more to the point, it functions equally well, that is, equally *loosely*, in all of them. Rather than insisting on a clear temporal relationship among the events it connects, "while" acts as a fulcrum around which those events swirl, supplying just enough of a sense of order to allow us to continue, but not so much that we feel compelled to arrange the components of the passage into an intelligible sequence. In short, "while" neither directs nor requires choice; instead, it *frees* us from choice and allows us—and I mean this literally—to be careless. This is also the effect of the two "ors" in the preceding couplet: "Through the Sweet-Briar or the Vine, / Or the twisted Eglantine."[4] The "ors" divide alternative images, each of which registers only for a split second before it is supplanted by the next. We are neither committed to any one of them, nor required to combine them into a single coherent picture. The effect of the couplet extends both backward—softening the outline of the window and of *who*ever or *what*ever has come to it—and forward—removing the pressure of specificity from the weakly transitional "while."

I intend the phrase "weakly transitional" precisely, for it exactly captures the balance Milton achieves by deploying his connectives. If there were no transitions, the freedom of the poem's experience would become a burden, since a reader would first notice it and then worry about it; and if the transitions were firmly directing, a reader would be obliged to follow the directions they gave.[5] Milton has it both ways, just as he does with a syntax that is not so much ambiguous as it is loose. Twentieth-century criticism has taught us to value ambiguities because they are meaningful, but these ambiguities, if they can be called that, protect us from meaning by protecting us from working. They are there, not to be noticed, but to assure that whatever track a reader happens to come in on, he will have no trouble keeping to it; no choice that he makes (of lark, poet, Goddess, etc.) will conflict with a word or a phrase he meets later. Anything fits with anything else, so that it is never necessary to go back and retrace one's effortless steps.

Rosemond Tuve has written that the pleasures enumerated in *L'Allegro* all have "the flat absence of any relation to responsibility which we sometimes call innocence."[6] What I am suggesting is that the experience of *reading* the poem is itself such a pleasure, involving just that absence; for at no point are we held responsible for an action or an image beyond the moment of its fleeting appearance in a line or a couplet. Moreover it is a *flat* absence in the sense that we are

not even aware of having been relieved of it. That is why Cleanth
Brooks is not quite right when he declares that the unreproved pleasures
of *L'Allegro* "can be had for the asking";[7] they can be had *without*
the asking.

The result is an experience very much like that described by
William Strode in "Against Melancholy," a poem that has been suggested by J. B. Leishman as a possible source for *L'Allegro*:[8]

> Free wandring thoughts not ty'de to muse
> Which thinke on all things, nothing choose,
> Which ere we see them come are gone.          (13–15)

"Take no care," Strode enjoins in line 18, but Milton goes him one
better by *giving* no care, by not asking that we put things together,
or supply connections, or make inferences, or do anything at all. Rather
than compelling attention, the verse operates to diffuse attention, either
by blurring the focus of its descriptions—the Sweet-Briar *or* the Vine
*or* the twisted Eglantine—or by breaking off a description if its focus
threatens to become too sharp, or by providing so many possible
and plausible sequences that it finally insists on none. As a result we
move from linguistic event to linguistic event with almost no hostages
from our previous experience and therefore with no obligation to
relate what we are reading to what we have read.

Critics have always been aware of the curious discreteness that
characterizes *L'Allegro*, both as an object and as an experience, but
in general they have responded either by downgrading the poem,
so capable, as D. C. Allen observes, of "desultory rearrangement,"[9] or
by attempting to rescue it from the charge of disunity and fragmenta-
tion. In 1958 Robert Graves went so far as to suggest that in the
course of composing *L'Allegro* Milton misplaced sixteen lines, probably
over the weekend. The lines beginning "Oft listening" (53) and ending
with every shepherd telling his tale under the hawthorn in the dale
(68) originally followed the account of the Lubber fiend as "Crop
full out of the door he flings, / Ere the first cock his matins rings"
(113–14). By restoring the original order, Graves asserts, we make
the poem very much less of a "muddle" (that is, we make *sense* of
it). Otherwise, he points out, we are left with this improbable sequence
of events:

While distractedly bidding good-morrow, at the window, to Mirth, with one
ear cocked for the hounds and horn . . . [he] sometimes, we are told, "*goes
walking, not unseen, by hedgerow elms, on Hillocks green.*" Either Milton had

forgotten that he was still supposedly standing naked at the open window—
(the Jacobeans always slept raw)—or the subject of "walking" is the cock, who
escapes from the barnyard, deserts his dames, ceases to strut, and anxiously
aware of the distant hunt, trudges far afield among ploughmen and shepherds
in the dale. But why should Milton give twenty lines to the adventures of the
neighbor's wandering cock? And why, "*walking not unseen*"? Not unseen by
whom?[10]

Graves is not unaware of the impression he is making. "Please
do not think I am joking," he implores, and at least one critic has
taken him seriously. Herbert F. West, Jr., admits that such an accident
of misplacement is "possible" and that Graves' emendation "does little
apparent danger to the text" and even seems to "smooth over some
difficult spots."[11] And so it does. The poet now looks out of his window
to say, quite naturally, "Straight mine eye hath caught new pleasures,"
and it is the Lubber fiend who walks not unseen on hillocks green
where he is espied, one assumes, by plowman, milkmaid, mower,
and shepherd. The sequence ends as he listens to each shepherd tell
his tale under the hawthorn in the dale, making for a perfect transition
to the next section, which begins with line 115: "Thus done the Tales,
to bed they creep." Yet Graves' emendation should, I think, be rejected
and rejected precisely *because* of its advantages; for by providing
continuity to the plot line of the poem, it gives us something to keep
track of, and therefore it gives us *care*. It is Milton's wish, however,
to liberate us from care, and the nonsequiturs that bother Graves
are meant to prevent us from searching after the kind of sense he
wants to make. "Not unseen by whom?" he asks, and he might well
have asked, why *not* unseen, a formula which neither relates the figure
of the walker to other figures nor declares categorically the absence
of such a relation, leaving the matter not so much ambiguous as unex-
amined. Or he might have asked (perhaps did ask) what precisely is
the "it" that in line 77 "sees"? This question would only lead to another,
for the pronoun subject is no more indeterminate than the object
of "its" seeing—the beauty who is the cynosure of neighboring eyes.
Is she there or is she not? "Perhaps," answers Milton in line 79, relieving
us of any responsibility to her or even to her existence. This in turn
removes the specificity from the adverbial of place which introduces
the following line: "Hard by, a Cottage chimney smokes." Hard by
what? Graves might well ask. In this context or noncontext the phrase
has no pointing function at all. It merely gets us unburdened into

the next line and into the next *discrete* scene, where with Corydon
and Thyrsis we rest in "secure delight" (91), that is, in delight *se
cura*, delight without, or free from, care.

It is the promise of "secure delight," of course, that is at the
heart of the pastoral vision, although it is the literary strength of the
pastoral always to default on that promise by failing to exclude from
its landscape the concerns of the real world. Milton, however, chooses
to sacrifice that strength in order to secure the peculiar flatness of
effect that makes reading *L'Allegro* so effortless. The details of this
landscape are without resonance; they refer to nothing beyond themselves and they ask from us no response beyond the *minimal* and
literary response of recognition. This lack of resonance is attributable
in part to the swift succession of images, no one of which claims
our attention for more than a couplet. Each couplet is self-enclosed
by ringing monosyllabic rhymes, and the enclosures remain discrete.
Continuity is provided by patterns of alliteration and assonance (moun-
tains-meadows), which carry us along but do not move us to acts
of association or reflection. The "new pleasures" which the eyes of
both speaker and reader catch are new in the sense of novel, *continually*
new, following one another but not firmly related to one another.
From lawns to mountains to meadows and then to towers, the sequence
is so arranged as to discourage us from extrapolating from it a composite
scene, the details of which would then be interpretable.[12] Neither
time's winged chariot nor anything else is at the back of these shepherds,
and the verse in no way compels us to translate them into figures
for the young poet or the weary courtier or the faithful feeder of
a Christian flock. In other words, we know and understand the quality
of their untroubled (careless) joy because it is precisely reflected in
the absence of any pressure on us to make more of their landscape
than its surfaces present. (This introduces the interesting possibility
that while *L'Allegro* is the easier of the two poems to read, it was
the more difficult to write. In *Il Penseroso* Milton can exploit the
traditions his verse invades; in *L'Allegro* he must simultaneously introduce them and denude them of their implications, employing a diction
and vocabulary rich in complex associations without the slightest gesture in the direction of that complexity. In *L'Allegro* it is not so much
what the images do, but what they do not do. The poem is a triumph
of absence.)

There is then here, as elsewhere, a one-to-one correspondence between the pleasures celebrated in the poem and the pleasure of reading it, and this correspondence inheres in the careless freedom with which *any* activity, including the activity of reading, can be enjoyed. The tournaments of lines 119–24 belong in *L'Allegro* because the knights and barons bold who take part in them hazard nothing, not life or death or even honor. Their high triumphs are triumphs of style and involve a fidelity to forms which have no meaning beyond the moment of their execution. Like us they are engaged in an activity from which the consequences (hostages to time) have been carefully removed.

The activities of *L'Allegro* are consistently like this, without consequences as they are without antecedents. Only once is a consequence even threatened, when the Lydian airs are said to "pierce" the meeting soul—"Lap me in soft *Lydian* Airs, / Married to immortal verse, / Such as the meeting soul may pierce" (136–38); but the first two words of the following line, "In notes," blunt the potential thrust of "pierce" exactly as the lances and swords of the knights and barons bold are blunted and rendered harmless. It has been suggested that Milton's conception of Lydian music is taken from Cassiodorus, who attributes to it the power to restore us with relaxation and delight, "being invented against excessive cares and worries."[13] Whether or not this is Milton's source, it is surely a description of the effect his music, *his* invention, has on us. We are delighted because we are relaxed, and we are relaxed because the cares to which other poems bind us—the care of attending to implications, the care of carrying into one line or couplet the syntax and sense of previous lines and couplets, the care of arranging and ordering the details of a poetic landscape, the care of rendering judgments and drawing conclusions, the care, in sum, of sustained (and consecutive) thought—these are here not present. The figure of Orpheus as he appears in lines 145–50 is thus a perfect surrogate for the reader; the music he hears calls him to nothing, as we have been called to nothing by the verse. He is enwrapped in its harmonies, resting on "heapt Elysian flow'rs" (147) as we rest, unexercised, on the heaped (not arranged) flowers of the poem's images and scenes, insulated from the resonances and complications which might be activated in another context (the context, in fact, of *Il Penseroso*). This music *merely* meets the ear and the ear it meets has no answering responsibility (of which there is the "flat absence") beyond the passive responsibility of involuntary delight. When Graves discovered that *L'Allegro* was "rather a muddle," it was after many years of reading the poem. I had however, he explains, never before "read it carefully."[14] The point that I have been making is that no one asked him to, and that his period of *mis*reading began when he decided to accord the poem the kind of careful attention from which it was Milton's gift to set us free.

## II

If I am right about *L'Allegro*, the other critics who have written on it are necessarily wrong; for to a man they have sought to interpret the poem, while it is my contention that interpretation is precisely what it does not invite, because its parts are arranged in such a way as to exert no interpretive pressures. Of course it would be easy to turn this argument into a criticism by saying that what I have demonstrated here is that *L'Allegro* lacks unity. This would certainly be true if unity were defined (narrowly) as the coherence of formal elements, but it is the absence of that coherence which is responsible for the unity I have been describing, a unity not of form, but of experience. That is to say, what unifies *L'Allegro* is the consistency of the demands it makes, or rather declines to make, on the reader, who is thus permitted the freedom from care ("secure delight") which is the poem's subject. It is this freedom which is banished when *Il Penseroso* opens by declaring "Hence vain deluding joys." "Vain" here is to be taken as fruitless or without purpose, and it refers not to an abstraction, but to a mode of experiencing, a mode in which the brain is quite literally "idle" because it is "possessed" by a succession of "gaudy shapes" and fancies "which ere we see them come are gone." This is of course the experiential mode of *L'Allegro*, and it should not surprise us to find that the experience of reading *Il Penseroso* is quite different.

Like *L'Allegro*, *Il Penseroso* offers alternative genealogies in its opening lines; but where in the first poem these are indifferently presented, in the second, one is specifically preferred to the other; and the fact of the preference is rooted in a judgment we are required to understand and in a distinction (or series of distinctions) we are pressured to make. That pressure is felt as soon as we hear, "Hail divinest Melancholy, / Whose Saintly visage is too bright / To hit the sense of human sight" (12–14). These lines turn on a paradox, and it is in the nature of a paradox that a reader who recognizes it is already responding to the question it poses. What kind of light is so bright that it dazzles and, in effect, darkens the sense of human sight? An answer to this question is readily available in the Christian-neo-Platonic opposition between the light of ordinary day and the "Celestial light" which "shines inward" revealing "things invisible to mortal sight" (*PL*, III, 52–55). There is no more familiar commonplace in Renaissance thought, but even so, in order to recall it, a reader must reach for it; that is, he must *do* something, engage in an activity, and it is an activity in which he is asked to continue as the passage unfolds:

> And therefore to our weaker view,
> O'erlaid with black staid Wisdom's hue.
> Black, but such as in esteem,
> Prince *Memnon's* sister might beseem,
> Or that Starr'd *Ethiop* Queen that strove
> To set her beauties praise above
> The Sea Nymphs, and their powers offended.
> Yet thou art higher far descended.                    (15–22)

The single word "therefore" in line 15 can stand for everything that distinguishes the companion poems. It is a word that could never appear in *L'Allegro* because it operates to *enjoin* the responsibility (to backward and forward contexts) from which that poem sets us free.[15] The lines that follow "therefore" add to the responsibility, for in the course of reading them we are asked to do several things at once. First we must suspend one line of argument and attend to another; but that argument in turn unfolds in stages, so that we are continually revising our understanding of what we have just read; and, moreover, the effect of our revised understanding extends in every instance backward to the Goddess Melancholy, whose precise characterization remains the goal of our consecutive attention. Obviously, that attention is not only consecutive, but strenuous. A phrase like "Black, but" asks us simultaneously to recall the pejorative associations of black and to prepare ourselves for a more positive view of the color; but no sooner has that view been established than it too is challenged, first by the imputation to Cassiopeia of impiety and then (more directly) by the qualificatory "Yet" of line 22. In this context (the context not of the verse, but of our *experience* of the verse), there are at least three possible readings of that line: (1) the obvious literal reading: "Your lineage is more impressive than that of Memnon's sister or Cassiopeia." (2) The secondary literal reading: "You come to us from a loftier height than does Memnon's sister or Cassiopeia, that is, from the stars." (3) What we might call the moral reading: "You are higher precisely because you have descended, because you have been willing to accommodate yourself to our 'weaker view' by being black and low rather than bright and high ('starry')."

In *L'Allegro*, the availability of alternative readings operates to minimize our responsibility to any one of them and therefore to any consecutive argument; here it is precisely because we have been following a consecutive argument that the alternative readings become available. In neither poem are we required to choose between the readings; but whereas in one the absence of choice is a function of the absence of interpretive pressure, in the other that pressure is so great that we are asked to choose every reading, because each of them goes with one of the interpretive strains we have been led to pursue and distinguish.

Here then is a way of answering the questions that have so often been put to these two poems. Do they share patterns of imagery, or is the presence in them of light and shadow consistently and meaningfully opposed? Are they to be read as the hyperbolic rhetoric of their invocations suggests, or are those invocations directed at the excess of the complementary means they present? Is there mirth in *Il Penseroso*'s melancholy and melancholy in *L'Allegro*'s mirth? So long as these (and other) questions have been asked in the context of an examination of the text, there has been no hope of answering them, for as the history of the criticism shows, the observable evidence will support any number of answers. But if we turn our attention from the text to the experience it gives, an unambiguous and verifiable answer is immediately forthcoming. Every point of contact is a point of contrast, not in the poems (where the details could be made to point in either direction), but in the nature of the activities they require of their readers. The activities required of us by *Il Penseroso* are consistently strenuous. Rather than permitting us to move from one discrete unit to another, the verse of the second poem continually insists that we carry into the present context whatever insights we have won from previous contexts, which are in turn altered or expanded retroactively. As a result our attention is not diffused but concentrated, and the distinction made in the opening lines—between an idle brain captive to a succession of unrelated images and a mind that is "fixed" —is precisely realized in the reading experiences of the two poems.

A fixed mind is one that keeps steadily before it an idea or a project to which it relates whatever new particulars come into its ken. Here the idea is the Goddess Melancholy and the project is the understanding of the way of life she presents. It is of course our project, and because it is ours, it gives interpretive direction to our movement through the poem, providing us with ready-made contexts— it is *we* who have made them—into which the details of the verse are immediately drawn. Thus when the Goddess Melancholy material- izes in the form of the "pensive Nun," the lines describing her habit and gait are resonant with significance because we bring the signifi- cances with us. The Nun's "robe of darkest grain" (33) is capable of any number of interpretations, but the reader who has negotiated the preceding lines will immediately identify its color as the dark hue of staid Wisdom and distinguish it from the boasting blackness of Cassiopeia. Forgetting oneself to marble and gazing downward with an unseeing stare (41–44) is at the very least ambiguous behavior, but it is disambiguated when the same reader recalls that the dimming of natural vision and the stilling of bodily motion are preliminary to the descrying of a light that is too bright to hit the sense of human sight. As a figure in the landscape, the Nun displays less and less energy, but at the same time she is being energized from within by the meanings *we* attach to her dress and actions, until at line 45 she stands (frozen) before us as an embodiment of all the mythological and philosophical associations to which we have been called by the verse.

In a way I am simply giving body to an observation made by D. C. Allen. In *L'Allegro*, Allen points out, "there is an abrupt division between the invitation and the main body of the poem," while in *Il Penseroso*, the transition is "more fluid and skillful."[16] For Allen, however, abruptness and fluidity are properties of formal structures, and his distinction is a value judgment (presumably if the transitions of *L'Allegro* were more fluid, it would be a better poem). But in my terms, abruptness and fluidity are properties of experiences, and the distinction is not between a skillful and an unskillful arrangement, but between the different experiences provided by arrangements that are indifferently skillful. The components of either poem offer ample possibilities for making connections (that is, for fluidity), but it is only while reading *Il Penseroso* that we are pressured to make them. The source of that pressure is the verse, and it is exerted both silently and explicitly: silently when we are asked to manage units of sense and syntax larger than the couplet, and explicitly when we are directed in line 49 to add ("And add to these retired Leisure"). What we are to add are Melancholy's companions, Peace, Quiet, Spare Fast, the Muses, retired Leisure, and first and chiefest (although last to be called) the Cherub Contemplation. Were this list in *L'Allegro*, we would receive its items discretely ("Straight mine eye hath caught new pleasures"); but here we are asked to relate them both to each other and to the master abstraction of which they are all manifestations. Moreover, the point of relation is not something they share on the surface—on its face the list is quite heterogeneous—but something that is available only when we extrapolate from the surface to an underlying pattern of significance. The content of that pattern is a two-stage sequence—withdrawal from the busy companies of men followed by an ascent to the realm of pure and heavenly forms— and this of course is precisely the sequence that has just been acted out by the pensive Nun, who is herself a realization of the paradoxes exploited in the opening lines. "The poetic components of *Il Penseroso*," declares Allen, "seem to glide out of each other by brilliant acts of association."[17] The point I have been making is that these acts are ours, and we perform them with a self-consciousness that is continually returning us to the first link in the associative chain, which in every case is found to be isomorphic with the last. The Cherub Contemplation is the first and chiefest even though he brings up the rear, because the values he declares explicitly, that is by name, were present in the first and in every other of their incarnations.

We see then that the pattern of experience in *Il Penseroso* is as consistent as the quite different pattern in *L'Allegro*. It is a pattern of continually exerted pressure, and it moves us to a set of sustained and related activities: generalizing, abstracting, reflecting, recalling, synthesizing. Not only are these activities sustained, but they have a single object, the precise elucidation of the nature of melancholy;

and this continues to be true when the focus of the poem shifts to the speaker, for in his wanderings he repeatedly acts out the sequence that joins the other figures we have encountered. Three times he retires from the light of day into an enclosure: first in some "removed place" (79) where light is taught to counterfeit a gloom, later in twilight groves (133) that have been sought specifically to escape the Sun's flaring beams, and finally in the "Cloister's pale" (156) where the light streaming through the windows is deemed religious *because* it is "dim." Three times as day's garish eye is shut out and earthly sounds are stilled, Il Penseroso becomes physically inactive, sitting in some high and lonely tower (86), or asleep by a hallowed brook (139), or standing motionless as the pealing organ blows to the full-voiced choir below (162). And three times, as his body forgets itself to marble, his spirit soars, in the company of Plato (as together they explore "what vast Regions hold / The immortal mind that hath forsook / Her mansion in this fleshly nook" [90–92]), under the aegis of "some strange mysterious dream" (147), and in response to the ecstasy-making sounds of the "Service high and Anthems clear":

> With antic Pillars massy proof
> And storied windows richly dight,
> Casting a dim religious light.
> There let the pealing Organ blow,
> To the full voic'd choir below,
> In Service high and Anthems clear,
> As may with sweetness, through mine ear,
> Dissolve me into ecstasies,
> And bring all Heav'n before mine eyes.          (158–66)

In this penultimate scene we are once again returned to the master images whose exfoliation has been the stimulus to our interpretive efforts. The worshiper in the "Cloister's pale" assumes exactly the position assumed earlier by the pensive Nun, and like her he is the very embodiment of Peace, Quiet, Spare Fast, the Muses, retired Leisure, and the Cherub Contemplation. Even the pattern of word play is the pattern we experienced in the opening lines, and we are moved by it to make the same distinctions we made then. The basic distinction is between two kinds of perception, the physical and the spiritual. They share a vocabulary, but that vocabulary is so placed that we cannot help but be aware of its two fields of reference. In line 160 the ruling adjective is "dim," but line 163 ends with a strong stress on the adjective "clear." The same apparent clash exists between the adverb "below" in line 162, which refers to the spatial positioning of the organ and the choir, and the adjective "high" in line 163. The clash in both cases is only apparent, because as we come upon them we understand "high" and "clear" to refer not to spatial and sensible, but to spiritual categories; but since that understanding follows immediately upon a sequence in which spatial and sensible categories *are* operative, it signals a transference from outer to inner space. That transference is completed by the pointed juxtaposition in lines 164 and 166 of "through mine ear" and "before mine eyes." No word in the poem is more emphasized than "eyes"; it marks the end of a line, of a couplet, and of a section; and as we read it we know, with the full weight of everything we have learned, that it cannot be read literally, and that this is the eye of the mind which now opens, as it has opened so many times before, to a light that is too bright to hit the sense of human sight. Milton, the *Variorum Commentary* observes at this point, "is here summing up the whole process of self-education described in the poem";[18] but whatever has been described in the poem (and that has long been a matter of dispute), the process and the education have taken place in the reader.

Let me say, lest there be any misunderstanding, that I am not here offering an interpretation of *Il Penseroso*, but arguing that interpretation is the activity to which the poem moves us, and that it is this which distinguishes it from *L'Allegro*. In another sense, however, the poems are not to be distinguished; for in both there is a congruence of experience with thematic materials. The bards in *Il Penseroso* sing of "Trophies hung" (118) and therefore of tournaments in which something more than the applause of ladies is at stake. In place of a domesticated goblin who performs kitchen chores in return for a "cream bowl," the voice of *Il Penseroso* speaks to us of Daemons "Whose power hath a *true* consent / With Planet or with Element";[19] and it is precisely this "power" that Orpheus displays when he bests Pluto in a line whose stresses communicate and create a sense of urgency that is wholly alien to *L'Allegro:* "And made Hell grant what Love did seek" (108).

The singing of Orpheus, like everything else in *Il Penseroso*, has both purpose and consequence; and purpose and consequence are also what characterize our efforts as readers. There is here as in *L'Allegro* a one-to-one correspondence between the activities *in* the poem and the activity of reading it, and these activities merge in a single line: "Where more is meant than meets the ear" (120). More is indeed meant by *Il Penseroso* than meets the ear, and the responsibility for that meaning rests with the ear that is met, an ear that is asked not only to take in a succession of sounds, but to relate them to each other and to a complex of significances in which they are implicated. It is just this kind of sustained mental effort, the effort of synthesizing, generalizing, and abstracting, to which the pensive man pledges himself in the poem's closing lines:

> Where I may sit and rightly spell
> Of every star that Heav'n doth shew,
> And every Herb that sips the dew;
> Till old experience do attain,
> To something like Prophetic strain.          (170–74)

To spell is to decipher, to puzzle out, to consider, to think; to engage in just those actions the poem requires of its readers. Here then is another point of contact between the two poems that is finally a point of contrast. In both, the speaker and reader are united by the kind of acts they do or do not perform. In *Il Penseroso*, as Bridget Lyons has observed, we are continually aware of a consciousness through which the phenomena of experience are being filtered.[20] In other words, we are continually aware of the presence in the poem of a mind, and our awareness takes the form of matching exertions. *L'Allegro*, on the other hand, is striking for the absence of mind; there is, it would seem, no one at home. The first-person pronoun only occurs once before the final couplet, and it is followed immediately by the lines that were the occasion of the *TLS* correspondence. They are in turn so variously interpretable that any sense of a continuous and controlling presence is progressively weakened; nor is it reinforced when the speaker appears again in line 69 as a disembodied eye: "Straight mine eye hath caught new pleasures." Even this synecdochical identity is blurred when it is absorbed into a speculation about "neighboring eyes" (the progression is from "I" to "eye" to "eyes") which may or may not be there. The same imprecision of reference and sequence that removes the pressure of consecutive thought also prevents us from finding in the poem a consecutive thinker; and in the absence of a consciousness whose continuing and active presence would give the poem unity, we are that much less inclined to unify it. If no one is at home, then we can be on holiday too.

In both poems, then, the speaker and the reader are to be identified, and this identification suggests a new answer to an old question: who or what are L'Allegro and Il Penseroso? L'Allegro and Il Penseroso are the reader; that is, they stand for modes of being which the reader realizes in his response to the poems bearing their names. The formal and thematic features of each poem are intimately related to its meaning, not because they reflect it, but because they *produce* it, by moving the reader to a characteristic activity. In short, the poems *mean* the experience they give; and because they so mean, the conditionals with which they end are false:

> These delights if thou canst give,
> Mirth with thee I mean to live.                    (15–52)

> These pleasures *Melancholy* give,
> And I with thee will choose to live.               (175–76)

These conditionals are false because the conditions they specify have already been met. The delights and pleasures of Mirth and Melancholy are even now ours, for in the very act of reading we have been theirs.

### III

In conclusion, I would like to turn away from the poems to consider the larger implications of my analysis. More specifically, I would like to pose a question. What is it that a procedure focusing on the reader's experience can do? First of all it can deal with *L'Allegro*, which has, for the most part, been unavailable to other critical vocabularies. This is not to say that the experience of *L'Allegro* has been unavailable, but that the readers who have had that experience have been compelled by their theoretical assumptions either to allegorize it or to devalue it. In fact it is difficult to see how a formalist criticism, committed as it is to "care" both as a criterion for composition and as a condition of serious reading, could accept my description of *L'Allegro*. For the formalist, reading poetry is equivalent to noticing and *sharing in* the craft and labor that produced it. A poem that asked for no such answering attention would therefore be suspect; and indeed when this paper was first read at a public meeting, a member of the audience rose to ask, with some indignation, why I was attacking *L'Allegro*.

Presumably it was inconceivable to him that an account of the poem
that did not tie up, but multiplied loose ends could be praise. In
this connection, the recently published *Variorum Commentary* is in-
structive. Time and again the editors note the presence in the poem
of interpretive puzzles, and time and again the sifting of evidence
leads to an indeterminate conclusion. The question, who comes to
the window at line 46?, is debated for a full four pages which end
with the recording of a difference of opinion between the two editors.
A discussion of alternative versions of line 104 breaks off with the
admission that in either version the syntax is "somewhat obscure"
and suggests a "degree of carelessness" (p. 295). (Carelessness indeed!)
Even the simple phrase "tells his tale" in "every Shepherd tells his
tale" (67) has had, we are told, "alternative explanations" (p. 287);
but after a survey of those explanations, we read that "all that is
certain is that the shepherds were sitting" (p. 288); anything else, "the
reader must decide for himself" (p. 289).

The point of course is that he need not, and that these and other
"obscurities" exist precisely so that he will not feel pressured to make
the sense the editors seek. These same editors are continually turning
up evidence for the reading offered in this paper (when for example
they gloss "wanton" as "uncontrolled by plan or purpose" and "giddy"
as "incapable of steady attention"), but they are unable to see the
evidence for what it is because they are committed to a single criterion
of formal unity (which is at base a criterion of cognitive clarity).
As it turns out, however, that is exactly the wrong criterion to apply
to a poem like *L'Allegro* which grows out of what Thomas Rosenmeyer
has recently called the "disconnective decorum" of the Theocritan
pastoral.[21] As Rosenmeyer describes it, this decorum is tied to "a perception of a world that is not continuous, but a series of discrete units,
each to be savored for its own sake" (p. 46). A poem displaying
this decorum will be "best analyzed as a loose combination of independent elements," since "the poet provides few if any clues . . . for
consolidation" (p. 47). The poem, Rosenmeyer continues, does not
have a plot, so that it is protected "against the profundities and syntheses
which . . . plot . . . is always on the verge of triggering" (p. 48).
"Consequently," he concludes, "the artlessness of the poem is not there
for a reason, but exists of itself, which also means that it is harder

to explain" (p. 48). An analysis in terms of the reading experience has, I submit, been able to explain it, because it is not tied to an evaluative bias which both directs and crowns its procedures.

This success (if you will agree that it is one) is finally attributable to a larger capability I would claim for experiential analysis: it provides a firm basis for the resolving of critical controversies. As I have argued elsewhere, formalist procedures are unable to settle anything, because in the absence of constraints the observable regularities in a text can be made to point in any number of directions.[22] But if the focus of analysis is the reader's experience, a description of that experience will at the same time be an interpretation of its materials. Rather than two operations (description and interpretation) whose relationship is problematical, there is only one, and consequently many of the directions in which values might have been irresponsibly assigned are automatically eliminated.

As a final example, consider the question most often asked of *L'Allegro* and *Il Penseroso*. Is the mode of being presented in one poem to be preferred to the mode of being presented in the other? As it is usually posed, this is a spatial question: that is, it is to be answered by examining the two poems as objects and toting up the attitudes or judgments they contain. Not surprisingly, this procedure has led only to disagreement and dispute. If, however, we turn the spatial question into a temporal one, an unambiguous answer is immediately forthcoming because preference or choice is no longer an issue. The pressure for choice is the creation of the assumptions of the critics who make it. The experience of the poems, however, exerts no such pressure, because in the order of their reading the faculties of judgment and discrimination come into play only in *Il Penseroso*.[23] Were that order reversed, the reflective self-consciousness encouraged by *Il Penseroso* would also encourage a critical attitude toward the flatness of implication characteristic of *L'Allegro*, and we would be unable to read that poem with the innocence (absence of responsibility) which is both its subject and its gift. The present order, the order Milton gave us, allows the pleasure of reading *L'Allegro* to be an unreproved pleasure free, and only then does it introduce us to another pleasure (by giving us another experience) which does not so much reprove the first as remove it from memory. Allen ends his fine essay on the poems by speaking of "a ceaseless passing from one chamber of experience to the next."[24] It is that passing, rather than any after-the-fact judgment one could make on it, that I have tried to describe.

The Johns Hopkins University


NOTES

This is an expanded version of a paper originally read before Section 6 of the MLA convention, December 1971.

1. V. B. Halpert, "On Coming to the Window in *L'Allegro*," *Anglia*, LXXXI (1963), 200.

2. Edith Riggs, "Milton's *L'Allegro*, 41-50," *Explicator*, XXIII (February 1965), item 44.

3. Cleanth Brooks and John E. Hardy, *Poems of Mr. John Milton* (New York, 1951), p. 136.

4. Lines 47-48. The text used throughout is from *John Milton: Complete Poetry and Major Prose*, ed. Merritt Y. Hughes (New York, 1957).

5. For a similar point, see Leslie Brisman, " 'All Before Them Where to Choose': 'L'Allegro' and 'Il Penseroso,'" *JEGP*, LXXI (April 1972), 239.

6. "Structural Figures of *L'Allegro* and *Il Penseroso*," in *Milton: Modern Essays in Criticism*, ed. Arthur E. Barker (New York, 1965), p. 61.

7. *The Well Wrought Urn* (New York, 1947), p. 54.

8. J. B. Leishman, "*L'Allegro* and *Il Penseroso* in Their Relation to Seventeenth-Century Poetry," *Essays and Studies 1951*, n.s., IV (1951), 5.

9. D. C. Allen, *The Harmonious Vision* (Baltimore, 1954), p. 6.

10. *5 Pens in Hand* (New York, 1958), p. 39.

11. Herbert F. West, Jr., "'Here's a Miltonic Discovery . . . ,'" *Renaissance Papers, 1958, 1959, 1960, 1961*, p. 73.

12. The discreteness of the details is noted by F. W. Bateson in "The Money-Lender's Son: 'L'Allegro' and 'Il Penseroso,'" in his *English Poetry: A Critical Introduction* (London, 1950), p. 159: "'Russet' is decidedly not the epithet one would have expected for 'Lawns' . . . nor is 'Gray' what one would have expected for 'Fallows.'" But Bateson then goes on to draw exactly the wrong conclusion: "Milton must have had his eye on a real field." I would say, rather, that Milton wanted to keep the reader's eye from going to the trouble of envisioning a real field.

13. See James Hutton, "Some English Poems in Praise of Music," *English Miscellany*, II (1951), 46.

14. Robert Graves, "John Milton Muddles Through," *New Republic* (May 27, 1957), p. 17.

15. I do not mean that the word itself could not appear in *L'Allegro*, but that it could not appear with its full logical force. It could appear if it operated (like "while" in line 49) in such a way as to gesture toward a sequence that was, in fact, not there. I would not wish to be understood as suggesting that the presence or absence of a word could automatically (that is, mechanically) be correlated with the presence

or absence of a particular effect. The specification of effect always requires a taking into account of the full experiential context.

16. *The Harmonious Vision*, p. 10.

17. Ibid.

18. *A Variorum Commentary on the Poems of John Milton*, vol. II, pt. 1, ed. A. S. P. Woodhouse and Douglas Bush (New York, 1972), p. 337. The commentary continues, "The end is to be read in the light of the beginning and particularly in that supplied by the image of the *Cherub Contemplation* when fully understood." The achieving of that full understanding is both the shape and the content of the reading experience.

19. (95–96). See the *Variorum Commentary*, pp. 324–26, for a full discussion of the symbols of power clustered in this passage.

20. *Voices of Melancholy* (New York, 1971), pp. 151–56. Professor Lyons goes on to point out that the central figure in *Il Penseroso* has an imagination of himself "as existing in time" (p. 152) and therefore lives in a world "of possibility and choice" (p. 155). The central figure of *L'Allegro*, on the other hand, "lives in a one day's world in which his imagined experiences follow each other as discrete and disconnected events or scenes" (p. 152). Similar points are made by Leslie Brisman, "All Before Them Where to Choose."

21. Thomas G. Rosenmeyer, *The Green Cabinet* (Berkeley and Los Angeles, 1969), p. 53.

22. "What Is Stylistics and Why Are They Saying Such Terrible Things About It?" in *Approaches to Poetics*, ed. Seymour Chatman (New York, 1973), pp. 109–52.

23. See Brisman, "All Before Them Where to Choose," p. 229: "The two may be conceived as choices, but choice is actualized when one has moved from the first to the second."

24. *The Harmonious Vision*, p. 23.

# MILTON'S PARAPHRASE OF GENESIS: A STYLISTIC READING OF *PARADISE LOST*, BOOK VII

## *Ernst Häublein*

The essay tries to evaluate Milton's paraphrastic techniques in his adaptation of the biblical account of the Creation in *Paradise Lost*, Book VII. The structure of *PL* VII, 216-632 and Milton's way of distributing the quotations from the Bible among additions and amplifications are reassessed. His use of various Bibles emerges from a meticulous comparison between the quotations and possible sources. Milton prefers the Authorized Version over the Geneva Bible by a ratio of approximately 2:1. He also consults the Vulgate and adapts the glosses of the English Bibles. Milton modifies the sources considerably in order to express his view of the Creation as a dynamic and logically structured process. He avoids repetitions, employs idiosyncratic and poetic diction, emphasizes significant words through position, and connects distant passages by verbal echoes. The syntax evinces a marked tendency toward extended units not contained in the Bibles. Milton fuses and condenses different biblical verses, notably in his adaptation of the creation of man, where he lets Raphael address Adam directly for the first time. Milton's techniques of transforming his sources by synthesizing, poeticizing, and imposing his own style upon the account of the Creation are illustrated by tables.

DESPITE THE proliferation of twentieth-century scholarship dealing with the significance of the Creation in *Paradise Lost*, we are still remarkably unaware of how Milton deals as a stylist with his biblical sources.[1] We are left with either inaccurate observation or vague generality. Is it sufficient, for example, to state that "the account of Creation is modelled on the first [*sic*] chapter of Genesis," without identifying the particular Bible,[2] or that Milton "largely" follows "the King James' Version, quoted as *closely* as metrical demands permitted"?[3] Obviously not. If we are to know how Milton functions as a stylist, we must look closely, even methodically, first at the nature of his sources, and second at his technique of stylistic adaptation.

We have already determined with some accuracy the nature of his sources. As Harris Francis Fletcher (among others) points out, Milton, while hardly familiar with the Coverdale Bible (1535), the Great Bible (1539), and the Bishops' Bible (1568), knew an English version of the Geneva Bible (1560), specifically the third edition of 1588, and a 1612 edition of the Authorized Version (1611). Also, Milton preferred the King James Bible later in life. He probably never owned a copy of the Latin Protestant Bible of Junius-Tremellius (1510–1580) but had read the Vulgate from grammar school onward.[4] Since they appear to be at least the most immediate sources for his treatment of the Creation in *Paradise Lost*, the Authorized Version, the Geneva Bible, and the Vulgate, then, should constitute a solid basis for a consideration of Milton's paraphrastic techniques.

In my analysis of those techniques, I shall focus upon Raphael's extended narration in Book VII of *Paradise Lost*. Specifically, I shall explore how closely Milton quotes his sources, what changes he introduces, and why he departs from his sources. To make the task manageable, I shall concern myself with a minute and detailed stylistic analysis of a few selected passages, a procedure well established in studies of this kind.[5] Such an approach will provide a perspective for viewing the stylistic techniques implicit not only in Raphael's account but in corresponding accounts of the Creation discernible in Milton's epic.[6] To prepare for that procedure, I shall engage in a rather wide-ranging survey of how Milton's paraphrases are embedded in the amplifications of *Paradise Lost*, Book VII, lines 216–632. Embracing the passages that will receive detailed consideration, this portion of Book VII will then allow me to construct the groundwork for the local analyses that follow.

The structure of Raphael's account is determined not only by the days of Creation, but more exactly by the Son's single creative acts, which are introduced by the *inquit*-formula "God said." By separating the steps of God's creating the new world, we arrive at the following outline:

Quotations from Genesis appear in the following lines of Book VII:

| Day | Act of Creation | Corresponding Passage from PL, VII |
|---|---|---|
| I | 1. Heaven and earth | 216–42[7] |
| | 2. The *Urlicht* | 243–60 |
| II | 3. The firmament | 261–75 |
| III | 4. The earth separated from the waters | 276–309 |
| | 5. Vegetable life on earth | 309–38 |
| IV | 6. Sun, moon, and stars | 339–86 |
| V | 7. Animals (water, air) | 387–448 |
| VI | 8. Animals (earth) | 449–504 |
| | 9. Man | 505–50 |
| VII | 10. The Son's resting and blessing of the World | 551–632 |

| Act of Creation | Passage from Genesis | Corresponding Passage from PL, VII |
|---|---|---|
| 1. | Chap. i, 1–2 | 232–35 |
| 2. | Chap. i, 3 | 243–45 |
| | Chap. i, 4–5 | 249–52 |
| | Chap. i, 5 | 260 |
| 3. | Chap. i, 6 | 261–63 |
| | Chap. i, 7 | 263–64, 267–69 |
| | Chap. i, 8 | 274–75 |
| 4. | Chap. i, 9 | 282–84 |
| | Chap. i, 10 | 307–09 |
| 5. | Chap. i, 11 | 309–12 |
| | Chap. i, 12 (main part) | 313–31 passim |
| | Chap. ii, 5 (second part) | 331–33 |
| | Chap. ii, 6 | 333–34 |
| | Chap. ii, 5 (first part) | 334–36 |
| | Chap. ii, 4 ("God . . . made") | 336 |
| | Chap. i, 12 (end) | 337 |
| | Chap. i, 13 | 338 |

| Act of Creation | Passage from Genesis | Corresponding Passage from PL, VII |
|---|---|---|
| 6. | Chap. i, 14–18 | 339–53 |
|  | Chap. i, 19 | 386 |
| 7. | Chap. i, 20–22 | 387–98 |
|  | Chap. i, 23 | 448 |
| 8. | Chap. i, 24 | 450–53 |
|  | Chap. i, 25 | 453–504 passim |
| 9. | Chap. i, 26 | 516–23 |
|  | Chap. ii, 7 | 524–26, 528 |
|  | Chap. i, 27 | 526–28, 529–30 |
|  | Chap. i, 28 | 530–34 |
|  | Chap. ii, 8 (ii, 15) (partly) | 535–38 |
|  | Chap. ii, 9 (partly) | 538–39 |
|  | Chap. ii, 16 ("freely") | 540 |
|  | Chap. i, 29 (partly) | 540–41 |
|  | Chap. ii, 17 | 542–44 |
|  | Chap. i, 31 | 548–50[8] |
| 10. | Chap. ii, 2 | 551–52, 581–82, 591–92 |
|  | Chap. ii, 3 | 592–93[9] |

It is interesting how Milton distributes the quotations from Genesis among the amplifications. Most frequently, he introduces a creative act with a biblical paraphrase, followed by an amplification. He usually quotes one or several verses at the beginning and places the rest in the middle (for example, VII, 243–45, 249–52) or—more often—at the end of the amplification (for example, VII, 309–12, 331–38; see table on p. 106). As a rule, the quotation at the end marks the conclusion of the respective day of Creation except in Book VII, lines 307–09.[10] If the Bible contains more than the mere reference to the day, Milton does not separate the parts of the concluding verse (for example, VII, 251–52, 274–75, 548–50).

Wherever the Bible is repetitive, the verses are not paraphrased *in toto* but are dissolved and scattered in the amplifications. Thus, Genesis i, 12, where the earth is described as obeying God's command, is totally broken up after Book VII, line 313: "He scarce had said" (VII, 315, 317, 324). Likewise, in Book VII, lines 453–504, Milton inserts only a few tags from Genesis i, 25 (VII, 457, 460, 475) after Book VII, lines 453-54: "The Earth obey'd, and straight / Op'ning her fertile Womb."[11] These tags are used as points of departure for the description of a variety of animals breaking out of the ground.

The most significant method of distributing the paraphrases, however, can be found in those passages where Milton prefixes a sizable introduction to the direct biblical reference.[12] Thus, the biblical summary of the Son's first creative act in Book VII, lines 232-35 is introduced by his address to the waves and the abyss, his inroad into chaos, and the circumscription of the universe. The detailed account of his forming of the earth follows the paraphrase, which, as a whole, is clearly placed between an introduction and an amplification. Thus, part of the paraphrase summarizes the introductory addition while the other part precedes an amplification.[13] Consequently, the logical adverb "Thus" at the beginning of line 232 indicates a summary; the second "thus" points ahead.[14]

In Book VII, lines 276-82, Milton also introduces the biblical paraphrase, this time characterizing the state of the earth before the division of sea and land. These lines belong to the quotation of Genesis i, 9 (VII, 282-84): from the embryonic unity of the two elements we are led toward the birth of the earth. Accordingly, this passage, which is also syntactically linked to the paraphrase,[15] functions as a transition between two days of Creation and as a preparatory explanation of the next creative act, which in turn is explained in detail (VII, 285-306) and concluded by the Son's act of naming (Genesis i, 10, in VII, 307-09).

The most notable instance of introductory addition occurs in Book VII, lines 505-16, before the creation of man. This addition follows a highly interesting summary in lines 499-504, where all the previous creative acts are surveyed in a famous and brilliant example of correlative verse: "Air, Water, Earth, / By Fowl, Fish, Beast, was flown, was swum, was walk't," a progressive correlation of three trimembered series or units ($A_1$—"Air," $B_1$—"Fowl," $C_1$—"was flown"; $A_2$—"Water," $B_2$—"Fish," $C_2$—"was swum"; $A_3$—"Earth," $B_3$—"Beast," $C_3$—"was walk't").[16] In the introductory addition, Milton again prepares for God's words, this time contrasting the *whole* Creation of six days with the last creative act in Raphael's *ex negativo* definition of man, the "Master work, the end / Of all yet done; a Creature who not prone / And Brute as other Creatures." Man is the nodal rung of the scale of being because he is able to bridge the gap between the newly created world and the realm of the spirit. In this sense, he should be conscious of God's expectation of gratitude, devotion, and worship. Such an addition, then, serves a major didactic aim.

It seems significant that Milton uses this structural method at three vital points of the Creation: before the first creative act, the creation of heaven and earth; before the separation of the earth from the waters; and before the creation of man. (Without the first, there would be no Creation at all; without the second, there would be no life; without the last, the Creation would be incomplete.)

Milton's way of arranging the quotations in Book VII within the amplifications and additions is indicated by the following table:

| Introductory Paraphrase | Paraphrase after Introductory Addition | Intermediary Paraphrase | Scattered Quotation | Concluding Paraphrase |
|---|---|---|---|---|
| | 232–35 | | | |
| 243–45 | | 249–52 | | 260 |
| 261–64 | | 267–69 | | 274–75 |
| | 282–84 | | | 307–09 |
| 309–12 | | | 313–31 | 331–38 |
| 339–53 | | | | 386 |
| 387–98 | | | | 448 |
| 449–53 | | | 453–504 | |
| | 516–44 | | | 548–50 |
| 551–52 | | 581–82 | | |
| | | 591–93 | | |

In his structuring of the paraphrase, Milton usually introduces a new act of Creation with one or several verses of Genesis, which he amplifies; at the most important stages of the Creation, he prefixes an introductory addition, pointing to the paraphrase.

Let us now turn to the handling of the sources in the quotations themselves. I will select three larger coherent passages and try to elucidate Milton's technique of transforming the Bible into his own form of poetic expression by comparing his paraphrase of Genesis with the Authorized Version (AV), the Geneva Bible (Geneva), and the Vulgate (Vulg.).[17] Examples from other passages will indicate the prevalence of a chosen technique.

The Authorized Version account of the fourth day of Creation starts out with:

And God said, Let there bee lights in the firmament of the heaven, to divide the day from the night: and let them be for signes and for seasons, and for dayes and yeeres. (Genesis i, 14)

Milton's version reads as follows:

> Again th' Almighty spake: Let there be Lights
> High in th'expanse of Heaven to divide
> The Day from Night; and let them be for Signs,
> For Seasons, and for Days, and circling Years.          (VII, 339–42)

Substituting "again" for "and," Milton emphasizes the repetitive and temporal aspect of God's acts. He also departs from the formula "God said" by characterizing the Creator periphrastically[18] and by introducing the stronger, slightly archaic "spake" (VII, 339). In the next line, the addition of the adjective "high" explains the position of the lights and hints at the vastness of the firmament. Since the insertion is placed in a metrically prominent position by inversion, it lends a specifically Miltonic rhythm to the line. Furthermore, Milton does not retain "in the firmament of the heaven," but reuses his amplification of line 264 ("expanse of liquid"),[19] thus connecting the two passages.[20] After that, he follows the Authorized Version (Geneva has "to separate"), leaving out only the definite article in line 341 and the conjunction in line 342, obviously for metrical reasons,[21] a fact which might also account for the insertion of "circling." This insertion reflects Milton's tendency to clarify nouns through telling adjectives.[22]

To continue:

And let them be for lights in the firmament of the heaven, to give light upon the earth: and it was so. (Genesis i, 15)

> And let them be for Lights as I ordain
> Thir Office in the Firmament of Heav'n
> To give Light on the Earth; and it was so.          (VII, 343–45)

In this passage, the main departure from the Bible is the addition of the subordinate clause "as I ordain / Thir Office." This might be inspired by Geneva's gloss o belonging to Genesis i, 16: "to give it [the day] sufficient light, as instruments appointed for the same, to serve to mans use"; the latter part of this sentence appears in Book VII, lines 346–47. Such an insertion changes the meaning of the biblical verse because "in the Firmament of Heav'n" can be related to both the subordinate clause and the noun "Lights." The syntax, although not nearly as involved and complex as outside the paraphrase (for example, VII, 375–84), assumes a marked Miltonic quality through this use of the ἀπὸ κοινοῦ position, which Milton borrows from the Greek. In Book VII, line 345, he only shortens the Bible's "upon" to "on" in order to attain metrical ease[23] and, for once, retains the "and it was so" formula, which he regularly leaves out elsewhere.[24]

Next:

And God made two great lights: the greater light to rule the day, and the lesser light to rule the night: he made the stars also.
And God set them in the firmament of the heaven, to give light upon the earth:
And to rule over the day, and over the night, and to divide the light from the darkenesse: and God saw that it was good. (Genesis i, 16–18)

> And God made two great Lights, great for thir use
> To Man, the greater to have rule by Day,
> The less by Night altern: and made the Stars,
> And set them in the Firmament of Heav'n
> To illuminate the Earth, and rule the Day
> In thir vicissitude, and rule the Night,
> And Light from Darkness to divide. God saw,
> Surveying his great Work, that it was good.          (VII, 346–53)

Here Milton somewhat condenses the Bible through syntactical zeugma, one of his favorite devices.[25] He leaves out the subject in Book VII, line 348, where he cuts "also," and in line 349, where he drops the article before "Heav'n." Through zeugma, Milton manages to weld together three sentences of his English sources—the Vulgate has only two—into one long, but lucid syntactical unit (VII, 346–52), which is further complicated by insertions (VII, 346–47, 351). The passage evinces a tendency to lengthen the sentences and to approach something like a Miltonic paragraph without obscuring its indebtedness to the more paratactic style of the Bible. The varying use of the verb "to rule" seems to result mainly from metrical demands. In Book VII, lines 350–51, however, Milton achieves what Frank Kermode calls "pseudo-rhyme"[26] by placing antithetical words ("Day," "Night") at the end of the lines. The pseudo-rhymes are supported by syntactical parallelism and rhythmic identity in both lines. This tendency toward coherence is also reflected in the substitution of "altern" for a subordinate clause in line 348[27] and in the addition of its synonym "In thir vicissitude" in line 351,[28] which stresses the division of day and night. Furthermore, Milton substitutes the highly ornate and almost technical "to illuminate" for "to give light" (Geneva has "to shine"),[29] a rendering probably inspired by the Vulgate's "illuminent" (Genesis i, 15).[30] The verb obviously was not chosen because of its metrical adaptability since "to give Light on" (see VII, 345) would equally accord with the meter. It was chosen, rather, to avoid the repetitive style of his English sources. The fact that Milton takes over Geneva's "less" in line 348 indicates that he compared or remembered both English versions.[31] In line 352 he places the verb "to divide" at the very end of the sentence, thus lending greater emphasis to the nouns central in this passage.[32] The insertion of "Surveying his great Work" in line 353 both clarifies and stresses the end of the creative act, which is followed by an amplification in lines 354–84 and a summary in lines 384–386:

And the evening and the morning were the fourth day. (Genesis i, 19)

> then first adorn'd
> With thir bright Luminaries that Set and Rose,
> Glad Ev'ning and glad Morn crown'd the fourth day. (VII, 384–86)

The quotation from the Bible is embedded in a longer syntactic unit, in which the achievement of the day is surveyed. Milton adds a very telling adjective ("glad") and, engaging in one of his favorite devices, substitutes a verb denoting action ("crown'd") for the Bible's rather colorless form of "to be."[33]

A first tentative survey of our findings shows the compositional strategies employed by Milton in his paraphrase of Genesis in Book VII of *Paradise Lost*:

1. Through substituting temporal adverbs (for example, "again" for the Bible's monotonous "and") and verbs denoting action or praise (for example, "crown'd" for "to be"), Milton expresses his view of the Creation as a dynamic process, which is fully developed in the additions and amplifications.

2. He tries to avoid the repetitions of the biblical account by using synonyms and periphrases. He usually transforms biblical tags like "God said" and "the evening and the morning were the . . . day."

3. The diction becomes more ornate and expressive through the substitution or insertions of colorful adjectives and nouns and the use of *personificatio* and verbs derived from Latin. Occasionally the verbs show a tendency toward scientific precision.

4. The sentences of the paraphrase are made markedly longer and more complicated than those of the sources through the use of zeugma and syntactical insertions. The "straightforwardness" and "simplicity" of the Bible are further reduced by rhetorical figures like parallelism and ἀπὸ κοινοῦ. The extended Miltonic syntax imparts a different kind of rhythm to the paraphrase.

5. Milton adapts the text to the meter by cutting articles, the preposition "to" before verbs, and conjunctions. Such adaptation leads to condensation and pseudo-rhyme.

6. He frequently changes the word order for emphasis, most notably by placing certain words at metrically prominent positions or by postponing the verb, a typically Miltonic habit.

7. He occasionally adds to his sources in order to make a paragraph more coherent.

8. He also takes up specific expressions from other, more distant passages, thus connecting different parts of Raphael's account by verbal echoes.

9. He derives his paraphrases not only from biblical sources, but, as I shall demonstrate, from the glosses that accompany them.

In order to provide further support for these findings, let us turn to Book VII, lines 387–98 and 446–48, the account of the creation of fish and birds. This passage will serve chiefly to illustrate Milton's use of the Authorized Version, the Geneva Bible, and the Vulgate. I quote all three sources here and indicate in italics the version chosen by Milton.

*And* God said, Let the waters bring foorth *aboundantly* the moving creature that hath life, and *foule* that may flie *above* the earth in the open firmament *of heaven.*
*And* God created great whales, and every living creature *that* moveth, which the waters brought forth aboundantly after their kinde, and every *winged* foule *after* his kinde: and God saw that it was good.
*And* God blessed them, saying, *Be fruitfull*, and multiply, and fill the waters in the Seas, and let the foule multiply in the earth.
And the evening and the morning were the fift day. (AV, Genesis i, 20–23)
Afterwarde God said, Let the waters bring forthe in abundance every creping

thing that hathe life: & *let* the foule flie upon the earth in the open firmament of the heaven.

Then God created *the great whales*, & every thing living & moving, which the waters broght forthe in abundance, according to their kinde, & every fethered foule according to his kinde: & God sawe that it was good.

Then God blessed them, saying, Bring forthe frute and multiplie, and fil the waters in the seas, & let *the* foule multiplie in the earth.

So the evening & the morning were the fifte day. (Geneva, Genesis i, 20–23)

Dixit etiam Deus: Producant aquae *reptile* animae viventis, et volatile super terram sub firmamento caeli.

Creavitque Deus cete grandia, et omnem *animam viventem* atque motabilem, quam produxerant aquae in species suas, et omne volatile secundum genus suum. Et vidit Deus quod esset bonum. Benedixit*que* eis, dicens: Crescite, et multiplicamini, et *replete* aquas maris: avesque multiplice*ntur super* terram. Et factum est vespere et mane, dies quintus. (Vulg., Genesis i, 20–23)

> And God said, let the Waters generate
> Reptile with Spawn abundant, living Soul:
> And let Fowl fly above the Earth, with wings
> Display'd on the op'n Firmament of Heav'n.
> And God created the great Whales, and each
> Soul living, each that crept, which plenteously
> The waters generated by thir kinds,
> And every Bird of wing after his kind;
> And saw that it was good, and bless'd them, saying,
> Be fruitful, multiply, and in the Seas
> And Lakes and running Streams the waters fill;
> And let the Fowl be multipli'd on the Earth.        (VII, 387–98)

> The Waters thus
> With Fish replenisht, and the Air with Fowl,
> Ev'ning and Morn solémniz'd the Fift day.        (VII, 446–48)

Regarding the stylistic evidence in general, we again observe that Milton prefers more poetic or scientific sounding verbs and nouns. He introduces variation through synonyms ("abundant," "plenteously") and eases the metrical flow by choosing a shorter preposition ("by"), by cutting articles and one conjunction (VII, 396), and by lengthening the verb "to multiply" (VII, 398), which is put into the passive voice. Milton also uses syntactical zeugma (VII, 395), by which two long verses are connected, again striving for a longer paragraph (VII, 391–97). The last verse is embedded in a longer sentence summarizing the creative act of the fifth day. The passage shows traces of Milton's habit of changing the word order, for example, postponing the main

verb or the participle (VII, 389–90; 397), and his preference for participial constructions (VII, 388, "living Soul"). Furthermore, he em-
bellishes and details the biblical account through little amplifications
(VII, 388, "with Spawn"; 397, "And Lakes and running Streams"). In
lines 389–90, the meaning of the sentence is unobtrusively changed
by the addition of "with wings / Display'd," because "on the op'n
Firmament of Heav'n" can be connected with "above the Earth" only
by disregarding the comma. Thus the last part of the sentence may
be related to both the preceding parts (ἀπὸ κοινοῦ). The same holds for
the adjective "abundant" (VII, 388), which belongs to both "with
Spawn" and "Reptile."

The following table shows Milton's indebtedness to his English
sources and the changes and additions made by him. The parentheses
indicate the exact wording of the sources and/or the verse or gloss
from which it is taken.

| Line | Borrowing from AV | Borrowing from Geneva | Milton's own Variants |
|---|---|---|---|
| 387 | And | | generate |
| 388 | abundant (abound-antly) | | adds: with Spawn |
| | living Soul (soule, gloss l: 20; a living soule, gloss l: 30) | living Soul (soule of life, gloss-es p and r) (?) | |
| 389 | Fowl (no article) | and let . . . fly (syntax) | adds: with wings |
| 390 | of Heav'n (no arti-cle) | | adds: Display'd on |
| 391 | And | the great Whales (article) | each |
| 392 | that . . . (relative clause) | crept (creeping, i, 20) | each |
| | plenteously (aboundantly) | Soul living (thing living) | plenteously (posi-tion changed) |
| 393 | | | generated by |
| 394 | of wing (winged) after | | |

| | | | |
|---|---|---|---|
| 395 | and | | And saw (zeugma) |
| 396 | Be fruitful | | cuts: and (et) |
| | | | rearranges: in the Seas |
| 397 | | | adds: And Lakes and running Streams |
| | | | postpones verb (fill) |
| 398 | | the Fowl (article) | |
| 446 | | thus (So) (?) | |
| 447 | replenisht (re-plenish, i, 28) | | |
| 448 | | | drops: articles poetic diction (Morn) verb denoting praise (solémniz'd) |

We notice that Milton favors the Authorized Version over Geneva where the two versions are not identical. Thus, he takes over certain words, for example, "abundant," "wing," "after" (Geneva has always "according to"), "Be fruitful," the adverb in line 392, and—most importantly—a syntactical variant (the relative clause in line 392) from the Authorized Version. If my tracings are correct concerning "replenisht" (VII, 447) and "living Soul" (VII, 388), Milton may be said to telescope vocabulary from other verses and glosses where the context is similar. In this passage, he for once adopts the Authorized Version's frequent "And." There are only five identifiable variants from Geneva, among them one syntactical feature, the main clause in line 389, where the Authorized Version has a second direct object plus a relative clause. Here, Milton follows the more logical source; the Authorized Version suggests that the birds, too, are created in or by the waters. The varying use of the definite article can be accounted for by metrical demands. Most of the wording stems from the Authorized Version.

A survey of all the other relevant passages in Book VII may help to determine more exactly which prevalent stylistic traits of the English Bibles are taken over by Milton.

| Line | Borrowing from AV | Borrowing from Geneva |
|------|-------------------|------------------------|
| 234 | | but |
| 251 | Divided | |
| 252 | | Thus |
| 261 | | Again |
| 267 | | partition (parted) |
| 269 | Dividing | |
| 274 | | So |
| 284 | | Into |
| 308 | called (postponed) | |
| 310 | Grass (not contained in Geneva, no article) | |
| | Herb yielding Seed (participle) | |
| 311 | Fruit Tree yielding Fruit (participle) | |
| | after . . . kind | |
| 312 | Whose Seed is | |
| 315 | Grass (see 310) | |
| 333 | | a . . . Mist / |
| 334 | ground | Went up (normal word order) |
| | | all the (without: the face of) |
| 338 | | So |
| 340 | divide | |
| 348 | | less |
| 352 | divide | |
| 452 | Creeping things (participle) | |
| | Beast | |
| 520 | | rule |
| 522 | | Beast |
| 523 | creeping thing that creeps (participle) | |
| 524 | form'd | |

| | | |
|---|---|---|
| 525 | nostrils | in |
| 526 | breath (no article) | |
| | own | |
| 528 | becam'st | |
| 529 | Male (word order) | he created (normal word order) |
| 531 | Be fruitful | fill |
| 532 | Dominion | |
| 534 | living thing | |
| 539 | | Delectable . . . to (no relative clause) |
| 540 | food | |
| 541 | Gave thee (no preposition) | all th'Earth (without: the face of) |
| 542 | but of the Tree | |
| 543 | | knowledge (no article) |
| 544 | in the day | |
| 548 | | all that |
| 549 | behold | |
| 550 | | So |

All in all, the ratio of borrowings is about 2 (AV) to 1 (Geneva) (43:25).[34] From the Authorized Version Milton certainly derives his preference for participial constructions (Geneva has mostly relative clauses) and the tendency toward more complicated word order (inversions and postponed verbs) hardly ever employed in the Geneva Bible. The Authorized Version frequently leaves out the definite article, which Milton imitates wherever metrically necessary. A few of his verbal preferences can also be traced to the Authorized Version ("after . . . kind," "be fruitful" instead of "bring forthe frute," and "to divide" instead of "to separate") and to Geneva ("all the" instead of "the face of all the"). He is definitely indebted to Geneva concerning his use of logical and temporal conjunctions, which help to structure the process of the Creation. Possibly, his tendency toward complicated hypotactical sentences can be traced back to Geneva's preference for subordinate clauses.

As regards the Vulgate, Milton seems to consult it chiefly for vocabulary. Occasionally he imitates the Latin word order. His use of zeugma could stem from the Latin version, too. The following table shows the paraphrase's indebtedness to the Vulgate.

| Line | Borrowing from Vulg. | Wording of Vulg. |
|------|----------------------|------------------|
| 234 | Abyss | abyssi |
| 252 | He nam'd (zeugma) | appellavit (zeugma) |
| 308 | Of congregated Waters | congregationesque aquarum |
| 350 | illuminate | illuminent (Genesis i, 15) |
| 385 | Luminaries | luminaria (Genesis i, 14, 16) |
| 388 | Reptile | reptile |
|  | living Soul | animae viventis |
| 392 | Soul living (position of adjective) (?) | animam viventem |
| 395 | and bless'd (zeugma) | benedixitque (zeugma) |
| 398 | be multipli'd on | multiplicentur (passive voice) super |
| 447 | replenisht (?) | replete (Genesis i, 22) |
| 520 | In our similitude | ad similitudinem nostram |
| 530 | and said (zeugma) | et ait (zeugma) |
| 537 | delicious Grove (?) | paradisum voluptatis (Genesis ii, 8, 15) |
| 538 | the Trees of God / | pulchrum visu, et ad vescendum |
| 539 | Delectable both to behold and taste (infinitive, no relative clause) | suave |

A look at the glosses of the Authorized Version and the Geneva Bible provides further proof that Milton was by no means committed to either of the sources. In Book VII, lines 247–48 he adapts glosses c and e from Geneva: "for as yet the light was not created"; "the light was made before either sunne or moone was created." The amplificatory "expanse of liquid" in line 264 (and 340) is possibly taken from the Authorized Version's gloss to Genesis i, 6: "*Hebr. expansion.*" The amplification in lines 313–14 ("the bare Earth, till then / Desert and bare, unsightly, unadorn'd") may stem from Geneva's gloss h to Genesis i, 11: "it is onely the power of Gods worde that maketh the earth fruteful, which els naturally is barren." The inserted adjective "tender" in line 315 can be traced back to the Authorized Version's gloss to Genesis i, 11: "*Heb. tender grasse.*" Book VII, lines 343–44 ("as I ordain / Thir Office") and lines 346–47 ("great for thir use / To Man") are based on gloss o in Geneva, Genesis i, 16: "as instruments appointed for the same, to serve to mans use." The reference to the appearance of the moon and the stars to human sight in lines 367–69 could go back to Geneva's gloss n to Genesis i, 16: "here he speaketh as man iudgeth by his eye: for els the moone is lesse then the planete Saturnus." Finally, in the introduction to the Creation of man, Milton uses Geneva's gloss s to Genesis i, 26 ("to make an excellent work above all the rest of his creation") to characterize God's "Master work" in Book VII, lines 505–07.[35]

Let us now turn to the longest paraphrase in Book VII, lines 516–50, which has only a small amplification in lines 545–47. Since Milton blends several verses from Genesis i and ii in this passage, I quote the Bible (AV) according to his arrangement.

And God said, Let us make man in our Image, after our likenesse: and let them have dominion over the fish of the sea, and over the foule of the aire, and over the cattell, and over all the earth, and over every creeping thing that creepeth upon the earth. (Genesis i, 26)

> therefore th' Omnipotent
> Eternal Father (For where is not hee
> Present) thus to his Son audibly spake.
>   Let us make now Man in our image, Man
> In our similitude, and let them rule
> Over the Fish and Fowl of Sea and Air,
> Beast of the Field, and over all the Earth,
> And every creeping thing that creeps the ground. (VII, 516–23)

And the LORD God formed man of the dust of the ground, & breathed into his nostrils the breath of life. (Genesis ii, 7)

> This said, he form'd thee, *Adam*, thee, O Man
> Dust of the ground, and in thy nostrils breath'd
> The breath of Life.                        (VII, 524–26)

So God created man in his owne Image, in the Image of God created hee him. (Genesis i, 27)

in his own Image hee
Created thee, in the Image of God
Express.                                              (VII, 526-28)

and man became a living soule. (Genesis ii, 7)

and thou becam'st a living Soul.              (VII, 528)

male and female created hee them. (Genesis i, 27)

Male he created thee, but thy consort
Female for Race.                                      (VII, 529-30)

And God blessed them, and God said unto them, Be fruitfull, and multiply, and replenish the earth, and subdue it, and have dominion over the fish of the sea, and over the foule of the aire, and over every living thing that moveth upon the earth. (Genesis i, 28)

then bless'd Mankind, and said,
Be fruitful, multiply, and fill the Earth,
Subdue it, and throughout Dominion hold
Over Fish of the Sea, and Fowl of the Air,
And every living thing that moves on the Earth.   (VII, 530-34)

And the LORD God planted a garden Eastward in Eden; and there he put the man whom he had formed. (Genesis ii, 8)[36]

Wherever thus created, for no place
Is yet distinct by name, thence, as thou know'st
He brought thee into this delicious Grove,
This Garden.                                          (VII, 535-38)

And out of the ground made the LORD God to grow every tree that is pleasant to the sight, and good for food. (Genesis ii, 9)

And the LORD God commanded the man, saying, Of every tree of the garden thou mayest freely eate. (Genesis ii, 16)

And God said, Behold, I have given you every herbe bearing seede, which is upon the face of all the earth, and every tree, in the which is the fruit of a tree yeelding seed, to you it shall be for meat. (Genesis i, 29)

planted with the Trees of God,
Delectable both to behold and taste;
And freely all thir pleasant fruit for food
Gave thee, all sorts are here that all th'Earth yields,
Variety without end.                                 (VII, 538-42)

But of the tree of the knowledge of good and evill, thou shalt not eate of it: for in the day that thou eatest thereof, thou shalt surely die. (Genesis ii, 17)

> but of the Tree
> Which tasted works knowledge of Good and Evil,
> Thou may'st not; in the day thou eat'st, thou di'st.　(VII, 542–44)

And God saw every thing that hee had made, and behold, it was very good.
And the evening and the morning were the sixt day. (Genesis i, 31)

> Here finish'd hee, and all that he had made
> View'd, and behold all was entirely good;
> So Ev'n and Morn accomplish'd the Sixt day.　(VII, 548–50)

In spite of many verbal reminiscences, Milton does not follow the Bible slavishly, for he telescopes various verses from the second chapter of Genesis into the first and leaves out Genesis i, 30, entirely. Thus the passage combines Genesis i, 26, the first part of Genesis ii, 7, the first part of Genesis i, 27, the second part of Genesis ii, 7, the second part of Genesis i, 27, Genesis i, 28, the part of Genesis ii, 8, that resembles Genesis ii, 15, part of Genesis ii, 9, "freely" from Genesis ii, 16, part of Genesis i, 29, ii, 17, and i, 31. This technique of blending entails a radical transformation and condensation of the Bible unique within the paraphrase. It seems that the last act of Creation was viewed by Milton as a challenge for his utmost craftsmanship.

The analysis of the section is rather complicated because of this method of telescoping and condensation. A survey of the most important compositional strategies, which may also serve as a kind of summary of our findings, can be attempted here.

Again, we have an addition to,[37] and transformation of, the *inquit*-formula, which is once more embedded in a larger syntactical unit (VII, 516–18). A long periphrasis is substituted for the sources' "God," which is amplified by an explanation: "(For where is not hee / Present)."[38]  Again we have the stress on the temporal aspect of the Creation in Book VII, line 519 ("now")[39] and the tendency to impose a kind of logical order on the account (VII, 516, "therefore," and 529, "but"). Furthermore, Milton frequently leaves out articles (VII, 521, 522, 533, 550) and conjunctions (VII, 531, 532, 544), adverbs (VII, 544, "thereof," "surely") and prepositions (VII, 521, 522, 523, 530, 533, 534)[40] to meet metrical demands. With an eye on both the meter and the succinctness and force of the sentence, Milton employs the syntactical zeugma, for example, in Book VII, line 530 ("then bless'd Mankind, and said"), through which he arrives at larger syntactic units.[41]

At one point, he even makes use of ellipsis in order to lend special weight and pith to the sentence:

> but of the Tree
> Which tasted works knowledge of Good and Evil,
> Thou may'st not.                    (VII, 542–44)

Here Milton leaves out the verb "to eat," which, however, does not occur at all in the preceding passage, because he fuses two wholly different verses of Genesis. The reader has to telescope "taste" (VII, 539, 543) into line 544 in order to understand the line. Milton obviously intends to throw full emphasis on the negation, which receives a major stress. In the same line, he shortens the Bible's "for in the day that thou eatest thereof, thou shalt surely die" to "in the day thou eat'st, thou di'st" (VII, 544). Through this adaptation the warning receives a stronger rhythmical emphasis. Furthermore, Milton condenses longer sentences by using a participial construction or an adjective instead of a full verb, for example, in Book VII, line 538 ("planted") and line 539 ("Delectable"). More importantly, he rearranges the word order of a few sentences in order to place significant words—mostly verbs—at metrically prominent positions. Thus, in Book VII, line 525 ("breath'd"), line 527 ("Created thee"),[42] line 541 ("Gave thee"), and line 549 ("View'd"), the verb appears at the beginning of the respective line. Although in lines 529–30 Milton takes up the inversion from the Authorized Version ("Male he created thee, but thy consort / Female for Race"), he changes the syntax drastically by inserting a zeugmatically connected antithesis, which is also reflected in the position of both "Male" and "Female" at the beginning of the two lines. Thus Milton arrives at what I would call initial pseudo-rhyme.[43] Some of the small additions are also placed in prominent positions, most importantly the repetition of "Man" in lines 519 and 524.[44] Furthermore, Milton again uses words and expressions more "poetic" than those of the sources, for example, "View'd" (VII, 549), "entirely" (VII, 549), and "accomplish'd" (VII, 550), where he changes the meaning considerably.

As we have noticed, the whole passage dealing with the creation of man not only differs structurally from the treatment of other verses, but also highlights Raphael's report and mission: the Angel—besides

quoting God's words in lines 519-23 and 531-34—directly addresses
Adam throughout, thereby contributing to a dramatic rise in emotional
pitch.[45]

| | |
|---|---|
| This said, he form'd thee, *Adam*, thee O Man | (524) |
| and in thy nostrils breath'd | (525) |
| The breath of Life; in his own Image hee | (526) |
| Created thee, . . . | (527) |
| and thou becam'st a living Soul. | (528) |
| Male he created thee, but thy consort | (529) |
| Female for Race; . . . | (530) |
| thence, as thou know'st | (536) |
| He brought thee into this delicious Grove, | (537) |
| This Garden, . . . | (538) |
| And freely all thir pleasant fruit for food | (540) |
| Gave thee, . . . | (541) |
| but of the Tree | (542) |
| Which tasted works knowledge of Good and Evil, | (543) |
| Thou may'st not; in the day thou eat'st, thou di'st. | (544) |
| lest sin | (546) |
| Surprise thee. | (547) |

Through such direct address, Milton dramatically underscores
Raphael's function as God's mediator (see V, 224-45). At the same
time, Raphael's references both to Adam's own experience (VII, 536,
"as thou know'st")[46] and to his new but as yet nameless abode (VII,
537-38) emphasize the *hic et nunc* quality of the scene.

The departures from the biblical sources in lines 516-50, then,
indicate most strikingly Milton's attempts to fuse biblical quotations
in his paraphrases. While adhering faithfully to the content of the
Scriptures, the paraphrast concurrently transforms his sources by synthesizing, poeticizing, and imposing his own style on the verses of
Genesis. If this is true of the foregoing passage, the same may be
said of Milton's paraphrastic techniques throughout Book VII of *Paradise Lost*. As my study has indicated, an analysis of those techniques
suggests both the subtlety and artistry of Milton's handling of the
Creation in his major epic.

University of Würzburg, West Germany

## NOTES

1. See the comments of J. L. Summers, "*Paradise Lost:* The Pattern at the Centre," in *Milton's Epic Poetry*, ed. C. A. Patrides (Harmondsworth, 1967), pp. 179–214; B. A. Wright, *Milton's Paradise Lost* (London, 1962), pp. 147–53; M. H. Nicolson, *John Milton: A Reader's Guide to His Poetry* (London, 1964), pp. 261–70; M. Lieb, *The Dialectics of Creation* (Amherst, 1970), pp. 42, 56–63, 67–68; H. Blamires, *Milton's Creation: A Guide through Paradise Lost* (London, 1971), pp. 171–87. The theological background is discussed by A. S. P. Woodhouse, "Notes on Milton's Views of the Creation: The Initial Phases," *PQ*, XXVIII (1949), 211–36, and J. H. Adamson, "Milton and the Creation," *JEGP*, LXI (1962), 756–78.

2. Blamires, *Milton's Creation*, p. 177; see also M. Y. Hughes, ed., *John Milton: Complete Poems and Major Prose* (New York, 1957), pp. 187, 352, nn. 235–37; A. W. Verity, ed., *Paradise Lost* (Cambridge, Eng., 1910), pp. 537, 540; J. H. Hanford, *A Milton Handbook*, 4th rev. ed. (New York, 1961), p. 207; Summers, "Pattern at the Centre," p. 206; and J. Carey and A. Fowler, eds., *The Poems of John Milton* (London, 1968), p. 428.

3. Nicolson, *A Reader's Guide*, p. 265 (italics added); see also J. H. Sims, *The Bible in Milton's Epics* (Gainesville, Fla., 1962), pp. 4, 33–34. Sims does not aim at comparing the sources with the poetry of *PL;* rather, he wants to show "what poetic effects Milton achieves" through allusions to the Bible (p. 64); he analyzes the "aesthetic effect on, and the ethical insight gained in, the mind of the reader" (p. 2).

4. H. F. Fletcher, *The Intellectual Development of John Milton* (Urbana, Ill., 1961), vol. II, pp. 103–06, and Sims, *Bible in Milton's Epics*, p. 5. Both Diodati's Italian version of the Vulgate (1607), which is similar to Geneva in many respects, and the Douay version (1609), which, according to my examination of it, has no influence on *PL*, can be neglected here. I have not seen the Antwerp Polyglot (1584), from which Milton probably translated directly. I quote from *The Authorised Version of the English Bible* (1611), ed. W. A. Wright (Cambridge, Eng., 1909), vol. I; *The Geneva Bible: A Facsimile of the 1560 Edition*, ed. L. E. Berry (Madison, Wis., 1969); and from *Biblia Sacra iuxta Vulgatam Clementinam*, ed. A. Colunga and L. Turrado, 4th ed. (Madrid, 1965).

5. See, for example, William B. Hunter, Jr.'s methodical procedure of selecting a few illustrative passages in "Milton Translates the Psalms," *PQ*, XL (1961), 487.

6. The Creation is discussed by God (III, 64–69), who foresees the Fall (III, 86–92), by Eve (IX, 553–66), Michael (XI, 335–46), and Uriel (III, 708–35). Uriel's account, which informs Satan about the location of "Adam's abode," is perhaps the most concentrated and coherent presentation of the Creation before Raphael's extended narration in Book VII and Adam's reminiscences in Book VIII. However, Raphael's account, to which I will confine myself here, is most consistently based on Genesis, which Milton amplifies considerably by letting the angelic narrator propound in detail the Son's creation of a dynamic and harmonious universe. In these amplifications, Raphael enlarges upon cosmological, astronomical, and theological concepts developed by Milton himself or inherent in the matrix of his world view.

7. Significantly Milton adds two *inquit*-formulas in Book VII, lines 217 and 230, to be followed by two direct addresses of the Son which are not contained in the Bible. Quotations from Milton in my text are taken from Hughes, *John Milton: Complete Poems and Major Prose*.

8. The fact that these verses of the second chapter of Genesis are inserted and Genesis i, 30, is left out entirely strongly contradicts the notion that Milton follows

only Genesis, chapter i (Blamires, *Milton's Creation*, p. 177), or that he follows the Bible "closely." The rearrangement escapes Hughes and—to some extent—even Bush in his *Milton: Poetical Works* (London, 1966), pp. 352–53.

9. The only editors aware of Milton's complicated fusion of Genesis, chapters i and ii, seem to be Carey and Fowler, in *The Poems of John Milton*, pp. 806–07, who, however, fail to notice the tags from Genesis i, 29, in Book VII, lines 540–41. Sims' examination of *PL*, VII and Genesis (*The Bible in Milton's Epics*, pp. 266–67), is not exact enough; see my analysis below, pp. 117–20.

10. As in the Bible, the end of this creative act is, however, indicated by another fixed formula (VII, 309): "And saw that it was good"; see also VII, 337, and Genesis i, 12. In the sources, this formula is always connected with the reference to the day except in Genesis i, 20–23. The Bible also differentiates animal life from man with this formula (Genesis i, 25), whereas Milton chooses an extensive summary (VII, 499–504). See p. 105 and nn. 15 and 16.

11. The suddenness of the Creation, which the Angel has to describe in its time sequence (VII, 176–79), is also alluded to in Book VII, line 239 ("then . . . then"), line 243 ("forthwith"), line 285 ("Immediately"), line 291 ("Hasted"), line 294 ("For haste"), line 317 ("sudden"), line 319 ("and these scarce blown"), line 462 ("Pasturing at once"), and line 475 ("At once"). See also lines 399 and 453.

12. The introduction of Book VII, lines 449–50, is too small to justify its treatment as an introductory addition, although it clearly marks off the fifth and sixth days.

13. The introductions will be more precisely called additions, whereas the passages following the paraphrases are amplifications proper.

14. Milton tends to impose a kind of logical and temporal order on the process of Creation by replacing the biblical "and" with adverbs; many of them are taken from Geneva; see pp. 114–15.

15. Milton uses syntactic linkage also between smaller amplifications and the quotations, for example, in Book VII, lines 267–69, 449–50, 548, 591–92, and most notably lines 384–86 and 446–48, where the amplifications recapitulate the creative act.

16. See D. Alonso, "Versos plurimembros y poemas correlativos," *Revista de la biblioteca archivo y museo del ayuntamiento de Madrid*, III (1944), 159. Another instance of correlative verse occurs in Book VII, line 521, a two-membered progression consisting of two series; see also Book VIII, lines 338–41, a three-membered progression of two series also based on "Earth," "Sea," "Air," etc.

17. In longer citations I will quote the Authorized Version and indicate Milton's indebtedness to the other sources. I have slightly modernized the spelling of the English Bibles.

18. See also Book VII, line 516 ("th'Omnipotent"), line 551 ("the Creator"), and line 587 ("The Filial Power").

19. The gloss of the Authorized Version, Genesis i, 6, has "*Hebr. expansion*"; the use of this noun, therefore, does not prove that Milton translated directly from the Hebrew as Sims contends (*The Bible in Milton's Epics*, p. 91).

20. Milton occasionally takes up expressions or even compositional strategies from other places to attain coherence, for example, Book VII, line 234 ("Abyss," which stems from Vulg. Genesis i, 2) and line 211; Book VII, lines 247–49 and 360; the correlative verses in Book VII, lines 502–03 and 521.

21. This is, of course, the most obvious and frequent change; in this section see also Book VII, lines 344, 349, and 352.

22. See also Book VII, line 233 ("profound"), line 267 ("partition firm and sure"),

line 310 ("verdant"), line 313 ("bare"), line 314 ("desert and bare, unsightly, unadorn'd"), line 315 ("tender"), line 324 ("stately"), and line 537 ("delicious").

23. He prefers the shorter preposition to eliding ("th'Earth"), perhaps in order to keep up the anapestic flow of the line; see also Book VII, lines 234, 262, and 525.

24. As indicated in n. 11, he substitutes "Immediately" (VII, 285), "He scarce had said, when" (VII, 313), "The Earth obey'd, and straight" (VII, 453) for it, or leaves it out altogether.

25. See Book VII, lines 249–52, 307–09, 544, etc.

26. Frank Kermode, "Adam Unparadised," in *The Living Milton*, ed. idem (London, 1960), p. 97; see also Book VII, lines 251–52 ("Night"—"Morn").

27. According to M. Jarrett-Kerr ("Milton, Poet and Paraphrast," *Essays in Criticism*, X [1960], 384), "that ugly word 'alterne'" ruins the smoothness of the line. I do not think he is justified in assuming that Milton's "reverence for Scriptural literalism" (p. 386) led to artistic failure.

28. I disagree with Blamires, who thinks that lines 349–52 refer only to the stars (*Milton's Creation*, pp. 180–81). All the sources have a period after Genesis i, 16.

29. A fairly frequent trait; see also Book VII, line 245 ("Sprung from the Deep"; AV and Geneva Genesis i, 3, both have "was"); lines 387 and 393 ("generate"; AV and Geneva Genesis i, 20: "bring forthe"); line 532 ("Dominion hold"; AV "have dominion," Geneva "rule over" in Genesis i, 28); line 539 ("Delectable" instead of AV and Geneva's "pleasant" in Genesis ii, 9); line 552 ("Desisting"; AV and Geneva Genesis ii, 2: "ended").

30. See also Book VII, line 385 ("Luminaries") and Vulg. Genesis i, 14 and 16 ("luminaria").

31. The borrowing of logical and temporal conjunctions and the use of the glosses of Geneva indicate this convincingly; see pp. 112–17.

32. This is typically Miltonic; see also Book VII, lines 235 ("outspread"), 251 ("Divided"), 252 ("He nam'd"), 269 ("Dividing"), 308 ("he call'd"), 525 ("breath'd"), and 549 ("View'd").

33. Except for the first day (VII, 252, 260), Milton regularly makes morning and evening come alive, mostly through verbs denoting speech or song; see Book VII, lines 274–75, 338, 448, and 550: the whole Creation joins in the Creator's praise.

34. In the face of this evidence, Sims' contention that "no evidence of use by Milton of the Geneva Bible has been discovered in his poetry" (*Bible in Milton's Epics*, p. 5, n. 4) seems completely unfounded. I fully agree with Fletcher, who advises to "guard against assuming that he was committed to either English text. . . . In general . . . throughout his lifetime Milton used the Genevan and the 1611 versions of the Bible" (*Intellectual Development of John Milton*, vol. II, p. 104).

35. See also above, p. 112, concerning AV's gloss to "living Soul," which is mentioned by H. Darbishire, ed., *The Poetical Works of John Milton*, 2d ed. (Oxford, 1961), vol. I, p. 302, n. 451.

36. See similarly Genesis ii, 15: "And the LORD God took the man, and put him into the garden of Eden, to dresse it, and to keepe it."

37. "Audibly" (VII, 518) emphasizes the significance of God's last utterance, which is addressed to the whole universe.

38. See also Book VII, lines 535–36 ("for no place / Is yet distinct by name").

39. See also Book VII, line 524 ("This said"), line 530 ("then"), line 536 ("thence"), and the addition in line 548 ("Here finish'd hee"), which lends weight to the conclusion.

40. He also uses shorter prepositions in Book VII, line 520 ("in") and line 534

("on"); in line 530 he leaves out "unto them" altogether. In Book VII, 525, where "of" is missing, Milton follows the Hebrew version; see AV's gloss to Genesis ii, 7.

41. See also Book VII, lines 525-26, 540-41, and 548, where the subject is not repeated either; see also line 539, where two sentences are fused into one by the zeugmatic adjective "Delectable."

42. Here Milton anticipates the word order of the next clause in Genesis i, 27, and leaves out one verb; through rearranging the sentence he arrives at ἀπὸ κοινοῦ.

43. For normal pseudo-rhyme in this section see Book VII, lines 521-22, 533-34 ("Air"—"Earth"; the latter appears very often at the end of the line) and possibly lines 543-44 ("Evil"—"di'st").

44. See Book VII, line 528 ("Express"), line 529 ("thy consort"), line 536 ("as thou know'st"), line 537 ("Grove"), line 542 ("Variety"), line 545 ("Death"), line 546 ("sin"), and line 547 ("Death").

45. Elsewhere in the account of the Creation, only three lines indicate Adam's presence: Book VII, lines 296 and 493-94. It seems that Milton deliberately refrains from letting Raphael address Adam directly, for example, in lines 332, 368-69, and 505-18. Except for the end, Raphael's report is surprisingly impersonal.

46. The only exception, outside God's discourse with the Son in Book VII, lines 519-23, and with Adam and Eve in lines 531-34, where Raphael does not use the personal pronoun, occurs in line 530 ("Mankind"). Here the whole human race is included in God's blessing. The noun also separates the direct addresses of Raphael and God.

# MILTON AND DIODATI:
# AN ESSAY IN PSYCHODYNAMIC
# MEANING

## *John T. Shawcross*

A reading of *Epitaphium Damonis* implies a homoerotic relationship, with Diodati as the more dominantly "masculine" and Milton
as the more recessively "feminine." An examination of letters and
other poems, as well as what we know of Milton's biography, leads
to the conclusion that Diodati and Milton had discussed male-
female love and that Milton had resisted entanglement. But there
was clearly some disruption in their relationship prior to the end of
1629, and during 1629–1630 Milton underwent an identity crisis.
His works at this time and through 1637 evidence an unsuccessful
attempt to develop heterosexual drives. The 1634 *Comus* and the
alterations in the 1637 *Comus* reflect the changes in Milton's ideas
of sexuality: his attitudes are more certain and less rigid by the end
of 1637 than they were in 1629–1630 or 1634. The homoerotic attitude toward Diodati was dissipated, or at least repressed, by the
rupture of their relationship and by sublimation. Further examination of letters, poems, and epigraphs indicates Diodati's homosexual nature and Milton's latent homosexualism, which was
repressed consciously and subconsciously from becoming overt,
except perhaps with Diodati. Accordingly new interpretations of
the works examined emerge.

## I

AT THE conclusion of *Epitaphium Damonis,* a Latin elegy on the
death of his friend Charles Diodati, John Milton makes a curious
pagan-Christian collocation. Of Diodati's apotheosis he wrote:

> You, encircled around your glorious head with a shining crown
> and riding in happy bowers entwined with palm leaves,
> shall pursue eternally the immortal marriage

127

> where song and mingled lyre rage with blessed dances,
> and festal orgies revel under the thyrsus of Sion.                    (215-19)[1]

Diodati, now an angel of pure air (203-04), is haloed and resident
in the happy bowers of paradise. Earthly bowers of earthly bliss are
made, we know from *Comus*, of "hyacinth and roses" (male and female
symbols);[2] in contrast such bowers as Diodati's are created by "Flowers
of more mingled hew," entwined with palm leaves—the palm of the
victor in life's struggle, of the multitude singing before the throne
of God (Revelation vii, 9). But Diodati does not simply rest in his
bower: he is "riding" ("gestans"). The word has the obvious meaning
of spinning round in his heavenly orbit like all angelic intelligences,
but also the commonplace physical meaning of sexual intercourse.
The sexual meaning is evident from the association of "bowers" and
"marriages," if nothing else. The imagery here has kinship with the
allegoric lines of the epilogue to *Comus* (992-1011), where Milton
contrasts the bower of Adonis with that of Cupid and Psyche, "farr
above in spangled sheen." Adonis "oft reposes" and Venus sits sadly
on the ground, no continued coition being possible. On the other hand,
the marriage of heart (or body) and soul (after its "wandring labours
long") will bring an eternal wedding (note that Psyche is Cupid's
eternal *bride*, not *wife*), and through an immaculate birth ("from her
fair unspotted side") will come "Youth" (immortality; without decline)
and "Joy" (heavenly bliss). In his bower, Diodati will pursue his immortal marriage with God,[3] one made possible through the love which
is God and the perseverance of his soul (a female symbol) through
the mazes of life. The expression of apotheosis as union with God
is not unusual; yet the metaphor of human union to express that divine
union, though frequent in such mystical writers as St. Teresa of Avila,
has been little examined in literary work such as Milton's.

The psychodynamic propensities of this metaphor are major ave-
nues of literary investigation. Man's creative act becomes the metaphor
to explain God's Creation, and man's closest form of oneness, the
metaphor for unity with God. The realization that all men are female
counterparts in the divine marriage (in *Comus* made obvious through
Psyche, the soul) leads to awareness of many mortal symbols of worthiness: motherliness, celibacy, love, tears, music, aesthetic leanings, charity, humanitarianism, etc. Further, man as supine receiver of God's
insemination helps explain the antiheroic view of life, although Milton

would stress that this is a *union*, demanding reciprocal action by both partners for consummation.[4] The initial failings of Satan can be explained as his refusal to submit to the demands of supineness, which is the prelude to fruitful union with God.[5] The antihero, in his great self-hate, cannot accept nonaction but wishes to assert his "maleness." When assertion of one's "maleness" is denied, it becomes the psychological source of self-hate similar to the female's "loss" of a penis as the source of the castration complex hypothesized by Freud.

It should be noted, of course, that such concepts imply a male point of view only. Man in his inability to bring forth creation, since he is only an agent, develops a self-love of agency (the penis) and of action-driven life, involving "male" symbols of worthiness: heroism, sexual potency, war, nonsentimentalism ("emotional strength"), mechanical and technological leanings, etc. We can see in the preceding the sources of our commonplace separation of things in terms of sex: careers, sports, the activities one engages in, handwriting, attire, physical beauty. Man's view of the female thus focuses on creation and the achievement of continuance (through birth and nurture, through love, through the arts), and to counter such female qualities within himself he praises destructive, mechanical, short-lived action. The male's inadequacy to generate and maintain develops self-hate, by reversal, when he is denied "male" command and dominance. Satan, as his interview with Chaos and Old Night in Book II of *Paradise Lost* makes clear, is dedicated to uncreation—not *non*creation but *un*creation, the reversal of that which is created back to its "original" elements. As archetypal antihero he must nullify totally the achievement of the creative spirit. Unfortunately, since Judeo-Christian societies have been male-oriented, our philosophies and literatures have reflected only this male point of view.

In the *Epitaphium*, Diodati is worthy because of his "sweet and holy simplicity," his "radiant virtue," his "blushing modesty," his "youth without blemish," and because he did not taste of "the delight of marriage" (199–214). The reward of virginity is salvation, according to Revelation xiv, 4: "These are they which follow the Lamb whithersoever he goeth." Likewise in his friendship for Milton, Diodati has shown his worthiness (37–56). The apotheosis is certain, to Milton, and implied when he cites the passing of the eleventh day. He says that Diodati will not crumble to dust in an unwept sepulchre "if there

is any worth in having cultivated the ancient faith and piety and the
arts of Pallas" (33–34), but "now daylight is present after the eleventh
night" (156). He has reached that point in time when he must "weep"
for Diodati.[6] But this also suggests Twelfth Night, after he has completed his poem; Twelfth Night thus becomes the epiphany, or manifestation of divinity (for Milton), of Diodati. The poem itself becomes
the epiphany.

The apotheosis involves "song and mingled lyre," which "rage
['furit'] with blessed dances," and "festal orgies," which "revel under
the thyrsus of Sion." The Bacchic dance of ecstasy is a frenzied simulation of sexual intercourse; here there is harmony and yet also enfevered
movement. The marriage is continually celebrated as this line imports.
It is "festal," that is, sacred, and yet orgiastic; and capping the pagan-
Christian collocation is the thyrsus of Sion. The thyrsus was a staff
twined with ivy and vine shoots borne by Bacchantes, and Sion is
the heavenly city of God, that is, God himself. The phallic image
is obvious; and the ivy and vine shoots symbolize immortality and
generation. The vision of God with such human attributes is startling,
yet to one like Milton it must have been further evidence of God's
mysterious being which He tries to communicate to man through man's
awareness of himself. But undoubtedly it has worked the other way:
man in his attempt to galvanize himself against the void of death
and nonbeing has fashioned a myth built on personal observation.
Since life ensues for man only through coitus, with the implications
of sexual differentiation before, during, and after the act, he can make
"Death the Gate of Life" (*PL* XII, 571) only through a like act. Life
emerges from intercourse; therefore, eternal life must ensue upon intercourse with God.

Even the metaphor of "gate" is dependent upon sexual meaning,[7]
and the common meaning of "to die" is played on. The "gate" suggests
the enclosed garden (paradise) to be reached through entrance. The
enclosed garden, or *hortus conclusus* of Song of Solomon iv, 12, is
a womb symbol,[8] and the womb as symbol of return brings the metaphor full circle. Exit through the "gate" of the enclosed garden as
womb of generation is birth, from the secure, known world into the
uncertain, unknown world of life; entrance through the "gate" of the
enclosed garden as womb of return is death, from the trials and tribula-
tions of this our life to the bliss and serenity which are God. There

is, of course, a reversal in sexual relationship implied in this metaphor from that of God as Father to God as Mother figure, that aspect underlying the feminine attributes of the Son.[9] That is, God as Father effects creation, God as Mother bears, God as Mother admits man to return, and God as Father unites man to him.

The ending of *Epitaphium Damonis* thus places Diodati in heaven as the eternal bride of the Bridegroom; the marriage is accompanied by a dance of life, harmony, and "sexual" motion. This immortal marriage receives particular significance because Diodati has "tasted not at all" of "the delight of marriage" (213). Indeed he has "rejected the rainbow with his foot" (204). The imagery is involved: the rainbow is the sign of God's covenant with Noah; it appears after the storms of life, after "tears"; and Diodati is now in the pure air above the middle air in which storms are generated. Implicitly, however, he has rejected a covenant involving water (a specifically female symbol), and he has rejected it with his foot (a specifically phallic symbol). The passage is thus seen to be underpinned by the worthiness of celibacy. The fire (a male image) in the festal orgies under the thyrsus of Sion implies not only a balance to the destructive flood but also the sexual fulfillment that has come for Diodati through death, his death becoming the gate (an explicitly female symbol). As Milton writes of Diodati's death and his apotheosis, he views his dead friend as "female" whose death is metaphorically a gate, who is united to God by the immortalizing thyrsus of God, and who has assured himself of this position by his actions in life, primarily his celibacy. Diodati has not been antiheroic in matters of faith; his life has shown "sweet and holy simplicity," "radiant virtue"; he is "Among the souls of heroes" (200–05). But one wonders why there has been so much emphasis on this mythic statement. Beneath the remarks are a sense of wrongness in human sexual activity and a celebration of those who can conquer and control such human bodily needs. "Blushing modesty" was dear to Diodati, according to Milton, but the participle is Milton's word, as also "youth without blemish" ("sine labe juventus") (212).

Although the metaphor is not unique, one is struck, I think, by the imagery, which suggests psychodynamic significance. In addition to this ending the reader recalls the prior statements of the poem which present the poet's sense of loss, lines 37–49, 83–86, 94–111. Implied is a homoerotic relationship, with Diodati as more dominantly "masculine" and Milton more recessively "feminine." The poet surely reflects here the tears and music and aesthetic leanings associated with the female. Such an interpretation gives further meaning to lines like "with what *incessant* complaints he vexed the *caves* / and *rivers*, the wandering *streams* and *recesses* of the woods" (5–6); "as the evil / southwind rattles all the *doors*, and whistles in the *elm above*" (48–49); "hidden in the *shade* of an *oak*, / and the nymphs return to their well-known haunts beneath the *waters*, / and the shepherds lie concealed, the farmer snores under a hedge, / who will bring back to me your flatteries, who then / your laughter and Attic salt, your cultured graces?" (52–56); "Alas, how entangled with insolent weeds are my once cultivated / *fields*, and the *tall grain* itself is *drooping* with *neglect*, / the *unmarried grape withers* on its *slighted vine*, / nor do *myrtle groves* delight" (63–66); and "What is to become of you, Thyrsis? / What do you wish for yourself? that brow of youth is not wont to be / melancholy, nor its eyes grim, nor its countenance severe; / these things justly desire dances and nimble sports / and always love; twice miserable he who loved late" (82–86). That Milton has purposefully used here female imagery of space, water, and enclosure, and phallic male imagery seems unavoidable, once we observe the hint. Milton, we understand, is both consciously and unconsciously reporting his sense of loss of a dear companion who had supplied a need. Whether that need was recognized overtly and perhaps satisfied is unclear from the remarks of this elegy, but that it was felt is apparent. The imagery suggests the female personality bereft of male companionship, and sexual overtones arise from the darkness evoked and the flatteries given. Amaryllis and Neaera seem not to have joined the poet, ever, in those shades. Diodati is less certainly identifiable, for we cannot be sure that Milton's statements of his celibacy are in fact accurate. What is important is that Milton apparently thought they were. This, of course, says more about Milton and his concept of his relationship with Diodati than about the dead friend. Although there is the possibility that these remarks concerning Diodati's sexual life refer only to heterosexual love, not homosexual love, Milton's insistence on Diodati's celibacy makes sense, really, only if Milton knew of or suspected nonheterosexual orientation on Diodati's part. For even if Diodati professed virginity to Milton and if they had seen each other soon before Milton left for the Continent, Milton's statement could still, he must have realized, be in error.

Because the imagery of the poem points to this suggestion, we should not take the suggestion to reason why the imagery was used. That goes in circles. Yet we do ask ourselves the reason for this imagery, and the answer seems to be Milton's "solitudinem," at age thirty. If there is any psychological validity in man's responses to given stimuli—in our language, in our way of thinking—then Milton's choice of certain images and allusions may have been governed by his, at least subconscious, relationship with Diodati. That it was conscious, however, will appear as we proceed through all the evidence. Sometime before, Milton had professed a desire for wife, family, and independent home,[10] and sometime well before that he seems to have been enamored of one Amelia (see the Italian poems) and "bands of maidens, stars / emitting seductive flames" (*Elegia prima*, 51–52) as well as "one surpassing all others" (*Elegia septima*, 61), the latter perhaps to be associated with the background for *Sonnet 1* and perhaps too with Amelia. But we know little of romance in Milton's life. Is perhaps this innocence of sexuality part of the difficulty some three years or so after he wrote *Epitaphium Damonis* that he encountered in his first marriage with Mary Powell?[11] We know nothing really of the circumstances of the marriage, though there have been speculations concerning financial matters and romanticizing about love at first sight. And the reason for her almost immediate departure from his household—the differences in ages (thirty-three and sixteen), the ages of her nephew-charges, Edward and John Phillips (twelve and eleven), the differences of background (social, religious, and political), and totally new surroundings—may have already been told. But a personality such as here hypothesized may hold part of the key to the abruptness of the marriage, the seeming familial and financial "arrangement," and the problems of those first two months.

II

Diodati was born in 1609, the son of a very important medical doctor, Theodore, and nephew of the well-known Swiss theologian, John. He lived with his family in the parish of St. Mary Magdalen, Castle Baynard Ward, London, from 1617 or 1618,[12] then in the parishes of Christ Church and St. Faith's, Castle Baynard Ward, by 1625, and finally in the parish of St. Anne's, Blackfriars, by 1638. His first home in London was only a few blocks from Milton's home, and both were only a few blocks from Alexander Gill's St. Paul's School, where both were students. Milton entered the school around 1620, remaining through 1624; Diodati may have entered in 1617 or 1618 and left in 1622. He matriculated at Trinity College, Oxford, on February 7, 1623. He was admitted B.A. on December 10, 1625, and proceeded through the M.A., awarded on July 8, 1628. Milton, though older, apparently went to St. Paul's later, left later, was only in his first year in college when Diodati was being graduated from college, and received his bachelor's degree nine months after Diodati received his master's.

The extant writing connecting Milton and Diodati are two Greek letters to Milton, *Elegia prima* addressed to Diodati, *Elegia sexta* addressed to Diodati, *Sonnet 4* addressed to Diodati, and two Latin letters to Diodati (plus *Epitaphium Damonis*). The two letters in Greek[13] from Diodati to Milton are undated; they have been assigned to 1625 and spring 1626, but the latter date may well be inaccurate since the letter probably does not specifically relate to *Elegia prima*. The first talks of the poor weather which seems to counter their plans to meet to "enjoy learned and philosophical discourse together." Diodati prophesies good weather will come and they will be able to proceed as planned. Like many letters of the time, it is written in the graceful style and is ornamented by classical allusion. It is thus unwise to explore deep significance in "so much do I long for your society," for such fulsomeness was expected. The second letter, however, has some provocative language in it. After saying that he is enjoying himself in the country, missing only "some noble soul skilled in conversation" (that is, Milton), Diodati admonishes his correspondent for overstudiousness and for not enjoying his youth. Diodati is Milton's better in only one thing, "knowing the proper limit of labor," a point Milton was to make much later in his verse epistles to Edward Lawrence and Cyriack Skinner (*Sonnets 20* and *21*, written around fall 1655). The differences in interests, activities, and philosophy of life between Milton and his good friend are more fully explored in *Elegia sexta*. But the differences implied in the letter smack of the commonplace attitudes toward "male" and "female" attributes: the one who plans and the one who follows; the one who is concerned with the here and now and the one who is concerned with lastingness; the one who is carefree and nonstudious and the one who is serious and overstudious; the one who is outgoing and the one who is withdrawn. And then in the letter's "ornament," Diodati writes: "and be joyous—

though not in the fashion of Sardanapalus in Cilicia [Soli]." Sardanapalus was an Assyrian king (seventh century B.C.) who was effeminate and voluptuous. While advising Milton to partake of lightness in life, Diodati also counsels moderation; but surely he had no fear that one of such "inexcusable perseverance" would move to a polar position. In fact the allusion contrasts with an allusion just before, that if Milton were with Diodati, Diodati "would be happier than the King of Persia," meaning, apparently, one who enjoys complete abundance of all things.[14] The aura of this allusion is male; that to Sardanapalus is female. It is fraught with possibilities: such a joyous life as Milton would lead involves those things considered effeminate; a tendency toward the effeminate has already been observable; ironically, Milton has not previously shown a tendency toward voluptuousness (that is, Diodati pokes fun at Milton's not being voluptuous by warning him against being voluptuous); the general context of Milton's life and attitude had already been discussed between them. The allusions sound like an inside joke. Diodati as potential King of Persia must be one given to overeating, excessive drinking, leisure, and sexual fulfillment.

Diodati's two letters attest to their friendship; they attest to the differences between them—differences of personality and thus of complementary personalities; they attest to Diodati's "male" role and Milton's "female" role in the commonplace separations of such role-playing; and the reference to Sardanapalus suggests that these friends had discussed their personality differences, Milton's tendency toward the "female" life, and Milton's abstemiousness toward things of a sensual nature. The "joke" of this allusion—there are others in Milton's two Latin letters to Diodati later on—shows us the way in which meaningful things can be said obscurely, if one can be sure of the reader's understanding (in this case, Milton's), and the letters contribute to our awareness of a closer bond between the two than simply friendship.

*Elegia prima*, written in April 1626, is concerned with Milton's rustication from Cambridge because of a disagreement with his tutor, William Chappell. This is almost the earliest extant writing we have of Milton's, only the paraphrases on Psalms cxiv and cxxxvi, *Apologus de Rustico et Hero*, the two fragments entitled *Carmina Elegiaca*, and the prolusion "Mane citus lectum fuge" being datable in 1624–1625. The first elegy is in response to a (nonextant) letter from Diodati,

who was sojourning in Chester. Although Milton has been required
to return to his home in London (probably that on Bread Street),
he is not unhappy to be there and says that he does not even care
to see the rushy Cam again. What his argument with Chappell was
and what his relationship with fellow students was can only be surmised.
But in the first case the rigidity of Chappell as tutor, the nature of
the program of study at Christ's College (criticized heavily some years
later in *Of Education*, 1644), and Chappell's religious leanings (a clearly
episcopal attitude which Milton, who was then studying for the ministry, might have disputed) probably supply the reasons. How "activist"
Milton may have been in expressing his disagreement with the establishment of his day, we do not know, but at least he seems not to have
been totally silent.

His relations with fellow students would also seem to have been
strained, for two years later in *Prolusion 6*, written in July 1628, he
talks of there having been "disagreements over our studies" and of
"an absolutely hostile and unfriendly spirit."[15] We know likewise that
he was called the Lady of Christ's, an epithet deriving perhaps from
his fine features (compare his portrait at age twenty-one, the "Onslow"
portrait, and his remark in *Sonnet 7* at age twenty-three or twenty-
four that his "semblance might deceave the truth / That I to manhood
am arriv'd so neer") and from his eschewing those activities of a frivo-
lous, perhaps romantic, perhaps athletic nature common to the male
college student. The circumstance is not much different from that
today which evokes the term "sissy"; our world's penchant for as-
signing certain attributes to the male or to the female, as referred
to before, lies behind Milton's sobriquet. What no one seems to have
remarked is that at Christ's, a community of about 265 people in
those days, Milton was called *the* Lady of Christ's, indicating no slight
notoriety and probably no localization to that one college only. In
the sixth prolusion he discusses this nickname, working from the title
of Father assigned to the master of ceremonies at the exercises preceding the long vacation, a role Milton acted in 1628, through ribald
puns. The omission of this event the year before is explained as perhaps
resulting from the fact that "those who were about to become 'Fathers'
conducted themselves so turbulently in town that he, to whom this
duty was assigned, taking pity on their great exertions ['tantorum
laborum'], of his own accord decreed that they should be relieved

of this anxiety." The irony that he, Milton, the Lady of Christ's, should now be "father" is immediately seized upon:

But indeed how comes it that I have so suddenly been made a "Father"? Ye gods, grant me your protection! What prodigy is this, surpassing the strange tales of Pliny! Have I by killing a snake suffered the fate of Tiresias? Has some Thessalian witch smeared me with magic ointment? Or finally, violated by some god, like Caeneus of old, have I bargained for manhood as a reward for dishonor, so that suddenly I might be changed from a woman into a man?[16]

The reference to Tiresias is particularly noteworthy. Seeing two serpents in copulation, Tiresias killed the female of the pair with a stick and so was changed into a female; seven years later he regained his sex by killing the male. The story allegorizes a man's rejection of maleness (later femaleness) and subsequent "femaleness" (later "maleness") through sexual inhibition. The appropriateness to male student turned Lady turned Father is patent. Within this passage of *Prolusion* 6, the allusion indicates Milton's opposition to sexual licentiousness and his subsequent "femaleness" in the eyes of his fellow students (now as "Father" regaining his sex). (The association of the story with Tiresias, who foresaw the future, relates to his blindness, for this is a symbol of castration; see also note 36.) The reference to Caeneus also involves a change of sex from woman to ,man, as Milton here changes from "Lady" to "Father" by the "dishonor" of having been "violated by some God" (as Caenis was by Neptune). The analogy suggests Apollo, god of poetry and song, of moral and intellectual pursuits. Perhaps, too, there is a pun in the term "Lady of Christ's" involving Milton's pursuit of these "female" interests controlled by Apollo, who is equated with the Sun (the Son) and Christ, and thence the college. A similar pun on Phoebus-Sun-Son-Christ-Christ's is employed in *Elegia prima*, line 14.

But the most obvious pun—amazingly not recognized before— is the equation of "Lady" with "Mother," suggested not only by the replacement of "Father" but by its qualifying phrase "of Christ's." That is, Milton to his fellow students was like the Virgin Mary, most apparently because of his virginity. What they might have come from his (like Psyche's and Mary's) unspotted side is interesting to contemplate. For the term "Lady" suggests hauteur, and the term "Father" not only indulges his "return" to maleness but requires sexual intercourse resulting in a pregnancy. His attitude toward his fellow students' philistinism implies such hauteur; his children are those students who took part in the Vacation Exercise, and those who have been identified were all younger than he. He plays upon this family situation in the verses called *At a Vacation Exercise*, which make clear the appropriateness of both terms. He continues, "From some I have lately heard the epithet 'Lady.' But why do I seem to those fellows insufficiently masculine?" and cites as answer his lack of "masculine" activities like wrestling, or plowing, or whoring.[17] The view of Milton which one sees is not quite that which his biographers have tried to rationalize.[18] He exhibited those qualities which the male-oriented world considered female: delicate physical features, certain kinds of interests and activities, avoidance of and perhaps even objection to sexual behavior. But we should also recognize that he was aware of all this, and that he himself, as this occasion demanded, engaged in sexual punning. He may not have approved, but he did not totally abstain from obscenities, and this is not uncommon in the sexually inhibited. Then too, in order to understand a double entendre, as those who argue against censorship of the stand-up comic or the television talk show point out, one already has to understand the joke before he hears it to recognize its off-color quality. Case in point: Milton next adds the line, "verum utinam illi possint tam facile exuere asinos, quam ego quicquid est foeminae" ("But would that they could as easily lay aside their asshood as I whatever belongs to womanhood"); the pun on "exuere ['uncover' or 'lay bare'] asinos ['asses']" is obvious, and bawdy.

In *Elegia prima* he remarks his joy at being able to read the classic drama (25–46) now that he is at home, and in contrast in *An Apology Against a Pamphlet* (1642) he castigates his fellow students and the stage fare in the colleges:

when in the Colleges so many of the young Divines, and those in next aptitude to Divinity have bin seene so oft upon the Stage writhing and unboning their Clergie limmes to all the antick and dishonest gestures of Trinculo's, Buffons, and Bawds; prostituting the shame of that ministery which either they had, or were nigh having, to the eyes of Courtiers and Court-Ladies, with their Groomes and *Madamoisellaes*. There while they acted, and overacted, among other young scholars, I was a spectator; they thought themselves gallant men, and I thought them fools, they made sport, and I laught, they mispronounc't and I mislik't, and to make up the *atticisme*, they were out, and I hist. (First ed., p. 14)

The picture of Milton that emerges is that of a youth so intellectually driven and so morally upright that he must have struck associates as their concept of the "female" personality. This is definitely not to say that Milton was overtly effeminate in attitude or had sexually exercised such personality traits (although he may have). But it is to suggest that his orientation involved sexual inhibition and compensation in study, vicarious experience, and male attachment (the apparently singular close attachment to Diodati). In *Elegia prima* he remarks that "the hours of spring do not hasten by without effect on me" (48) and recounts the beauty of maidens whom he observed beneath "the celebrated shade of a suburban spot" (50). But it is only observance from afar; he has not communed with any of these young women of Britain. The lines seem to be trying to prove to Diodati that he is not exclusively studious, "bending over books and studies day and night," and that he has not totally despised "the gifts of nature," that he is living, laughing, enjoying his youth and the hours—these being phrases from Diodati's second extant letter. Indeed Cupid's indulgence permits Milton to prepare to return to Cambridge, much as he does not wish "to leave the favorable walled city" (86). Curiously, and evidencing his sexual-moral attitudes and his inhibition, he is preparing "to escape from afar the infamous halls of faithless Circe, / preparing with the help of divine moly" (87-88). For Milton, here in 1626, sexual alliance implies "roul[ing] with pleasure in a sensual stie" (*Comus*, 77), which is the way he expressed succumbing to bodily temptation in 1634. The "divine moly" which exists within him to resist the charms of Circe is his moral sense and his transmutation of such bodily urges to an aesthetic plane. The seductive maidens he has espied are likened to maidens of classic literature or history and to stars in the heavens. His maidens entice by shaking their hair, a symbol of sexuality ("hair") and thus of sexual activity ("shaking"; "tremulosque capillos"); and hair for Milton is that "by which deceitful Love extends his golden nets" (*Elegia prima*, 60). Others, of course, frequently find themselves in "the tangles of *Neaera*'s hair."

*Elegia sexta*, addressed "To Charles Diodati, sojourning in the country," pursues the differences in their personalities we have noted before. Diodati apparently ate much, and Milton opens with an ironic contrast: "On an empty stomach I send you a wish for health, / which you, stuffed full, can perhaps do without." He also says that Ceres is favorable toward Diodati. His friend imbibed noticeably; he talks of "the French wines consumed beside agreeable fires" and of Bacchus (in various guises) repeatedly. The nature of the poetry which Diodati might produce is Bacchian or Dionysian; his overeating and overdrinking should not inhibit his poetizing. That Diodati indulged himself is clear, and so is the fact that he is given to bodily satisfaction. The Bacchian reference in *Epitaphium Damonis* may, thus, have more personal meaning than has been noted. Apollo, as god of poetry and song, will have his effect on Diodati also, Milton contends, and one can hope for "gay Elegy" or amatory verse as the result. (Diodati had apparently been a medical student, and Apollo was associated with healing.) But for a poet such as Milton (in December 1629 when he was composing *On the Morning of Christ's Nativity*) frugal life is the norm. The work on which he was engaged—a birthday present for Christ—awaits Diodati's judgment.[19] The emphasis certainly is placed on Diodati's fleshly world and Milton's aesthetic one; the pair appear to Milton's way of thinking as complements to each other. Diodati is vacationing, he is feasting, he is drinking; he is outgoing in manner and surrounded by people. Milton is at work, he is abstemious of food and partakes of only "nonintoxicating potions from the pure spring ['Castalia']," and he is alone. He is also embarrassed to talk of his work.

Two odd phrases appear in the poem which suggest something more for their relationship than the above dichotomy, which in itself has earmarks of a male-female relationship. "You would like to know by song," Milton writes, "how I return your love and revere you; / believe me, you can scarcely learn this from song, / for my love is not confined by brief measures, / nor does it itself proceed unimpaired on halting feet" (5-8). The apparent fact that Diodati has requested such a statement makes Milton's lines more than a commonplace avowal of friendship in a verse letter. Perhaps Milton had not written to Diodati in a while, or had not answered a letter prior to that of December 13, cited in the headnote. The possible anxiety on Diodati's part that such a question implies places an odd construction on their friendship. If we can read the implied question as a symptom of anxiety—that emotional state caused by anticipation of future failing of a present desire—then we recognize an attitude on Diodati's part suggestive of homoeroticism. It would seem that, by whatever actions would be usual—letters, meetings, exchanged avowals of friendship or love—Diodati has not recently been reassured of Milton's attitude toward him. It appears that Diodati does not think himself in the wrong for the disruption in their relationship but is anxious lest it be totally disrupted. On Milton's part is a tone that says, If friendship were confinable to song, it would not be very deep. And then there is a tone that suggests that Milton is questioning Diodati's sincerity as friend. Diodati appears the insensitive one; Milton, the sensitive. Diodati appears the uncomprehending male; Milton, the long-suffering female of many a sentimental novel. Secondly, an aside casts a curious light on Milton's attitude toward Diodati at this time: "But if you will know what I am doing (if only at least / you consider it to be important to know whether I am doing anything)" (79–80). Here the situation implied is that sometime in the not too distant past Diodati has seemed unconcerned, perhaps aloof and airy, has been less than seriously communicative about Milton's hopes and activities. The parenthesis hints that there has been a strain in their relationship, just as lines 5–8 do, and that Milton has come to a kind of decisive stage in his view of that relationship by recognizing one who is less worthy of his intimate friendship than he had thought him in the past. The inference to be made, I think, is that Diodati was friendly with many people (perhaps especially males) and that Milton was not, holding their relationship rather exclusive. The strain in their relationship arose from these contrasting attitudes, with Milton now in 1629 proceeding to a conscious assimilation of his subconscious drives. While the evidence does not prove homosexualism, suggestions are strong that overt actions grew out of Milton's and Diodati's homoeroticism. Later evidence, as we shall see, makes such suggestions warranted and leads to the conclusion that Diodati was fickle and irresponsible in human relationships, while Milton was inhibited and guilt-ridden.

At least after having received an M.A. at Oxford in July 1628, Diodati seems to have floundered in his career and in any kind of noticeable accomplishment. Whether or not we should assume that, like Milton, he retired to his father's home in London for medical study cannot be determined, but his family situation was unlike Milton's: his father was in good health and active in his medical practice and there was a younger sister, Philadelphia, at home. (His brother John was at school, and we do not know whether his mother was

then living, though it seems probable that she was, since his father
did not remarry until sometime around 1637.) It is assumed that his
studies in college had been to prepare him for medicine and then
speculated that he pursued further study or practice upon gradua-
tion. He might rather have been preparing for the ministry—but we
just do not know. Not long after the sojourn referred to in *Elegia
sexta*, Diodati was abroad, enrolled as an English student of theology
in the Academy of Geneva on April 16, 1630. His move to Geneva
is explained by probable dissatisfaction with theological training in
England and by his uncle's residence there. He remained at the academy
through at least September 15, 1631. When he returned to England
we do not know. What he did thereafter we do not certainly know
either, but he eventually began the practice of medicine before the
end of 1637, outside London.

    In other words, around the time of *Elegia sexta* the friendship
of Milton and Diodati may have cooled, partially because they were
following such different patterns of life—Diodati, as in the poem,
given to the vacationing spirit and Milton to the compulsiveness observable throughout his life—and partially because of Diodati's apparent decline from what seems a kind of precociousness in earlier
life. Milton's parenthesis hints that he has learned that he cannot trust
Diodati's avowal of interest in his activities, and the picture that arises
from the total poem is of a Diodati more or less pleased with himself
and insensitive to Milton. The poem suggests that, though their friendship continued, it was to be less intense and less frequently reinforced
by close associations than in the past.

    Milton's own immediate activities after this time are less difficult
to chart, for during the next year, from April 17, 1630, to around
January 1631, Cambridge was closed because of the plague, and Milton
was at his family's home (probably Bread Street since they seem to
have moved to Hammersmith in 1631, although it is also possible
that there was a suburban home in the parish of St. Martin's in the
Fields from around 1623-1624). The spate of poetizing which has been
sometimes assigned to this period is corroborated by his freedom
from required study and by its nature. *The Passion* attempts to recap-
ture the mood of the Nativity ode, while he was still at Cambridge
(March 1630), but *Elegia septima*, the lines appended to that elegy,
*Song On May Morning*, *Sonnet 1*, the Italian poems, and *On Shakespear*

(all perhaps 1630 and some around May) suggest different and more leisurely concerns. There is an amatory veneer on *Elegia septima*, the lines, *Song*, and *Sonnet 1* that has seldom struck critics as very convincing. (These poems have sometimes been dated 1628 or 1629.) Perhaps their literary problem is that Milton seems to be *trying* to write this kind of verse (and not succeeding very well), and their subject matter may be, at least partially, at fault. The Italian poems, however, are another matter.

Our first problem with the Italian poems is date. Since Milton purchased his volume of Giovanni della Casa's *Rime e Prose* in December 1629, and since the Italian poems reflect Casa's influence, the poems are often dated after that time. The freedom of being off from graduate study and the possible date of the other poems allows 1630 as their date, and there is no reason to place individual poems of the sequence at different times. But *Sonnet 4* is addressed to Diodati, and he was in Geneva by the middle of April. Of course, there is no requirement that Diodati be nearby when Milton wrote, no requirement that the poem or the sequence be communicated to him. Still the date is only conjectural. Next, why does Milton choose Italian as his vehicle? Most thinking has centered around the "Donna leggiarda" whose name, Amelia, is given cryptically in *Sonnet 2*. It is suggested that she was one of the Italian colony in London, associated with the Diodatis, perhaps introduced to Milton by Charles, and so the address in *Sonnet 4*. In turn this implies that Milton sent or intended to send the verses to her (he says that she reads Italian). In *Sonnet 3* he writes that "Love on my alert tongue / awakens the new flower of foreign speech . . . by my good countrymen not understood." Pose is certainly involved, but is it pose in order not to be scoffed at? (According to *Canzone* he was.) Or is it simply experimentation in another language under the influence of having read Casa enthusiastically? Another problem is the substance and thus sincerity of this little sonnet sequence. The enamoring seems to be only on Milton's part, unexpressed to the girl, although the *Canzone* implies that others have read these verses. I think that the inference is invalid and that the *Canzone* represents a pose, a consideration of what others' reactions might be should they read these verses. I have previously suggested[20] that the sequence is concerned with love of heavenly being rather than human love, though working through human love and an actual experience (compare such lines as "grace alone from above enables him to withstand / the amorous desire which would lodge itself in his heart" [*Sonnet 2*, 13–14]; "Oh! were my sluggish heart and hard breast / as good soil for him who plants from heaven" [*Sonnet 3*, 13–14]), but there is no need to repeat that argument here. In any case, the sonnet in which Diodati is addressed says that Milton has been stubborn ("ritroso") about matters of love, that he used to contemn love ("amor spreggiar soléa") and frequently scoffed at its snares ("E de' suoi lacci spesso mi ridéa"), and that he has fallen where upright man (with physical pun) sometimes entangles himself ("Già caddi, ov' huom dabben talhor s'impiglia"). He has not been enticed by golden hair or vermeil cheeks (compare *Elegia prima*) but by foreign beauty.[21]

The poem leads to a major, general realization: Diodati and Milton have discussed male-female love in the past, and Milton has resisted entanglement. He who falls is deceived, Milton believes, and is no longer upright; the moral stricture placed on love and the implication in the pun of imminently ensuing physical sex are to be noted. Such sexual inhibition and the pall of "sinfulness" which lies over heterosexuality seem never fully to have left Milton, even in the innocent love of Adam and Eve depicted in Book IV of *Paradise Lost*. I would suggest that the Italiam poems related Milton's certain yet embarrassed reaction to a sexual stimulus around spring or summer of 1630 (?), one more emotional than that described in *Elegia prima;* that Diodati would be surprised at this reaction; that Milton assumes the role of Petrarchan lover through the influence of such sonneteers as Casa, thus employing a pose, language, imagery, and "narrative" appropriate to that influence; that he recognizes a parallel between sexual love and spiritual love, such as we have noted at the beginning of this paper, and professes (surely as pose) his lack of sufficient spiritual inspiration; and thus that the sexual love of the sequence is basically vehicle. Why does he address *Sonnet 4* to Diodati? Probably because their past discussions have little supported his reaction to this sexual stimulus ("I will say it to you with wonder," Milton admits). And probably because shortly before in *Elegia sexta* their strained relationship came to the surface. It tells Diodati that he can be enticed by the siren's eyes and voice, and since to fly himself he is in doubt (*Sonnet 6*, 2), he will devotedly render his heart to his lady and remain faithful. His heart is above "chance and envy [and] the fears and

hopes of common men." While the sequence may be an honest statement of his attitude toward Amelia, it also serves to deny a continued
relationship with Diodati as in the past. For in distinction from their
relationship of the past, these poems claim that Milton is capable
of becoming a partner in a different relationship with a different person.
The question which we perhaps cannot answer with certainty is, Do
the poems often assigned to 1630 (*Elegia septima*, etc.) register a
concerted effort to force heterosexual attitudes? Their superficiality
and the spiritual overtones in the Italian poems as well as the break
in relationship with Diodati suggested in *Elegia sexta* lead to an affirma-
tive answer. The sequence may, therefore, serve Diodati fair warning
that the kind of close relationship shared in the past is at an end.[22]

## III

The foregoing discussion of *Elegia sexta* and the Italian poems
points to an identity crisis for Milton in 1629–1630, possibly extending
backward and forward. With the removal of Diodati from a close
relationship with Milton, there were two specific compensatory reactions: a superficial and ultimately ineffectual attempt to pursue male-
female relationships, without concepts of sexual morality and inhibition
being overcome, and with the attempt abandoned thereafter; and
a deeper plunge into study and writing. The Nativity ode may represent part of that reaction as well as the inept and overreaching *Passion*,
and possibly we can add *On Shakespear*. In 1631–1632 he seems to
have written two or three Hobson poems, *Epitaph on the Marchioness
of Winchester*, *L'Allegro*, and *Il Penseroso* (and possibly the academic
*Naturam non pati senium* and *De Idea Platonica*). The seventh prolusion heralds his studious retirement to Hammersmith and Horton
(1632–1638). However, the retirement may have been a result also,
we should note, of his father's and mother's advanced ages, since his
sister Anne was married with children and his younger brother Christopher was at school. The sublimation which such removal from the
mainstream of life effected is seen in the organized and systematic
program of study which we can infer from his remarks in the seventh
prolusion concerning the attainment of a full circle of knowledge of
the past and from those in a letter to Diodati, dated November 23,
1637. In the latter he says that he has "by continuous reading brought
down the affairs of the Greeks as far as to the time when they ceased

to be Greeks" and that he has "long been occupied by the obscure business of the Italians under the Longobards, the Franks, and the Germans, to that time when liberty was granted them by Rodolph, King of Germany."[23] Additionally during this period he wrote *Comus* and other poems.[24] The foregoing, of course, describes the personality called anal-retentive.[25]

The identity crisis, reflective of sexual repression, of a lack of familial individuation, and of uncertainty of career, would seem to have emerged because of the break in the complementary subconscious which Diodati provided for Milton. Perhaps Milton came to recognize at this time the need to alter his sexual indecision. The tightness of the view Milton presents of himself in *Elegia sexta*—with its rejection of hunger (and thus sex) drives, not simply a control of such drives, and their replacement with spiritual justifications—leads eventually to the studious retirement. During most of 1630 he was ostensibly retired to his father's house, but the planned retirement of 1632–1638 specifically avoids identity decision. The decision of career in the fall of 1637, for which I have argued in the past, came finally through familial individuation (provoked apparently by the death of his mother in April 1637) and a subsequent acceptance of a male role in life. The death instinct which this retirement points to must be replaced by positivity and by matters of the future rather than of the past. The move to act positively to bring forward the future (not simply to prepare until such time that one is ready) can be seen, I believe, in the Letter to an Unknown Friend, in the writing during this period, in the letters to Diodati from November 1637, which indicate that Milton thought of taking residence in one of the Inns of Court, and in his trip to the Continent. While Milton seems not totally to reject the concept of continuing to try to be prepared (see remarks in *The Reason of Church-Government*, 1642), still while he was preparing he was also acting: plans and subjects for creative works are recorded in the Trinity MS during 1639–1642, and *Paradise Lost* was begun during this time, with some of that writing remaining in the completed poem more than twenty years later. We do not see that "doing" during the years 1632–1637, if my reading of this period and the works produced during it is correct, but we do see that "doing" in 1637–1638.

In the Letter to an Unknown Friend,[26] Milton talks of his "tardie moving," which has not, however, been held back only by "the meere love of Learning." The fact is, he says, that he is now moving and thereby he is not one who "cutts himselfe off from all action and becomes the most helplesse, pusilanimous and unweapon'd creature in the world, the most unfit and unable to doe that which all mortals most aspire to either to be usefull to his freinds, or to offend his enimies." While the retirement may have been planned as a means to an end, according to this sentence, Milton seems only with this moving to recognize the significance of his having cut himself off from the world. The adjectives describing what has been his implied former helplessness, his pusillanimity, and his being "unweapon'd" suggest "female" attributes which the "tardie moving" will controvert into "male" attributes of independent action, courage, and active opposition. "Helplesse" and etymologically "pusilanimous" suggest Milton's awareness of his dependence upon his parents and his continued immaturity, and "unweapon'd" certainly points to the ideal of the soldier conquering by use of his sword, the "warfaring" Christian. (The sexual overtones of the last adjective are also interesting.) As might be expected from someone who wrote the preceding letter, Milton had, to us, a curious concept of his age and a seemingly interminable "youth." For example (and it is only example), in the Preface to *The Judgement of Martin Bucer* (1644), referring to the first edition of *Doctrine and Discipline of Divorce* (1643), when he was thirty-five years old, he wrote of himself, "he knew not that what his youth then reason'd without a pattern, had bin heard already" (first ed., p. [xii]). Such immature views of the self are frequently attendant on those of homoerotic orientation.

*Comus* too offers evidence of concerns during the period of the studious retirement and changes in attitude by 1637. The *Comus* we read today is not the masque presented at Ludlow Castle on September 29, 1634.[27] The Trinity MS and the dating of at least parts thereof (around fall 1637) on the basis of handwriting point to renewed creativity and inspired hopes for literature,[28] but the changes in *Comus* have been insufficiently studied. Although the poem is offered as a commemoration of the Earl of Bridgewater's assumption of the Presidency of Wales, and although a scandal in the family circle throws up an intriguing backdrop for the work,[29] it provides meaningful analysis of the attitudes of the 1634–1637 Milton toward virginity, chastity, sex, and divine relationships. A full discussion cannot be undertaken

here, but briefly the earlier *Comus* seems to have been less specific
in its detailing of the Lady's resistance to Comus and in the Attendant
Spirit's description of heaven and the rewards for the virtuous. The
masque is an elaboration of the temptation in the wilderness in mortal
terms: in the dark forest of life (to use Dante's phrase) the Lady,
en route to her father's house (with its obvious divine meaning), becomes victim of the hypocritical and sensual Comus, who has im-
mobilized her body but who cannot control her mind. His offer of
"all manner of deliciousness" and "his Glass" (the first temptation of
need, *concupiscentia carnis*), his admonishment that one should partake
of the bounties poured forth by nature "With such a full and unwith-
drawing hand" (the second temptation of fraud, *concupiscentia ocu-
larum*), and his *carpe diem* and *carpe rosam* argument against "the
same vaunted name virginity" (the third temptation of violence,
*superbia vitae*) are rejected, for she discerns the "false rules pranckt
in reasons garb." Yet to free her bodily the intervention of God is
needed in the person of Sabrina, proving that "if Vertue feeble were,
/ Heav'n it self would stoop to her" (1022–23).[30] Comus' temptation
was originally given in one long speech without interruption by the
Lady (659–62, 666–71, 706–55, 672–78, 688–90, with some variations),
the glass being unspecified in the stage direction and its specific offer
being made only later, in lines 811–13. The Lady then reacts with
lines 662–65, 693–96, 701–03, and 756–79; she counters Comus' arguments by pointing out his falseness and stressing that it cannot touch
the freedom of her mind. But her remarks about the "Sun-clad power
of Chastity" and Comus' inability "to apprehend / The sublime notion,
and high mystery" which unfolds "the sage / And serious doctrine
of Virginity" (782–87) are missing. These lines, added in 1637 or early
1638 just before the masque was published (our only source for them),
pick up the Elder Brother's description of chastity and its "sun-clad
power" in lines 381–82, 419–21, and 425. In 1634 there seems to be
a confounding of chastity and virginity; note the Elder Brother's "No
goblin . . . has hurtfull power o're true virginity" (436–37) and ensuing
reference to "the arms of chastity" (440), the Spirit's request that Sabrina
"undoe the charmed band / Of true virgin heer distrest" (904–05),
and Sabrina's " 'tis my office best / To help insnared chastity" (908–09).
But chastity, by which is meant purity in conduct and intention, is
not the same as virginity (with its implications of celibacy and the

rewards of Revelation xiv, 4), and the Lady's added lines differentiate the two.

She attests to a belief in the doctrine of virginity in contradiction to Comus' interpretation of meaning in the gift of beauty; yet she is basically speaking out against his "profane tongue" and "contemptuous [earlier, 'reproachfull'] words" which have condemned "lean and sallow abstinence" (not total abstinence, but such as the abstemiousness discussed in *Elegia sexta*). In lines 690–705, a passage which was reworked with new lines in 1637, the Lady indicts Comus' dishonesty and refuses his proffered drink, since "that which is not good is not delicious / To a well-govern'd and wise appetite" (these lines were added in 1637). In question, of course, is not virginity, but a general doctrine of chastity; the close relationship between food and drink and sex is fundamental in pre-Freudian literature, the interpretation of *concupiscentia carnis* being the most obvious evidence. The doctrine of virginity involves concepts of the sinfulness of sex and the rewards awaiting those not so "defiled"—basically a form of innocence supposedly approaching the prelapsarian world. Milton had not yet moved to all the implications in "Assuredly we bring not innocence into the world" (*Areopagitica*, first ed., p. 12), but he was presenting in *Comus* a picture of a nonfugitive and noncloistered virtue, one which was being exercised. The Lady is a clear prototype of the warfaring Christian. Though she is a virgin, the real test is her chastity. Her lines do not make chastity the same as virginity; she recognizes that Comus has argued against chastity as well as virginity; but the "ideal" of virginity remains as a powerful force in Milton's thought.

There is a subtle change between the confusion of virginity and chastity in 1634 and their separation in 1637. The Milton of 1634 seems not to realize that the purifying trial which he has plotted does not demand virginity. Untried, really, himself, surely virginal, Milton had seen opposition to the "cursed place" which is both Comus' palace and urban life coming only through inhibition and escape: this was his answer in *Elegia prima* and afterward. By 1634 there is recognition of the importance of trial and the control of chastity by freedom of the mind. Milton has changed since his pre-1629 days, but he has not yet, in 1634, accepted sexual life. Comus' words are reasonable: the good of beauty "Consists in mutual and partak'n bliss, / Unsavoury in th' injoyment of it self" (741–42),[31] but since the intention of his words is unchaste, their concept is not developed in the *Comus* of 1634. However, with the Spirit's revised epilogue we do have a reconsideration of the question.[32] The earlier epilogue (generally consisting of 976–79, [1014–15], 980–83, 980–96, 998–99, 1012–23) describes heaven as a world of eternal summer and flowers, watered by Iris, goddess of the rainbow. The 1637 epilogue shows that Milton is clearly aware that this is a mortal heaven "Where young *Adonis* oft reposes"—a heaven peopled by the "lovers" of this world, who, though they are "wounded" by sexuality, may still ascend to "Beds of hyacinth and roses." But such a heaven is not the preferred eternity, that which is available to the virgins. For "farr above in spangled sheen" is Psyche, the eternal bride of Cupid, that is, the soul that has undergone "wandring labours long" (trials such as the Lady has overcome in the masque) and that has maintained its "fair unspotted side."[33] Psyche becomes the bride of the God of Love (that is, of the Son). Chastity is acknowledged in 1637 as a wider concept than in 1634 and one which will be rewarded; but virginity, a more rarefied part of chastity (a smaller circle, as it were, within the larger whole), is the greater ideal and more clearly delineated than in 1634.

By the end of 1637, Milton's attitudes are more certain and less rigid than in 1629–1630 or 1634. During the studious retirement, he avoids identity decision, familial individuation, and career decision. In career he was moving toward the world of the scholar and creative artist and more certainly away from the ministry. As late as 1641–1642, in *The Reason of Church-Government*, he was to link the ministry and writing as parallel endeavors. The acceptance of creative art as career acknowledges the significance of "female" worthiness and his predilection toward such attempted achievement. The rejection of the ministry as career acknowledges his inability to function successfully as "father" surrogate through direct and personal action. His whole life had shown his withdrawn and anal-retentive personality, hardly the kind not to "deale worse with a whole congregation."

The decision of a career is well entwined, I believe, with the resolution of identity, still unclear in 1634 and more certain in 1637. Subconscious psychological acknowledgment of his "femaleness" and homoeroticism had to occur before identity could be established. Probably the clarification of virginity and its rewards is a result of this identification of self as a justification of his past lack of heterosexual intercourse and the expected continuance of that life. Unfortunately the specter of celibacy seems to have hung over him through at least the period just before his marriage to Mary Powell. The break with Diodati in 1629–1630 must have left Milton in a limbo of nondirection, such as underlies *Sonnet 7* (in 1632) as well, really, as the 1634 *Comus*. Only with a total rejection of forced sexuality (as seen in the poems of 1630) and of the relationship with Diodati (which had not sufficiently occurred even when *Sonnet 4* was written) was Milton to conceive of himself as being able to move (as he says in the Letter to an Unknown Friend) and to think of family and home and to aspire to publishing the fruits of his attempted achievement.[34] The letter presents one who has finally rejected escape and the solitary life and who is now ready to compete in the world of men. Milton's identification with family and his implied immaturity aided in avoidance of decision and in maintenance of his sexual nonidentity. The death of his mother must have presented a crossroads, although there is no evidence one way or the other. The psychological disruption which a mother's death can create for a son, particularly an unmarried son living at home, perhaps was the major catalyst to Milton's "tardie moving." *Ad Patrem* suggests that there had been some question on the part of Milton's father as to what his son was going to do with his life. And the letter to Diodati implies decision of a poetic career, but with a transferred continuance of his former life to a world of men in London, only now with direction. The additions and changes in *Comus* in 1637 reflect an acceptance of the world of trial, of the chaste sexual life, and of the differentiations possible among good men. Milton's apparent removal to London and then his trip to the Continent place him in the middle of such life forces.

The ideas worked out in *Comus* seem to have stayed with Milton through the writing of *Epitaphium Damonis*, or perhaps they reemerge because they were subconsciously associated with Diodati and Milton's identity crisis. The 1634 *Comus* ended (except for the Spirit's epilogue) with songs and dances. The final (second) song presents the Lady and her brothers to their parents as youths who have earned "a crown of deathless praise" (973) and who are thus enabled "To triumph in victorious dance / O're sensual folly, and intemperance" (974–75). The dance is much less clearly defined than it is in *Epitaphium Damonis*. Here the dance caps the defeat of temptation, seen as assertion of chastity; but it does not emphasize the contrast with Comus' rout's dance (144 ff.), since it seems to reject any kind of sensuousness (although "dance" by itself contains such an implication) and all thought of excess. The allegory of the children's reaching their father's home after the trial of the dark forest of life would suggest that the triumphal dance engages all senses rightly used and without surfeit. The dialectic really demands such contrast; but it is not until "song and mingled lyre rage with blessed dances, and festal orgies revel" for Diodati that Milton pushed the point toward which he was heading in 1634 to its conclusion: sexuality is good but it must be chaste. Still, virginity rather than successful trial remains as an ideal; the wisdom of trial is not to be fully realized until the mid-1640s with the divorce tracts, *Areopagitica*, and the first attempts at *Paradise Lost*.

Whereas in 1634 heaven is seen as lying in the realms of Iris, goddess of the rainbow, with its lack of distinction between the chaste lover and the virgin, in 1637 heaven is divided between the lower Elysium of Adonis and the celestial heaven of Cupid and Psyche. The latter, lying above "the spheary chime," is the paradise which the followers of the Lamb, the virgins, may aspire to. And in *Epitaphium Damonis*, Diodati, as we have seen, has rejected the rainbow—the lower Elysium of Adonis—to ascend to the higher heaven with God. Now, with our fuller background in the *Comus* of 1634 and of 1637, we see the apotheosis in the elegy more firmly as I suggested at the beginning of this paper. The poem becomes an excursion in nostalgia and in wish fulfillment. For example, see the opening of the last verse paragraph, with its questions concerning Diodati's disposition after death. The wishful answer that he has ascended to the higher heaven comes through a continued belief in the rewards of virginity. If not, what is the worth of virginity? Is Milton in 1639 on the verge of realizing his assertions about good and evil that we find in *Areopagitica* in 1644?

The view of Diodati which the foregoing yields is of one who represented a dominant counterpart to Milton, one whose sexual life cannot be described but whose rough personality outlines—his excesses, his fickleness in friendship, his sensual nature, his drifting life—would not deny a rather promiscuous homosexuality. On the other hand, Milton would seem to be somewhere on the fringes of homosexuality through religious and ideological repressions of "natural" attitudes toward sex, high-mindedness, and "female" qualities of appearance, interests, and abilities. That there were homosexual experiences with Diodati does not demand a label of "homosexual" for Milton; rather a latent homosexuality which on occasion might emerge and a homo-erotic personality would seem to fit the total evidence of Milton's life. Of significance in corroborating these statements are the epigraphs given on the title pages of *Comus* (1637) and the *Poems* (1645). The first ("Eheu quid volui misero mihi! floribus austrum / Perditus" ["Alas! what have I brought on my miserable self? I have let the south wind ruin my flowers"]) is from Virgil's second eclogue, which tells of the shepherd Corydon's love for the beautiful Alexis. Alexis is aloof and cares nothing for Corydon's songs; the shepherd then laments his at-tempt to win Alexis by his poetic gifts. He concludes, "If Alexis treats you with contempt, you'll find another." The parallel with Milton and Diodati is unavoidable. The use of this epigraph has never before been adequately explained,[35] but we can now see it as consciously reflective of Milton's firm farewell to his former liaison with Diodati. *Comus* by 1637 has exalted the virginal to a high estate, and taken in the Virgilian context the quotation shows that Milton realized that he had been neglecting (in his studious retirement, in the type of poetry he had written) his proper work. It is easy to understand why *Lycidas* begins with "Yet once more" and ends with "To morrow to fresh woods and pastures new." (Should the male symbol of *woods* and the female symbol of *pastures* be especially noted?) Additionally, though, Eclogue 2 is a major source for *Epitaphium Damonis*, not only in its statement of homoerotic love but in its very language: from Corydon's seeking out lonely spots and the imagery of nature, to recalling their activities together, to the gifts (writing) he is saving for Alexis, to the changes in mood and employment of "disordered shreds of song." Milton rehearses within the elegy the "proper work" that he is planning, but with Diodati's death he berates himself for having turned to it and thus for having seemingly forsaken Diodati. Recognition of the epigraph and the significance of the eclogue for the elegy informs us that Milton, at least in 1637–1639, understood the full implications of their relationship. Even past homosexual activity would not of necessity have forced upon Milton's consciousness all the implications which the use of this epigraph indicates were now viable. Probably the relationship had to be repressed in some way before it could be recognized for what it was.

The second epigraph ("Baccare frontem / Cingite, ne vati noceat mala lingua futuro" ["Crown my brows with foxglove, lest a hostile tongue harm the destined poet"]) comes from *Eclogue 7* and is spoken by Thyrsis in a singing match with Corydon. The point of the quotation is that excessive praise heaped upon the rising poet may bring envy from the gods; Thyrsis (Milton) asks to be bewreathed with foxglove to ward off such excessive (envious) praise. But the main point is that Corydon wins the match, and Corydon is the shepherd of she-goats while Thyrsis is the shepherd of sheep. "Goats" alludes to licentiousness and thus to the kind of poetry so often popular and praised by the rabble, while "sheep" implies the followers of God and thus vatic poetry, such as Milton rightly considered his own. The quotation registers faith in his future accomplishments (he had already begun what became *Paradise Lost*). The dichotomy, however, suggests that in *Elegia sexta*, and the sexual overtones of licentiousness (popular and rewarded in this life) and of high morality (rare and rewarded by God) should be noted. The name Thyrsis, besides, recalls *Epitaphium Damonis*, implying Milton's ultimate dedication and faith in himself in that poem. In the eclogue, Thyrsis addresses the handsome Lycidas to spend more time with him in a passage whose imagery is trees—the ash, the pine, the poplar, and the fir. The tree is a male and phallic symbol, and again a submerged homosexual strain breaks through.

The homoerotic attitude toward Diodati can be seen to be dissipated, or at least repressed, by the breach in their relationship and by sublimation. Conscious effort would have little effect—and Milton's seems to have had little. Yet this psychological *Affekt* left its toll on Milton's life and work, matters too involved for discussion here.[36] Certainly his marriages should be restudied, as should his attitude toward woman and undoubtedly the divorce tracts. Is not all this— his appearance, his "female" attributes, his high-mindedness concerning sex—responsible for Salmasius' calling him a catamite? I presume any young man who rejected the available Italian ladies of the night, whom he must have seen frequently enough and probably had thrust upon him by his Italian friends, would have his manhood questioned.

So Milton during his *wanderjahr*—one quite different from that of the typical sower of wild oats. Was the anxiety potential in the married man with latent homosexual tendencies contributory to the psychosomatic problems which seem to have advanced Milton's blindness?[37] And what of Milton's frequent young friends, of whom Parker wrote: "As he grew older, Milton was more and more attracted to the young, and he gathered about him a group of devoted disciples"?[38] But this paper, dealing as it does with Diodati and Milton, cannot investigate these matters and must return now to the remaining evidence of their relationship, two Latin letters of late 1637.

## IV

The two letters written to Diodati in November 1637[39] inform us that Milton had tried to communicate with him "in the beginning of autumn" (that is, apparently, late September) and to see him in London sometime around October, and that he has more to say about himself and his studies "but would rather in person." I interpret this to refer to his "tardie moving"—his decision of a career and his familial individuation. In the second letter (having received an answer to the first) he talks of his studies and the possibility that he will take up residence in one of the Inns. We learn too that Diodati is living somewhere in the north, though making trips to London, but not near Horton, Bucks., where Milton's country residence was. Diodati was practicing medicine at the time, as the second letter remarks.

The letters establish the conclusions which have been advanced in this paper. Milton begins the first letter by saying that "Now at length I see plainly what you are doing: you are vanquishing me finally by obstinate silence." That there has been a falling out and off is evident;[40] that Milton has written or otherwise tried to communicate with Diodati is clear; and that Diodati has not only not answered or sought out Milton but has also not even kept his promises to visit Milton is explicitly stated. "Behold!" Milton says, "I write first," but if there may be any "contention" about this, "beware you think that I shall not be by many respects ['partibus'] the more excused." The word puns on the meaning "genitals," and Milton goes on to differentiate Diodati as one easily "drawn into literary correspondence" "by nature or by habit ['consuetudine,' meaning 'intercourse']" and himself as one whose nature is "slow and lazy to write [the Greek says that he is 'cowardly' in the use of his 'pencil']"—and he adds, "as you properly ['probe,' with a moral implication] know." The puns without doubt point to a sexually active Diodati, thus an aggressive type ("male") who should not manifest this kind of silence, and to a sexually inhibited Milton, thus a recessive type ("female") who would be understandably slow to engage in any kind of "correspondence" ['προσφώνησις,' literally, and with sexual meaning, speech sounds made face to face]. "I know your mode of studying ['studendi,' also 'being zealous toward someone'] to be so arranged," Milton writes with hidden meaning, "that you repeatedly breathe in between ['crebro interspires,' implying breaths that come close on one another as in coition], visit your friends, write much, sometimes make a journey." The puns simply do not let us imagine that Milton was ignorant of sexual activity and the physical actions accompanying climax. But Diodati apparently can be sexually diverted by other matters. Milton appears the serious and intense one, whose probably infrequent excursions into homosexual situations (there is no hint that there were any besides that with Diodati) were guilt-ridden, and Diodati, the libertine whose attitude was blasé. In contrast, Milton says that he cannot delay "until I reach ['pervadum,' 'penetrate'] where I am being driven, and complete, as it were, some great period of my studies" (Conficiam, "complete," likewise means "diminish," and studiorum implies also "desires" and "affection" and "zeal"). Because of this he "more slowly approach[es] discharging [his] offices spontaneously"; again there are easily recognizable puns, including ultro as "wantonly" or "gratuitously." But he wonders whether in the area where Diodati now lives there are "any young learned people with whom [he] can associate with pleasure and chat, as [they] were accustomed." But the erudituli are "those experienced in love"; and consuevimus jokes that what they were accustomed to doing was "having sexual intercourse."

The obscene puns suggest prior relationships as frank and as sexually involved. But the tone of these puns does not suggest that Milton is now emotionally upset by Diodati's manner and their lack of close relationship as he once was. Rather it points to a Milton who has accepted the situation, replaced whatever remains or could have developed into a "married" attitude on his part with resignation and humor, and recognized finally the uncomplementary differences between them. The break can be understood as Milton's demand or Diodati's attitude toward what he considered Milton's demand for a steady and exclusive relationship. The tone of the puns is in no way like that of the parenthesis, "if only at least / you consider it to be important to know whether I am doing anything," in *Elegia sexta*. And he notes that when he heard that Diodati was visiting in London, he "hastened to [his] chamber ['cellam,' 'a room in a brothel']," a comment which, coupled with the remark concerning Diodati's repeated breathing in between, suggests that Milton suspected that Diodati's visits included carnal fulfillment. But did he mean that Diodati might have visited a brothel? The statements in *Epitaphium Damonis* hardly support that. Instead he seems to be joking—though perhaps not seriously—that Diodati's room may have been the focus for homosexual assignation. The total view of Diodati seen from the extant evidence certainly points to a homosexual nature; of Milton, to a latent homosexualism which was probably repressed consciously (as well as subconsciously) from becoming overt except with Diodati.

Such a view in turn suggests that Milton's father's opposition to his son's poetic career may have been kindled by the son's outward personality traits and by commonplace ideas of "male" and "female" roles. Milton, of course, argues that his father has likewise pursued certain aspects of the kind of role he is proposing for himself. Milton writes: "Now since it has fallen to me to have been born a poet" (*Ad Patrem*, 61), a line susceptible of more meaning when we consider physical-emotional-psychological make-up and categoric role-playing. Further, the end of *Ad Patrem* clarifies the source of the argument: outsiders' gross aspersions about Milton. (Perhaps the Unknown Friend was only one of several who criticized Milton, though he did so kindly and without slander.) The poem reads:

> Begone, sleepless cares; begone, complaints,
> and the twisted gaze of envy with oblique goatish leer.
> And do not open your serpentine jaws, fell Calumny;
> you can do nothing disagreeable to me, O most detestable band,
> nor am I under your authority, and with heart secure
> I shall walk, lifted high from your viperous stroke.   (105–10)

We can only guess what the sleepless cares and complaints were, although the Latin connotations are suggestive of anxiety and self-hate. The gaze ("acies"), however, may also be a verbal contest and the envy ("invidiae") may be ill will, while the "transverso hirquo" implies a voluptuous person who has been misled. Does not the line

therefore observe for the informed father that Milton is casting aside
as defeated the false view of himself that has been given by some
who are voluptuaries (rather than morally minded) out of their ill
will and envy? Certainly calumny is this kind of false accusation and
slander. Such people are detestable ("foedissima"), that is, dishonorable, filthy, but is this not the way the average person may view
the unmarried and totally unattached man (less seldom woman) of
thirty? With the publication of *Comus*, if the suggested dating of
*Ad Patrem* is accurate, Milton was able not only to show that his
study and retired life have been meaningful, but also that questions
of sexual morality have been answered. Suddenly the revised epilogue
with its two-leveled heaven and its emphasis on virginity becomes
powerfully psychological: it is a conscious effort to offset slander. (And,
too, we remember the epigraph on the title page.) Does the epilogue
represent a truly believed or primarily a hopeful view? Does it resolve
the sexual anxieties that Milton must have felt? Are indeed the "que-
reles" of *Ad Patrem* banished?

In April 1638, Milton went to the Continent, and a few months
later Charles died (from the plague?) and was buried at St. Anne's,
Blackfriars (August 27, 1638). From the headnote to *Epitaphium Damonis* we know that Milton heard of the death while abroad. William
R. Parker argues that he learned of the death when in Naples in December 1638, but this requires that mail would have been sent to him
there. Since Naples may not have been on his original itinerary—
certainly the aborted trip to Sicily and Greece was not—and since
his times of arrival and departure at any point along the way, other
than Venice, were and had to be uncertain, it seems unlikely that
mail would have been sent to him there.[41] Venice was, traditionally,
the last port visited by English travelers before their return, primarily
because of an important English embassy and colony there. One often
returned to England from Venice by boat; Milton tells us in the *Second
Defense* that he spent a month there and sent back his books by
boat.[42] Possibly Milton heard of Diodati's death in mail sent to him
in Venice;[43] at least soon afterward he proceeded to Geneva to visit
with Charles' uncle John (for about a month), with whom he spoke
everyday ("quotidianus versabar"). He returned to England toward
the end of August 1639 and wrote the epitaph around October or
so (see lines 58–61).

*Epitaphium Damonis* may not tell us much about Diodati bio-
graphically, but it is a major clue to Milton's personality in his younger
years and nostalgically provides evidence of its transcendence. The
guilt and self-hate which the foregoing analysis predicates seem to
have been sublimated in or around 1637, with a flaring up in 1639
when the reality of Diodati's death led Milton to deprecate his rejection of their relationship on Diodati's terms. Whether such guilt and
self-hate, and indeed such latent homosexualism, did not flare up in
later years must be left unconsidered here.

City University of New York

NOTES

1. Poetic quotations are from my edition of *The Complete Poetry of John Milton*,
2d ed. (New York, 1971).
2. The rose as female symbol is well documented in literature (for example, in
*Roman de la rose* and Dante). The hyacinth as male symbol arises from the myth
of the youth beloved and accidentally killed by Apollo. Upon completion of the present
paper, the reader should return to consider Milton's use of the symbol and myth in
*On the Death of a Fair Infant Dying of a Cough*, lines 22-28, in *Comus*, line 998,
and in *Lycidas*, line 106.
3. The metaphor implies that Milton already accepted creation *ex deo*, which
he was to make a focal point in *Paradise Lost*, for return for man means return to
unification with the substance of God. Accordingly Michael leads back ("reduces")
the faithful angels who are "Under thir Head imbodied all in one" (*PL* VI, 779).
4. A type of this ultimate marriage appears in Milton's seventh sonnet when he
concludes that whatever he achieves in life will be the result of his own worthiness
and action and of God's grace upon him. It lies central to *Comus*, for the Lady evinces
resistance to the lures of the Satanic and maintains her chastity of mind (soul), but
only through the divine agency of Sabrina can she be freed bodily: "If Vertue feeble
were, / Heav'n itself would stoop to her" (1022-23).
5. But compare his relationship with Beelzebub:

> Sleepst thou Companion dear, what sleep can close
> Thy eye-lids? and remembrest what Decree
> Of yesterday, so late hath past the lips
> Of Heav'ns Almightie. Thou to me thy thoughts
> Wast wont, I mine to thee was wont t' impart;
> Both waking we were one.          (*PL* V, 673-78)

Here he is asserting maleness or, indeed, playing God; but the tone and language
suggest a homosexual attitude, which both denies a maleness like that of God the
Father and implies an assertion of latent femaleness. The disapproval implied in assign-

ing homosexuality to Satan, as in *In quintum Novembris*, lines 90–101, where Satan bids the Pope rise, is not uncommon in the homosexual personality who feels guilt at his own sexual orientation. However, angels were reputedly bisexual and capable of assuming either form. (Plato's *Symposium* recalls much of this traditional lore which tries to rationalize sexual differentiations.) When, on the second day of battle, Satan reveals his discovery of gunpowder and development of cannon (note also the relationship between imagery of war and of love), it is in male and sexually aggressive terms; see *PL* VI, 482–90, 558–91, and Michael Lieb, *The Dialectics of Creation: Patterns of Birth and Regeneration in Paradise Lost* (Amherst, 1970), pp. 116–17. His overt sexualism implies a disorientation (understandable in terms of antiheroics) and an assertion to convince himself of his male attributes and capabilities.

6. The "weeping" is metaphoric; the poem is the "wept sepulchre." Milton ends the poem by saying, "neither do [literal] tears for you befit, nor shall I shed them more. / Away, my tears" (202–03). He alludes to Revelation xxi, 4 (as also at the end of *Lycidas*, line 181, and *PL* XII, 645): "And God shall wipe away all tears from their eyes; and there shall be no more death, neither sorrow, nor crying, neither shall there be any more pain; for the former things are passed away." They have passed away, perhaps Milton believed at this time, for Milton too.

7. "Gate" is a yonic symbol, that is, a symbol implying the vagina and its entrance. Natural openings (mouth, anus) function similarly, both as symbols and as surrogates.

8. For the most extensive and illuminating literary discussion of this metaphor, see Stanley Stewart's *The Enclosed Garden* (Madison, Wis., 1966).

9. Much as religious minds dislike this characterization of the Son, one need point out only that the Father loved the Son so much, and the Son the Father, that they begot the Holy Spirit. We might also note such Christ figures as Nathanael West's Miss Lonelyhearts, Dostoevski's Sonia or Alexis, and Shakespeare's Antonio. "Feminine" attributes depend on the previously cited male concepts of "worthiness" and on the female's role as mother.

10. In the Letter to an Unknown Friend in the Trinity MS.

11. H. R. Hays, in *The Dangerous Sex: The Myth of Feminine Evil* (New York, 1964, 1966), chap. 17, "The Bosom Snake," discusses Milton's "passively homosexual potential." Hays errs on some biographical statements and proceeds on some questionable (though not unusual) interpretations of the works, but infers rightly that Milton's sexual orientation had its effect on *Comus, Paradise Lost*, and *Samson Agonistes*, as well, obviously, as on his personal life and the divorce tracts.

12. See Donald C. Dorian's *The English Diodatis* (New Brunswick, N.J., 1950), for a full biographical treatment, which, however, does not consider such psychodynamic matters as are raised here.

13. See *Works of John Milton*, ed. Frank Allen Patterson et al. (New York, 1931–38), vol. XII, pp. 292–95; hereafter cited as CM.

14. See *Complete Prose Works of John Milton*, ed. Don M. Wolfe et al. (New Haven, 1953-), vol. I, p. 337, n. 1; hereafter cited as YP.

15. CM, XII, 207. He had previously written "It is not pleasant constantly to submit to the threats of a stern tutor / and to other things which are foreign to my nature" (*El. 1*, 15–16).

16. CM, XII, 241 (and 238).

17. The translation in CM obscures the point; see Phyllis B. Tillyard's translation in YP, I, 284. While Milton does mean physical combat between men and manual labor, he also puns obscenely.

18. Compare, for example, William Riley Parker's statement, "His reaction to a nickname may be another instance of misjudging friendliness, although we know too little of the circumstances to be sure. Nicknames are informal tributes of recognition, sometimes cruel but often ironically affectionate. . . . It is inconceivable, however, that his widow regarded it as a slur or as evidence of unfriendliness; one must assume that her husband had told her the anecdote with a masculine chuckle" (*Milton: A Biography* [Oxford, 1968], p. 43).

19. The translation which has suggested that Milton had additional poems awaiting Diodati's judgment is simply ignorant of Latin; the *quoque* goes with *Te* (in addition to Christ, that is), not with *meditata*.

20. "Milton's Italian Sonnets: An Interpretation," *University of Windsor Review*, III (1967), 27–33. In such an interpretation the name "Aemilia" would imply one worthy of emulation or one who is a rival (as in the opposition between human and divine love—or is it rival to Diodati?).

21. Hays points out that Milton's first marriage (to Mary Powell) was to one not of his own political and religious persuasion (a kind of "foreign" wife), just as Samson was to choose outside his nation. While the appeal which the exotic holds for most people is pertinent, still psychologically such choosing implies a subconscious desire to thwart the success of the union. Theories of complementarity may help account for Milton's attraction to Amelia; the association with Diodati—also Italian and in physical appearance different from Milton—suggests that subconsciously Amelia, whether real or fancied, was a surrogate for Diodati.

22. What the reader should do, of course, is return to these poems and read them in this suggested light to see whether such a view is tenable. For me, this view does stand up in such rereading and leads to important differences in understanding of the sequence. It nullifies the apparent problem of double addressees (the lady and Diodati); it makes more understandable the references to divine love and spiritual need with which the poems are punctuated; and it poses the real uncertainty about the sequence—that is, confusion between human (bodily) love and divine (spiritual) love which underlies attitudes in *Comus*, the divorce tracts, and *Paradise Lost*. One may do well to exalt the bodily to a union with the spiritual (as seen in Adam and Eve's innocent love), but the rejection of bodily satisfaction of and by itself serves to describe the "sinfulness" of sex and thus a major failing of the author of such pamphlets as *The Doctrine and Discipline of Divorce*.

23. Cited from my translation in *The Prose of John Milton*, ed. J. Max Patrick (New York, 1967), p. 611.

24. Probably *Arcades*, the Greek translation of *Psalm 114, On Time, Upon the Circumcision, At a Solemn Music, Lycidas, Ad Patrem*, and perhaps *Philosophus ad regem*. Whether it was in the fall of 1637 that he firmly rejected a clerical career and adopted a poetic one may still only be speculative (see my "Milton's Decision To Become a Poet," *MLQ*, XXIV [1963], 21–30); nevertheless *Lycidas* (November 1637) established that decision, and *Ad Patrem*, which may have been written in March 1638 (although some would date it much earlier), seems to most scholars to corroborate such a decision.

25. This character trait cannot be discussed fully here, but its manifestation in Milton's biography should be examined. The anal character shows tendencies to conceit, suspicion, and ambition (the anal expulsive) and to meticulousness, orderliness, and obstinacy (the anal retentive). Frequently the conscious thoughts and actions of the anal character become compulsive due either to failure of repression of those wishes

rejected as incompatible with the self-image or as an indication of alienation through a failure at self-recognition. Doubt of one's abilities or success for one's wishes generally forces one to withdraw from the external world. What we note in Milton's biography as just described is the orderliness of his life and study, one that did not disappear throughout his life and one even exhibiting a kind of pedantry, which, when extreme, is psychologically categorized as a neurotic trait of unconscious defense against overt action. Milton's failure with male-female relationships suggests that his studious retirement, at least partially beyond familial concerns, was conditioned by self-doubt. An obstinacy toward changing his way of life can be read in his remarks in *Ad Patrem* and in a letter to an unknown friend (to be discussed in a moment); it may be in part due to continued self-doubt, and in any case again suggests the anal-retentive. While Milton shows a strong conceit and ambition in various works—his abhorrence of the rabble in the "Ode to Rouse," for example, is a reversed manifestation—and thus evidences tendencies of the anal-expulsive, it was not until he published *The Reason of Church-Government* in January (?) 1642 that he acknowledged authorship of his work openly. His publications prior to that time are anonymous or initialled only, a clear indication of the repression of the expulsive tendency.

26. See *The Prose of John Milton*, ed. J. Max Patrick, pp. 604–07.

27. See my "Certain Relationships of the Manuscripts of *Comus*," *Papers of the Bibliographical Society of America*, LIV (1960), 38–56, and "The Manuscripts of *Comus*: An Addendum," *Papers of the Bibliographical Society of America*, LIV (1960), 293–94.

28. See my "Speculations on the Dating of the Trinity MS. of Milton's Poems," *MLN*, LXXV (1960), 11–17, as well as "The Manuscript of 'Arcades'," *N&Q*, n.s., VI (1958), 359–64. The question of the Commonplace Book cannot be examined here, but the usual dating for entries is given as 1637 or after, except that a period of 1635–1637 has been suggested (erroneously?) for some few. The question has much light cast upon it by Milton's remarks in his letter to Diodati in November 1637, cited before. See my article surveying Milton's prose works in *Achievements of the Left Hand: Essays on the Prose of John Milton*, ed. Michael Lieb and John T. Shawcross (Amherst, 1974), pp. 291–391.

29. See Barbara Breasted, "*Comus* and the Castlehaven Scandal," in *Milton Studies*, III, ed. James D. Simmonds (Pittsburgh, 1971), pp. 201–24. Rosemary Karmelich Mundhenk, in "Dark Scandal and the Sun-Clad Power of Chastity: The Historical Milieu of Milton's *Comus*," *SEL*, XV (1975), 141–52, argues that Milton's alterations to the text after 1634 (see below) were necessary because the Lady would be played by others than Alice Egerton, who was known to be virtuous and chaste, after the initial performance.

30. Note also the Elder Brother's "So dear to Heav'n is saintly chastity, / That when a soul is found sincerely so, / A thousand liveried angels lackey her" (453–55).

31. The reference to masturbation is obvious enough as a polarity to mutual sexuality, but Milton's citation of it should be noted. It is rejected by Comus, arguing in "reasons garb," as unsavory ("morally offensive"), hardly an adjective that the Satanic Comus would credit. And the mutual sexuality is heterosexuality, although the ambiguous phraseology would allow homosexuality.

32. My disagreement with E. M. W. Tillyard's reading of these revisions will be evident; see his "Action of *Comus*," with an addendum, in *Studies in Milton* (London, 1951), pp. 82–99.

An article complementary to the present study is Irene Tayler's "Say First! What Mov'd Blake? Blake's *Comus* Designs and *Milton*," in *Blake's Sublime Allegory*, ed. Stuart Curran and Joseph Anthony Wittreich, Jr. (Madison, Wis., 1973), pp. 233–58.

Professor Tayler cogently argues that "Blake saw the lady's encounter with Comus as the product of that frightened girl's fantasy: her bondage, the bondage of sexual fears; her release, the release from them" (p. 235). While we see the additions to the masque which set forth the doctrine of virginity espoused by the Lady a bit differently, we agree that the Lady—that is, Milton—"reached maturity by breaking free of her benighted state of self-isolating fear of her own desires" (p. 248).

33. Milton contrasts Adonis' wound; a boar had gored him in his side. The contrasting sexes of Adonis in the mortal heaven and Psyche in the superior heaven owe their being to concepts previously raised in this paper: the male as exerciser of maleness; the female (whether man or woman) as exerciser of femaleness.

34. Milton's first published work was *On Shakespear*, which appeared in the second folio of Shakespeare's *Works* in 1632, and his second was *Comus*, 1637 according to the title page but possibly early 1638. Both were anonymous, possibly a further sign of his anal-retentive personality.

35. Cf. Parker, *Milton: A Biography*, pp. 142–43.

36. Ernest Sirluck's discussion of some of these matters in "Milton's Idle Right Hand," *JEGP*, LX (1961), 749–85, is faulted by antagonism toward certain controversies (generally chronological hypotheses advanced by Parker), but his examination of Milton's attitude toward virginity (or celibacy, as he calls it) is most significant, for he sees it as inhibitory of achievement in marriage and creative activity.

37. See William B. Hunter, Jr., "Some Speculations on the Nature of Milton's Blindness," *Journal of the History of Medicine*, XVII (1962), 333–41. Blindness has often been associated psychologically with castration. Samson, who is finally galvanized to act by "inward eyes," is a good example; the cutting of his hair reinforces the psychodynamic significance of the blinded hero.

38. *Milton: A Biography*, p. 473.

39. Dated November 2 and 23; see W. Arthur and Alberta Turner in YP, I, 325 n., for redating of the month. I quote from my translations in *The Prose of John Milton*, ed. J. Max Patrick, pp. 607–09, 610–12.

40. Note in the second letter this remark: "I did indeed, since it had been so agreed, long expect your letters; yet, in fact, never having received any, I did not, believe me, on that account allow my old good-will toward you to cool in the least; rather that same excuse for delay which you used in the beginning of your letter I had anticipated already in my own mind that you would offer, and that rightly and consistently with our relationship."

41. See Rose Clavering and John T. Shawcross, "Milton's European Itinerary and His Return Home," *SEL*, V (1965), 49–59, for a full discussion of the problem.

42. CM, VIII, 127.

43. "The care of the flock / left behind" (*Epitaphium Damonis*, 14–15) suggests that his sister Anne may have died between April 1638 and May 1639 and that the flock were his nephews Edward and John Phillips, who joined his household soon after his return. Ralph Hone's argument that Anne was alive on 29 December 1639 on the basis of a real estate document of that date seems questionable to me ("New Light on the Milton-Phillips Family Relationship," *Huntington Library Quarterly*, XXII [1958], 63–75). The reference in the document may simply repeat the wording of the previous deeds; Anne did not sign or witness the document. Her death is the only reasonable answer for the boys' actually living with Milton. Perhaps this was the main communication that Milton received in Venice, the information about Charles being additional.

# MILTON'S NATIVITY POEM
# AND THE DECORUM OF GENRE

## *Philip Rollinson*

Although Milton's Nativity poem is usually considered to be an
early example of the English ode, it is probably a literary hymn. In
it the young poet is consciously emulating and reworking elements
traditionally associated with literary hymns. Viewed from this
generic perspective, the Nativity poem is, as a poem, a lofty
"hymn" (17), and at the same time, devotionally considered, a
"humble ode" (24). Milton's fiction of his muse presenting his
hymn as a gift to the Christ-child is neither original nor particularly
fanciful. Rather, it is a version of a commonplace of the hymn
tradition. The traditional uses of feigned liturgical occasions to
introduce literary hymns explain some of the ways in which the
Nativity poem may be considered liturgical. The important function of narrative in previous literary hymns and in Renaissance
critical theory about hymns also provides the standard for evaluating the importance and function of narrative in the Nativity poem.
Finally, the prominence of the pagan gods in the Nativity hymn
is best explained by the Renaissance controversy concerning the
revival of an essentially pagan literary form. Milton's Christian
hymn incorporates, while nullifying, its pagan predecessors and
competitors.

T HERE ARE various analytical means by which scholars and critics
customarily discuss, explain, and evaluate literary works. Depending on the precise circumstances of author, culture, and the kind of
work in focus, one critical approach may be more particularly relevant
and valuable than others. I confess that my own predilections are
quite definitely non-Kantian and are in the area of what is commonly
called historical criticism. I believe that however else you may wish
to dissect, analyze, or evaluate a poem, you must first understand
it as a creative expression brought into existence in historical time

and place by an act of intentional, authorial will. Admittedly the process of arriving at such an understanding is substantially inferential, and the product is hypothetical guesswork based on whatever evidence is available.

For European poetry prior to romanticism, one of the most important kinds of available evidence is the classification of poems according to genre. Although literary genres cannot be defined except as loose groupings of poems which appear to be similar in purpose, subject, form, and technique, what particular poets and critics have thought and said about genres may often be ascertained with considerable certainty. In Milton's age, generic groupings were an important means of understanding and evaluating literary art. Indeed it is probably not overstating the case to say that the intrinsically related concepts of decorum and genre provided most Renaissance poets, given as they were to imitation and emulation, with their fundamental standard for measuring artistic achievement.

Consequently, for the historical critic, basic artistic questions about the typical Renaissance poem are answered by perceiving it in relationship to its generic antecedents—antecedents, that is, with which the author may reasonably be said to have been familiar. Included in this generic framework are not only previous poems but also critical theories and practical criticism, available to the poet and his milieu, about the reading and writing of the kind of poem which he has written or apparently thought he was writing. For a variety of reasons, Milton's Nativity poem has never been placed in its proper generic surroundings. I propose to do so here, first, because it ought to be done, and more importantly because by so doing very satisfactory answers are suggested to many of the questions about the Nativity poem which have continued to interest and sometimes vex scholars and critics in this century.

The first task is to determine what kind of poem Milton thought he was writing. The overwhelming view among twentieth-century scholars and critics, based primarily on the careful strophic form of the "hymn" section, is that the Nativity poem is an ode, more particularly an early example of the emerging English ode, and that it is indebted variously to Pindar, Horace, neo-Latin odes, and in the native tradition to the simple Christmas carol.[1] This view, seeing the young Milton as an originator or innovator, has tended mainly to look forward from the Nativity poem to subsequent odes in English. When generic antecedents have been examined, as in Carol Maddison's *Apollo and the Nine*, the numerous lyric poems in antiquity and the Renaissance identified as hymns (with an unmistakably literary *vice* liturgical intention) have been classified as species of the ode, similar in form and structure, and differing only in their subject matter.[2] The editors of the recent *Variorum Commentary on the Poems of John Milton* endorse this reasoning to explain how the lyric portion of the Nativity poem, identified by Milton as "The Hymn," is after all an ode.[3]

This position is understandable if one sees, as modern critics and scholars have tended to see, the essential defining quality of the poem as its particular lyric, stanzaic form. However, in Milton's day and in antiquity, the praise of gods or God and all forms of epideictic literature were analyzed, described, and evaluated in terms of rhetorical theory and practice, and justifiably so, since there are extant literary hymns from antiquity in heroic hexameters, in elegiac couplets, in lyric stanzas, and in prose. Indeed the most extensive discussion of hymns and their species in antiquity that I know of, that by the third-century rhetorician Menander, completely disregards such distinctions except occasionally to disparage poetic in favor of oratorical eloquence.[4] Because it intentionally excludes attention to the hexameter, elegiac, and prose hymn, Maddison's interesting and informative *Apollo and the Nine* provides an inadequate generic introduction to Milton's Nativity poem.[5]

Although modern scholars and critics have customarily ignored the generic existence of such a thing as the literary hymn, it is empirically demonstrable that there existed in antiquity and Renaissance Europe a long, well-defined tradition of literary hymns as well as a rather considerable body of critical theory and practical criticism relating to the reading and writing of them.[6] Limiting this tradition simply to lyric hymns or ignoring it completely, as the case usually has been, explains, I think, the obvious inadequacies of the two most prevalent kinds of attempts to establish Milton's Nativity poem in some traditional context. The one, exemplified in Albert S. Cook's early annotative study and more recently in a well-known essay by Rosemond Tuve, has searched randomly throughout Western literature for similar themes, analogous images, and verbal echoes reflected in the Nativity poem without generic delimitation or organization.[7] The other method has involved the diligent examination of previous English verse for thematic, imagistic, and structural analogues and parallels. Such studies are certainly useful, but their limitations are painfully obvious when they lead to the kind of generic conclusion implicit in Leishman's recent remark that Spenser's *Epithalamion* is "the only preceding poem of similar length that may be compared with the Nativity Ode, not merely in diction and imagery, but in design and organic unity" (*Milton's Minor Poems*, p. 53). In fact Spenser's *Hymn of Heavenly Love*, his other hymns, Chapman's, Ronsard's, du Bellay's, Scaliger's, Vida's, Pontano's, those by Prudentius, Proclus, Callimachus, and Homer, to name a few, are considerably more comparable and more pertinent to the questions of Milton's diction, imagery, and design in the Nativity poem. I believe it can safely be said that Milton, at twenty-one, did not primarily intend to improve Drayton's and others' innovations and to found the English ode. It is rather more likely that he intended to write a literary hymn, which he could expect his readers to compare with other literary hymns in English, neo-Latin, French, Italian, Latin, and Greek.

To be sure, it has often been argued (most recently in the *Variorum Commentary*, vol. II, pt. 1, pp. 39–40) that reviewing his life and literary ambitions a few years later in the preface to Book II of *The Reason of Church-Government*, Milton himself equates rather than distinguishes the terms hymn and ode.[9] In this well-known passage Milton discusses various literary genres in which he has considered writing. They are mentioned in this order: the epic (YP, I, 813–14), tragedy (YP, I, 814–15), and odes and hymns with a side reference to "all the kinds of Lyrick poesy" (YP, I, 815–17). In very conservative fashion, but typical of medieval and Renaissance Christian apologists, Milton finds Hebrew precedents for these genres and pairs them with their classical counterparts. Job is a model for the brief epic (none is available for the longer). The Song of Solomon is a pastoral drama and the book of Revelation a tragedy. The remarks on odes, hymns, and lyrics, which subsequently broaden to include Milton's general thoughts on the function of all worthwhile poetry, merit quotation in full:

Or if occasion shall lead to imitat those magnifick Odes and Hymns wherein *Pindarus* and *Callimachus* are in most things worthy, some others in their frame judicious, in their matter most an end faulty: But those frequent songs throughout the law and prophets beyond all these, not in their divine argument alone, but in the very critical art of composition may be easily made appear over all the kinds of Lyrick poesy, to be incomparable. These abilities, wheresoever they be found, are the inspired guift of God rarely bestow'd, but yet to some (though most abuse) in every Nation: and are of power beside the office of a pulpit, to imbreed and cherish in a great people the seeds of vertu, and publick civility, to allay the perturbations of the mind, and set the affections in right tune, to celebrate in glorious and lofty Hymns the throne and equipage of Gods Almightinesse, and what he works, and what he suffers to be wrought with high providence in his Church, to sing the victorious agonies of Martyrs and Saints, the deeds and triumphs of just and pious Nations doing valiantly through faith against the enemies of Christ, to deplore the general relapses of Kingdoms and States from justice and Gods true worship. (YP, I, 815–17)

That Milton means to say that odes and hymns are more or less equivalent and indistinguishable cannot legitimately be inferred from the references here to Pindar and Callimachus, "those magnifick Odes and Hymns wherein *Pindarus* and *Callimachus* are in most things worthy." Pindar was reputed to have authored a number of different kinds of lyric poems, which served to define the lyric canon in antiquity. These included hymns, paeans (originally hymns to Apollo), and dithyrambs (celebrations of Dionysus), the top three lyric genres. However, excepting a few fragments, none of Pindar's hymns, paeans, or dithyrambs have survived. Only four books of epinician odes, celebrating victorious athletes, remain. Consequently Milton is probably not describing as "in most things worthy" Pindar's hymns, which were simply not available to him or anyone else. The case is the same with Callimachus, from whose extensive writings in prose and verse only some fragments, a few epigrams, and six literary hymns remain. These hymns, to which Milton alludes, are not even in lyric measures, five being in hexameters and one in elegiac couplets. The probable sense of Milton's remark is that the odes of Pindar and the hymns of Callimachus are two poetic forms, along with the epic and tragedy, worthy of imitation or emulation.

As the passage continues, Milton shows himself to be sympathetic to the most careful kinds of generic distinctions. The fundamental critical distinction relating to hymns, whether in prose, lyric, elegiac, or heroic verse, is that they celebrate God or gods, while other kinds of encomia celebrate different objects of praise—men, cities, and so on.[10] Odes and several other kinds of poems are appropriate for men, not gods (see Scaliger, *Poetices* I. iii, xliv, and xlv). To be sure, this distinction is by no means universally maintained. There are French, English, Italian, and Renaissance-Latin poems identified as odes celebrating God and some identified as hymns celebrating men.[11] In the non-Christian, especially neo-Platonic tradition, the power (*numen*) of the gods is extended into forces of nature and the universe. Aspects of these forces are celebrated in hymns.[12] From Prudentius onward in the Christian tradition various saints and martyrs as well as the persons of the Trinity are celebrated in hymns.

As an English Protestant with Calvinistic leanings, Milton must have found it easy to endorse the critical distinction that hymns celebrate God and odes men;[13] and it is, I think, unquestionable, that Milton implies this distinction when he syntactically separates "glorious and lofty Hymns," celebrating "the throne and equipage of Gods Almightinesse, and what he works" from the singing of "victorious agonies of Martyrs and Saints."[14] Milton clearly indicates that the gods celebrated in Callimachus' hymns are overshadowed by Christian and Old Testament celebrations of God. In the same parallel manner, Pindar's celebrations of victorious Greek athletes are clearly inferior to the greater celebrations of "victorious agonies of Martyrs and Saints." It is difficult not to believe that Milton chose the terms "victorious" and "agonies" with their athletic implications to describe saints and martyrs with careful reference to Pindar's epinician odes.

Although with conventional Christian enthusiasm Milton endorses the superiority of subject matter and form of the odes and hymns in the Old Testament, he does refer favorably to other literary hymns and odes, which are, formally and rhetorically speaking, good models but deficient in not having Christian objects of praise ("some others in their frame judicious, in their matter most an end faulty"). The legitimate inference to be drawn from this passage is that Milton is aware of a poetic tradition, classical, Hebrew, and Christian, which celebrates gods in hymns and men in odes. Granted this, and I think it must be granted, the Nativity poem may be understood as a Miltonic venture into the Christian literary hymn, a venture in the lyrical manner of Pindar only insofar as Milton may have imagined his poem to be an imitation of what Pindar's hymns might have been like.

Another important factor in the modern attempt to realize with some degree of probability Milton's own generic conception of his poem is his use in the four prefatory stanzas of both terms, ode and hymn. In the exordium he writes:

> Say Heav'nly Muse, shall not thy sacred vein
> Afford a present to the Infant God?
> Hast thou no vers, no hymn, or solemn strein,
> To welcom him to this his new abode.          $(15-18)$[15]

In the next stanza, imagining the approach of the Wise Men, Milton calls on his Muse to hurry and present his hymn as a gift before the Magi arrive; only he calls it an ode:

> See how far upon the Eastern rode
> The Star-led Wisards haste with odours sweet:
> O run, prevent them with thy humble ode,
> And lay it lowly at his blessed feet.          $(22-25)$

Some years ago, Ernst Robert Curtius noted that when Milton concludes the Nativity poem with the remark, "Time is our tedious Song should here have ending" (239), he is employing a version of the *topos* of affected modesty or humility.[16] Milton does not think or expect his reader to think that his poem is "tedious" any more than he considers it to be simply a "humble ode." His hymn, a "solemn strein," is a "humble ode" only in the special sense of a devotional version of the humility *topos*. The context for understanding Milton's particular use of the *topos* here is provided by the tradition of the literary hymn, especially as revived in the Renaissance, and by critical norms concerning hymns.

One of the problems recognized by Renaissance critics in writing Christian hymns was that of developing an appropriate style. Great or lofty subjects normally would call forth the grand style and heroic verse, or in lyric measure, a formal stateliness (Scaliger's term is *nobilitas* [*Poetices* I. xliv]). Several times Scaliger discusses the special problem of rhetorical display potentially having a detrimental rather than a suitably ornamental and elevating effect in hymnic celebrations. For Scaliger, rhetorical virtuosity might interfere with and impede the reader's appreciation of those aspects of God which were being praised. He remarks of Vida's *Hymns:* "For as much as they add splendor from their own rules of the Muses, they take away from the heavenly light."[17] God cannot be rhetorically elevated. Hence, Scaliger asserts, paradoxically, in writing hymns the style should be elevated, but modestly with restraint (*additis verecunde proprietatibus*) "as pious Poets are accustomed to do," not like "peevish disputants" displaying their rhetorical skills (III. cxii, p. 162, col. 1D).

Scaliger, of course, is in one sense simply accommodating classical rhetorical theory and practice to a Christian subject. In antiquity, as even the anti-Sophistic Cicero and Quintilian admit, and as is quite apparent in the Sophist Menander's discussion of hymns, the purpose of epideictic eloquence of all forms was primarily to display the poet's or orator's skill. Except for neo-Platonic appropriations of the traditional gods, the Olympians were an occasion for rhetorical display, not for reverent adoration. The celebration of God in a Christian culture obviously alters the situation. In this context Milton's expression, "humble ode," reflects the rhetorical paradox of celebrating the Deity and the related devotional *topoi* of humility and inexpressibility.[18] Milton's hymn does have lyric formality, *nobilitas;* it is a *gravis oratio* (another Scaligerian phrase describing the style of a hymn [*Poetices*, p. 180, col. 2D]), a "solemn strein," celebrating Christ. However, when considered through the eyes of Christian humility as an adequate rhetorical and poetic expression of Deity, the poem becomes humble and odic. As compared to similar literary celebrations and insofar as its object of praise is concerned, it is neither humble nor an ode.

The *topoi* of humility and inexpressibility are closely associated in the tradition of the literary hymn with the idea of the hymn as a gift to the god it celebrates. Curtius observes that a common version of the inexpressibility *topos* is that, while the subject is beyond the powers of the author's expression, the whole world or everything expresses and/or celebrates it.[19] In the hymn tradition, this *topos* frequently takes the form of authorial humility manifested in the fiction of the writer himself or some other group singing his hymn as a gift to the god. This, of course, is precisely the form it takes in the Nativity hymn. Milton imagines his Muse presenting the hymn as a gift to the Christ-child and joining her voice (probably singing his hymn) to the angelic choir. Although the researches of Albert S. Cook, M. M. Ross, and more recently W. J. Roscelli have uncovered at least two other versions of this *topos* in early seventeenth-century English verse (neither is developed to such as extent as in Milton),[20] a general unawareness of the tradition of the literary hymn has led some scholars and critics to dismiss the singing-gift *topos* in the Nativity hymn as an unfortunate flight of youthful poetic fancy or to characterize it as an adolescent manifestation of religious devotion in a poem generally characterized by unquestioned poetic skill and mastery of technique.[21] That neither is quite the case is shown by even a casual survey of the tradition of the literary hymn, for the singing-gift *topos* in various forms is a commonplace of long association with that tradition.

The peroration of Theocritus' *Hymn to the Dioscuri* (xxii) refers to the *Homeric Hymns* and Theocritus' own as gifts.[22] In the conclusion of one hymn in the *Peristephanon Liber* (iii), Prudentius imagines himself presenting his hymn as another pilgrim gift at the shrine of Eulalia.[23] At the end of another (vi) he visualizes a huge chorus of Spaniards singing his own hymn around a Spanish martyr's relics (II, 213). Vida's first and longest hymn, to God the Father, cleverly inverts the *topos*.[24] About halfway through (beginning at line 303), Vida has a vision, like Isaiah's, of the angelic choir surrounding the Father. He proceeds to record his poetic version of this angelic celebration and thus adds the angelic voices to his own. Very close to Milton's version is that in another nativity hymn, this one by Pontano, celebrating the birth of the Virgin Mary.[25] Pontano imagines himself arranging for a celebration of the Feast of the Nativity. Among the arrangements is the poet's gift of his own hymn to be sung by a fictional choir: "Ipse ego, quod possum, tanti natilis honores / voce feram et patrio carmine digna canam" (13–14) ("I myself, as I am able, will raise my voice in honor of so great a birth and sing worthy things in native song"). Closer still to Milton in time and place is Spenser's employment of the same *topos* in his hymnic celebration of Venus:

> Then *Iö tryumph*, O great beauties Queene,
> Aduance the banner of thy conquest hie,
> That all this world, the which thy vassals beene,
> May draw to thee, and with dew fealtie,
> Adore the powre of thy great Maiestie,
> Singing this Hymne in honour of thy name,
> Compyld by me, which thy poore liegeman am.[26]

Milton, of course, in *Elegia sexta* characterizes the Nativity hymn as a gift (line 87). The larger implications of the gift *topos*, as, I believe, Rosemond Tuve was the first to point out, involve the question of a potentially liturgical intention of the poem. Arguing correctly that Milton's primary goal in the Nativity poem is to celebrate, Tuve observes that "a hymn is not only a 'praise', but usually a liturgical act of praise, by definition usually written as Sidney says '*to imitate the inconceivable* excellencies of God'" (*Images and Themes*, p. 42). J. B. Broadbent has objected that "Milton's Ode is not liturgical in any way in which the *Benedicite* . . . , *Benedictus, Cantate Domino, Magnificat* or *Nunc Dimittis* are: it lacks their comprehensiveness and unity, and their dedicated generosity."[27] This objection begs the essential question of just in what way, if any, the Nativity poem may be called liturgical. The question is not really answered by Lawrence W. Kingsley's recent observation, though true enough, that "the act of writing a poem [the Nativity hymn is the poem in question] therefore becomes 'liturgical' by way of the ancient bard-priest identification which Milton acknowledges in Elegy VI."[28]

Again, the question can only be adequately and fully answered by examining the tradition of the literary hymn and its relationship to liturgical hymns, that is, hymns actually composed for or used in public worship. The Greek lyric was of course intended to be sung to the lyre or to be accompanied by music and dance. It was surmised in the Renaissance, probably correctly, that Pindar's hymns were intended for public worship.[29] The scarcity of extant Greek lyrical hymns may be due to their basically liturgical function. The earlier *Homeric Hymns*, however, seem to have been, as Thucydides calls the hymn "To Delian Apollo," preludes or prefaces to epic recitations.[30] Callimachus' and Theocritus' adoption of the heroic hymn is clearly literary, as is the Roman adoption of the Greek lyric hymn. The Latin lyric did not have to be accompanied by music,[31] and of numbers of lyrical hymns in classical Latin only Horace's Sapphic *Carmen Saeculare*, sung by a chorus to open the Century Games in 17 B.C., seems to have been actually performed. Prudentius adopts Horatian lyric measures for the hymns in his *Liber Cathemerinon* and the *Peristephanon Liber*. Comparison of these hymns, particularly as to length, with the liturgical hymns of Prudentius' contemporary, St. Ambrose, clearly shows at the beginning of the Christian era the difference between literary and liturgical hymns, a difference not of course characterized by inequalities of devotional piety, sincerity, or religious conviction.[32] Although during the Middle Ages the liturgical hymn prevailed, and hymnic composition was again reidentified with music, singing, and public worship,[33] in Renaissance Italy the Prudentian kind of lyrical literary hymn, the elegiac, and the heroic hymn were revived.

The Reformation also introduced developments which bear on Milton's poem. Protestants were generally split over the question of the propriety of using man-made hymns without such scriptural basis as had metrical versions of the Psalms.[34] Although the Lutherans wrote new hymns and freely adopted translations from the Roman Breviary, the church at Geneva took another course and adopted a metrical psalmody which influenced the national Protestant movements in England and Scotland.[35] The first English Psalter of Sternhold and Hopkins (1562) contains a translation of the Roman hymn, "Veni, Creator Spiritus," but it excludes the other translations of Latin hymns which had appeared in the *Sarum Primer* of 1538 and the *Queen's Primer* of 1559. Similarly, under Cranmer's influence both the first and second Prayer Books (1549 and 1552) omit all translated hymns except the "Veni, Creator." The customary practice of English poets in the Renaissance, including Milton, of experimenting with metrical versions of the Psalms (to improve on Sternhold and Hopkins) relates directly to the Anglican practice of excluding nonscripturally based hymns from the liturgy.

Consequently the evidence of Milton's cultural situation, as well as the evidence of the Nativity poem itself, especially its length, suggests that it is surely intended to be a literary hymn. In this light Broadbent's objection, calling to mind the likes of the *Nunc Dimittis* (which is liturgical and scripturally based) is entirely beside the point. Milton expects his readers to see his poem in the tradition of the literary, not the liturgical, hymn.

Literary hymns, however, frequently and understandably have liturgical associations. Since the occasion for a liturgical hymn, its ritual purpose, is lost in a hymn of purely literary intention, fictional occasions must be invented or feigned to justify the poet's celebration. Callimachus was very sensitive to this necessity and develops elaborate fictional frames to introduce and conclude his *Hymns*. One of these fictions, introducing his celebration of Athena, is the ritual occasion of the annual Bath of Athena ("On the Bath of Pallas," v). In the exordium the poet addresses an imagined group of Greek women coming to participate in the ritual Bath of Athena. He then addresses the goddess herself, calling to her attention the group of devotees that awaits her. All of this introduces a mythical narrative of how Tiresias was blinded when he inadvertently saw the goddess bathing. In the conclusion the poet again addresses the women and Athena, who is imagined arriving.

Following Callimachus, ritual occasions understandably become a commonplace means of artfully introducing a hymnic celebration.[36] Furthermore, in both the *Homeric Hymns* and those by Callimachus a great deal of attention is paid to the ritual associations of various myths. A favorite subject of the *Homeric Hymns* is the origin, nature, and efficacy of some ritual associated with the god being celebrated.[37] Callimachus continues this interest in ritual and liturgy, as do Prudentius and Catholic writers of Christian literary hymns in the Renaissance.

Finally there is another sense in which the literary hymn, as a gift, is privately and philosophically liturgical. It is in this sense, I think, that Rosemond Tuve characterizes the Nativity hymn as liturgical. The ultimate source of Sidney's brief definition of hymns as imitations of God's excellence, which Tuve quotes in this respect, is probably a longer definition by the neo-Platonic philosopher, Proclus, himself a writer of literary hymns.[38] In his *Commentary on the Chaldean Oracle*, Proclus defines hymns as gifts back to god of his own symbolic truths (he consequently recommends a restrained style):

According to the ORACLE, the soul is perfected by celebrating divine things. This results in carrying to the Father, and placing before him the Father's own ineffable symbols, which in the original progression of essences the Father himself had implanted in the soul. . . . Therefore let us not imagine that the Master of true discourses could be persuaded by strange hurricanes of words, nor by ornamental parades in artificial rites: for God loves the simple, unadorned beauty of form. A hymn properly consecrated to God would therefore consist of assimilation to Him, becoming like Him.[39]

Milton's hymn, like so many literary hymns, feigns a liturgical, festival occasion (Christmas Day). Although it does not directly treat liturgical or ritual material as its subject, it may be said to be liturgical in a private, devotional sense and in the artistic-philosophical sense that it humbly gives back to Christ a poetic imitation of Christ's own true manifestation. The singing-gift *topos*, adopted by Milton, is a rhetorical commonplace associated with the tradition of the literary hymn, and in that same tradition, as manifested in neo-Platonic hymns and neo-Platonic thinking about the function of hymns, it has a liturgical propriety which transcends rhetoric and moves into the realms of philosophy and theology. It is not at all unlikely that the young Milton, interested in and influenced, as he was, by Platonism at Cambridge, may well have considered his hymn as a gift in precisely this latter, Proclean way.

Although the fictional introduction of the Nativity poem with its liturgical implications is traditional, Milton's emphatic separation of that introduction from the main body of his celebration by means of markedly different verse forms is unusual. The one is slightly modified rime royal, associated with heroic narrative and the epic hymn in English,[40] and the other a lyric measure. It is also somewhat unusual that there is no corresponding return to the verse form of the introduction for the conclusion, and indeed there is of course practically no conclusion to the poem at all. I cannot recall any previous literary hymns in which the framing introduction and conclusion are distinguished in any other way than rhetorically. Somewhat less frequent is careful attention to balancing a conclusion against the introduction to make a rhetorically symmetrical frame. Spenser's first two hymns, celebrating love and beauty, do balance the conclusion against the introduction. However, his *Hymn of Heavenly Love*, introduced with three stanzas, lacks any formal conclusion. Possibly not much more can be said than that Milton draws on and reflects both the epic and the lyric forms of the literary hymn. To be sure, a lyric measure better fits the imagined singing of the hymn by his Muse than does an epic recitation. It is similarly more appropriate to the motif of harmony and music as developed in the hymn and as implied in the philosophically liturgical ramifications of the singing-gift *topos*.

The larger fictional frame, which includes the hymn as gift presented at the manger, has occasioned considerable critical comment about the whole structuring of the Nativity poem, especially about the significance and propriety of the hymn's narrative element. Rosemond Tuve emphasizes the hymn's laudatory as opposed to a narrative purpose. Broadbent justly observes that Milton has chosen to narrate only part of the traditional nativity story anyway (*The Living Milton*, p. 13), and an earlier, well-known essay by Arthur Barker argues for

the patterning of the poem's images as its structurally controlling principle.[41] It has remained for Frank S. Kastor to show that Tuve has
established an unnecessary opposition between praising and narrating
and that the function of what narrative aspects there are in the Nativity
poem needs to be evaluated.[42] The long tradition of the literary hymn,
and especially critical theory relating to that tradition current in the
Renaissance, generally provides a basis for affirming Kastor's argument
and his analysis of the poem. It also refines and necessitates slight
changes of emphasis in his important critical conclusions about the
artistry of the Nativity poem.

Kastor points out that Milton has used selected elements of the
traditional nativity story as a skeletal framework on which to build
his celebration ("Miltonic Narration," pp. 341–46). Such was not original
with Milton, and from many other similar exploitations of the nativity
story Kastor picks out a literary hymn by Prudentius (*Cathemerinon*
xi) as "the only poem concerning the nativity" which he has found
"to closely resemble Milton's" (p. 343). My only quibble with Kastor's
very just observation here is that, like so much previous criticism of
the Nativity poem, it ties down a rhetorical or poetic technique to
a particular subject matter, in this case the advent of Christ, and
to a particular poem. Prudentius organizes all twelve of the hymns
in the *Liber Cathemerinon* around different kinds of frameworks which
serve as foundations for appropriate reflections and comments. Like
many writers of lyrics, he frequently does not develop simple linear
organizations even when, as in "A Hymn for the 25th of December"
(xi), he might reasonably have done so with the narrative details of
Christ's birth. Actually *Cathemerinon* xi pays somewhat less attention
to the traditional narrative of the nativity story than does Milton's
poem. The quantitative emphasis on narrative details in the Nativity
poem would seem to stand somewhere between *Cathemerinon* xi and
*Cathemerinon* ix ("A Hymn for Every Hour") in which clusters of
lyrical remarks are developed around the more or less chronological
pegs of the major narrative events of Christ's earthly ministry and
passion. The point is, though, that Milton is imitating a poetic genre,
not a particular poem.

Although Kastor justly uses the evidence of the poem itself to
correct Tuve on the matter of narrative, by ignoring the tradition

of the literary hymn and focusing on content alone he misses an enormous amount of corollary support for his argument. One of the principal and understandably likeliest means of celebrating a god or saint is through the development in brief or at length of one of the important myths or stories associated with him. As a framework or for its own sake, narrative was traditionally an important element in dozens of literary hymns available to Milton and his milieu.

This importance is also reflected in literary criticism of antiquity and the Renaissance. Scaliger's detailed classification of hymns, based on Menander, is illustrative. Six species of the classical hymn are distinguished (III. cxiii–cxv): (1) the invocatory (Scaliger cites the theurgic hymns of Proclus); (2) valedictory (examples cited are the *Homeric Hymns* involving divine departures); (3) physical, celebrating the *numen* of a god or other natural or astronomical force (Marullo's neo-Platonic *Hymni Naturales* are mainly of this sort); (4) mythical; (5) genealogical; and (6) inventional (or fictional—an original addition to or a newly imagined myth of a god). Narrative provides the basic ingredient for half (the last three) of these species and could easily be developed in valedictory and even physical hymns. Both Menander and Scaliger allow for the characteristics identifying these species to be mixed in particular hymns. For example, almost all hymns, long or short, invoke the god, God, or saint they celebrate, especially and appropriately in the exordium and in the conclusion. (In this respect it is interesting that Milton invokes his Muse and not Christ.)[43] On the other hand there are many hymns of the briefer sort from some of the *Homeric Hymns* onward which are purely invocational. According to Scaliger's system of classification Milton's hymn might be considered a combination of the inventional (the fictional frame imaginatively bringing Milton's Muse to the scene at Bethlehem), the genealogical (the skeletal framework of details of Christ's birth as well as the poetic comment on the significance of that event), and the mythical (or rather mythological—the elaborate catalogue of pagan gods silenced by the Christ-child).

The important position of the pagan gods in Milton's Christian celebration continues to provoke critical interest. A recent article is still asking and formulating answers to the question: "Why in a poem dedicated to the birth of Christ does Milton place so much emphasis on these pagan gods?"[44] Certainly there have been many illuminating suggestions about this question from stylistic, imagistic, theological, and other perspectives. Another significant perspective, as yet unexplored, is that of the Renaissance adaptation and imitation of the classical literary hymn.

There was considerable controversy in the sixteenth century over the proper objects of praise in literary hymns. Should Christian poets adopt only the form of the literary hymn, or should they imitate as well the celebrations of various pagan gods, demigods, and quasi-philosophical forces, frequently identified (especially in neo-Platonism) as being manifested in or as the gods? Critical opinion was divided and so was poetic practice.[45] One of the more interesting aspects of this poetic controversy was the writing of what Sears Jayne appropriately calls "counter-hymns."[46] Marullo's pagan-philosophical objects of praise in his *Hymni Naturales* are, for example, deliberately countered by the first three of Vida's *Hymns*, celebrating God in his triune aspects. Spenser counters his own earlier pair of *Hymns*, celebrating Cupid and Venus, with a pair celebrating Christ and Sapience.[47]

As one would expect from his subsequent remarks in *The Reason of Church-Government*, Milton opts for the Christian variety in his Nativity hymn. His learned catalogue of pagan gods cleverly accomplishes two things. First, Milton sets up the pagan gods, so often celebrated in Renaissance and classical hymns, as appropriate strawmen to be silenced theologically before the Christ-child and to be dispraised or dethroned as fitting objects of literary praise. In this sense the Nativity hymn counters the whole tradition of pagan celebrations, classical and Renaissance, to which its learned catalogue alludes. Secondly there is a stylistic aspect relating to the decorum of hymns. Learned catalogues, especially those involving classical allusions, were of course a standard device for elevating style in Renaissance poetry. Callimachus introduced into the literary hymn the self-conscious and even pedantic display of mythological erudition. In the Renaissance both Marullo and Ronsard imitate Callimachus in this respect. However, writers and critics of Christian hymns disagreed in theory and practice over the propriety of using such display as a means of elevating the style of hymns. Spenser's *Four Hymns* are remarkably restrained.[48] Even the first two are only mildly allusive, and the third, the *Hymn of*

*Heavenly Love*, celebrating Christ, does not have one classical allusion. Both Spenser and Vida depend on other rhetorical effects. On the other hand, Scaliger's *Hymns* rely heavily on displaying classical erudition.[49] By cleverly posing the opposition of pagan gods to Christ, Milton can have his cake and eat it too. He manages a legitimate excuse in a Christian hymn of displaying extensively his classical erudition and appropriately elevating his style.

It is a point of only minor and incidental interest that another area of the poem's content, Platonic-Pythagorean harmony, which has justly received considerable critical attention,[50] is a commonplace motif in many literary hymns, especially those reflecting neo-Platonic, Stoic, and other philosophical interests.[51] The same is true of the prevailing light-dark imagery, a favorite poetic approach to the mystery and paradox of divinity in celebrations both pagan and Christian.[52] Such imagery, of course, and the motif of heavenly harmony are certainly not limited to literary hymns and occur in many other contexts. However, Milton's use of them would certainly appear more original were they not associated with the tradition of the literary hymn.

Milton's originality lies in his reworking, modifying, and adapting traditional poetic resources. For him and for most Renaissance poets, I believe, the ideological boundaries which organize and define these resources are literary genres, as probably understood, of course, by the poet and his milieu. I have attempted here to point out some of the more important resources on which Milton drew to compose the Nativity hymn and to suggest some conclusions about Milton's artistic achievement which seem to me to be implied by the relationship of his poem to its literary tradition. Certainly the young author of the Nativity poem foreshadows the mature poet of *Paradise Lost*. He is sensitive and responsive to literary tradition, adopting many of the motifs, *topoi*, and other conventions of the literary hymn— but never slavishly. He has mastered the tradition and is not mastered by it. He is learned and already enjoys displaying his mythological erudition, but he does so by cleverly and decorously integrating his learning into the fabric of his celebration. He chooses a Christian theme but reveals his awareness of pagan literary hymns, which his own hymn and its object of praise discredit. He consciously sets out to emulate and outdo his ancient and Renaissance predecessors, and,

if without quite the success of *Paradise Lost,* he nonetheless achieves
a poetic creation which can, without embarrassment, be compared
to any in the genre.

University of South Carolina

NOTES

An abbreviated version of this paper was read before the English 6 (Milton) Group
at the 1972 Annual Meeting of the MLA.

1. Robert Shafer asserts that in Milton's Nativity poem "almost at a single bound
the English ode springs into full-blown life" (*The English Ode to 1660: An Essay
in Literary History* [1918; reprint ed., New York, 1966], pp. 93–94). A similar study
by George N. Shuster identifies the Nativity poem as an ode (*The English Ode from
Milton to Keats,* Columbia University Studies in English and Comparative Literature,
no. 150 [New York, 1940], pp. 67–68). For the same identification see Louis L. Martz,
*The Poetry of Meditation: A Study in English Religious Literature of the Seventeenth
Century,* rev. ed. (New Haven, 1962), p. 164; Marjorie Hope Nicolson, *John Milton:
A Reader's Guide to His Poetry* (New York, 1963), p. 31; Don Cameron Allen, *The
Harmonious Vision: Studies in Milton's Poetry,* enl. ed. (Baltimore, 1970), p. 25; and
Carol Maddison, *Apollo and the Nine: A History of the Ode* (Baltimore, 1960), pp.
320–27. Maddison emphasizes the point that the odic "hymn" section is indebted to
the Christmas carol (p. 321), as do James Holly Hanford and James G. Taaffe, *A
Milton Handbook,* 5th ed. (New York, 1970), p. 113; and Louis L. Martz, "The Rising
Poet, 1645," in *The Lyric and Dramatic Milton: Selected Papers from the English
Institute,* ed. Joseph H. Summers (New York, 1965), p. 24. Rosemond Tuve rejects
the putative association of the Nativity poem with the carol in *Images and Themes
in Five Poems by Milton* (Cambridge, Mass., 1957), p. 42. Specific formal indebtedness
to Horace or Pindar has occasionally been a matter of dispute. Nicolson (pp. 32–33)
and Maddison implicitly opt for Horace and the classical Latin ode, while David B.
Morris has recently fixed on Pindar in "Drama and Stasis in Milton's 'Ode on the
Morning of Christ's Nativity,'" *SP,* LXVIII (1971), 212.

2. Maddison explicitly classifies such lyric hymns as odes (for example, pp. 83,
186) and frequently refers to them as "hymn-odes" (for example, pp. 83, 125, 174)
or "ode-hymns" (p. 65).

3. A. S. P. Woodhouse and Douglas Bush, eds., *The Minor English Poems, A
Variorum Commentary on the Poems of John Milton,* gen. ed. Merritt Y. Hughes
(New York, 1970–), vol. II (1972), pt. 1, p. 69.

4. *Peri Epideiktikon,* in *Rhetores Graeci,* ed. Leonardi Spengel (Leipzig, 1853–56),
vol. III, pp. 329–446. I am indebted to Michael Washburn for translating the section
on hymns, pp. 333–43. Menander's comments on one species, the valedictory hymn,
especially reflect an antipoetic bias (p. 336).

5. Maddison, for example, ignores Pontano's elegiac hymns (p. 68) and Scaliger's
hexameter ones (pp. 111–13). She ignores Vida altogether and pays little attention
to Marullo's four hexameter hymns except to identify one as "a hexameter ode" (p.

83). Similarly excluded from discussion are Ronsard's heroic hymns (p. 272). In n. 3, p. 272, Maddison remarks that the longer *Homeric Hymns* are "epic fragments" but that the shorter ones (although in hexameters, too) are lyric. She similarly decides that the short, hexameter *Orphic Hymns* are "odic," as are the (long) hexameter and elegiac *Hymns* of Callimachus. The basis for these arbitrary judgments is unclear.

6. I have surveyed briefly the main lines of the Renaissance revival and imitation of the classical literary hymn in "The Renaissance of the Literary Hymn," in *Renaissance Papers 1968*, ed. George Walton Williams (Durham, N.C., 1969) pp. 11-20, and discussed Spenser's *Four Hymns* in the light of that tradition in "A Generic View of Spenser's *Four Hymns*," *SP*, LXVIII (1971), 292-304.

7. The *Variorum Commentary* (vol. II, pt. 1, pp. 34-110) incorporates most of Cook's findings in "Notes on Milton's Ode on the Morning of Christ's Nativity," *Transactions of the Connecticut Academy of Arts and Sciences*, XV (1909), 307-68. Rosemond Tuve's essay, "The Hymn: *On the Morning of Christ's Nativity*," appears in her *Images and Themes in Five Poems by Milton*, pp. 37-72. With some justification J. B. Broadbent criticizes Tuve's emphasis on Milton's use of traditional images and themes ("The Nativity Ode," in *The Living Milton: Essays by Various Hands*, ed. Frank Kermode [London, 1960], pp. 12-31). Finding some problems with the appropriateness of the particular traditional images and themes Tuve elucidates, Broadbent responds by rejecting tradition altogether as a significant critical factor in the interpretation and appreciation of the poem. Balachandra Rajan similarly chooses to stress the unique originality of the poem ("*The Nativity Ode:* in order serviceable," in his *Lofty Rhyme: A Study of Milton's Poetry* [Coral Gables, Fla., 1970], pp. 11-22, esp. p. 12). At the same time, apropos of the Nativity poem and the generality of Milton's poetry, Rajan asserts that "Milton was among the most refined of generic artists" (p. 16). Blossom Feinstein has searched for parallels within the tradition of the literary hymn but limits her comparison to only one earlier writer of Christian literary hymns ("On the Hymns of John Milton and Gian Francesco Pico," *CL*, XX [1968], 245-53). The editors of the *Variorum Commentary* find the parallels too general and "unconvincing" (vol. II, pt. 1, p. 38). Feinstein fails in not extending her perspective to the numerous other examples of literary hymns in the Renaissance and antiquity.

8. The most exhaustive is J. B. Leishman's posthumous study, *Milton's Minor Poems*, ed. Geoffrey Tillotson (Pittsburgh, 1969), pp. 51-67. Also typical of this approach is M. M. Mahood's argument that the Nativity poem is heavily indebted to Fletcher's *Christ's Victory* (*Poetry and Humanism* [New Haven, 1950], pp. 171-76). Louis L. Martz emphasizes Milton's "indebtedness" in the poem "to his predecessors in the line of English poetry" (*The Lyric and Dramatic Milton*, p. 25). While justly recognizing the inconclusiveness of researches into earlier English verse alone, Rajan, following Broadbent, is unwilling to allow for the possibility of any tradition playing a very important role in the composition of the Nativity poem (*Lofty Rhyme*, pp. 12, 149, n. 8).

9. Citations from *The Reason of Church-Government* are to the *Complete Prose Works of John Milton*, ed. Don M. Wolfe et al. (New Haven, 1953-), vol. I, hereafter cited as YP.

10. Menander has already been mentioned. Other comments on hymns may be found in: Minturno, *De Poeta* (Venice, 1559), pp. 379-80; Viperano, *De Poetica Libri Tres* (Antwerp, 1579), pp. 26, 148, 153; Julius Caesar Scaliger, *Poetices Libri Septem* I. iii, xliv, xlv, and III. cxi-cxviii (citations from Scaliger in this paper are to the facs. of the 1561 ed. [Stuttgart-Bad Cannstatt, 1964], George Puttenham, *The Arte of English Poesie*, ed. Gladys D. Willcock and Alice Walker (Cambridge, Eng., 1970), pp. 24-36,

152; and Philip Sidney, *An Apology for Poetry*, ed. Geoffrey Shepherd (London, 1965), pp. 101–02.

11. A listing would be tedious and is probably unnecessary. A few random examples are: Beaumont's *Ode of the Blessed Trinity;* Herrick's *Ode of the Birth of Our Savior;* Fabricius' *Odarum Libri Tres ad Deum Omnipotentem* (see Maddison, *Apollo and the Nine,* pp. 136–37); Chapman's "Hymnus ad D. Russelium defunctum" (sung by Poesie in the epicedion, *Eugenia*); and Crashaw's *Hymn to the Name and Honor of the Admirable Sainte Teresa.* Of course, among Catholic writers in the sixteenth and seventeenth centuries, saints were regularly celebrated in "hymns."

12. Michael Marullo's *Hymni Naturales* are the best Renaissance examples. See *Michaelis Marulli Carmina,* ed. Alessandro Perosa, Thesaurus Mundi (Zurich, 1951). In addition to various gods, Marullo celebrates the heavens, eternity, the stars, and so on.

13. Discussing panegyrics (III. cix) and encomia (cx), Scaliger lists as topics of poetic praise: God, the heavens, the elements, men, animals, and plants (cxi). Only celebrations of God (Scaliger indicates explicitly how each person of the Trinity is to be praised) are properly hymns (cxii). In the same chapter Scaliger observes that the ancients simply pluralized God into specific attributes. Similarly, when the ancients celebrated nature and fortune, they were (unwittingly) celebrating the power and will of God. The same argument could justify hymnic celebrations of saints, since their lives reflect and glorify God's love and power. Scaliger himself wrote hymns celebrating the Virgin Mary and John the Baptist. In a subsequent chapter (cxvi) Scaliger rejects the appropriateness of classifying celebrations of heroic, legendary, or semilegendary figures as hymns.

14. The hymns celebrating saints and martyrs in Prudentius' *Peristephanon Liber* and in collections of hymns by Catholic writers in the Renaissance usually pray to the saint for assistance. This practice was, of course, distasteful to Protestants, who did not like to credit mortals with divine or intercessory powers.

15. Citations from Milton's poetry are to *The Poetical Works of John Milton,* ed. Helen Darbishire, 2 vols. (Oxford, 1966).

16. *European Literature and the Latin Middle Ages,* trans. Willard R. Trask (1953; reprint ed., New York, 1963), p. 85. Curtius first discusses this *topos* generally (pp. 83–85) and later its purely devotional manifestations in Excursus II (pp. 407–13). The evidence Curtius marshals of the commonplace use of this *topos* discredits the recent subjective judgment of T. K. Meier that Milton's reference to his celebration as a "tedious song" puritanically "denigrate[s] both the poet's art and his subject" ("Milton's 'Nativity Ode': Sectarian Discord," *MLR,* LXV [1970], 10).

17. My translation here and throughout. This criticism of Vida (p. 311, col. 2B) is certainly justified. For a brief analysis and some examples of the rhetorical exuberance of Vida's *Hymns,* see my "Generic View of Spenser's *Four Hymns,*" pp. 297–99.

18. For the latter, a favorite *topos* for devotional and other subjects in the Middle Ages, see Curtius, *European Literature and the Latin Middle Ages,* pp. 159–62.

19. Ibid., p. 161. The formula, "what or how shall I sing of you," is originally Homeric and is sometimes used to introduce the narrative of the longer *Hymns* (for example, in iiia and b). See *Hesiod, The Homeric Hymns, and Homerica,* trans. Hugh G. Evelyn-White, Loeb Classical Library, rev. ed. (Cambridge, Mass., 1964), pp. 327, 339. So too in Callimachus' celebration of Zeus; see *Hymns and Epigrams,* trans. A. W. Mair, Loeb Classical Library, rev. ed. (Cambridge, Mass., 1960), p. 37.

20. See the *Variorum Commentary,* vol. II, pt. 1, pp. 64–67.

21. E. M. W. Tillyard writes in *Milton*, rev. ed. (New York, 1967): "In the opening stanzas Milton pictures himself present at Bethlehem and hastening to offer his hymn, before the Wise Men, who have just appeared in sight, can arrive with *their* offering. It is a quaint idea, which most poets, had they thought of it, would have dropped when once stated. Not so Milton" (p. 33). Tillyard, of course, has read the passage a bit carelessly, since in the fourth stanza Milton is probably still apostrophizing his Muse and urging her (not himself) to present the hymn-as-gift. Regrettably, William Riley Parker's admirable *Milton: A Biography*, 2 vols. (Oxford, 1968) shares the same view: "The idea is far-fetched and naïve, but the poet's youthful vitality and seriousness give it charm" (vol. I, p. 64). A. S. P. Woodhouse supposes that in the singing-gift *topos* we have "whatever there is of simple personal religion in the experience from which the *Nativity Ode* sprang" ("Notes on Milton's Early Development," *UTQ*, XIII [1943-44], 76). Woodhouse may be quite correct in seeing genuine religious conviction expressed in Milton's use of the singing-gift *topos*, and I suppose it would be unfair to say that he is implicitly contrasting poetic skill with personal religious inspiration. However, it does misrepresent the poem to single out this one element as peculiarly manifesting personal devotion, especially since it is as traditional a commonplace as the other two ideas (heavenly harmony and the routing of the pagan gods) discussed by Woodhouse (pp. 75-77). Intense personal devotion may conceivably be conveyed by a writer with either artistic ineptness or great skill and may or may not use or adapt traditional motifs and *topoi*. Neither the quality of a piece of literary art nor its proportionate use of traditional as opposed to original materials has any bearing on the question of the nature or the degree of personal devotion being manifested.

22. In *Greek Bucolic Poets*, ed. and trans. J. M. Edmonds, Loeb Classical Library (London, 1912). This hymn is textually incomplete (part of a speech is missing between lines 170 and 171), but 223 hexameters remain, including the peroration.

23. In *Prudentius*, trans. H. J. Thomson, Loeb Classical Library (Cambridge, Mass., 1962), vol. II, pp. 155-57.

24. Citations from Vida are to the *Poemata Quae Extant Omnia*, 2 vols. (London, 1732). The thirty-five hymns are in vol. II.

25. "Hymnus ad Divam Mariam," *De Laudibus Divinis Liber* ii, in *Ioannis Ioviani Pontani Carmina*, ed. Johannes Oeschger, Scrittori D'Italia, no. 198 (Bari, 1948). Like so many literary hymns (including Milton's), this one opens with an imagined scene at daybreak.

26. *Hymn in Honor of Beauty*, 267-73, in the Variorum *Works of Edmund Spenser*, *The Minor Poems*, ed. Charles Grosvenor Osgood and Henry Gibbons Lotspeich (Baltimore, 1943), vol. I.

27. "The Nativity Ode," in *The Living Milton*, p. 29.

28. "Mythic Dialectic in the Nativity Ode," in *Milton Studies*, IV, ed. James D. Simmonds (Pittsburgh, 1972), p. 171.

29. Scaliger refers to Greek lyrical hymns "qui ad aras diis dicebantur" ("which were chanted before the altars of the gods") (*Poetices*, p. 48, col. 1B). So does Viperano, in a passage apparently indebted to Scaliger or some other common source (*De Poetica Libri Tres*, p. 153).

30. Thomas W. Allen and E. E. Sikes comprehensively discuss this question and include full quotation of all classical references to the *Hymns* in the Introduction to their edition of *The Homeric Hymns* (London, 1904), pp. lv-lxiii.

31. See C. M. Bowra, *Greek Lyric Poetry from Alcman to Simonides*, 2d ed. (Oxford, 1961), p. 1.

32. The hymns in the *Peristephanon Liber* are long narratives of the exploits of martyrs and saints, but even the hymns in the *Cathemerinon* are much too long for liturgical use. Only one is under a hundred lines (no. viii, 80 lines), and three of the twelve are over two hundred (nos. iii, vii, and xii). The typical Ambrosian hymn has thirty-two short, iambic dimeter lines. To be sure, lines and stanzas of Prudentius' hymns were incorporated into the hymnody of the Roman Church and some in toto into the Mozarabic Breviary. See F. J. E. Raby, *A History of Christian-Latin Poetry from the Beginnings to the Close of the Middle Ages*, 2d ed. (Oxford, 1953), pp. 45, 50; and John Julian, ed., *A Dictionary of Hymnology: Setting Forth the Origin and History of Christian Hymns of All Ages and Nations*, 2d ed. (New York, 1957), vol. II, p. 915.

33. Raby quotes the well-known passage from the *Confessions* (IX. vii) where Augustine describes the introduction of hymn-singing (*History of Christian-Latin Poetry*, p. 32). The essential components of Isidore's definition are that a hymn must praise God and be sung (*Etymologiae* VI. xix. 17).

34. See Louis F. Benson, "The Relation of the Hymn to Holy Scripture," in *The Hymnody of the Christian Church* (New York, 1926), pp. 57–95. It was an old question by the time of the Reformation.

35. For the Calvinistic settlement see Benson, "Relation of the Hymn to Holy Scripture," pp. 79–86. Benson fully explores the English and Scots resolution of the hymn-psalm question in *The English Hymn: Its Development and Use in Worship* (1915; reprint ed., Richmond, Va., 1962), pp. 25–45.

36. Of many classical examples employing this fiction a few are: Tibullus' song of the Ambarvalia (II. i); the anonymous *Pervigilium Veneris;* and the conclusion of Horace's hymn to Apollo (*Carmina* IV. vi). All twelve hymns of the *Liber Cathemerinon* are occasioned by certain hours of the day or annual festivals. Marullo imagines himself with a ritual group of Bacchantes in "To Bacchus" (*Hymni* I. vi. 13–18). Birthdays are the occasion for the Homeric "To Delian Apollo" (iiia) and for Callimachus' "To Delos" (iv) and "Hymn to Zeus" (i). In the Renaissance various feast days are common real or feigned occasions for Christian literary hymns. Christmas, of course, is a favorite.

37. The long "To Demeter" (ii, 495 lines) makes recurrent reference to the rituals of Demeter (for example, in the Loeb text, pp. 307–09 and 323). A ritual lesson about the proper manner of appeasing Persephone is also included (p. 315). In "To Pythian Apollo" (iiib) the poet describes Apollo's establishment of the ritual procession to his temple at Delphi (pp. 359–61). This account includes instruction by Apollo to his new priests on the proper ritual to be followed. The singer then describes the first such ritual procession. The hymn "To Delian Apollo" (iiia) tells of the birth of Apollo and describes the particular ritual associated with his worship at Delos.

38. The *Hymns* of Proclus usually appear with the *Orphic Hymns*, the *Homeric Hymns*, and *Hymns* of Callimachus in MSS which have survived. All four collections were in print, in the original Greek, Latin, and some modern languages, by 1600. See my "Renaissance of the Literary Hymn," p. 13. A good introduction to Proclus is Lawrence J. Rosan's *The Philosophy of Proclus: The Final Phase of Ancient Thought* (New York, 1949). On the *Hymns* see Rosan, pp. 52–53. Citations from Proclus in this paper are to the modern translation by Kenneth Sylvan Guthrie, *Proclus's Biography, Hymns, and Works*, Master-Key ed. (Yonkers, N.Y., 1925).

39. Guthrie's translation, pp. 3–5 (the *Hymns* are separately paginated). Like Sidney (and possibly Sidney's source), Scaliger echoes Proclus' definition. He emphasizes the

seriousness of the artistic task of writing hymns as a poetic imitation of God in a rhetorically restrained style (III. cxii).

40. Spenser's *Four Hymns* are, of course, in rime royal (Milton only alters the last line to an alexandrine). Early English criticism identifies rime royal as a proper verse form for serious and elevated subjects. In *Certayne Notes of Instruction*, Gascoigne observes that "it is a royall kinde of verse, serving best for grave discourses" (*The Complete Works of George Gascoigne*, ed. John W. Cunliffe [Cambridge, Eng., 1907–10], vol. I, p. 471). Puttenham similarly remarks that it "is the chiefe of our ancient proportions vsed by any rimer writing any thing of historical or graue poeme" (p. 65).

41. "The Pattern of Milton's *Nativity* Ode," *UTQ*, X (1940–41), 167–81.

42. "Miltonic Narration: 'Christ's Nativity,' " *Anglia*, LXXXVI (1968), 339–52.

43. Not infrequently in Renaissance literary hymns the poet will invoke both a muse or other source of artistic inspiration as well as the god or saint celebrated. Marullo, for example, invokes Athena, all the Muses, and Calliope to inspire his celebration of Pan (*Hymni* II. i. 1–5) and begins his celebration of Venus by invoking Erato (II. vii). In both these hymns he invokes the god(dess) celebrated.

44. Lawrence Hyman, "Christ's Nativity and the Pagan Dieties," in *Milton Studies*, II, ed. James D. Simmonds (Pittsburgh, 1970), p. 103. Understandably, most critical examinations of the Nativity poem of any length perforce discuss the pagan gods. Even more recently than Hyman, Lawrence W. Kingsley devotes significant attention to them ("Mythic Dialectic in the Nativity Ode," *Milton Studies*, IV, pp. 168–71, 175).

45. For a brief discussion of this question see my "Renaissance of the Literary Hymn," pp. 17–20. Pontano, who wrote Christian literary hymns, also imitates Horace and Catullus in his "Hymnus in Noctem" (*Parthenopei Liber* I. vii), as does Flaminio, a writer of liturgical hymns in Ambrosian dimeter, in his famous "Hymnus in Auroram" and several other poems. For text and comment see Carol Maddison, *Marcantonio Flaminio: Poet, Humanist, and Reformer* (Chapel Hill, 1966), pp. 57–68. There are similar poems in English, for example, Jonson's "Hymne" celebrating Diana (set to music) in *Cynthia's Revels* V. vi. Jonson opens his collection, *Under-wood*, with three Christian literary hymns (one on Christ's Nativity). Philosophical implications like those in Marullo's *Hymni Naturales* are developed in Chapman's two hymns in *The Shadow of Night* (1594). The preponderance of literary hymns in English verse of the earlier seventeenth century have Christian themes.

46. In an unpublished monograph, "The Making of Spenser's *Hymnes*." A short version of this monograph was read by Professor Jayne before English Section I at the MLA Annual Meeting in 1971.

47. See my "Generic View of Spenser's *Four Hymns*," pp. 293–97.

48. Ibid., pp. 297–301.

49. Of course, Christian poets as early as Prudentius adopted classical mythology to their own purposes. Piccolomini's Prudentian "Hymnus de Passione" (sapphic stanzas, 140 lines) adopts the proverbial trilogy of Venus, Bacchus [*Liber* in Terence], and Ceres (see Terence, *Eunuch* IV. v. 6) to contrast man's gluttony with Christ's mastery of the flesh (lines 23–28). This hymn appears in *Poeti Latini del Quattrocento*, ed. Francesco Arnaldi et al., La Letteratura Italiana, vol. 15 (Milan, 1964), pp. 148–56. Pontano's "Hymnus ad Divam Mariam" (ii), cited earlier, refers to Heaven as Olympus (line 21) and God the Father as "Thunderer" (line 23—a commonplace Prudentian epithet for God; see, for example, *Psychomachia*, line 640 and *Cathemerinon* xii. 83).

Chapman's long (300 lines, heroic couplets) "Hymn to Our Savior on the Cross" is relatively free of classical allusions. Although a dedicated classicist, Jonson, like Spenser, avoids classical allusions in his Christian literary hymns.

50. For example, in Tuve, "The Hymn," and Barker, "Pattern of Milton's *Nativity* Ode." See also Lawrence Stapleton, "Milton and the New Music," *UTQ*, XXIII (1953–54), reprinted in *Milton: Modern Essays in Criticism*, ed. Arthur E. Barker (New York, 1965), pp. 31–42.

51. Proclus' *Hymns* and the *Orphic Hymns* are obvious examples, as are some of Marullo's (see I. iv and II. iii). The harmonizing influence of Venus is the principal theme of *Hymni* II. viii. See also II. i. 69–76. Scaliger's critical remarks about hymns (III. cxii) are of some interest in this respect. The poetic process of writing hymns is conceived of as being itself related to the harmony of the spheres. According to Scaliger the poet must achieve in his mind and hence in his poetic celebration a reflection or offspring of the divine harmony which organizes the universe:

> Ac Dei quidem laus semper in toto animo, universaque cogitatione nostra versari debet. Quicquid sine eius communione facias, id vero factum ne putes. quanto magis appellendus animus ad eas modulationes, quae quantum illius complectuntur, tantum eius concipiunt divinitatis: fiuntque illorum affines concentuum, qui caelestibus anfractibus atque rotationibus sunt ab opifice attributi. (p. 162, col. 1C)

> [Accordingly, our whole being and every thought truly ought to reflect always the praise of God. Do not imagine that whatever you may do is really done without such communion. How compellingly ought our soul to be driven to those measures which embrace as much of that divinity as they can comprehend—and thereby become associated with those harmonies which were bestowed by the maker on the celestial revolutions and rotations.]

52. On Spenser's and Vida's employment of such images in literary hymns, see my "Generic View of Spenser's *Four Hymns*," p. 299. Visual images of light and dark are also common in Marullo's *Hymns* and, of course, many others.

# THE DOUBLE TIME SCHEME
# IN *PARADISE REGAINED*

## *A. B. Chambers*

*Paradise Regained* in part depends on Milton's manipulations of two very different concepts of time and on the resulting interreactions of alternate chronologies for divine and human history. From one point of view, time is linear in its nature, and on the line are unique moments, never repeatable, when God chose to intervene in history. From another point of view, time is not linear but cyclic, always and necessarily repetitive as recurrent intervals replace one another. Milton employs linear time, since the Wilderness Temptation of Christ was a unique event, but he adds other moments to the line, some of which are unorthodox. Milton also uses repetitive time in an unusual way since his cycles spin round with enormous rapidity. The point is that linear and cyclic time schemes, divine plans and human experience, must be compatible with one another for the work of salvation to occur and for paradise to be regained. If so, then Milton's views in the poem, however idiosyncratically, approach those of the Anglican church. Indeed, the church's prayer for the Wilderness Temptation supplies a surprisingly satisfactory statement of one of Milton's meanings.

S OME OF the structural patterns of *Paradise Regained* and one of the poem's fundamental meanings arise from Milton's curious handling of two different concepts of religious time. One of these concepts has been referred to as "Christian" time, though "sacred" or "divine" might be more accurately descriptive adjectives; the other probably should be labeled "liturgical" time in this case, but "Platonic" would serve almost as well were it not for the subject matter of Milton's poem. The first kind of time is essentially linear and depends on the idea of *kairos* (καιρός), defined by Liddell and Scott as "*exact* or *critical time, season, opportunity.*"[1] The second is cyclic or repetitive and depends on the idea of *chronos* (χρόνος), time in the more general sense of recurrent interval. A brief exposition of each term will be required before I can try to apply both toward an understanding of *Paradise Regained*.

"Christian" time, to use Oscar Cullmann's term,[2] is time as it might be seen from the perspective of God, "beholding from his prospect high, / Wherein past, present, future he beholds" (*PL* III, 77–78).[3] From this exalted point of view, time progresses straightforwardly and inexorably from a pre-time, when as yet the world was not, to an eternity whose limits no other eye than God's can perceive. It moves, that is, from a timeless beginning to an infinite end, and it thus can be understood fully by the mind of God alone. Certain moments along the line of sacred time may be comparable to one another— especially the theoretical "beginning" and "end" when God once was and shall again be "All in All" (*PL* III, 341), but none is an exact duplicate of any other, and the most important of them are genuinely unique. These special moments are the divine *kairoi*, the due seasons which God with omniscience and omnipotence perceives or chooses to be inevitably right for certain events. No other time or place, no other occurrence, however comparable, would serve. Only once, to mention random examples, did God create, did he single out a chosen seed, did he become incarnate. Only once shall he appear in glory to call into existence new heavens and earth. By means of *kairoi* such as these, time does indeed march on from beginning to end. An appropriate diagram for Christian or divine time is therefore a straight line, infinitely extended in both of its possible directions, upon which certain exact or critically important points must be observed. Without points like the Creation or Incarnation, after all, the line could neither progress nor even exist.[4]

Liturgical time also is linear, at least in part, since it depends in many ways upon the chronology of events in the life of Christ.[5] The church year, for example, begins with Advent season, the preparation for the coming of Christ on Christmas Day. It proceeds to such events as the Circumcision and Epiphany and then to the incidents of Holy Week, including the Passion and Resurrection. And it ends, in one sense, with Christ's ascent into heaven on Ascension Thursday and with the sending of the Holy Ghost from heaven, on Pentecost or Whitsunday, to be a comforter to mankind until the *Parousia* or last coming of Christ himself on Judgment Day. In Roman and Anglican use, it is true, observance of these events occupies no more than half of any given liturgical year, but the chronological or linear sequence nevertheless controls the whole. Romans count liturgical time after Pentecost by numbering subsequent Sundays as first Sunday after Pentecost, second Sunday after Pentecost, Pentecost III, and so on, until the first Sunday of Advent renews the cycle. Anglicans, until recently,[6] have begun the count with Trinity Sunday, one week after Pentecost, but their system of marking time has otherwise been the same: Trinity I, II, III, and so on lead eventually and once again to Advent I.

Liturgical time, therefore, is quite obviously repetitive or recurrent in practice, despite its linear foundation. Advent and Christmas, Good Friday and Easter, the Ascension and Whitsunday—all of these recur each year, and in more senses than one. First of all and most apparently, the church annually and thus cyclically observes these *kairoi* in the life of Christ. More importantly, for Christians, each person is asked to engage in the imitation of Christ, for the liturgy demands that these events be constantly reviewed and renewed within the arena of the human imagination or, to use George Herbert's term, the human heart, in order to base the activity and thoughts of one's own life on the exemplary history recorded in the Gospels. Each *kairos* is thus a model, an exemplum in a moral tale, a type or standard against which to measure the patterns into which mortal behavior falls. Liturgical time, in short, is both linear (because of its basis) and cyclic (because of its applications) simultaneously.

Liturgical time is thus a Christian variant of Platonic time because of its revolving nature.[7] But Plato's Great or Cosmic Year, perhaps thirty-six thousand normal years in duration, has been subsumed within the single, though recurrent, time span of the church's Year of Grace, and the high prospect of God has been accommodated to the more limited perspectives of merely human participants in the divine plan for universal history. *Kairoi* indubitably remain supremely important in and of their own right, for they are indeed "critical" moments, to quote Liddell and Scott again. But one of the very reasons for their momentousness, in liturgical terms, is their recurrence in lesser forms and in lesser degrees of importance in the lives of the individual members of the church, of Christ's body as it now exists on earth. *Kairoi* and *chronoi*, though based on very different perspectives and

interpretations of time sequences, must therefore be compatible in
at least some ways.

For illustrative proof of this compatibility, one might notice a
Nativity sermon preached by Lancelot Andrewes in 1623.[8] Andrewes'
text for the day is Ephesians i, 10, "That in the dispensation of the
fulnesse of times, hee might gather together in one all things in Christ,
both which are in heaven, and which are on earth, even in him."[9]
Andrewes first explains that "the fulnesse of times" actually means
"the fulnesse of seasons," since the word in the Greek text is *kairoi*.
He next distinguishes between *kairoi* and *chronoi* and gives a knotty
exposition of Christian or divine time. Yet Andrewes also compares
God's due seasons to those of the natural year, and he argues at some
length for the "good congruities" between his text and the liturgical
day on which he expounds it. Andrewes ends with an anticipation
of "the *fulnesse of eternity*, and in it the *fulnesse* of all *joy*. To which,
in the several *seasons* of our being *gathered to our fathers*, He vouch-
safe to bring us; that (as the yeare, so) the *fulnesse* of our *lives* may
end in a *Christmas*, a *merry joyfull Feast*, as that is." Andrewes' point
seems to be that recurrent times and unique seasons are both on their
way to eternity; by means of cyclic celebrations the church and mankind
travel in that direction as well.

For this conclusion Andrewes probably took a hint from the liturgy
itself, since some of the rite's appointed lessons—or pericopes, to use
the technical term—refer to *kairos*. One example is the ritual for the
first Sunday of Lent. The Epistle for Mass or Eucharist is taken from
2 Corinthians, chapter vi, and includes St. Paul's pronouncement, modeled on Isaiah lxii, 2, that "now is the accepted time [*kairos*] . . . now is
the day of salvation" (verse 2). Balancing the Epistle is the Gospel
lesson, taken in this case from Matthew, chapter iv, of a *kairos*, the encounter between Christ and Satan in the wilderness. Yet the Anglican
Collect stresses not the uniqueness of Christ's wilderness temptation
but its exemplary function as a model of abstinence appropriate for the
annual beginning of Lent and for the whole of Christian life. The Collect is this:

O Lord, which for our sakes diddest fast fourtie dayes and fourtie nights:
give us grace to use such abstinence, that our flesh being subdued to the
Spirit, wee may ever obey thy godly motions in righteousnesse and true holi-
nesse, to thy honour and glory, which livest and reignest, &c.

The Anglican rite for Lent I in effect reverses the normal applications of *kairoi* and *chronoi*. The revolving time when salvation is continually offered to mankind is referred to in the Epistle as a *kairos;* one of the *kairoi* in Christ's life is treated in the Collect as if it were recurring in *chronos*. The liturgical point of this reversal of meanings is multiple in significance. The wilderness temptation, because unique, can only be a *kairos*, yet it must be viewed as a recurrent event because of its importance in the lives and memories of mimetic Christians. The accepted time for salvation—to paraphrase the Epistle —did, does, and shall recur, thanks among other things to Christ's victory in the desert. But for each individual, "that *time*," as Andrewes noted in another sermon, "is at this *time, now*."[10] From these perspectives, every cyclic hour in Christian life can be unique, and every act in the life of Christ necessarily is intervallic. *Kairoi* and *chronoi* thus cooperate in the work of salvation and in the lengthy process whereby both become eternity.

This historical background can be summarized by quotations from three seventeenth-century authors. The first is Edward Leigh, whose third edition of *Critica sacra* or "philologicall and theological observations upon all the Greek words of the New Testament" appeared in 1650. As Leigh points out:

The Greeks make a difference between χρόνος[*chronos*], *Time*, and καιρός[*kairos*], *Season;* and in the Scripture they are also distinguished. . . . *Time* is more generall; *Season* . . . implyeth that part which is fit for doing a thing. Καιρός [*kairos*] signifieth in a large acceptation, Seasonablenesse of circumstance, whether of time, place, or any occasion; but most properly a seasonable time . . . or present occasion, that present fit time, wherein any thing to be done may be done fitly and happily . . . with relation to the good that may be done, even for that fit opportunitie, and fit occasion offered of well doing.[11]

The second author is John Diodati, the famous uncle of Charles Diodati, the closest friend of Milton's youth. The elder Diodati asks himself, in effect, just what the *kairos*, or acceptable time, mentioned by Isaiah and by St. Paul, might be. It is, he says, "the new and happy age of God's grace, answerable to the ancient year of Jubilee, wherein all bondages, and mortgages of Lands were cancelled . . . here Christ punisheth the tyranny of the Devil and all his ministers."[12] The third author is Cornelius à Lapide, probably the most useful, certainly the most comprehensive Bible commentator of the seventeenth century.

Concluding his survey of the opinions of the Fathers of the first five centuries of the Christian church, Lapide states that the *kairos* to which St. Paul refers ultimately means that indeterminable time in which God offers his ire but also his grace to mankind, his "acceptance, benevolence, paternity, glory, and all those primal goodnesses which were ours in paradise in a state of innocence."[13]

What God offers to mankind, in short, is a return to paradise and the primeval virtue known in that place and God makes the offer by means of his own divine *kairoi*, the sacred seasons acted out in terms of human chronology, those due moments which occur in terms of merely regular time. More evidence could be gathered for these arguments from John Boys, the Dean of Canterbury Cathedral when he published, in 1615, his exposition of the Epistle and Gospel for Lent I.[14] Or one might cite the sermons collected by Father Toal as appropriate for the first Sunday of Lent; the homily of St. Ambrose— Father Toal entitles it "The Acceptable Time"—would be especially relevant.[15] At this point, however, enough of the background surely has been presented to enable a turning to *Paradise Regained*.

Milton's version of the wilderness temptation places extraordinarily heavy emphasis on *kairos*. The initial, but *only* the initial point of this emphasis—even though it is so rigorously underscored that no one ought to miss it—is that the moment has not yet arrived when Christ should do or say any of the things which Satan suggests. All in due season Christ will perform most of that which Satan commands here. Christ will perform miracles, become a true oracle to his people, administer a Eucharistic Last Supper, establish a kingdom, and so on, but not until his "season comes" (*PR* IV, 146) for public action. Now is merely the occasion for "deeds / . . . in secret done" (I, 14–15), deeds concluded when Christ "unobserv'd / Home to his Mother's house private return'd" (IV, 638–39). From this perspective, much of Satan's argument is a devilish *carpe diem*, an insidious temptation to force the pace of Christian time, to confuse critical opportunities with untimely actions and with temporal means of accomplishing them. And much of Christ's wise fortitude consists of a stern refusal to do more than "endure the time" (IV, 174) until the season for his divine kingdom falls due. A characteristic example of these divergent positions is one of the confrontations described in Book III. Satan remarks:

> Zeal and Duty are not slow,
> But on Occasion's forelock watchful wait.
> They themselves rather are occasion best,
> Zeal of thy Father's house, Duty to free
> Thy Country from her Heathen servitude;
> So shalt thou best fulfill, best verify
> The Prophets old, who sung thy endless reign,
> The happier reign the sooner it begins.
> Reign then; what canst thou better do the while?  (III, 172–80)

What Christ can better do is simply wait.

> To whom our Savior answer thus return'd.
> All things are best fulfill'd in their due time,
> And time there is for all things, Truth hath said:
> If of my reign Prophetic Writ hath told
> That it shall never end, so when begin
> The Father in his purpose hath decreed,
> He in whose hand all times and seasons roll.  (III, 181–87)

The point is unmistakably clear, but the provocative image in Christ's speech is the "roll" of the last line, particularly because Milton's primary source, Acts i, 6–7, contains no verbal counterpart:

When they therefore were come together, they asked of him, saying, Lord, wilt thou at this time [ χρόνῳ] restore again the Kingdome to Israel?
And hee said unto them, It is not for you to know the times [χρόνους] or seasons [καιροὺς], which the father hath put in his owne power.

What the verb "roll" thus reveals is that in the mind of Milton and of his Christ, unique *kairoi* and repetitive *chronoi* cannot be totally alien to one another. For if both seasons and times roll, both must in some sense revolve and therefore in some sense be cyclic. Satan also offers a relevant comment, but it takes, appropriately, a muddled form.

> Long the decrees of Heav'n
> Delay, for longest time to [God] is short;
> And now too soon for us the circling hours
> This dreaded time have compast, wherein we
> Must bide the stroke of that long threat'n'd wound,
> At least if so we can, and by the head
> Broken be not intended all our power
> To be infring'd, our freedom and our being
> In this fair Empire won of Earth and Air;

For this ill news I bring, the Woman's seed
Destin'd to this, is late of woman born.          (*PR* I, 55-65)

Self-contradictory though this statement is in its simultaneous emphasis
on swift and slow time, it describes the chain by which Satan ines-
capably is bound. The links of the chain are circling hours and the
due seasons which time brings forth, each a vehicle of the other,
and both, depending on one's point of view, either short or long.

Milton, like the authors of the liturgy, thus finds it necessary to
blend two time schemes in setting forth the meanings of the wilderness
temptation. Even in asserting this parallel, however, one must notice
that Milton is far more interested in liturgical patterns than in ritualistic
details. Milton, for reasons shortly to be explained, does not even
follow the order of events given by Matthew in the pericope for
Lent I; instead, he adopts the order given by Luke. In addition, Milton
invents more *kairoi* for Christ's early life than the Bible records and
causes the *chronoi* to circle far more repetitively than in the liturgy.
These departures from liturgical and biblical norms can be accounted
for in biographical terms by remembering that Milton was in many
ways heterodox in his opinions when he wrote *Paradise Regained*,
recognizing no formal church and observing no set forms in his private
devotions. The explanation for these departures in terms of the poem
is rather different, since in *Paradise Regained* they represent extensions
of the liturgy for Lent I in both of its possible directions, to greater
circularity but also to more numerous moments of linear time. The
result of these strategies is that *Paradise Regained*, even though it
departs from the liturgical order of events, presents the devotional
and moral meanings of Lent I in exaggerated form. In arguing this
point I shall first look at Milton's *chronoi*, then at his *kairoi*, and then
at the way in which they cooperate together.

One reason why the hours circle in *Paradise Regained* is the generic
form of the poem. Since an epic, even a brief epic, customarily "hastes
into the midst of things," as the argument to Book I of *Paradise Lost*
puts it, the structural principle cannot be based on sequential time
but must depend on inverse chronology. *Paradise Regained* accordingly
begins *in medias res* with the baptism of Christ. The temptation scenes
shortly follow, while events prior to the baptism are summarized in
retrospective speeches by the various characters and by the narrator.
Milton's reviews of antecedent action, however, are not typical of

normal epic practice. Virgil, to cite only one standard against which Milton has often been measured, places all of the narratively important prior action in one extensive speech, Aeneas' narration to Dido of what befell him and his companions in Troy and on their voyage to Carthage. The equivalent speech in *Paradise Regained*, insofar as any can be found, is Christ's internal soliloquy in Book I. The monologue includes not only a survey of those past events which Christ himself remembers but also a doubly internal speech, the one at some time delivered by Mary to Christ and now quoted by him as a part of his own internal statements. This doubly internal speech looks further back than Christ can; it refers to the Annunciation, the Nativity, and the Purification, occasions too remote for Mary's son to recall them but indispensable for even a partial understanding of his nature and mission and therefore introduced as indelible but indirectly acquired parts of Christ's own memory.

Even the device of incorporating one retrospective speech within another cannot, however, provide enough past history for sufficient understanding. The narrator finds it necessary to remind his hearers of the first temptation in the Garden; God recalls to Gabriel the Annunciation and the temptation of Job; Christ mentions to Satan the forty-day fasts of Moses and Elijah; and Satan speaks of his own expulsion from Heaven, of Job and Ahab, and of his success as an oracle among the Gentiles. These examples, no more than a sampling of those available from the first book alone, indicate that Milton's handling of the *in medias res* device differs from Virgil's in important ways. First, instead of depending on one principal narrative of prior events, Milton distributes accounts of significant past action through the poem, presenting that action in various ways and from multiple points of view. Second, there is of necessity not one major dislocation of time in *Paradise Regained* but a series of minor dislocations. Given Aeneas' narration, Virgil's story can move straightforwardly along, but Milton repeatedly glances at the past even as each present event moves into the future. As a result, one reads nearly every scene of *Paradise Regained* with a sense of *déjà vu*, of having encountered the present moment at some earlier past time. Milton strengthens this impression in several ways. The trial of Job, for example, continually recurs as an analogue for the temptation of Christ. The Dove descends three times within the first 280 lines, once as described by the narrator,

again as mentioned by Satan, and a third time as remembered by
Christ. Three different characters in three separate incidents allude
to Christ's appearance in the temple at the age of twelve. Christ recalls
it as an early indication of his surprising knowledge (I, 209 ff.); Mary,
as a cause for hope that her son's present absence, like the earlier
one, is in pursuit of "his Father's business" (II, 96 ff.); and Satan, as
an excuse to survey Greek philosophy and to tempt Christ to secular
wisdom (IV, 215 ff.). At the beginning of the second book, Andrew
and Simon "began to doubt" because of Christ's inexplicable absence;
"plain Fishermen" are similarly troubled but resolve to "wait," thereby
extracting "new hope" from their "perplexity"; Mary next expresses
"troubl'd thoughts," asking "where delays he," but decides to "wait
with patience." In the meantime Christ "into himself descended" in
an effort to resolve self-doubt, and Satan, "doubting," speaks to his
devilish cohorts. The plain fishermen, moreover, assume that "the Kingdom shall to *Israel* be restor'd," a notion later to be tested in the
temptation of the kingdoms of Parthia and Rome. But even earlier,
God had intimated to Gabriel that the Son's warfare and kingdom
were to be matters of the soul, and Christ had identified "the promis'd
Kingdom" with the "work" of "Redemption" (I, 265–66). Earlier still,
John the Baptist proclaimed "Heaven's Kingdom nigh at hand" (I,
20), yet much later Christ waits until his "season comes to sit / On
*David's* Throne" (IV, 146–47), and at nearly the end of the poem
Satan continues to wonder whether the kingdom is "real or Allegoric"
(IV, 390).

    With an insistence which these examples no more than suggest,
the poem doubles back upon itself as thematic motif, typological parallel, or significant image recurs and then recurs again. For everything
in *Paradise Regained* happens not once but repeatedly. Yet the poem's
line of time is rectilinear as well as circular. One reason is that the
cycles recur as repeated points of reference whereby to gauge the
successive events by which Christ's character is developed and to
measure the understanding of that development by Christ himself
or, at times, by other characters in the poem. Only for one of the
poem's characters, Satan, is this statement completely untrue. Incapable
of understanding the process which unfolds before him, Satan approaches each repetitive event with greater bewilderment. He attacks
Christ's progressively greater strength with temptations successively

more weak and remains baffled until, "smitten with amazement," he falls (IV, 549). Milton has been criticized for the ineptitude which Satan displays in this poem, but it is difficult to see how Satan could have reacted more wisely. In *Paradise Lost* he at least knew the identity of those to whom he chose to be the Adversary. In *Paradise Regained* not only does he never recognize whom he opposes, but also his opponent's changing character presents a conundrum even more mysterious than the one described in orthodox Christianity.

First of all, orthodoxy insists that Christ at all times was *Theanthropos*, or God-man, even though some of his experiences on earth, among them the desert temptation, may have had relevance primarily or exclusively to his human nature.[16] Prior to the Incarnation, according to this theology, the Son existed as God; after the Incarnation, he existed and exists as both God and man. This is a point established by the angelic chorus at the end of Milton's fourth book. Speaking of Satan and addressing the triumphant Christ, this chorus recalls that "him long of old / Thou didst debel, and down from Heav'n cast / With all his Army," and the chorus also remarks that "now thou hast aveng'd / Supplanted *Adam*, and by vanquishing / Temptation, hast regain'd lost Paradise" (IV, 604–08). Christ therefore is "heir of both worlds" (633), a "queller of Satan" (634) both as God and as man. But Christ's identity as *Theanthropos*, however obvious to the angelic chorus, never occurs to Satan. God's "first-begot we know," he says, "and sore have felt, / When his fierce thunder drove us to the deep; / Who this is we must learn" (I, 89–91). It does not occur to him that the first-begot and newly-begot are both the only-begotten Son of God; and having mistaken his ground at the outset, Satan never thereafter recovers. He probes and questions and tests, ever more vainly and impotently, without ever learning even the orthodox truth. But even had Satan unexpectedly stumbled on this hard rock of traditional Christianity, in this case it probably would have done him no good because the orthodox view, difficult to rational thought though it is, is less difficult than Milton's view. Milton makes large gestures toward orthodoxy, the angelic hymn of Book IV being a notable example, and incorporates into his interpretation of Christ's character large quantities of traditional material, particularly Old Testament typology and the three offices normally attributed to Christ of prophet, priest, and king.[17] The *Theanthropos* of this poem nevertheless is unusual because, for purposes of the poem, his two existences as God and as God-man remain almost completely distinct. In *Paradise Regained*, as elsewhere, Christ was at one time the unincarnate Son who debelled Satan and other rebels from heaven. At the end of *Paradise Regained*, Christ once again is the Son of God, miraculously standing on a narrow pinnacle, causing Satan to fall again, receiving the ministration of angels who recognize him for what he is. But until the pinnacle scene, Christ confronts Satan only as a man. Even this fact in itself is not necessarily unusual since biblical commentaries regularly state that Christ suffered and overcame these temptations only in his human capacities. Milton, however, goes further. He indicates that at the beginning of the poem this Christ was merely Jesus, a rather confused and potentially culpable man emerging from a childhood in which he set himself ungodly aims. This is the point at which the *kairoi* described by Milton begin to seem strange.

When this Christ was a child, his "mind was set / Serious to learn and know" (I, 202–03), but his mind was devoid of any memories of his former and divine existence and it occasionally reached false conclusions in the process of educating itself. At one time, for example, this Jesus entertained hopes of a worldly empire founded on martial prowess. "Victorious deeds," he says,

> Flam'd in my heart, heroic acts; one while
> To rescue *Israel* from the *Roman* yoke,
> Then to subdue and quell o'er all the earth
> Brute violence and proud Tyrannic pow'r,
> Till truth were freed, and equity restor'd.     (I, 215–20)

This is, of course, the ambitious aim to which Satan is to appeal with the temptations of the kingdoms, but Satan acts too late. When he offers the worldly kingdom and earthly throne, Christ knows enough to refuse, though at one time the offer would have been tempting. Even the moment when the poem begins might have been a propitious occasion for this temptation since Christ, in his initial soliloquy, admits to confusion and uncertainty: a "multitude of thoughts at once / Awak'n'd in me swarm" (I, 196–97). By this point he already has been instructed by Mary's narration of events from the Annunciation to the Purification, by his reading in the prophets, by John the Baptist, by the Spirit descending "like a Dove" (282), and by his "Father's voice" (283). Even so, Christ has arrived at a wrong conclusion. "I knew," he says, "the time / Now full, that I no more should live obscure, / But openly begin, as best becomes / The Authority which I deriv'd from Heaven" (286-89). Yet the time is not yet full nor is this season due; the deeds which immediately follow are done not openly but "in secret" (I, 15), and they are concluded when he "private return'd" (IV, 639) to his mother's house. He even enters the desert in ignorance of why he journeys there:

> And now by some strong motion I am led
> Into this Wilderness, to what intent
> I learn not yet; perhaps I need not know;
> For what concerns my knowledge God reveals.     (I, 290-93)

No revelation from God, however, is needed, for Christ, prodded by Satan's various temptations, instructs himself as to his internal nature and his external responsibilities. He learns to avoid distrust and intemperance, for example, to distinguish between oracles and the living Word, to prefer the kingdom of God to earthly thrones and sacred learning to secular wisdom. He learns too much, in fact, and learns it too subtly for a brief summary to be satisfactory, but one can note that his education is a process and that the process ends precisely where God foresaw it would when he referred to Christ as "this perfect Man, by merit call'd my Son" (I, 166). It ends when the chorus can identify Christ as the heir of both worlds.

The Christ of *Paradise Regained* thus is an emergent deity, a son of man who grows into godhead and becomes, by merit more than birthright, Son of God. Given this interpretation of Christ's character and of his earliest *kairoi*, it would have been impossible for Milton to follow the order of temptations described by Matthew in the pericope for Lent I. In Matthew's order the pinnacle scene comes second, not last, but of the biblical temptations only the pinnacle scene potentially contained a revelation that Christ had so matured that he could at last put on divinity. And even for Milton to extract this meaning it was necessary for him to adopt the minority view that the pinnacle—in the Greek text a πτερύγιον or "little wing"—was a narrow spire from which any normal man would fall rather than a flat turret on which any right-minded mortal might stand.[18]

> *Jerusalem,*
> The holy City, lifted *high* her Towers,
> And *higher* yet the glorious Temple *rear'd*

> Her *pile*, far off appearing like a *Mount*
> Of Alabaster, *top't* with golden Spires:
> There on the *highest* Pinnacle [Satan] set
> The Son of God.                    (IV, 544-50; italics added)

In giddy heights like these, Satan's comment to Christ, "to stand upright
/ Will ask thee skill" (IV, 551-52), becomes gross understatement;
yet Christ miraculously stood, and, with less ambiguity than has sometimes been perceived, he first rebuked Satan, "Tempt not the Lord
thy God" (IV, 561). On the pinnacle, for the first time in the poem,
Christ exercises powers exceeding those of man. He becomes *Theanthropos*, and Satan, smitten with amazement, falls.

Milton's Christ thus progresses through more points on the line
of Christian time than the church would care to recognize. He begins
not merely as mortal man but as a child, uninstructed and mistaken
as to himself and his mission. He slowly matures to become a perfect
man and then, by means of the wilderness temptation, to resume
his status as God. From the perspective of *Paradise Regained*, moreover, these are the crucial *kairoi* in Christ's life. Milton suggests that
something might have gone wrong at any one of them, that Christ
had the free will to choose, and therefore just conceivably might have
chosen, the worldly kingdom he dreamed of as a child or the roles
of false prophet and priest which Satan offers him. This is not to
say that Christ reveals any weakness in his confrontation with Satan.
Throughout the wilderness trial he acts as he should, discovering each
correct response as it is needed and displaying the wise fortitude
of a true hero. Even so, Milton has introduced within Christ's mind
remembrance of less admirable thought, and he suggests that this
*kairos* in the desert is the last one whose issue could be in doubt.
Christ now can "enter" on his "glorious work" and "begin to save
mankind" (IV, 634-35). Other *kairoi* of necessity must follow. But
the end of the work now is assured:

> For though that seat of earthly bliss be fail'd,
> A fairer Paradise is founded now
> For *Adam* and his chosen Sons, whom thou
> A Savior art come down to reinstall,
> Where they shall dwell secure, when time shall be.   (IV, 612-16)

In a "now" long since past, paradise was regained as a habitation
for men when time shall be. The *kairos* of the past thus insures the

result of the *chronos* to come, and this is one reason why Milton has stressed both seasons and times throughout the poem. Another reason is that man's *chronoi* must be modeled on God's *kairoi* if Adam's sons are to find their way out of the wilderness. Just as Christ's own *kairoi*, though unique, imitated and fulfilled their Old Testament ante-types—the forty-year sojourn in the desert of God's chosen seed, for example, or the forty-day fasts of Moses and Elijah—so the *kairoi* themselves must be imitated in the "now" when the day of salvation continually recurs. Indeed, those who refuse to subdue their time to God's due seasons will discover that paradise remains lost and will say on Judgment Day what the Satan of this poem said long ago: "And now too soon for us the circling hours / This dreaded time have compassed." The final reason for Milton's strategies, then, is that when this Christ, at this moment, became able to begin to save man-kind, a corner in history irrevocably was turned and a fundamentally important "now" was permanently located in time. Prior to that "now" was the whole of preceding history, from Adam and the happy garden which Milton erewhile sang to the events which Mary narrated to her son. All of that past takes its meaning from Christ since everything imperfectly was until he came. The "now" of the present is this unique *kairos* in the desert, one among many along the line of Christian time, but supremely important in Milton's treatment in that it not only an-swered the demands of the past but insured the progress of the future. The future itself included and includes Christ's own subsequent *kairoi* and the acceptable times of salvation for all future men, the unique but recurring moments when they may discover an internal garden in this world's wilderness and prepare toward a paradise happier far. Milton's concept of Christ again is relevant to this view of times and seasons. All prior to Christ were attempting the maturity he alone achieved. Thanks to his example, all subsequent men can hope by timely imitation to become justified and to sit with Christ on the right hand of God. When that final time and season would coincide, Milton could not know. But he could argue, however heterodox his way, the point made by St. Paul in the Epistle for Lent I, that now is the acceptable time, now is the day for salvation. And Milton, what-ever his specific differences with the established church, seems to have embodied in his poem that church's Collect for Lent I. The lesson of Milton and of the liturgy and of the time schemes of the poem may be unpalatable to modern tastes, but *Paradise Regained*, as I read it, indicates that they who would seize the day, the Christian "now," may thus be enabled, in the words of the Collect, to subdue their flesh to spirit and to obey Christ's godly motions in righteousness and true holiness to the honor and glory of God.

The University of Wisconsin, Madison

## NOTES

1. H. S. Jones and R. McKenzie, eds., *A Greek-English Lexicon*, new ed., rev. and aug. (Oxford, 1961).

2. See *Christ and Time*, tr. Floyd V. Filson (Philadelphia, 1950).

3. Quotations from Milton are taken from *John Milton: Complete Poems and Major Prose*, ed. Merritt Y. Hughes (New York, 1957).

4. Laurie Zwicky is surely correct in stressing the importance of *kairos*, but most of my research is not based on hers, and I believe, as she apparently does not, that *chronos* also is important for an understanding of the poem ("Kairos in *Paradise Regained*: The Divine Plan," *ELH*, XXXI [1964], 271–77).

5. I know of no exposition of liturgical time comparable to Cullmann's account of "Christian" time, but Dom Pius Parsch supplies much basic information in *The Breviary Explained*, tr. William Nayden and Carl Hoegerl (St. Louis, 1952).

6. Liturgies now in trial use among some Anglican churches also count time in the Roman way; see, for example, *The Church Year: Prayer Book Studies 19* (New York, 1967).

7. For Plato's theory of time, see *Timaeus*, 37C–39E. Francis M. Cornford takes up the question, in his words, of "how came it that Time was conceived, not as a straight line, but as a circle" in *Plato's Cosmology* (New York, 1957), p. 103.

8. *XCVI Sermons*, 4th ed. (London, 1641), pp. 148–58.

9. Quotations from the Bible and *The Book of Common Prayer* are taken from editions printed in London in 1619. As was often the case, the works have separate title pages but were bound together.

10. *XCVI Sermons*, p. 202; the sermon was preached on Ash Wednesday, 1619.

11. *Critica sacra* (London, 1651), p. 130. The copy I have used is bound with the second edition (London, 1650) of Leigh's philological remarks on Hebrew roots of the Old Testament.

12. *Pious and Learned Annotations Upon the Holy Bible*, 4th ed. (London, 1664), s. v. Isaiah lxii, 2.

13. Translated from *Commentaria in omnes divi Pauli epistolas* (Antwerp, 1635), f. 367. Lapide (a Latinized form of the original van den Steen) published massive commentaries on all books of the Bible except for Job and the Psalms.

14. *Dominical Epistles and Gospels*, pt. II (London, 1615), pp. 1–36. Boys published commentaries on the Gospels and Epistles for each Sunday of the year.

15. *The Sunday Sermons of the Great Fathers*, ed. and tr. M. F. Toal (Chicago, 1958), vol. II, pp. 1–36.

16. Elizabeth M. Pope supplies heavy documentation for the belief that Christ suffered the wilderness temptation only in his human nature (*Paradise Regained: The Tradition and the Poem* [Baltimore, 1947], chap. II).

17. Barbara K. Lewalski discusses typology and the offices of Christ at length (*Milton's Brief Epic* [Providence, 1966]).

18. Leigh supports the minority view adopted by Milton (*Critica sacra*, p. 229, s. v. πτερύγιον). For a comprehensive survey of majority opinion, see Lapide, *Commentarius in quatuor evangelia* (Antwerp, 1639), vol. I, f. 104.

# THE MOSAIC VOICE
# IN *PARADISE LOST*

## *Jason P. Rosenblatt*

---

A limited perception of Moses' relation to the epic narrator in
*Paradise Lost* derives from the tendency to regard his brief role
as hierophant in an early draft of a tragedy as a paradigm of his role
in the great epic. Placing Moses within an exclusively neo-Platonic
perspective and elevating him to virtually godlike status obscure
the human features of the imperfect Minister of the Law. In fact,
*two* distinct Moses traditions—the neo-Platonic and the typological—help to define Milton's epic voice. If the transition from
Edenic perfection to sin in *Paradise Lost* is attended by a shift
from predominantly neo-Platonic to predominantly typological
symbolism, then these shifts might be assisted by our recognition
of a changed emphasis upon the character of Moses. Though lines
ought not be drawn too sharply, it is generally true that the epic
voice depends on the neo-Platonic tradition of Moses as poet-
illuminator in passages that describe a prelapsarian world. When
the Fall of Man is evoked, the epic narrator exploits a complex
typological conception of Moses as at once a symbol of Old
Testament obscurity and a mediator who leads to Christ.

RECENT ATTEMPTS to isolate the component parts of the epic
voice of *Paradise Lost* demonstrate the value of a rhetorical approach to narrative and to the narrating *personae* whose mediating
voices present the text to us. Recognizing that the role of inspired
poet-narrator is in some sense an artifact, critics have been especially
attentive to those voices which Milton himself invented—the night
bird, the blind bard, and the Christian poet who defines himself with
reference to the characters in his poem.[1] A presence felt early in the
poem—inherited rather than invented—is that of Moses, though the
example he sets in the Bible and in Milton's work of fortunate beginnings and incomplete endings is reflected in the tendency of critics

to relate him to the epic voice only in the first quarter of *Paradise Lost*. Moses is the figure who ultimately falls short.

James Holly Hanford is Moses' strongest advocate, but even he limits Moses' appearance in *Paradise Lost* to the two earliest invocations. Hanford elaborates the importance of two of the four drafts of a tragedy on the theme of paradise lost which have been preserved in the Cambridge Manuscript in the Library of Trinity College.[2] These jottings, set down within a year of Milton's return from the Continent in 1639, are related by their mutual assignment of a prominent role to Moses, who is first among "the Persons" in the second draft, and who serves as Prologue in the third draft. Actually, the second draft is nothing more than a *dramatis personae*, and the third can be described as a minimal scenario. Hanford makes the most of these sketches by treating Moses' role of Platonic philosopher in the third draft as a paradigm of his role in *Paradise Lost*. The Platonic bias of Hanford's thesis leads to a characterization of Moses as the inhabitant of a Hellenistic universe, whose symbolic office is exclusively that of hierophant, interpreting inaccessible divine truth to the unpurged faculties of his audience. Hanford concludes his study by observing that Milton's exalted notion of Moses' character presents similar problems in both the third draft and the epic poem. It seems that Gabriel, whose gift of perfect vision is the result of an angelic nature that requires no special explanations, supplants the more difficult Moses as Prologue in Milton's fourth draft in the Trinity Manuscript. Similarly, argues Hanford, Milton's early invocation in *Paradise Lost* of the inspired "Shepherd, who first taught the chosen Seed" (I, 8)[3] is succeeded by the invocation of a less troublesome model of divinity: "Milton loses sight of Moses and elaborates the Platonic and poetic symbolism of Urania."[4]

Hanford's suggestive note invites anyone attempting to understand the character of Moses in *Paradise Lost* to examine the Hellenistic tradition which portrays him as a sort of all-knower and bringer of *gnosis*. Following Hanford's suggestion, Don Cameron Allen searches Philo for a mystical interpretation of the Sinai theophany. Allen conceives of Moses' role in *Paradise Lost* as that of illuminator, and the relevant biblical verse is Exodus xx, 21: "And the people stood afar off, and Moses drew near unto the thick darkness where God was." The oxymoron "bright darkness," implied and expressed in the writings of Philo and of Alexandrian Christian theologians interested in mysticism, conveys the notion that the divine light "hides itself in the dark and one must enter the cloud to find it."[5] Allen demonstrates that Moses and the blind narrator apprehend divinity in darkness.

It is hardly surprising that Hanford and Allen begin their search for the artifact of the role of inspired poet-narrator in the Hellenistic Jewish apologetics of Philo and Josephus—specifically, in their accounts of the life of Moses. There one finds a portrayal of "the divine (and) holy Moses,"[6] whose mediatorial office is unexcelled and whose human limitations are seldom, and then only grudgingly, admitted. It would, of course, be a mistake to suggest that wholly approving interpretations of Moses' life are limited to non-Christian sources. Though more restrained than Philo and Josephus, patristic interpreters such as Origen, Eusebius, Theodoret, Gregory of Nyssa, and others present Moses as a mediator whose exemplary life is set before the faithful as an ideal. Moreover, the extensive historical and allegorical tradition of Moses as poet-prophet extends into Milton's England and sheds light on the first two invocations of *Paradise Lost*. The only problem here is that this tradition fails to account for other attitudes toward Moses which we are forced to adopt in the course of the poem.

Placing Moses within an essentially Hellenistic perspective and elevating him to virtually godlike status obscure the human features of the imperfect "Minister / Of Law" (*PL* XII, 308–09). By stressing Moses' fallen nature, the last quarter of *Paradise Lost* brings him into an even closer relationship with the narrator than Hanford and Allen suggest. An almost limitless Christian tradition views Moses in the light of the history of redemption which culminates in Christ, and the outlines of this tradition must be traced if we are to understand that in *Paradise Lost* we gain access to God through a "Mediator, whose high Office now / *Moses* in figure bears, to introduce / One greater, of whose day he shall foretell" (XII, 240–42). An examination of the Moses-Christ typology should aid our comprehension of the poetics of accommodation by means of which the reader is led to Christ. The reader, who is asked, with the help of the Holy Spirit, to adjust Old Testament meanings to the fuller intent of the entire Scripture, is drawn closer to the epic voice, for whom the adoption of a Mosaic character represents the devout hope to be fulfilled and transcended by Christ.

It should be noted at the outset that the boundaries between various Moses traditions in patristic writings are at times more fluid than this paper might indicate. St. Augustine, for example, treats two central, conflicting points of view in one breath when he states: "There is no doubt that Moses . . . represents two different persons. In the first instance he is an image of the one who participates in the divine truth (for he entered the cloud on Mt. Sinai); but secondly he represents the Jews, who set themselves against the image of the grace of Christ. They did not understand and did not join in the covenant."[7] If, as William G. Madsen suggests, the transition from Edenic perfection to sin in *Paradise Lost* is attended by a shift from predominantly neo-Platonic to predominantly typological symbolism,[8] then these shifts might be assisted by our recognition of a changed emphasis upon the character of Moses. Though lines ought not be drawn too sharply, it is generally true that the early invocations depend on the neo-Platonic view of Moses as poet and prophet, inspired author of the Pentateuch, and "image of the one who participates in the divine truth."

Among the changes signaled by the opening lines of the lyrical prologue to Book IX is an altered conception of the role of Moses:

> No more of talk where God or Angel Guest
> With Man, as with his Friend, familiar us'd
> To sit indulgent . . .
>
> .    .    .    .    .    .    .    .
>
>                        I now must change
> Those Notes to Tragic; foul distrust, and breach
> Disloyal on the part of Man, revolt,
> And disobedience.                        (IX, 1–3, 5–8)

Todd notes that "Milton was here instructed . . . by the divine historian himself, *Exod.* xxxiii.11 'And the Lord spake unto Moses face to face, *as a man speaketh to his friend.*'"[9] The inspired narrator of the Pentateuch, then, is describing his own relationship with God, a relationship now rendered inappropriate to the poet's concerns by the introduction of sin. The fallen narrator replaces Raphael, himself the "Divine / Historian" (VIII, 6–7), because "now," in our fallen state, we require communication with someone acquainted with distrust and disobedience. Later in the poem, Moses is united with Adam as a sinner excluded from sacred ground by sin (XII, 307–14), and in *Christian Doctrine* Milton identifies Moses' sin at the waters of

Meribah (Numbers xxvii, 12-14) as "distrust of God."[10] Moses is the single historical figure who spans the abyss between perfection and sin—unique and inimitable as a result of his communion with God, yet somehow like us in our sinfulness and in our dependence on Christ's redemptive force. This is the paradox which the inspired narrator of *Paradise Lost* attempts to embody. Though he prays for the inward illumination to "see and tell / Of things invisible to mortal sight" (*PL* III, 54-55), he admits his kinship with us as a sinner who requires one greater man to restore us, to redeem us in the midst of all our "woe" (I, 3; IX, 11).

Since the paradox can be understood largely in terms of a changed dependency on typological rather than on Platonic and neo-Platonic Moses traditions, the remainder of this paper will examine the complex of attitudes toward Moses which characterizes these different traditions. The portrait of Moses as Platonic illuminator will be traced first, and traced somewhat lightly, since it offers an interpretation of Moses' role in the early invocations of *Paradise Lost* that has already been recognized.

The portrait of Moses as poet-illuminator is shown to best advantage in a setting where the threat of continued and necessarily damaging comparisons of Moses to Christ is absent. Milton provides such a setting in *Areopagitica,* where he attests to the sufficiency of the individual to separate good from evil by exercising his gift of reason. At the very start of the second argument ("what is to be thought in generall of reading Books, what ever sort they be"), Moses is cited as an example of an individual "skilfull in all the learning of the Aegyptians, Caldeans, and Greeks, which could not probably be without reading their Books of all sorts."[11] In addition to relying on the summary account of Moses' education that appears in the New Testament ("And Moses was learned in all the wisdom of the Egyptians," Acts vii, 22), Milton would have known the fuller account in the work of Philo, whom he calls "a writer of weight . . . who wrote a lengthy commentary on all the Mosaic law and was most learned in its lore."[12] Philo includes prosodic principles among the subjects that Moses learned from the three cultures:

Arithmetic, geometry, the lore of metre, rhythm and harmony, and the whole subject of music as shown by the use of instruments or in textbooks and treatises of a more special character, were imparted to him by learned Egyptians. These further instructed him in the philosophy conveyed in symbols, as displayed in the so-called holy inscriptions. . . . He had Greeks to teach him the rest of the regular school course, and the inhabitants of the neighbouring countries for Assyrian letters and the Chaldean science of the heavenly bodies.[13]

Drawing on his youthful instruction in poetry and music, Moses would have sung a hymn to God and an ode to Israel (Exodus, chap. xv, and Deuteronomy, chap. xxxii), both composed in structurally classical hexameter verse. Israel Baroway has already charted the underground patristic stream that carried the myth of scriptural prosody from Philo and Josephus to the Renaissance literary critics.[14] Transmission of the myth is also aided by the spirit of controversy, which has thrived on the association of Moses and Scripture with classical prosody. Though their ends require different emphases, Philo's coreligionist Flavius Josephus confuted the learned grammarian and anti-Semite Apion with an argument substantially similar to one used later by Sidney against the Puritan attack of Gosson. Josephus dignified Moses by attesting to his composition of an "Ode in Hexameter verse, containing the prayses of God, and a thanksgiving for the favour he had done to them [the Israelites]."[15] Sidney's justification of literature and figurative expression in general depends partly on the support of "Moses and Deborah in their Hymns," which demonstrate that the chief among poems, "both in antiquity and excellency, were they that did imitate the unconceivable excellencies of God."[16] It is in this same spirit of self-justification that Milton writes of "those frequent songs throughout the law and prophets" that surpass the odes and hymns of Pindarus and Callimachus.[17]

The deliverance at the waters of the Red Sea prompted Moses' first song, "the most auncient song that is extant in the world,"[18] and the seventeenth-century exegete William Attersoll strictly discriminates the lofty style of the song in expounding the doctrine that "Poetry is ancient and commendable":

Poetry is ancient in the Church of God, and commendable among the godly. The setting forth of the workes of God, not onely truly, soundly, and simply in a plaine forme & frame of words, but strictly, poetically, artificially, is worthy of praise and commendation. . . . See the examples of Moses singing the praises of God after their deliverance out of Egypt, after the overthrow of Pharaoh, and after their passage over the red sea; he footed it not in a

low, but in a lofty stile, praising God in verses, not in prose, for the greater
efficacy of the matter, and the better expressing of their affections. The like
we might say of his sweet song sung not long before his death, Deut. 31,
19, 22 & 32, 1, 2, & c. which he taught the children of Israel.[19]

We can believe that Milton promises a poem composed in lofty
style when he adopts a distinctive Mosaic personality in *Animadver-
sions*. There he prays to God for the perfection of the Reformation
in a mood of chiliastic exaltation:

O perfect, and accomplish thy glorious acts; for men may leave their works
unfinisht, but thou art a God, thy nature is perfection; shouldst thou bring
us thus far onward from *Egypt* to destroy us in this Wildernesse though wee
deserve; yet thy great name would suffer in the rejoycing of thine enemies,
and the deluded hope of all thy servants. When thou hast settl'd peace in
the Church, and righteous judgement in the Kingdome, then shall all thy Saints
address their voyces of joy, and triumph to thee, standing on the shoare
of that red Sea into which our enemies had almost driven us. And he that
now for haste snatches up a plain ungarnish't present as a thanke-offering
to thee, which could not bee deferr'd in regard of thy so many late deliverances
wrought for us one upon another, may then perhaps take up a Harp, and
sing thee an elaborate Song to Generations. (YP, I, 706)

Though such a victory and such hosannas are not forthcoming, the
narrator of *Paradise Lost*, speaking more softly than the youthful Milton, records at least a limited sort of Exodus deliverance. Intimations
of the Exodus myth in the epic have been treated in learnedly provocative essays by Harold Fisch and John T. Shawcross.[20] One might also
recall Milton's announcement, in the conclusion to his defense of "The
Verse," that his Heroic Verse without Rime sets an example, "the
first in *English*, of ancient liberty recover'd to Heroic Poem from
the troublesome and modern bondage of Riming." Moreover, faint
echoes occasionally sound in passages not overtly concerned with the
Exodus. Thus the invocation to Book III of *Paradise Lost* suggests
a comparison between the narrator's flight, borne by his Muse, and
the Israelites' flight from Egypt on eagles' wings (Exodus xix, 4). The
narrator has "Escap't the *Stygian* Pool, though long detain'd / In that
obscure sojourn" (III, 14–15). We recall references in the latter books
of the epic to the lengthy "sojourn" in Egypt (XII, 159, 190–92), as
well as the first Exodus simile in the poem, which compares Satan's
broken legions in the fiery lake to Pharaoh's army beheld by "The

Sojourners of *Goshen*" (I, 309). The narrator's sense of relief here—
of escape—is explained at least partly by reference to the dramatic
context of the Exodus.

The vibrations of the Sinai theophany are recorded rather more
emphatically than those of the Exodus in the early invocations of
*Paradise Lost*. The Old Testament insisted on the united functions
of prophet and legislator (Exodus, chaps. xx, xxi, and xxxiv), and the
Apocrypha embellished the argument that Moses' mystic ascent authen-
ticated his role as lawgiver. An apocalyptic tenor characterizes God's
account of Moses' visions: "I brought him up on to Mount Sinai; and
kept him with me for many days. I told him of many wonders, showing
him the secrets of the ages and the end of time, and instructed him
what to make known and what to conceal" (2 Esdras xiv, 4–5). Jesus
the son of Sirach, in his praise of famous men, also sees the ascent
of Sinai as the occasion for the revelation of mysteries:

He gave him commandments for his people and showed him a vision of
his own glory.
For his loyalty and humility he consecrated him, choosing him out of all
mankind.
He let him hear his voice and led him into the dark cloud.
Face to face, he gave him the commandments, a law that brings life and
knowledge. (Ecclesiasticus xlv, 3–5)

Philo's interpretation of the Sinai ascent as Moses' induction into
kingship and prophecy is of some importance in understanding the
Hellenistic conception of the mediatorial office—a conception that
must at least have influenced Milton in the Trinity Manuscript drafts
of the "Paradise Lost" tragedy. Moses is assigned an intermediary
status between God and the rest of men:

For he was named god and king of the whole nation, and entered, we are
told, into the darkness where God was, that is into the unseen, invisible, in-
corporeal and archetypal essence of existing things. Thus he beheld what
is hidden from the sight of mortal nature, and, in himself and his life displayed
for all to see, he has set before us, like some well-wrought picture, a piece
of work beautiful and godlike, a model for those who are willing to copy
it. Happy are they who imprint, or strive to imprint, that image in their souls.[21]

Where Philo treats Moses as supreme prophet, priest, and king,[22]
Josephus somewhat more moderately stresses the roles of author-editor
and legislator. Just as Moses was a lawgiver, so was he devoted to

natural philosophy. This is evident from his method in the Pentateuch of prefixing the Genesis cosmogony to the legal prescriptions of the other books. The prophet "deemed it above all necessary, for one who would order his own life aright and also legislate for others, first to study the nature of God, and then, having contemplated his works with the eye of reason, to imitate so far as possible that best of all models and endeavour to follow it."[23] Moses' narrative method is a paradigm for Josephus, who states: "I therefore entreat my readers to examine my work from this point of view."[24]

Milton acknowledges the influence of Josephus in shaping his understanding of the merged functions of author and legislator. He realizes that the purpose of divine inspiration is not only to "see and tell / Of things invisible to mortal sight" but also to "justify the ways of God to men." Thus he writes in the preface to Book I of *Reason of Church-Government:*

*Moses* therefore the only Lawgiver that we can believe to have been visibly taught of God, knowing how vaine it was to write lawes to men whose hearts were not first season'd with the knowledge of God and of his workes, began from the book of Genesis, as a prologue to his lawes; which *Josephus* right well hath noted. That the nation of the Jewes, reading therein the universall goodnesse of God to all creatures in the Creation, and his peculiar favour to them in his election of *Abraham* their ancestor, from whom they could derive so many blessings upon themselves, might be mov'd to obey sincerely by knowing so good a reason of their obedience. (YP, I, 747)

In Milton's view, all knowledge—even the inspired wisdom of poetic song—must be regarded as the base upon which virtuous action is founded, and the poetry of creation is only the preface to legal instruction.

That this principle remains with Milton is evident from its practical application in *Christian Doctrine*. There he justifies the editorial insertion of a description of the Sabbath into the second chapter of Genesis by appealing to Moses' primary role as lawgiver. Milton notes the scriptural anachronism of referring to the institution of the Sabbath before the account of the promulgation of the Law and concludes that "Moses . . . inserted this sentence from the fourth commandment, into what appeared a suitable place for it; where an opportunity was afforded for reminding the Israelites, by a natural and easy transition, of the reason assigned by God, many ages after the event itself, for his command with regard to the observance of the Sabbath by the covenanted people" (CM, XV, 117). In both passages, Milton finds Moses' narrative method to be grounded on the reason of obedience.

In works close to Milton, Moses' Sinai ascent becomes the source of apocalyptic knowledge as well as legal regulation. Indeed, both Clement of Alexandria, whom Milton cites early in his *Commonplace Book*, and Eusebius, the poet's favorite church historian, present fragments of a verse drama by Ezekiel, an otherwise unknown author, in which Moses himself narrates the ascent as a dream-vision. Standing before "a mighty throne that reached to heaven's high vault," Moses surveys the prospect:

> Thence I looked forth
> Upon the earth's wide circle, and beneath
> The earth itself, and high above the heaven.
> Then at my feet, behold! a thousand stars
> Began to fall, and I their number told,
> As they passed by me like an armed host.[25]

In the interpretation of the dream that follows, Moses learns of his combined role of legislator and seer.[26]

The narrator of Book III of *Paradise Lost* assumes a role analogous to that of Moses. Dealing with what Isabel MacCaffrey calls "divine epistemology, the ways whereby men can know, or come to know, God,"[27] he aspires to a vision of the timeless realm of light and to the justification of Christian doctrine as it is expounded by God himself. The poet evokes the Sinai theophany in Book III by modulating the significance of "cloud" and "ever-during dark." We remember that the Sinai narrative employs the imagery of covering: Moses is enveloped by the thick cloud (Exodus xix, 9), shaded by the hand of God (Exodus xxxiii, 22), and concealed by the veil (Exodus xxxiv, 33–35). These images suggest at once initiation and revelation as well as obstruction and concealment. A consideration of the invocation to Book III should indicate a relationship between the epic voice and Moses by bringing into similar play the varied meanings of the imagery of concealment.

The poet's ascent to knowledge is first described as a "flight / Through utter and through middle darkness borne / With other notes than to th' *Orphean* Lyre" (*PL* III, 15–17). Then, both clinically and poetically, the narrator describes the cloud covering his eyes: "So thick a drop serene hath quencht thir Orbs, / Or dim suffusion veil'd" (25–26).

"Drop serene" is a literal translation of *gutta serena*, the medical term for the form of blindness which Milton suffered. The term furnished the poet with some consolation, and in the *Second Defence* he wrote that his eyes were "as clear and bright, without a cloud, as the eyes of men who see most keenly" (YP, IV, 583). Yet the consolation here is immediately canceled when the image of a cloud covering the eyes is suggested by the alternate description of blindness, "or dim suffusion veil'd."

The association of darkness and song appears soon after in the description of the bird: "as the wakeful Bird / Sings darkling, and in shadiest Covert hid / Tunes her nocturnal Note" (*PL* III, 38-40). This somewhat fuller consolation is also canceled immediately, by the dissociation of the bird, who is in tune with nature and who knows when night comes, from the speaker:

> Thus with the Year
> Seasons return, but not to me returns
> Day, or the sweet approach of Ev'n or Morn,
> Or sight of vernal bloom, or Summer's Rose,
> Or flocks, or herds, or human face divine;
> But cloud instead, and ever-during dark
> Surrounds me, from the cheerful ways of men
> Cut off, and for the Book of knowledge fair
> Presented with a Universal blanc
> Of Nature's works to me expung'd and ras'd,
> And wisdom at one entrance quite shut out.          (III, 40-50)

The "cloud" and "ever-during dark" surrounding the poet are not, at this point, transmitters of consolatory wisdom, and the invocation ends with the prayer that the Celestial Light

> Shine inward, and the mind through all her powers
> Irradiate, there plant eyes, all mist from thence
> Purge and disperse, that I may see and tell
> Of things invisible to mortal sight.          (III, 52-55)

The speaker must wait longer for the next consolation, which comes in the form of a dark mystery at the upper limit of human poetic vision. Through a sort of divine peripeteia, the speaker's prayer for illumination is answered in an unexpected way when he joins the angels in the next apostrophe to the Divine Light of God the Father:

> Fountain of Light, thyself invisible
> Amidst the glorious brightness where thou sit'st
> Thron'd inaccessible, but when thou shad'st
> The full blaze of thy beams, and through a cloud
> Drawn round about thee like a radiant Shrine,
> Dark with excessive bright thy skirts appear,
> Yet dazzle Heav'n, that brightest Seraphim
> Approach not, but with both wings veil thir eyes.     (III, 375–82)

"Fountain of Light" takes us back to the eighth line of the invocation that begins Book III, and, like the wandering epic voice (III, 27), we traverse the same ground, our interpretation transformed by vision. The cloud that blinds the poet becomes the vehicle of the beatific vision. The blind speaker, "from the cheerful ways of men / Cut off," imitates the Father who sits "Thron'd inaccessible." Surrounded by a cloud and by ever-during dark, he is like God, who draws a cloud about Him, and like the dazzled Seraphim who voluntarily veil their eyes. Here, indeed, the oxymoron "Dark with excessive bright" reminds us especially of Moses, who "drew near unto the thick darkness where God was." We are also reminded of Exodus xxxiii, 18–23, where God reveals himself in a cloud to Moses alone atop Mount Horeb, while the Israelites (the "society of men") watch from a distance and wonder. The epic narrator ascends the mount of inspiration and, after praying and waiting, he is granted a veiled glimpse of eternity. The beatific vision becomes a function of his blindness.

The radical alterations of meaning of the cloud image in Book III enable it to represent fully the paradox that divine mysteries are apprehended in darkness. When the epic narrator is associated with Moses, the cloud becomes a symbol of authenticity as well. God tells Moses: "Lo, I come unto thee in a thick cloud, that the people may hear when I speak with thee, and believe thee for ever" (Exodus xix, 9). For Milton, too, the cloud of blindness becomes a mark of inspirational authenticity.

The complex of attitudes toward Moses examined so far affirms, among other things, the possibilities of human endeavor. Primarily Hebraic or Platonic rather than Christian, these traditions offer an ultimately partial understanding of Moses' symbolic role in Milton's work. Moses' genuine achievements without the aid of Christ's mediation are recalled most often in Milton's prose tracts of the 1640s. These represent Milton's part in a program for achieving religious, political, and domestic freedom. Attacking abuses of institutional authority, Milton sought to transfer power and freedom to his regenerate countrymen. The example of Moses' reproof to Joshua (Numbers xi, 29) sustained Milton in his hope that the culmination of the Reformation could be achieved. In a passage in *Areopagitica* preceded by the announcement that "great reformation is expected," Milton foresaw a holy community in England: "For now the time seems come, wherein *Moses* the great Prophet may sit in heav'n rejoycing to see that memorable and glorious wish of his fulfill'd, when not only our sev'nty Elders, but all the Lords people are become Prophets. No marvell then though some men, and some good men too perhaps, but young in goodnesse, as *Joshua* then was, envy them."[28] That this is one of Milton's noblest visions of human capability is dramatized by Blake's selection of the verse on which it is based as the epigraph for his brief epic, *Milton*. Blake's Milton is redeemed by becoming a liberating prophet.

Though hardly unconcerned with the effects of the Fall, Milton addressed himself in the 1640s to problems of the present and the immediate future. Eden he called simply "another world" (*Doctrine and Discipline of Divorce*, YP, II, 316). Counseling acceptance of Moses' divorce laws, he argued that it is no comfort to recall Adam and Eve in paradisiacal bliss when one is saddled with an unfit wife: "In such an accident it will best behove our sobernes to follow rather what moral *Sinai* prescribes equal to our strength, then fondly to think within our strength all that lost Paradise relates" (ibid.).

Milton's later, altered opinions regarding unmediated human achievement are reflected in the poetry of *Paradise Lost* and *Paradise Regained* and in the prose of *Christian Doctrine*. The disinclination to expect redemption in the material world through solitary human action is marked by a relentless emphasis on the need for divine intervention. Fallen human history becomes the record of "supernal Grace contending / With sinfulness of Men" (*PL* XI, 359–60).

As a poet, Milton chooses to exploit his fallen opinions of mankind by expressing them in *Paradise Lost* as a consequence of Adam's fall. In paradise, before the Fall, Raphael offers himself as a model of perfection, advising that Adam can alter his own nature from human to angelic simply by obedience. It is only a matter of time, he suggests,

"Till body up to spirit work" (V, 478). He underscores his claim that
the body's work is to be mediated only by the action of time (V,
497–98), adding the postscript "If ye be found obedient" (V, 501).

After the Fall, we understand that all of the verses treating Eden
were written in the subjunctive mood and that Raphael's postscript
must now be reinterpreted as a most unsettling codicil. In the soteriol-
ogy of the last books, Christ replaces Raphael as a pattern for Adam—
a pattern ultimately matchless. As an earlier Adam had twice repeated
the word "obedience" (V, 514), incredulous at the thought that his
could be doubted, so a newly startled Adam hears the word repeated
by Michael (XII, 403, 408), who discloses the effects of a sin so terrible
that only Christ can atone for it.

Adam is told that Christ must destroy Satan's work

> In thee and in thy Seed: nor can this be,
> But by fulfilling that which thou didst want,
> Obedience to the Law of God, impos'd
> On penalty of death, and suffering death,
> The penalty to thy transgression due,
> And due to theirs which out of thine will grow.   (XII, 395–400)

In the passage that follows immediately (401–50), Michael dispels the
fallacy of simple self-reliance. The complex system of imputations—
of human sin to Christ, of Christ's righteousness to all believers, and
of Adam's sin to all his descendants—is founded on the mediateness
of vicarious substitution.

Michael, unlike Raphael, treats the progression from body to spirit
in a context of the relation of Law to Justification by Faith—a context
that forecloses the possibility of redemption without Christ's intervention:

> So Law appears imperfet, and but giv'n
> With purpose to resign them in full time
> Up to a better Cov'nant, disciplin'd
> From shadowy Types to Truth, *from Flesh to Spirit,*
> From imposition of strict Laws, to free
> Acceptance of large Grace, from servile fear
> To filial, works of Law to works of Faith.
>                         (XII, 300–06; italics added)

In a prose paraphrase of the verses that follow (307–14), Milton identifies
the Law with Moses and concludes that "the imperfection of the law
was manifested in the person of Moses himself; for Moses, who was

a type of the law, could not bring the children of Israel into the land of Canaan, that is, into eternal rest; but an entrance was given to them under Joshua, or Jesus."[29]

This passage evokes Christ's redemptive reenactment of a mission uncompleted by Moses: to bring mankind home safe from wandering to "eternal Paradise of rest" (XII, 314). In Michael's presentation of history, Moses is the minister of a Law that brings the awareness of sin but not the power to overcome it. Only Christ has the power to enter Canaan and to regain paradise. The development in the reader of an awareness of incompleteness and a desire for fulfillment is part of a strategy in the later books of *Paradise Lost* which translates principles of mediation, of redemption and intercession, into a poetic technique. Examining Moses and his relationship to Christ—a relationship that can be defined partly in terms of the office of mediator—can afford us some insight into the Mosaic component of the epic voice as well as a convenient point of entry into this poetic technique.

The remainder of this paper, then, examines Milton's increased dependency on typological Moses traditions in the later books of *Paradise Lost*. Placed within a typological perspective, Moses is diminished, and his inferiority to Christ in person and office is emphasized. Neglect of these traditions and their relevance to Milton's poetics has led to the rejection of Moses as an informing presence in *Paradise Lost* by critics interested in typology. Thus, for example, William G. Madsen discredits the suggestion "that Milton thought of himself as a kind of Moses Anglicus, 'a revealer of truth in the Platonic sense.'"[30] The reason for his quarrel with this interpretation becomes clear when Madsen announces as one of the principal goals of his study the demonstration that the images and themes of *Paradise Lost* are essentially typological rather than Platonic or neo-Platonic: "Indeed, I hope to show that the poem may be described in some respects as anti-Neo-platonic, not only in its symbolic method but also in its central thematic concerns."[31] Madsen's dismissal of Moses traditions, then, is founded on the certainty that the recognition of a Moses persona involves the acceptance of a neo-Platonic orientation in *Paradise Lost*. A brief discussion of the tradition which views Moses in the light of the New Testament should indicate its compatibility with the symbolic method and thematic concerns that Madsen articulates.

That the application of the Gospel accomplishes the partial transformation of Old Testament events and personages is dramatized by
a reexamination of the images of "cloud" and "ever-during dark."
In emphasizing the limitations of the Law, the Pauline Epistles submit
Moses' Sinai ascent to the judgment of Christian experience. Moses,
the minister of the Law, is involved in obscurities of vision and language:

Seeing then that we have such hope [of glory], we use great plainness of
speech: And not as Moses, *which* put a vail over his face, that the children
of Israel could not stedfastly look to the end of that which is abolished: But
their minds were blinded: for until this day remaineth the same vail untaken
away in the reading of the old testament; which *vail* is done away in Christ.
But even unto this day, when Moses is read, the vail is upon their heart.
Nevertheless when it shall turn to the Lord, the vail shall be taken away.
Now the Lord is that Spirit: and where the Spirit of the Lord *is,* there *is*
liberty. But we all, with open face beholding as in a glass the glory of the
Lord, are changed into the same image from glory to glory *even* as by the
Spirit of the Lord. (2 Corinthians iii, 12–18)

In the Pauline letters, Moses is identified with the covenant which
has passed away ("when Moses is read"), and he is contrasted with
the new covenant in Jesus. This passage alludes constantly to Exodus
xxxiv, 29–35, though Paul departs from the biblical text by suggesting
that Moses' veil was meant to conceal the loss of his glory from the
Israelites. Paul's purge of Moses is complete. The last verse, with
its image of a mirror and its theme of transformation by beholding,
is an ironic reminder of the very similar passage in Philo dealing with
the establishment of *Moses* as a paradigm of virtue.

The passage from Corinthians proves that the imagery of covering
is not possessed of an inalienably sublime meaning. In Hebrews xii,
18–22, the verses' antitheses oppose terror to serenity, clouds and darkness to light, Sinai to Sion, the Law to the Gospel. Samuel Mather
interprets both sets of verses while discussing Moses as a type in regard
of his dispensation ("a Type of the Law"): "There was a *darkness*
also in that Dispensation, *Heb.* 12.18. *Ye are not come unto blackness,
and darkness, and Tempest.* Hence *Moses* had a Veil upon his Face,
*Exod.* 34.29, 30, 33. But there was a further Mystery in this Veil;
it signifieth a spiritual Veil, a Covering upon the Heart, 2 *Cor.* 3.13,
14. a Veil upon their Mind, *Act.* 13.27. they understood not the Prophets
though Read every Sabbath-day."[32]

Exegetes often saw Moses' thick cloud as equivalent to the "shadows and figures" of the Old Testament which are then opposed to the clarity of the Gospel.[33] That Moses embodies the obscurities and the limitations of the Old Law is brought home when we recall some of the titles, and the still more revealing subtitles, popular among seventeenth-century Protestants: William Guild's *Moses Unvailed: Or, Those Figures Which Served unto the Patterne and Shaddow of Heavenly Things* (London, 1620); Thomas Godwin's *Moses and Aaron: Civil and Ecclesiastical Rites, used by the ancient Hebrews: observed and at large opened* (London, 1625); and Thomas Taylor's *Moses and Aaron, or the Types and Shadows of the Old Testament Opened and Explained* (London, 1653).

Few could equal William Guild in compressing images opposing "Evangelicall light" to "Legal obscuritie." In his epistle dedicatory to the Bishop of Winchester, Guild remarks that "Moses covered with a vaile stood before the people: Even so (Right Reverend) in the detection of the glorious worke of mans Redemption, mysticall promises went before mercifull performance, darke shadowes were the fore-runners of that bright substance, obscure types were harbingers to that glorious Anti-type the Messiah."[34]

The New Testament verses and their various interpretations all agree that Christ and the new dispensation he embodies must be reached without clouds and darkness. This is evident when we return to Book III of *Paradise Lost*. The Son, participating in the heavenly dialogue with God the Father, foresees his final ascension after defeating death:

> Then with the multitude of my redeem'd
> Shall enter Heav'n long absent, and return,
> Father, to see thy face, wherein no cloud
> Of anger shall remain, but peace assur'd,
> And reconcilement; wrath shall be no more
> Thenceforth, but in thy presence Joy entire.      (III, 260–65)

The opposition of the old and new dispensations is subtly but definitely suggested by the association of "cloud" with anger and of anger with wrath. In *Christian Doctrine*, opposing the Covenant of Grace to the Mosaic Law, Milton quotes successively Romans iv, 15 ("the law worketh wrath") and v, 20 ("moreover the law entered, that the offence

might abound; but where sin abounded, grace did much more abound")
(CM, XVI, 107). Similarly, in *Paradise Lost,* wrath is used as a virtual
synonym of Law ("over wrath grace shall abound," XII, 478); and
this meaning is not absent from God's reply to the Son, whom he
addresses as "the only peace / Found out for mankind under wrath"
(III, 274–75).

In the same book, just after his veiled vision of God the Father,
the epic narrator addresses the Son as

> Divine Similitude,
> In whose conspicuous count'nance, without cloud
> Made visible, th' Almighty Father shines,
> Whom else no Creature can behold.          (III, 384–87)

Thomas Taylor reinforces the Mosaic allusion: "Never was God so
clearly seene by the eye of flesh as to *Moses,* who talked face to
face: But never did creature see his face but Christ, Joh. 1.18."[35]

God the Father is covered by a cloud before Moses in the Bible
and before the epic narrator in the poem. When he is alone with
the Son, he is "without Cloud, serene" (XI, 45). The Son of God experiences the ultimate perfection from which even Moses and the narrator
are excluded. Unlike the Son, they cannot experience a totally unmediated vision of divinity. "Without Cloud, serene" describes the
calm of the Father, whose countenance is not darkened by the Son's
desire to mitigate man's punishment; it alludes to the clouds of mystery
which can be removed when the Father and Son deliberate together;
it reminds us by contrast of the limitations of Moses' mediatorial office
and of the Law that works wrath; and, finally, it reminds us of the
"*gutta serena,*" the "drop serene" and "dim suffusion" that cloud the
eyes of a blind narrator.

The heart of every typological relationship is what William Guild,
throughout *Moses Unvailed,* calls "congruity" and "disparity." Though
the Pauline letters develop the negative typology, the "disparity," other
New Testament books treat as well the congruities between the person
and office of Moses and Christ. Moses, who is mentioned more frequently in the New Testament than any other Old Testament per-
sonage, is portrayed as the fullest type of Christ. Indeed, as St. Augustine
tells us, Jesus characterized himself by reference to the person of
Moses ("Se autem figuraverat in persona Moysi").[36] In Acts vii, 18–44,
Moses is depicted as the leader of the Israelites who mediates between

them and God. The rebellion of the Israelites against Moses prefigures the unbelief of the Jews with regard to Christ. Of primary importance in the typological relationship of Moses and Christ is the account of the Transfiguration in the Synoptic Gospels (Matthew xvii, 1–13; Mark ix, 2–13; Luke ix, 28–36). Here Moses is Christ's harbinger, a forerunner. As Jean Daniélou remarks, "the parallel between Moses and Christ terminates in the Transfiguration, with its numerous references to the Exodus: Moses himself, the cloud, the Divine voice, the tabernacles."[37]

Regarding the prefiguration of Christ's mediatorial office, William Guild notes that Moses "was King, Prophet, and Mediatour of the people. Typing so Christ Jesus in all these his Offices, Heb. 9.13."[38] In *Christian Doctrine*, when Milton turns to a consideration of Christ's mediatorial office and its tripartite function, he turns to Moses as well: "The name and, in a sense, the office of mediator is also ascribed to Moses, as a type of Christ. . . . The nature of this office becomes apparent when we compare Acts vii.38: *this is he who has received the living words to pass on to us*, with Deut. v.5: *when I was standing between Jehovah and you to pass the word of Jehovah to you.*"[39] These verses refer directly to Moses, and it is of some interest that the very first scriptural citations to validate Christ's prophetic function in the mediatorial office indicate that Christ is regarded as the ful- fillment, the culmination, of the Moses type: "HIS FUNCTION AS A PROPHET IS TO INSTRUCT HIS CHURCH IN HEAVENLY TRUTH, AND TO DECLARE THE WHOLE WILL OF HIS FATHER. Deut. xviii.15 compared with Acts iii.22 and vii.37. 'Je- hovah thy God will raise up unto thee a prophet from the midst of thee'" (CM, XV, 287–89). These verses treat Moses as a witness of Christ's prophetic office and identify Christ as the eschatological figure of Jewish expectation, the "prophet like Moses" promised in the eighteenth chapter of Deuteronomy.

Throughout his prose writings, Milton regards even the obscurity and indistinctness of Moses' Law with sympathy. It is true that he is always at pains to distinguish between the plainness and light of the Gospel (as in his quotation from Corinthians: "we use great plain- ness of speech; and not as Moses" (*Christian Doctrine*, CM, XVI, 115) and "the obscurity necessarily arising from the figurative language of the prophets" (CM, XIV, 291). Yet Milton describes Moses as a good man whose message has been misunderstood by "the common observer," by "the Pharisaical tradition" which disregards the true intent of the Law, by "the Jewish obstinacy" in "false glosses that deprav'd the Law," and by seventeenth-century pamphleteers who set him among the crew of the Anabaptists, *"not onely* dipping Moses *the divine Lawgiver, but dashing with a high hand against the justice and purity of God himself."*[40] Moses was the first to announce the new dispensation of the Covenant of Grace, though obscurely and indistinctly (CM, XVI, 99, 103, 113). Afterwards Christ clarified the Law's obscurity and revealed the true Mosaic intention (CM, XV, 113).

Into the turmoil of misunderstanding and misinterpretation that confuses Moses' words, Christ always descends. He is Moses' only authoritative interpreter. As Milton remarks: "Ye have an author great beyond exception, *Moses;* and one yet greater, he who hedg'd in from abolishing every smallest jot and tittle contained in that Law, with a more accurat and lasting Masoreth, then either the Synagogue of *Ezra,* or the *Galilean* school at *Tiberias* hath left us" (*Doctrine and Discipline of Divorce,* YP, II, 230–31).

Just as Christ is required to complete Moses' meaning, so is he required to complete his mission. It is no surprise that the exclusively positive features of Moses' life are disclosed in those accounts which stress his marvelous birth. Milton recognizes Moses' life as an example of fortunate beginnings ("That Shepherd, who first taught the chosen Seed, / In the Beginning") and incomplete endings ("And therefore shall not Moses . . . his people into *Canaan* lead" (*PL* XII, 307, 309). In *An Apology Against A Pamphlet,* he drops abruptly his astringent style to offer a moving account of Moses' faith in ultimate fulfillment in Christ:

what reward had the faith of *Moses* an eye to? He that had forsaken all the greatnesse of *Egypt,* and chose a troublesome journey in his old age through the Wildernesse, and yet arriv'd not at his journies end: His faithfull eyes were fixt upon that incorruptible reward, promis'd to *Abraham* and his seed in the *Messiah,* hee sought a heav'nly reward which could make him happy, and never hurt him, and to such a reward every good man may have a respect. (YP, I, 950)

In the invocations of *Paradise Lost,* the narrator asks the Holy Spirit to clarify his obscurity ("What in me is dark / Illumine") and to find him a Christian audience that will understand the true intent of his words ("fit audience find, though few"). The narrator prays for the successful end to his journey: the completion of a great epic poem. The confidence of the beginning gives way to fear that the poet will fall short. The sense of strain is explicit in the lyrical prologue to Book IX, where the narrator prays for style answerable to his great argument and fears lest

> an age too late, or cold
> Climate, or Years damp my intended wing
> Deprest; and much they may, if all be mine,
> Not Hers who brings it nightly to my Ear.          (IX, 44–47)

Here the immense effort of flight is evoked by the image of a bird, which manages to support itself only by the ceaseless beating of its wings. The fear that cultural decline, cold climate, and old age may prevent his success is aggravated by the narrator's acute sense of the possibility of the withholding of inspiration. A waning of the narrator's powers is suggested by the transition from references to sight in the opening invocations to the reference to hearing in this prologue. The narrator no longer sees the Holy Light; he must depend entirely on the narration of his muse. Yet this dependence on a divine source is a sign of spiritual development in *Paradise Lost*. As Barbara K. Lewalski indicates, the transition from vision to narration in Michael's presentation of history symbolizes Adam's initial revelation through faith of a covenantal relationship with God.[41]

In *Paradise Lost*, the narrator retells Moses' historical narrative and depends on the Holy Spirit to transform that narrative by revealing its Christian meaning. The poem, then, is an implicit prayer for understanding. Milton himself reminds us: "It is not necessary that our prayers should be always audible; the silent supplication of the mind, whispers, even groans and inarticulate exclamations in private prayer, are available. *Exod.* xiv.15. 'Jehovah said unto Moses, Wherefore criest thou unto me?' though he was saying nothing with his lips, and only praying inwardly" (*Christian Doctrine*, CM, XVII, 87). In *Paradise Lost*, the Son hears the prayer of our first parents, who "sighs now breath'd / Unutterable" (XI, 5–6), and he intercedes on their behalf:

> Now therefore bend thine ear
> To supplication, hear his sighs though mute;
> Unskilful with what words to pray, let mee

> Interpret for him, mee his Advocate
> And propitiation, all his works on mee
> Good or not good ingraft, my Merit those
> Shall perfet, and for these my Death shall pay.          (XI, 30–36)

The Son, in his later role as Christ the Savior, transforms sighs and mute longing into articulate prayer, just as he transforms the mercy-seat of the Law (*PL* XI, 2; Exodus xxv, 17–23) into himself by serving as the true Propitiation (*PL* XI, 34; Romans iii, 25). William Guild identifies the "Mercy-Seat or Propitiatory" with Christ, and Samuel Mather interprets similarly: "*The Mercy-seat* which was upon the Ark, was a Type of the *Passive Obedience* and Satisfaction of Jesus Christ for our Sins, whom God hath set forth to be . . . *a Propitiation.*"[42]

The problem in *Paradise Lost* of communicating complex truth, which affects even the angels Raphael and Michael, is compounded for the epic narrator by the introduction of sin. A sense of anxiety about the ultimate incommunicability of his narrative is apparent at certain moments: in the doubts that attend the expression of the Holy Name; in the slow advances toward an understanding of God's judgment on the serpent; and, most striking of all, in the oblique and partial rendering of the new dispensation, "obscurely . . . foretold" (XII, 543) in a few lines near the end of the poem.

The narrator of *Paradise Lost*, involved in the necessary obscurities of figurative language, can be understood at least partly in relation to Moses, whose own cloudy formulations in the Old Testament must be understood by the Christian reader with the help of the Holy Spirit. That Moses' Law must always be interpreted in light of the Christian history of redemption is clear from Milton's observation in a chapter of *Christian Doctrine* (I, xxx) that the one true sense of the Old Testament is a combination of the historical and the typological (CM, XVI, 263). Of significance for *Paradise Lost* is the iterated emphasis in this chapter treating the Holy Scriptures on the transforming power of the Holy Spirit. In the dialectic of the chapter, the external Scripture of the written page is balanced by the internal Scripture, "WRITTEN . . . BY THE HOLY SPIRIT IN THE HEARTS OF BELIEVERS" (CM, XVI, 113, 269, 271). As Milton remarks: "We have, particularly under the gospel, a double scripture. There is the external scripture of the written word and the internal scripture of the Holy Spirit which he, according to God's promise, has engraved upon the hearts of believers, and which is certainly not to be neglected" (YP, VI, 587; CM, XVI, 273). For Milton, then, Scripture is as much process and experience as it is written record: "Hence, although the external ground which we possess for our belief at the present day in the written word is highly important, . . . that which is internal, and the peculiar possession of each believer, is far superior to all, namely, the Spirit itself" (CM, XVI, 275).

In *Paradise Lost*, as in Scripture, the operation of the Holy Spirit upon us is required if we are to effect the transformations that constitute a correct reading. As a poet, Milton refines his prayer for transformation into a sophisticated narrative device. The expansiveness of the mind's topography is the result of a sense of distance that is encouraged by a perspective of typological mediation. Thus Milton turns to poetic advantage John Calvin's observation on Moses and the Law: the ceremonies and institutions of the Law "were not to be rested in, unless we would stand at a stay in the middle way, making no reckoning to come to the marke."[43] Scripture is, in John Bunyan's image, a compass, pointing to Christ the pole, allowing pilgrims to plot their course "from Sin to Grace."[44]

We are familiar with Milton's employment of a typological method in the last books of *Paradise Lost*, which are heavily indebted to the eleventh chapter of Hebrews. The implied hope in those books is that Christ will invade the poem, fulfilling and superseding his types and transforming our vision in the process. I should like to conclude this paper by suggesting that the weight of multiple signification and progressively unfolding implication is first felt in the opening invocation of *Paradise Lost*, when the poet introduces the figure of Moses, "That Shepherd, who first taught the chosen Seed." At this point the reader is not permitted to rest with Moses "in the middle way." He is forced "to come to the marke" which is Christ. The reader is directed by the Holy Spirit from the "secret top / Of *Oreb* or of *Sinai*" to "*Sion* Hill," the "flaming Mount, whose top / Brightness had made invisible" (*PL* V, 598-99). There the Son is exalted: "Yet have I set my King upon my holy hill of Zion" (Psalm ii, 6). The same Holy Spirit, present from the first, who transforms Sinai into Sion, Moses' Covenant of Law into Christ's Covenant of Grace, and darkness into light, is asked to transform as well the poem, the reader, and the poet himself.

Georgetown University

NOTES

1. See Anne Davidson Ferry, "The Bird and the Blind Bard," in her *Milton's Epic Voice: The Narrator in Paradise Lost* (Cambridge, Mass., 1967), pp. 20-43; Louis L. Martz, *The Paradise Within* (New Haven, 1964), pp. 105-10; and especially William G. Riggs, *The Christian Poet in Paradise Lost* (Berkeley and Los Angeles, 1972), passim. The inevitable experiential result of Riggs' argument that "the epic characters of Milton's poem are drawn with continued reference to the poet" (p. 1) is an awareness of the argument's reciprocal nature: we see the characters in the narrator as surely as we see him in them.

2. " 'That Shepherd Who First Taught the Chosen Seed': A Note on Milton's Mosaic Inspiration," *UTQ*, VIII (1939), 403-19.

3. *John Milton: Complete Poems and Major Prose*, ed. Merritt Y. Hughes (New York, 1957), p. 211. Parenthetic line references to Milton's poetry are to this edition.

4. Hanford, " 'That Shepherd Who First Taught the Chosen Seed,' " p. 415.

5. *The Harmonious Vision: Studies in Milton's Poetry* (Baltimore, 1970), p. 136.

6. Philo, *Questions in Exodus*, trans. Ralph Marcus, Supplement to *Philo*, Loeb Classical Library (London, 1964), vol. II, p. 102. See also Flavius Josephus, *Jewish Antiquities*, trans. H. St. J. Thackeray, Loeb Classical Library (New York, 1930), vol. IV, p. 289.

7. *De Genesi ad Litteram*, in *Corpus scriptorum ecclesiasticorum latinorum*, ed. Joseph Zycha (Leipzig, 1894), vol. XXVIII, pp. 203 ff.

8. See *From Shadowy Types to Truth: Studies in Milton's Symbolism* (New Haven, 1968), pp. 85-144.

9. *The Poetical Works of John Milton*, ed. Henry J. Todd (London, 1809), vol. IV, p. 5.

10. *The Christian Doctrine*, in *The Works of John Milton*, gen. ed. Frank Allen Patterson (New York, 1931-38), vol. XVII, p. 55; hereafter cited as CM with volume and page number. See also CM, XV, 365.

11. *Areopagitica*, in *Complete Prose Works of John Milton*, gen. ed. Don M. Wolfe (New Haven, 1953-), vol. II, pp. 507-08; hereafter cited as YP with volume and page number.

12. *A Defence of the People of England*, YP, IV, 345. See also *Tetrachordon*, YP, II, 593, 646-47.

13. *De Vita Mosis*, in *Philo*, trans. F. H. Colson, Loeb Classical Library, vol. VI, pp. 287-89. Colson notes that the regular school course of the Greeks would include grammar or literature and rhetoric.

14. "The Hebrew Hexameter: A Study in Renaissance Sources and Interpretation," *ELH*, II (1935), 66-91. The best recent study of the church fathers' association of

Moses with the earliest Greek philosophers and poets is by Don Cameron Allen in *Mysteriously Meant* (Baltimore, 1970). Allen examines the belief of the early Christian apologists that "Moses . . . is the source of all Greek philosophy" (p. 3), and he discusses Eusebius' identification of Moses with Musaeus and Hermes (pp. 108–09).

15. *The Famous and Memorable Works of Josephus,* trans. Thomas Lodge (London, 1609), vol. I, p. 252.

16. *The Defence of Poetry,* in *Sir Philip Sidney: Selected Prose and Poetry,* ed. Robert Kimbrough (San Francisco, 1969), p. 110.

17. *Reason of Church-Government,* YP, I, 816. See also *Paradise Regained* IV, 334–49.

18. Andrew Willet, *Hexapla in Exodum* (London, 1608), vol. II, p. 210.

19. *A Commentarie Upon the Fourth Booke of Moses, called Numbers* (London, 1618), p. 847.

20. Fisch, "Hebraic Style and Motifs in *Paradise Lost,*" in *Language and Style in Milton,* ed. Ronald D. Emma and John T. Shawcross (New York, 1967), pp. 30–64; John T. Shawcross, "*Paradise Lost* and the Theme of Exodus," in *Milton Studies,* II, ed. James D. Simmonds (Pittsburgh, 1970), pp. 3–26.

21. *De Vita Mosis,* Loeb Classical Library, vol. VI, pp. 357–59. See also vol. II, pp. 471–73.

22. That Philo was not alone in ascribing to Moses the tripartite office is proven by the exhaustive scholarship of Wayne Meeks in *The Prophet-King: Moses Traditions and the Johannine Christology* (Leiden, 1967).

23. *Jewish Antiquities,* Loeb Classical Library, vol. IV, p. 11.

24. Ibid., vol. IV, p. 13.

25. Eusebius, *Praeparatio Evangelica,* ix. 29, in *Eusebii Pamphili, Evangelicae Praeparationis,* trans. E. H. Gifford (Oxford, 1903), vol. III, p. 469. See also the account in Clement of Alexandria, *Stromata, Patrologiae . . . Series Graeca,* ed. J.-P. Migne (Paris, 1857), vol. VIII, p. 902. For evidence of Milton's familiarity with Clement's *Stromata* in the edition of the *Opera* published by Carolus Morellus (Paris, 1629), see James Holly Hanford, "Milton's Private Studies," in his *John Milton: Poet and Humanist* (Cleveland, 1966), p. 86.

26. Eusebius, *Evangelicae Praeparationis,* vol. III, pp. 469–70. Here Moses is told that his mind will "survey all things in time, past, present, and to come." For Moses as a paradigm of the soul seeking heavenly mysteries, see Origen, *In Leviticum Homilia, Patrologiae . . . Series Graeca,* vol. XII, p. 544; and, in the same volume, *In Numeros Homilia,* p. 630.

27. "The Theme of *Paradise Lost,* Book III," in *New Essays on Paradise Lost,* ed. Thomas Kranidas (Berkeley and Los Angeles, 1969), p. 58.

28. YP, II, 555–56. A topical gloss of the biblical passage, to which Milton would undoubtedly have assented, is provided by William Attersoll in his *Commentarie Upon . . . Numbers:* "Hee [Joshua] was too much addicted to the person of his master, as many hearers are to their teachers . . . as in our dayes, many conceive too highly of *Luther,* otherwise a very worthy man: howbeit *Moses* tendring the good of all the people more than his owne glory, reproveth his corrupt affection . . . and sheweth a contrary disposition in himselfe, desiring that all the Lords people could prophesie. . . . Heere we see what *Joshua* would have *Moses* do: he counselleth him to restraine them. A young man, young counsell" (pp. 540–42).

29. *Christian Doctrine,* CM, XVI, 111. See also John Trapp, on Deuteronomy xxxi, 3, in *A Commentary or Exposition upon the Five Books of Moses* (1662; reprint

232 MILTON STUDIES

ed., London, 1867), p. 316; William Guild, *Moses Unvailed* (London, 1620): "Moses led the people onely into the sight of *Canaan*, and unto the borders thereof, but gave them not possession therein: but our Mediatour and Messiah hath purchased the same unto his Chosen, and hath gone before to prepare a place for us in that celestiall *Canaan*, that wee may possesse the same peaceably after the day of our dissolution" (p. 53).

30. *From Shadowy Types To Truth*, p. 19. An extended attack on Platonic and neo-Platonic Moses traditions appears on pp. 74–75 and 81–82.

31. Ibid., p. 83.

32. *The Figures or Types of the Old Testament* (Dublin, 1683; reprint ed., London, 1705), p. 93.

33. See the citations of, *inter alios*, Jerome, Ambrose, and Gregory of Nyssa, in Andrew Willet's *Hexapla in Exodum*, pp. 284–87, 443–47; John Calvin, *Commentaries on Exodus*, trans. John King (Edinburgh, 1847), vol. III, p. 315.

34. *Moses Unvailed*, sig. A₃.

35. *Christ Revealed* (London, 1635), p. 45.

36. *Sermo CXXXVII, Sermone De Scripturis, Patrologia Latina*, vol. XXXVIII, p. 758.

37. *From Shadows to Reality*, trans. Dom Wulstan Hibberd (London, 1960), p. 160.

38. *Moses Unvailed*, p. 52.

39. I prefer the translation of this passage in the new version of *Christian Doctrine* by John Carey, YP, VI, 431. The passage is also found in CM, XV, 287.

40. *Seriatim: Tetrachordon*, YP, II, 660; *Doctrine and Discipline of Divorce*, YP, II, 307, 319; *Tetrachordon*, YP, II, 583.

41. "Structure and the Symbolism of Vision in Michael's Prophecy, *Paradise Lost*, Books XI–XII," *PQ*, XLII (1963), 29–32.

42. Guild, *Moses Unvailed*, p. 99; Mather, *Figures or Types of the Old Testament*, p. 408.

43. *Jean Calvin, A commentarie on the whole epistle to the Hebrewes*, trans. C. Cotton (London, 1605), p. 5.

44. *The Pilgrim's Progress*, ed. James B. Wharey (Oxford, 1928), p. 298; cited by Roland M. Frye, in the course of a full examination of the doctrine of accommodation (*God, Man, and Satan* [Princeton, 1960], pp. 143–44).

# *PARADISE LOST* AND
# THE MYTH OF PROHIBITION

## *Michael Lieb*

In accord with the J text of Genesis, Milton incorporates into *Paradise Lost* the mythic and nonrational elements implicit in the prohibition against eating the fruit. In so doing, he formulates a view of the prohibition that at once dismisses the prevailing rationalist interpretation based upon a covenant theology and embraces a nonrationalist outlook that has ties with something associated with a covenant theology. This nonrationalist perspective allows Milton to exploit the mythic propensities latent in the prohibition. It allows him to conceive of the prohibition as a taboo, an approach decidedly in keeping with his anthropological approach implicit in *Christian Doctrine*. Through this outlook, all that surrounds the prohibition in *Paradise Lost* has affinities with cultic phenomena well known to the Renaissance. Accordingly, *Paradise Lost* embodies a "Theologia *Adamica*" that gives rise to the "*cultum institutum*" of all races. In that way, it reflects a view of sacred and profane that has ties with the Levitical code but that retains its essentially archaic and mythic basis.

## I

WHEN, IN the proem to Book I of *Paradise Lost*, Milton directs our attention to "Mans First Disobedience, and the Fruit / Of that Forbidden Tree" (I, 1–2),[1] he has in mind none other than Genesis ii, 16–17: "And the Lord commanded the man, saying, Of every tree of the garden thou mayest freely eat: But of the tree of the knowledge of good and evil, thou shalt not eat of it: for in the day that thou eatest thereof thou shalt surely die." That command forms the basis of the J or Jahwistic document of the Genesis account. Extending from Genesis ii, 5, to iii, 24, the J document is remarkably distinct from the P or Priestly document that precedes it. Whereas the P document, extending from Genesis i, 1, to ii, 4, is nothing more than a straightforward chronicle of the work of the six days, the J document is a complex narrative whose very origins are mythical "not only in the strictly anthropological sense of the term, but also in the vaguer poetic sense."[2] Indeed, as John M. Evans states, J is "a full-blooded, myth" with legendary and cultic elements that were "probably old even at the time the Jahwist was writing." Derived from an "ancient religious tradition," these elements exhibit an "incomplete assimilation into the structure of a monotheistic and ethical theology which makes some of J's features so puzzling."[3]

Not the least of these puzzling elements is the command not to eat of the interdicted tree. That command appears all the more puzzling when compared with the command issued to man in the P document: "Be fruitful, and multiply, and replenish the earth, and subdue it: and have dominion over the fish of the sea, and over the fowl of the air, and over every living thing that moveth upon the earth" (Genesis i, 28). Compared with the P command, which benevolently instructs man to follow his natural inclinations, the J command rather ominously prohibits man from following those inclinations. The one is self-evident in its rationale, the other decidedly perplexing.

Appropriately, the rationale for what we have defined as the J command became the subject of discourse from the time of the church fathers to the biblical exegetes of the Renaissance. Determined to make "sense" of the command, they almost universally appropriated it into a covenant theology founded upon natural law, on the one hand, and moral law, on the other. Thus, from the first point of view, we find Henry Vane, in *The Retired Mans Meditations* (London, 1655), maintaining that "when we speak of this Covenant in reference to the state of innocency, it is to be understood for the same thing with the law of nature, under which *Adam* was created" (pp. 60–61). From the second point of view, we find Andrew Willet, in *Hexapla in Genesin* (London, 1605), maintaining that "this precept . . . containeth the very foundation of all precepts, and of the whole morall law" (p. 33). Willet has in mind here Tertullian's assertion in *An Answer to the Jews* that God's divine command contains

in embryo [*condita*] all the precepts which afterwards sprouted forth when given through Moses; that is, Thou shalt love the Lord thy God from thy whole heart and out of thy whole soul; Thou shalt love thy neighbour as thyself; Thou shalt not kill; Thou shalt not commit adultery; Thou shalt not steal; False witness thou shalt not utter; Honour thy father and mother; and, That which is another's shalt thou not covet. For the primordial law was given to Adam and Eve in paradise, as the womb of all the precepts of God.[4]

In *A Treatise of the Divine Promises* (London, 1633), Edward Leigh sums up both points of view when he says that God's first prohibition constituted both a "*Faedus Naturale*, the *Covenant* of nature, because it was made by God with man at his first Creation, and because it is contained in the Law which is known to men by nature; and [a] *Faedus Legale*, the *Covenant* of workes, because workes were the condition of it" (p. 63). It was customary to combine the two laws, because they were both universally seen as having been founded upon the same principle. In his discussion of the written and unwritten laws in *Christian Doctrine*, Milton himself reflects that outlook when he says that "the law of nature has the same obligatory force, and is intended to serve the same purposes as the law of Moses."[5] It is an outlook that is given full expression by Robert Rollock in *A Treatise of Gods Effectual Calling* (London, 1603): "The couenant of workes, which may also be called a legall or natural couenant, is founded in nature, which by creation was pure and holy, and in the law of God, which in the first creation was ingrauen in mans hart" (p. 66). Both laws, in turn, are tied by the bond of reason. If Milton sees in the law of nature the expression of "right reason" (*Christian Doctrine*, CM, XV, 117), he sees in the moral law the expression of "morall reason" (*Doctrine and Discipline of Divorce*, CM, III, 410). As he says in *Brief Notes*, "that which is grounded on the light of nature or right reason [is] commonly call'd *moral law*" (CM, VI, 158). From that point of view, he maintains in *The Doctrine and Discipline of Divorce* that "what is against nature is against Law . . .: by this reckning *Moses* should bee most unmosaick, that is, most illegal, not to say most unnaturall" (CM, III, 458).

But this is precisely Milton's attitude in *Christian Doctrine* toward what is implied by God's issuing of the divine command. Taking into account both natural and moral law in his consideration of that command, Milton adopts a position that runs counter to the prevailing outlook. Of natural law, he says:

Seeing, however, that man was made in the image of God, and had the whole law of nature so implanted and innate in him, that he needed no precept

to enforce its observance, it follows, that if he received any additional commands. . . . these commands formed no part of the law of nature, which
is sufficient of itself to teach whatever is agreeable to right reason, that is
to say, whatever is intrinsically good. (CM, XV, 115–17)

Of moral law, he maintains that, although the divine command "is
sometimes called 'the covenant of works,' . . . it does not appear
from any passage of Scripture to have been either a covenant, or
of works. No works whatever were required of Adam; a particular
act only was forbidden" (CM, XV, 113). Milton's treatment of the
divine command, then, categorically dismisses both laws and, in so
doing, dismisses the principles upon which those laws are based. As
such, the command becomes for Milton "an act in its own nature
indifferent [*neque bonum in se esset, neque malum*]." "For since it
was the disposition of man to do what was right, as a being naturally
good and holy, it was not necessary that he should be bound by
the obligation of a covenant to perform that to which he was of himself
inclined; nor would he have given any proof of obedience by the
performance of works to which he was led by a natural impulse,
independently of the divine command" (CM, XV, 113–15).

At the same time, however, Milton refers elsewhere in *Christian
Doctrine* to the divine command as that which may be classifiable
with what he calls "contingent decrees" founded upon "implied conditions": "If thou stand, thou shalt abide in Paradise; if thou fall, thou
shalt be cast out; if thou eat not the forbidden fruit, thou shalt live;
if thou eat, thou shalt die" (CM, XIV, 69, 81). It is within this context
that the fallen Adam complains of God's justice in *Paradise Lost:*

> inexplicable
> Thy Justice seems; yet to say truth, too late,
> I thus contest; then should have been refus'd
> Those terms whatever, when they were propos'd:
> Thou didst accept them; wilt thou enjoy the good,
> Then cavil the conditions?                    (X, 755–59)

Despite Milton's declaration that the divine command is not a covenant
but "an exercise of jurisdiction" since "no command . . . can properly
be called a covenant, even where rewards and punishments are attached
to it" (*Christian Doctrine*, CM, XV, 115), that command embodies
even for him something that resembles a covenant psychology. Indeed,
he actually refers to the command as a "covenant" ("*in foedere, sive*

*mandata accipiendo"*) whose violation involves none other than "a transgression of the whole law" "written by Moses . . . long subsequent" to "the special command which proceeded out of the mouth of God" (CM, XV, 179–83).

What does this leave us with, then? It leaves us, on the one hand, with a dismissal of a covenant theology based upon moral and natural law as those laws are bound by the principle of reason and, on the other, with the acceptance of something associated with a covenant theology founded upon the "implied conditions" of "contingent decrees." That is, it leaves us with a command at once "unmosaick," "illegal," and "unnaturall," and at the same time indebted to the conditional terms of the Mosaic outlook. The result is a point of view that emphasizes the extralegal nature of the command while maintaining its dispensational ties. If such is the case, then, any consideration of the divine command must take into account a point of view that is decidedly complex. The way in which that view functions in Milton's thought will become clear if we explore further the implications of the divine command.

As a command that is "unmosaick," "illegal," and "unnaturall," the prohibition against eating the fruit has absolutely no basis for Milton in anything that governs rational behavior as that behavior is determined by natural or moral law. Having categorically dismissed natural and moral law as the underlying principle of the first prohibition, Milton postulates a situation in which a command is issued in order to impose upon man a deliberately arbitrary injunction that *by its very nature* runs counter to the dictates of human reason. Milton is unequivocal on this point. The arbitrariness of the command, its irrationality, is attested to by the fact that for Milton the idea of not eating of the tree of the knowledge of good and evil "would not have been obligatory on any one, had there been no law to enjoin or prohibit it" (*Christian Doctrine*, CM, XV, 117). Only the prohibition itself, imposed quite arbitrarily from without, makes the tree off limits. As Milton states in *Tetrachordon*, "For albeit our first parent had lordship over sea, and land, and aire, yet there was a law without him, as a guard set over him" (CM, IV, 74).

Were it not for this prohibition, man might very well have eaten of the tree, as he ate of the others, and suffered no punishment as a consequence. But because of the prohibition, the tree becomes forbid-

den, a circumstance which causes to attach to it the experience of
the fallen world, what God calls in *Paradise Lost* the "knowledge
of Good lost, and Evil got" (XI, 87). And after such knowledge what
forgiveness? "Be lowlie wise," Raphael admonishes Adam; "Think
onely what concerns thee and thy being" (VIII, 173-74). What the
fruit of the tree appears to offer does not concern Adam and his
being. Man's reason concerns other matters. The reason underlying
the prohibition is not for man to know: that reason is God's, not man's.
As Richard Hooker states in the *Laws of Ecclesiastical Polity*, "To
find out *supernatural laws*, there is no natural way, because they have
not their foundation or ground in the course of nature. Such was the
law before Adam's fall, which required abstinence from the tree of
knowledge touching good and evil. For by his reason, he could not
have found out this law, inasmuch as the only commandment of God
did make it necessary and not the necessity thereof procure it to be
commanded."[6] Although she slights God's prohibition by calling it
"Sole Daughter of his voice" (*PL* IX, 653), even Eve is aware of the
fundamental distinction between "supernatural" and "natural" law.
Distinguishing between what Milton earlier calls that "one restraint"
and the fact that she and Adam are otherwise "Lords of the World
besides" (I, 32), she says, "the rest, we live / Law to our selves, our
Reason is our Law" (IX, 653-54). God's reason, Eve thereby implies,
is his own law, to be obeyed because God is God.

From that point of view, the prohibition functions as a means
of establishing or testing man's ability to obey even that which is
arbitrarily imposed and to believe in the justness of that imposition
(*Christian Doctrine*, CM, XV, 115).[7] As God says to Adam, the interdicted tree becomes "The Pledge of thy Obedience and thy Faith"
(*PL* VIII, 325). Since the "seat of faith," Milton states in *Christian
Doctrine*, "is not in the understanding, but in the will" (CM, XV,
407), to obey the command becomes an act of the will, not of the
understanding. However, in refusing to compromise one's faith, Milton would maintain, one paradoxically demonstrates not only his freedom to choose but his ability to understand. As God states in *Paradise
Lost:*

> Freely they stood who stood, and fell who fell.
> Not free, what proof could they have given sincere
> Of true allegiance, constant Faith or Love,

> Where onely what they needs must do, appeard,
> Not what they would? what praise could they receive?
> What pleasure I from such obedience paid,
> When Will and Reason (Reason also is choice)
> Useless and vain, of freedom both despoild,
> Made passive both, had serv'd necessitie,
> Not mee.                                    (III, 102-11)

Ironically, Satan leads man precisely to the point of relinquishing his freedom, his power of choice, and thus his ability to reason, by tempting man to question the rational basis of what is deliberately without reason. He leads man, that is, to assume his own posture toward the divine command, a posture he assumes early in the epic after he has overheard Adam and Eve speak of the injunction:

> all is not theirs it seems:
> One fatal Tree there stands of Knowledge call'd,
> Forbidden them to taste: Knowledge forbidd'n?
> Suspicious, reasonless. Why should thir Lord
> Envie them that? can it be sin to know,
> Can it be death? and do they onely stand
> By Ignorance, is that thir happie state,
> The proof of thir obedience and thir faith?          (IV, 513-20)

Although Satan obviously misinterprets the motives behind the issuing of the command, his reaction is perfectly in keeping with the nature of the command as that which is deliberately "reasonless," even upon initial scrutiny "suspicious." It is precisely this "reasonlessness," this "suspiciousness," that Satan capitalizes upon in order to destroy man: "O fair foundation laid whereon to build / Thir ruin!" (IV, 521-22). He establishes that foundation, of course, by attributing to God those very motives that characterize his own personality—envy and jealousy. "Why then was this forbid?" asks the Tempter of Eve. "Why but to awe, / Why but to keep ye low and ignorant, / His worshippers" (IX, 703-05). In this sense, God becomes the "Threatner" (IX, 687), the "great Forbidder, safe with all his Spies" (IX, 815).

If this response to God runs directly counter to the doctrinal view that Milton establishes in *Paradise Lost*, it, like Satan's response to the divine command, has an ironic appropriateness. For it recalls none other than the Jahwistic Deity of the J document, as opposed to the Elohistic Deity of the P document. Whereas the Elohistic Deity is fundamentally an idea, the conceptualized expression of an elevated and sophisticated theology, the Jahwistic Deity is a "person" portrayed vividly and pictorially.[8] As such, the Jahwistic Deity betrays a personality whose "shortcomings" seem to be "more human than divine." "Appear[ing] to be jealous in denying his creatures knowledge," he is "envious and fearful in His desire to prevent them from . . . becoming like Him."[9]

Although the Deity of *Paradise Lost* is far removed in this respect from the Jahwistic Deity of the J document, he shares the same decidedly anthropomorphic characteristics that distinguish *Jahweh* from *Elohim*. Nowhere is this fact more dramatically apparent than in God's issuing of the divine command in *Paradise Lost*. As Adam recalls of God:

> Sternly he pronounc'd
> The rigid interdiction, which resounds
> Yet dreadful in mine ear, though in my choice
> Not to incur; but soon his cleer aspect
> Return'd and gracious purpose thus renew'd.     (VIII, 333–37)

Here, as elsewhere in *Paradise Lost*, the anthropomorphisms of the J document are dramatically apparent. Indebted to the anthropomorphic presence of God throughout the Old Testament, this vision of the Deity is, of course, perfectly in keeping with Milton's view of God as expressed in *Christian Doctrine:* "Our safest way is to form in our minds such a conception of God, as shall correspond with his own delineation and representation of himself in the sacred writings" (CM, XIV, 31). "If God habitually assign to himself the members and form of man, why," asks Milton, "should we be afraid of attributing to him what he attributes to himself?" (CM, XIV, 35). In that sense, "let us believe that it is not beneath the dignity of God to grieve in that for which he is grieved, or to be refreshed in that which refresheth him, or to fear in that he feareth. For however we may attempt to soften down such expressions by a latitude of interpretation, when applied to the Deity, it comes in the end to precisely the same" (CM, XIV, 35).

Such a view does much to legitimate the primitive resonances to which the issuing of the divine command gives rise in *Paradise Lost*. Rather than "softening down" those resonances, Milton intensifies them. For example, he assimilates into the prohibition the strictures not only against eating of the interdicted tree but against *touching* the fruit of that tree. Biblical precedent for that point of view may be found, of course, in Eve's statement to the serpent in Genesis iii, 3: "But of the fruit of the tree which *is* in the midst of the garden, God hath said, Ye shall not eat of it, neither shall ye touch it, lest ye die." From the very beginning, exegetes never tired of pointing to the fact that "touching" of the fruit had nothing at all to do with God's original prohibition to Adam in Genesis ii, 16–17. Either Adam himself communicated that aspect of the interdiction to Eve or Eve made it up at the time of the temptation. In either case, the addition of this further restriction was both unprecedented and unnecessary. Thus, according to the *Aboth de Rabbi Nathan*, the addition of that restriction was like making "a fence higher than the object which it is to guard," with the result that "the fence fell and crushed the plants."[10] That is, by adding to the prohibition, man helped pave the way for his own undoing.[11]

For Milton, on the other hand, the restriction against touching becomes a natural extension of the divine command, one that deliberately intensifies the rigor of its bearing. Although we never directly witness the pronouncement of that restriction to man by God or his messengers, Milton implies clearly enough that it is the office of the "affable Arch-Angel" to make sure that man is "Charg'd not to touch the interdicted Tree" (*PL* VII, 41–46). Touching and tasting, in a sense, become interchangeable, two acts derived from the same root, one *tangere* that implies them both. Thus, when Eve is tempted by Satan, she invokes the two acts as if they embodied one forbidden act: "But of this Tree we may not taste nor touch" (IX, 651) and "God hath said, Ye shall not eat / Thereof, nor shall ye touch it, least ye die" (IX, 662–63). Adam's initial response to Eve's transgression, in turn, not only reflects but elaborates upon that point of view: "Much more to taste it under bann to touch" (IX, 925). But Adam does not stop there: he carries the interdiction still further by suggesting that even looking upon or "coveting to Eye" the fruit represents a daring and perilous affront (IX, 921–23). From that point of view, the inherent "reasonlessness" of the command is additionally reinforced to the extent that the interdiction against tasting comes to involve both touching and seeing as well.

If such is the case, then the threatened punishment of violating the interdiction is perfectly in accord with what becomes, after all, most "unmosaick," "illegal," and "unnaturall." Within this context, God warns Adam that "The day thou eat'st thereof, my sole command / Transgrest, inevitably thou shalt dye" (VIII, 329–30). Despite the fact that God qualifies the warning by explaining that to "dye" means to be both "mortal" and "expell'd from hence into a World / Of woe and sorrow" (VIII, 331–33), Adam does not know in any absolute sense the meaning of death. Under the circumstances, his response to the threatened punishment is quite appropriate: "What ere Death is, / Som dreadful thing no doubt" (IV, 425–26). Thus Adam is not only given an arbitrary prohibition not to eat (and, by implication, touch and even look upon) that which would be acceptable under any other circumstances, but he is warned that, if he disobeys the prohibition, he will suffer a punishment the true signification of which he has absolutely no idea.

To understand the full impact of what God has imposed upon Adam, we might render the situation in the following terms: "Do not touch the tip of your left ear with your right forefinger, or else you will *squibbledydib*." Our response, like Adam's, would appropriately be, "what ere *squibbledydib* is, / Som dreadful thing no doubt." I project the situation in these terms not to make fun of it but to indicate the true nature of its reasonlessness. At its very source, *Paradise Lost* embodies a logic of illogic, a sense of nonsense. In so doing, it re-creates with deadly earnestness the irrationality of the Jahwistic account from which it is drawn.

Such a view is hardly alien to seventeenth-century thought. In his *Archaeologiae Philosophicae* (London, 1692), Thomas Burnet questions the rationality of God's caveat that disobedience of the prohibition will result in death: "*Mori!* Quid hoc rei est, inquit ignara virgo, quae nihil unquam mor tuum viderat, ne florem quidem" (p. 29).[12] In a work appropriately entitled *The Oracles of Reason* (London, 1693), Charles Blount translates Burnet's observation as follows: "Die! what does that mean, says the poor ignorant Virgin, who as yet had not seen any thing dead, no not so much as a flower" (p. 41). Although Burnet substitutes Eve (the "ignara virgo" or "poor ignorant Virgin") for Adam, the significance of the correspondence still holds. As C. S. Lewis states, the prohibition and the manner in which it is cast are quite simply "inexplicable," if not irrational,[13] but not for that any the less "dreadful."

Accordingly, Death becomes a "thing" whose "dreadfulness" is truly nightmarish: a "Goblin," "black . . . as Night / Fierce as ten Furies, terrible as Hell," a "Monster" shaking its "dreadful Dart" (*PL* II, 670–72, 688). Who would not be afraid? "Beware the Jabberwock, my son! / The jaws that bite, tha claws that catch! / Beware the Jubjub bird, and shun / The frumious Bandersnatch!" Milton veritably surrounds the disobedience of the prohibition with terror. Eden itself is enveloped in nightmare: once expelled, Adam and Eve look back to behold "thir happie seat, / Wav'd over by that flaming Brand, the Gate / With dreadful Faces throng'd and fierie Armes" (XII, 641–44; cf. Genesis iii, 24). Such are the consequences of disobeying the "rigid interdiction," the mere pronouncement of which by a stern-faced Deity resounds dreadfully in Adam's ear and still unnerves him long after it has been pronounced.

Its effects are quite in accord with the language that describes it. The word "rigid" itself tells the tale. We think of *Comus:*

> What was that snaky-headed *Gorgon* sheild
> That wise *Minerva* wore, unconquer'd virgin,
> Wherwith she freez'd her foes to congeal'd stone?
> But rigid looks of chast austerity,
> And noble grace that dash't brute violence
> With sudden adoration and blank aw.                    (447–52)

We recall once again the figure of Death in *Paradise Lost*. There, he appears with his "Mace petrific" and his "look" which binds "with Gorgonian rigor not to move" (X, 294–97). One is not certain whether he would rather be confronted by Minerva's shield with its "snaky-headed *Gorgon*" or with the "Goblin" Death with his "Mace petrific" and "*Gorgonian*" "look." In either case, the specter of violating a terrifying "rigidity" is not something that one would willingly contemplate. In the case of the "rigid interdiction," the only way of overcoming the effects of that violation is through fulfilling the momentous demands of an equally "rigid satisfaction." As God pronounces sternly in the heavenly council of Book III of *Paradise Lost:* Man "with his whole posteritie must die, / Die hee or Justice must; unless for him / Som other able, and as willing, pay / The rigid satisfaction, death for death" (III, 209–12).

As so many have recognized before, the fundamental terms upon which *Paradise Lost* is predicated are essentially archaic. Despite the complex logical superstructure of doctrinal explanation and rational discourse that characterizes Milton's epic, *Paradise Lost* retains, and even intensifies, that subimperative sense of myth that pervades the Jahwistic account of Genesis. As Wayne Shumaker maintains, *Paradise Lost* is, at its source, "an enormous 'tell-me-why' story, infinitely more complex than those told by children and savages but similar in basic nature."[14] Professor Shumaker is referring to the many *pour quoi* legends of a fall, "found everywhere in mythology," that is "regularly the effect of some transgression. For instance, among the Andaman Islanders, a Negrito people isolated for centuries in the Bay of Bengal, it resulted from the breaking of a taboo against the making of noise while the cicadas are singing. . . . As a result of the violation, say the Andamanese, 'a great storm came and killed many people, who were turned into fishes and birds.' The human survivors were dispersed, each pair being provided with a different dialect. Although reported versions of the myth vary slightly, we seem to have here an amalgam of three separate incidents in the Christian story—the fall, the deluge, and the building of Babel."[15]

## II

If invoking such a parallel seems at first glance a spurious way of underlining the so-called mythic elements in *Paradise Lost*, we would do well to remind ourselves that the attempt to bolster biblical truth through the discovery of cultural parallels was by no means new to either Milton or the Renaissance. Milton's expressed attitude toward the Fall in *Christian Doctrine* is that of a cultural anthropologist. We may take, for example, his treatment of the "principle" governing original sin and its effects upon the human race. For Milton, the truth of that principle is not only attested to by the "divine proceedings" of established doctrine but is "recognized by all nations and under all religions from the earliest period" (*Christian Doctrine*, CM, XV, 185). Drawing at once upon the testimonies of the Bible, the *History of the Peloponnesian War*, and the *Aeneid*, Milton points to the customs of the Hebrews and the Egyptians, on the one hand, and of the Greeks and the Romans, on the other, in order to establish the fact that the sins of the fathers are visited upon their offspring from one generation to the next as the result of divine enmity, which, in turn, can only be appeased through rituals of expiation (CM, XV, 184–91). "Hence," Milton states, "the penitent are enjoined to confess not only their own sins, but those of their fathers. . . . Thus also entire families become obnoxious to punishment for the guilt of their head" (CM, XV, 189).

Viewing the Genesis narrative in this way, Milton thereby attempts to establish the crosscultural basis of what he sees as religious truth. In doing so, he places himself within the tradition established by tracts ranging from Johanne Bompart's *Parallela Sacra et Profana* (Amsterdam, 1589) to John Owen's θεολογουμενα παγτοδαπα (Oxford, 1661).[16] Infused with the outlook of comparative religion, these tracts are the works of exegetes who sought to discover the universality of their own beliefs in the beliefs of other cultures. With them, Milton derives from the narrative of the Fall what John Owen calls a "Theologia *Adamica*" giving rise to the "*cultum institutum*" of all races.[17] It is precisely this cultural framework that helps establish even further the precise nature of what Milton understood as God's prohibition not to eat of the interdicted tree. For if, according to Milton, the principle governing original sin and its consequences finds expression in all cultures, the principle governing that command whose violation resulted in original sin might likewise be said to find expression in "all nations and under all religions from the earliest period." Although Milton never explicitly makes this point, his view of the command as the expression of a law totally removed from what underlies the rational dictates of natural and moral law invites a response that has its basis in cultural anthropology.

Milton hints at that approach when he suggests that God's ways in the issuing of such a command are reflected in the customs of men. Springing from what Milton calls God's "positive right," his absolute prerogative to do as he wishes, the injunction not to eat of the fruit has its counterpart for Milton in those injunctions issued when "any one invested with lawful power, commands or forbids what is in itself neither good nor bad" (*Christian Doctrine*, CM, XV, 117). Milton does not elaborate further upon the association here, but exegetes concerned specifically with what John Owen calls the "*cultum institutum*" do.[18] One thinks in particular of biblical commentators like Edward Stillingfleet. In his *Origenes Sacrae* (3rd ed., London, 1666), Stillingfleet defends the "reasonlessness" of the divine command by asking:

Hath not then a *Legislator* power to require any*thing*, but what he *satisfies* every one of his *reason* in commanding it? if so, what becomes of *obedience* and *subjection?* It will be impossible to make any *probative precepts* on this account; and the *Legislator* must be charged with the *disobedience* of his *subjects*, where he doth not give a particular *account* of every thing which he requires. [This is] contrary to all *Laws* of *Policy*, and the general sense of the world. This *Plutarch* gives a good account of when he discourseth so *rationally* of the *sobriety* which men ought to use in their inquiries into the *grounds* and *reasons* of *Gods actions; for*, saith he, *Physitians will give prescriptions without giving the patient a particular reason of every circumstance in them.* . . . *Neither have humane Laws alwayes apparent reason for them, nay, some of them are to appearance ridiculous;* for which he instanceth in that *Law* of the *Lacedemonian Ephori* . . ., to which no other reason was annexed but this . . .: *they commanded every Magistrate at the entrance of his office to shave himself, and gave this reason for it, that they might learn to obey Laws themselves.* He further instanceth, in the *Roman* custom of *manumission*, their *Laws* about *testaments, Solons Law* against *neutrality* in seditions, and concludes thence. . . . *Any one would easily find many absurdities in Laws, who doth not consider the intention of the Legislator, or the ground of what he requires.* . . . What wonder is it, if we are so puzled to give an account of the actions of men, that we *should be to seek as to those of the Deity?* This cannot be then any ground on the account of mere reason, to lay the *charge* of *mans disobedience* upon *God*, because he required from him the observance of that *positive command* of not eating of the *forbidden fruit.* (pp. 480–81)

Simply stated, Stillingfleet's approach to the divine command is that of an anthropologist who provides a rationale for the "reasonlessness" of the command by directing our attention to certain "customs" that seem to have no basis in rational behavior, such as the apparently "*ridiculous*" custom fostered by the "*Lacedemonian Ephori*" that "*every Magistrate*" must "*shave himself*" "*at the entrance of his office.*" What Stillingfleet is addressing himself to, of course, is the taboo, a phenomenon that was to become the particular concern of ethnologists in the centuries following the publication of *Origenes Sacrae*. First recorded by Captain James Cook in his 1777 voyage to the Pacific Islands, the taboo received extensive treatment in the nineteenth century by Robert Henry Codrington and others.[19] In its earliest definition, the taboo is spoken of by Captain Cook as that which "signifies that a thing is forbidden," a signification that has no basis in rational explanation.[20] Since Captain Cook's definition, the basic understanding of the taboo still prevails: it represents a "prohibition for which to the civilized mind, there is no obvious meaning."[21] "In proportion as a taboo becomes a custom and its sanctions fall into the background and are forgotten, its obligations thus transformed are one source of the categorical imperative, the distinguishing feature of which is that it is non-rational and instinctive."[22] In his own writings, Milton delighted in recounting such prohibitions. Thus, in the *History of Muscovia*, he is careful to note that one "*Antony Jenkinson*," having voyaged to "*Mosco*," "arriv'd while the Emperour was celebrating his marriage with a *Circassian* Lady; during which time the City Gates for three daies were kept shut; and all men whatsoever straitly commanded to keep within their Houses; except some of his Houshold; the cause whereof is not known" (CM, X, 372).

As the foregoing discussion has made clear, it is precisely this kind of prohibition that Renaissance exegetes who viewed the Genesis account anthropologically would apply to the divine command itself. To be sure, there are obvious differences between the prohibition that Milton cites in his *History* and the divine command of Genesis ii, 16–17. The command certainly does not give rise to a "custom" whose "sanctions fall into the background and are forgotten." As Milton's treatment of the command in *Christian Doctrine* makes clear, there is even a sense in which we can say that the "cause" of the command is "known." To use the language of Milton's *Art of Logic*, we can say that God himself is the "efficient cause" and man's ability to sustain the "test" occasioned by the command, the "final cause." Nonetheless, our discussion of Milton's understanding of the command has also shown that there is an equally compelling "reason" for maintaining that the command is one about which we can assuredly say, "the cause whereof is not known." That "reason," to continue in the language of Milton's *Logic*, is the "form" the command assumes in the world of "matter,"[23] that is, the context created by placing an interdiction against eating upon the fruit of a particular tree. The rationale underlying the context out of which these "causes" (both "formal" and "material") arise, according to Milton's point of view, is decidedly unknown: why does this particular interdiction fall upon this particular tree? Whatever the "reason," the situation is distinctly classifiable, as we have already seen, in anthropological terms. Specifically, it is a situation growing out of what Emile Durkheim in *The Elementary Forms of the Religious Life* calls a "negative cult," by which certain objects are forbidden or "withdrawn from common use" as the result of interdictions or "taboos" placed upon them.[24]

Such, of course, are the special trees of Genesis, the one taboo before the Fall, the other taboo after it. This fact contributes in part to their peculiarly "magical" quality, one that associates them with the animism that Northcote Whitridge Thomas, in his now classic essay on the taboo, suggests is an essential constituent of at least certain kinds of tabooed objects.[25] How closely such an outlook accords with Milton's handling of the special trees may, of course, be open to question. Indeed, judging by what he says in *Christian Doctrine*, that outlook would appear to run directly counter to his point of view. The tree of knowledge, for example, derives its name not from anything inherent in the tree itself but from the "event" ("*Dicta est autem scientiae boni et mali ab eventu*" ["It was called the tree of knowledge of good and evil from the event"], CM, XV, 114-15). Here, Milton's outlook seems to reflect that of St. Augustine, who says in his treatise *On Merits and Forgiveness of Sins*, whatever evil Adam and Eve brought upon themselves, the interdicted tree "did not produce it to their detriment from any noxious or pernicious quality in its fruit, but entirely from the fact of their violated disobedience."[26] It is from this point of view that Milton classifies the tree as nothing more than "a pledge, as it were, and memorial of obedience" (CM, XV, 114, 115). In the same way, the tree of life is "a symbol of eternal life" (CM, XV, 114, 115). Such, we recall, is precisely the language of *Paradise Lost*, where the trees become nothing more than "The Pledge" of "Obedience" and "Faith," on the one hand, and of "immortality," on the other (VIII, 325; IV, 200-01). It is none other than this attitude which prompts scholars such as Joseph Duncan to label the special trees of *Paradise Lost* as "chiefly physical realities."[27] How then do they become assimilated into the "*cultum institutum*" that forms the basis of the mythic point of view that we have been exploring? The answer lies in the nature of the first prohibition. With its "mythical" affinities, the prohibition causes that which is prohibited to share its mythos. Milton himself suggests something of that mythos when, discoursing upon the customs of "the Britains" in *The History of Britain*, he says that "thir Religion was governd by a sort of Priests or Magicians call'd *Druides* from the Greek name of an *Oke*, which Tree they had in greate reverence, and the *Missleto* especially grown thereon" (CM, X, 49-51).

Although Milton never directly makes the association, his tree of the knowledge of good and evil and his tree of life share much of this cultic aura. That aura has at its source "the sacred tree which figures largely in Babylonian religion."[28] There, we find "a sanctuary of the gods, 'the centre of the earth,' where was a grove 'into which no man hath entered' and . . . a famous oracle-tree, a sacred palm 'with a root of bright lapis.' "[29] "An old bilingual hymn, probably of Acadian origin, depicts the tree growing in the garden of Edin or Eden, placed by Babylonian tradition in the immediate vicinity of Eridu, a city which flourished at the mouth of the Euphrates between 3000 and 4000 B.C.: 'In Eridu a stalk grew overshadowing; in a holy place did it become green; / Its roots were of white crystal, which stretched towards the deep. . . . / Into the heart of its holy house, which spread its shade like a forest, hath no man entered.' "[30]

By drawing upon the Hesperian myth, Milton establishes a similar milieu. It is in the "groves" of Eden, after all, that the "*Hesperian Fables*" prove to be "true," that the trees actually do hang "with Golden Rind" (*PL* IV, 249–50), and that, in particular, "all amid them" stands "the Tree of Life, / High eminent, blooming Ambrosial Fruit / Of vegetable Gold" (IV, 218–20). This tree may not be precisely the one on which "The scaly harnest dragon ever keeps / His unenchanted eye," but it is close enough to the "golden tree" of myth to suggest similar associations.[31] Shakespeare's rendering of the idea in *Pericles* is particularly apt: "Before thee stands this fair Hesperides, / With golden fruit, but dangerous to be touch'd; / For death, like dragons, here affrights the hoard" (I, i, 27–29).[32] If there are no "dragons" surrounding the tree of life, there are those frightening angels assigned to "guard all passage" to that tree (*PL* XI, 120–22; XII, 641–44; Genesis iii, 24) once Adam and Eve have fallen. They certainly will not be able to steal any "golden apples" or, as Milton says, be "delude[d]" with "stol'n Fruit" (XI, 125).

If such mythic associations are true of the tree of life, they are particularly true of the tree of the knowledge of good and evil, which assumes an undeniable centrality to *Paradise Lost* because it is the object at which the divine command is first directed. That command bestows upon the tree an aura that characterizes primitive thought. In particular, it causes the tree to embody the archaic predisposition to reverence the tabooed object for the powers that are latent within it. The tree thereby assumes a magical cast by virtue of its supposedly indwelling powers. Animating and thereby sanctifying the tree, those powers, in their most archaic form, are demonic, giving rise to the idea that associates certain kinds of *jinn* or demons with trees in primitive thought. "In Hadramant," states W. Robertson Smith, "it is still dangerous to touch the Mimosa, because the spirit that resides in the plant will avenge the injury."[33] "A demonic plant of the northern Semites is the Baaras, described by Josephus . . ., which flees from those who try to grasp it, and whose touch is death."[34]

Such, we recall, is true of the interdicted tree, as Genesis introduces and *Paradise Lost* elaborates upon the relationship between touching and dying. Eve's repeated admonitions not to touch the tree in *Paradise Lost* are perfectly in accord with the primitive associations to which the magical trees of the Genesis account give rise. The *Pirkê de Rabbi Eliezer* dramatizes the situation in distinctly animistic terms: "The serpent went and touched the tree, which commenced to cry out, saying: 'Wicked One! do not touch me!' . . . The serpent went and said to the woman: 'Behold, I touched it, but I did not die; thou also mayest touch it, and thou wilt not die.' The woman went and touched the tree, and saw the angel of death coming towards her."[35] Accordingly, when Eve eats of the fruit in *Paradise Lost*, Milton depicts that event through a language that draws upon the animistic idea: Eve, says Milton, "knew not eating Death" (*PL* IX, 792), as if the "Goblin" resided in the fruit itself. As such, Eve implicitly becomes for Milton a kind of Pandora who, having disobeyed the command not to open the magic container, inadvertently allows its demonic contents to escape (IV, 714–19).

That event, in turn, brings the animistic figure of "Death into the World, and all our woe" (I, 3), as Sin and Death, "there in power before, / Once actual, now in body" (X, 586–87), fly up from the gates of hell in order to perpetuate "the Race of *Satan*" (X, 385–86) on earth. Adam and Eve, commanded to "*Encrease and multiply*" (X, 730), are their vehicles. Indeed, Eve, "deflourd" (IX, 901) by her fall, becomes Death's "consort" (IX, 954), through whom all that she and Adam "eat or drink, or shall beget, / Is propogated curse" (X, 728–29). In animistic terms, the consequences of the transgression are cosmic indeed: "Earth felt the wound, and Nature from her seat / Sighing through all her Works gave signs of woe, / That all was lost" (IX, 782–84), while the "Skie lowr'd, and muttering Thunder, som sad drops / Wept at compleating of the mortal Sin / Original" (IX, 1002–04).

Ironically, Eve's immediate response to her transgression fosters, in a perverse way, this animistic sense. First, she apostrophizes the

tree: "O Sovran, vertuous, precious of all Trees / In Paradise, of operation blest / To Sapience," and then bows in "low Reverence . . . as
to the power / That dwelt within" (IX, 795–97, 835–36). Both gestures
suggest Eve's willingness to worship the tree as the receptacle of a
power that animates it. Replacing God as the rightful recipient of
worship, the tree becomes for Eve the object of adoration. As its
votary, she promises to "cultivate" the tree by "caring" for it, "tending"
it with "Song" and "praise" "each Morning," and "easing" it of its
"fertil burden" until she becomes godlike in the special knowledge
that the tree is supposed to bestow upon her (IX, 799–804). In so
doing, she would become a priestess of the tree about which she
would create her own particular kind of "fetish," one which would
look upon the tree as magic, its fruit "infus'd" with "sciential sap,
deriv'd / From Nectar, drink of Gods" (IX, 834–38).

The application of the term "fetish" in this instance is not arbitrary.
Renaissance ethnologists were already quite familiar with the "fetish"
and its cultic manifestations. In treatises ranging from Samuel Purchas'
*Pilgrimage* (London, 1613) to John Ovington's *Voyage to Suratt* (London, 1696), the "fetish" had received ample elaboration. In his discourse
on Africa, for example, Purchas speaks of "strawen Rings, called *Fetissos*, or *Gods*," attended by their priests or "*Fetisseros*." To those who
worship them, the "*Fetissos*" are "sacred things," animated by a spirit
of one kind or another.[36] For our purpose, Purchas' observation about
the relationship of fetish worship and trees is particularly significant:

When the King will sacrifice to *Fetisso*, he commaunds the *Fetissero* to enquire
of a Tree, whereto he ascribeth Diuinitie, which he will demaund. He, with
his wiues, comes to the Tree, and in a heape of ashes, there prouided, prikes
in a braunch plucked off the Tree, and drinking water out of a Bason, spouts
it out on the braunch, and then daubeth his face with the ashes: which done,
he declareth the Kings question, and the Deuill out of the Tree makes answere.
The Nobles also adore certaine Trees, and esteeme them Oracles: and the
Deuill sometimes appeareth vnto them in the same in forme of a blacke Dogge,
and otherwhiles answereth without any visible apparition.[37]

The magical quality ascribed to the trees by the *Fetisseros* is not
lacking in the effects that the "fallacious Fruit" (X, 1046) has upon
Adam and Eve in *Paradise Lost*. First, it "intoxicates" with a deceptive
sense of godlike transcendence (compare Eve's dream [V, 28–92])
and then "enflames" with a carnal "Lust" (IX, 1008–15) that results
finally in humiliation, as Adam and Eve are "naked left / To guiltie

shame" (IX, 1057–58). In that state, they rush into "the thickest Wood"
and cover themselves with the leaves of the fig tree (IX, 1100–01),
itself traditionally associated with the tree of the knowledge of good
and evil.[38] Thus covered, they are reminiscent, Milton implies, of those
American savages "*Columbus* found" "so girt / With featherd Cincture,
naked else and wild / Among the Trees on Iles and woodie Shores"
(IX, 1115–18).

Before that humiliation occurs, however, Adam's response to the
transgression is no less desperate than Eve's, as he slights the prohibition by saying, "if such pleasures be / In things to us forbidden, it
might be wish'd, / For this one Tree had been forbidden ten" (IX,
1024–26). (Freudian psychology would see here the characteristic over-
reaction to having disobeyed the taboo, which, as a "primaeval prohibition . . . imposed [by some authority] from outside," is "directed
against the most powerful longings to which human beings are subject,"
longings that give rise to an incessant desire to "violate" the taboo.)[39]
From the cultic point of view, Adam, like Eve, desires to engage
in a "fetish," one that would create many forbidden trees to be violated
time and again. The absurdity of both Adam and Eve's responses
to their disobedience is made dramatically apparent in Book X. There,
Milton mythologizes the entire situation by recounting what becomes
purportedly the "annual humbling" (X, 577) of Satan and his accom-
plices.

Forcibly transformed into serpentine form, they are drawn to
a "Grove . . . laden with fair Fruit, like that / Which grew in Paradise,
the bait of *Eve* / Us'd by the Tempter" (X, 548–54). "Imagining /
For one forbidden Tree a multitude / Now ris'n," the snakes "greedily"
"pluck'd / The Fruitage fair to sight" (X, 553–61). Unable to "abstain"
in spite of the fact that the fruit is filled with "soot and cinders,"
the snakes "oft . . . assayd," only to be repulsed with "bitter Ashes"
at every turn (X, 558–70). Brought to our attention through local allusion
and contextual pattern, the cultic implications of the scene are manifold.

Locally, the sight of the trees with their "fair Fruitage" that contain nothing but "bitter Ashes" recalls the delusive Dead Sea apples
with their ashes and smoke, mentioned by commentators extending
from Josephus to John Mandeville.[40] These apples, implies Milton,
are like those "which grew / Neer that bituminous Lake where *Sodom*
flam'd" (X, 561–62; Genesis, chaps. 18–19). With this allusion, Milton

appropriately places his tree of the knowledge of good and evil within the context of the "*cultum institutum*." His tree thereby comes to inhabit the same mythos as the "rigid interdiction," a mythos that Milton even further enhances by associating his vision of the serpents' "climbing" "up the Trees" with the "snakie locks / That curld *Megaera*" (*PL* X, 558–60). Confronted with that Fury, we are returned implicitly to the Gorgonian rigidity of the interdiction itself. We are face to face with Death, a singularly appropriate circumstance considering the way in which Milton makes clear the fact that the tree of knowledge is no less than the tree of "Death" (IV, 220–21).

Contextually, the circumstances surrounding the serpents' devouring the fruit recalls the fetishism of Adam and Eve's response to their own transgression. If Adam desires not one but many trees to violate, they are present here, violated time and again by the serpents. If Eve desires to worship what she has just violated, here she may do so in the form of serpents that are unwitting and unwilling votaries, drawn to the trees by an irresistible force. But when they "ease" the trees of their "fertil burden," they do not sing "praises" to the trees. Rather, their songs are those of spewing and "spattering," as they spit out the "soot and cinders" "with hatefullest disrelish" (X, 567–70). Such "worship" they are "Yearly enjoynd" (X, 575) in an unwelcome process of self-humbling that parodies, like a perverse cult, the whole idea of the "fetish" as the Renaissance understood it. Creating his own "Theologia *Adamica*," based upon cultic parallels, then, Milton causes his tree of the knowledge of good and evil to reflect a point of view that associates the tree with that which is magical and demonic and about which perverse cults arise.

If such is the case, Milton's attitude toward the tree of knowledge is decidedly ambivalent. For while that tree accrues to itself demonic associations as a result of the interdiction, it also enjoys, we recall, the stature of that which is divine. In doing so, it subscribes to a pattern of religious thought which conflates demonic and divine. The tabooed object "diverges in two contrary directions": on the one hand, it embodies that which is "dangerous" and "forbidden" and, on the other, that which is "consecrated" and "sacred."[41] Such, for example, is true of the Semitic attitude toward the sacred tree. With its roots in the demonic, the tree of the Semite evolves into a sacred object of worship. As W. Robertson Smith states, "no Canaanite high place was complete without its sacred tree standing beside the altar." In fact, in the local sanctuaries of the Hebrews, altar-sanctuaries "were habitually set up 'under green trees'" or situated beside the *ashera*, a living tree or treelike post. "The *ashera* undoubtedly was an object of worship; for the prophets put it on the same line with other sacred symbols" (cf. Isaiah xvii, 8; Micah v, 12 ff.).[42]

Accordingly, Milton suggests in *Christian Doctrine* that to have disobeyed the first prohibition was to have engaged in a "sacrilege" ("*sacrilegus*") involving "the violation of things sacred (and such was the tree of knowledge of good and evil)" ("*rem sacram violasset, [sacra autem erat arbor ista]*") (CM, XV, 184–85). Such an outlook is reflected in Adam's response to Eve's disobedience in *Paradise Lost:* "how hast thou yeelded to transgress / The strict forbiddance, how to violate / The sacred Fruit forbidd'n" (IX, 902–04). Thereafter, Adam attempts to appease them both with this telling rationalization: "Perhaps," he says to Eve, "thou shalt not Die, perhaps the Fact / Is not so hainous now, foretasted Fruit, / Profan'd first by the Serpent, by him first / Made common and unhallowd ere our taste" (IX, 928–31).

The doctrinal answer to Adam's rationalization is to be found in *Christian Doctrine*. There, Milton maintains that, as an embodiment of God's "hidden things" ("*rerum occultarum*"), the tree of knowledge must remain inviolate at all costs. In that way, it resembles God's holy name (Genesis xix, 26; xxii, 19), his holy mount (Exodus, xix, 22), and his ark (1 Samuel vi, 19). Around these things, he has "set bounds," Milton suggests, so that they might not be profaned (*Christian Doctrine*, CM, XVII, 32–35). Milton is not alone in assuming such a posture. His outlook is part of a prevailing tradition, most notably expressed by Martin Luther in his *Lectures on Genesis:* whereas today we have altars and pulpits in our churches, for Adam "this tree of the knowledge of good and evil was Adam's church, altar, and pulpit," and if Adam had not fallen, "this tree would have been like a common temple and basilica to which people would have streamed."[43]

Such a statement springs from the common Renaissance predisposition to view both the tree of knowledge and the tree of life in ecclesiastical terms. Precisely how far Milton would have been willing to accept these terms might, however, be open to some question. One is inclined to feel that his outlook is more nearly "mythic" than "ecclesiastical" when it comes to the place of the interdicted tree in his understanding of the Genesis narrative. I make this distinction because those who embraced the ecclesiastical view did not hesitate to place their interpretation within a ceremonial context. In short, they sacramentalized not only the tree of knowledge but the tree of life. In so doing, they envisioned the special trees as sacramental prefigurations of God's will. Thus, John Salkeld observes in *A Treatise of Paradise* (London, 1617) that while the tree of knowledge fore-shadows "the tree of the crosse," the tree of life foreshadows "the sacred communion, and bread of life" (p. 51). Underlying such an observation is a point of view that we have already seen Milton, in one instance, reject in *Christian Doctrine*. That view is one which relates the divine command with the covenant of works. Expressing precisely that point of view in his *Compendium Theologiae Christianae*, Johannes Wollebius maintains that the covenant of works was "confirmed" by the "twofold sacraments" embodied in the trees.[44] So consistent was that view with reformed dogmatics that it was incorporated into the Westminster Confession.[45] Milton, of course, dismisses the view outright. Both the tree of knowledge and the tree of life, states Milton, are "not a sacrament, as [they] are generally called; for a sacrament is a thing to be used, not abstained from" (*Christian Doctrine*, CM, XV, 114-15). Taken at face value, such a statement would seem to suggest that Milton divorces his trees entirely from all but the most "literal" of considerations.

We have seen, however, that such is hardly the case, that because of the mythos implicit in the first prohibition, the special trees are a great deal more than the "chiefly physical realities" that Joseph Duncan and others have seen in them. Reflecting the *"cultum institutum"* engendered by Milton's handling of the first prohibition, they veritably inhabit the world of myth. Anthropologically, they share the aura of the "sacred" so integral to primitive thought. Because of the first prohibition, they become "taboo." We have already seen how "alive" that concept was for the Renaissance and how readily it was applied to the first prohibition. The question that now presents itself is what specific connection the concept of the taboo might have with the traditions of religious thought that Milton inherited from the Bible and what particular bearing that thought might have on Milton's under-

standing of the Genesis account. The answer lies paradoxically in that
very ceremonial law that Milton would appear to reject in his dismissal
of the sacramental basis of the special trees.

<h1 style="text-align:center">III</h1>

The aptness of that assertion becomes discernible in Milton's
treatment of the sacraments in general. The meaning of the term "sacrament," Milton maintains in *Christian Doctrine*, need not be confined
to the strict interpretation that has been imposed upon it by the churches
throughout the ages. Since the word "nowhere occurs in Scripture,"
"it is unnecessary to be very scrupulous" about its doctrinal significance
(CM, XVI, 215–17). The term finally may be understood as that which
is expressed by "religious emblems, or symbols of things sacred" ("*res
sacras significent*") (CM, XVI, 214–17). It is in this sense that the special
trees are to be understood. If the tree of the knowledge of good
and evil is not a "sacrament" in the sense of that which is "to be
used," it is "sacred" in the sacramental sense, as that which is to be
"abstained from" (CM, XV, 115). "Sacred to abstinence," Adam calls
it in *Paradise Lost* (IX, 924).

The ceremonial basis of that point of view may be found, of
course, in the Levitical code. It is there that exegetes were most inclined
to discover the "cultic" basis of the first prohibition. In a tradition
extending back to *The Babylonian Talmud*, the idea that Adam and
Eve might "freely eat" of "every tree of the garden" (Genesis ii, 16)
is contrasted implicitly with what they might not eat. That which
they might not eat is viewed within the context of the dietary injunction "not" to eat "flesh cut from a living animal."[46] Similarly, the *Mid-
rash Rabbah*, in its gloss of the same text, maintains that the interdicted
fruit takes on the forbidden character of "a limb torn from a living
animal" (Leviticus xxii, 18: "That which dieth of itself, or is torn *with
beasts*, he shall not eat to defile himself therewith: I *am* the Lord").[47]
This outlook is carried through to the Christian tradition in writers
extending from the church fathers to the Renaissance. Whereas Novatian, in his discourse *On the Jewish Meats*,[48] implies a relationship
between the interdicted fruit and the interdicted food of Levitical
law, such writers as Gervase Babington and Joseph Mede make that
relationship overt. Thus, in *Comfortable Notes Vpon the bookes of
Exodus and Leuiticus* (London, 1604), Babington suggests that, al-

though the interdicted fruit is not in itself unclean, it becomes so by virtue of the prohibition. In that way, the fruit assumes the character of unclean meat (p. 93). In *Diatribae* (London, 1648), Mede maintains that the interdicted fruit, as that which is cursed, is similar to those foods in Levitical law that are cursed (p. 400).

Milton undoubtedly had something of this idea in mind in *Paradise Regain'd* when he has Satan defend the "purity" of the feast that is set before Jesus by maintaining that "no interdict / Defends the touching of these viands pure" (II, 369-70): here, Jesus will find neither "Meats by the law unclean" (II, 328) nor "Fruits forbidd'n" (II, 369).[49] (Compare Leviticus xix, 23-25: "And when ye shall come into the land, and shall have planted all manner of trees for food, then shall ye count the fruit thereof as uncircumcised: three years shall it be as uncircumcised unto you: it shall not be eaten of. But in the fourth year all the fruit thereof shall be holy to praise the Lord *withal*. And in the fifth year shall ye eat of the fruit thereof, that it may yield unto you the increase thereof: I *am* the Lord your God.")

Appropriately, in *Paradise Lost*, when Adam and Eve do violate God's command, they contract the uncleanness of the fruit itself, thereafter to be reproached as both "unclean" (IX, 1097) and "impure" (X, 735).[50] (Compare Leviticus v, 2: "If a soul touch any unclean thing, whether *it be* a carcase of an unclean beast, or a carcase of unclean cattle, or the carcase of unclean creeping things . . . he also shall be unclean, and guilty.") As Sebastian Franck says, in *The forbidden fruit: or a treatise of the tree of knowledge* (London, 1640), the Fall was an "offense" to God, causing man to become "unclean": we will become clean again only when we "doe vomitt up the Fruit of the Tree of Knowledge of Good and Evill" (pp. 14-16). In the meantime, Adam and Eve must be expelled from paradise. As God declares in *Paradise Lost:*

> But longer in that Paradise to dwell,
> The Law I gave to Nature him forbids:
> Those pure immortal Elements that know
> No gross, no unharmoneous mixture foul,
> Eject him tainted now, and purge him off
> As a distemper, gross to air as gross.          (XI, 48-53)

The idea returns us to the original concept of the taboo and its effects upon the tabooed object. Those effects are such that the tabooed object becomes divine: it contains *manna*, the power to destroy upon contact. As such, it is distinct from that which is *noa* or common. That which is *noa* must never come in contact with that which is *taboo*. The *noa* must obey "a complicated etiquette" that surrounds the tabooed object.[51] To violate that etiquette is to suffer the wrath of the god who has made the object taboo. Emile Durkheim describes the situation in these terms:

> Owing to the contagiousness inherent in all that is sacred, a profane being cannot violate an interdict without having the religious force, to which he has unduly approached, extend itself over him and establish its empire over him. But as there is an antagonism between them, he becomes dependent upon a hostile power, whose hostility cannot fail to manifest itself in the form of violent reactions which tend to destroy him. This is why sickness or death is considered the natural consequence of every transgression of this sort; and they are consequences which are believed to come by themselves, with a sort of physical necessity. The guilty man feels himself attacked by a force which dominates him and against which he is powerless. Has he eaten the [tabooed] animal? Then he feels it penetrating him and gnawing at his vitals; he lies down on the ground and awaits death. Every profanation implies a consecration, but one which is dreadful, both for the subject consecrated and for those who approach him. It is the consequences of this consecration which sanction, in part, the interdict.[52]

Those consequences involve the subjecting of that which is profane to what Durkheim calls "the contagiousness of the sacred."[53] Thus, Eve in *Paradise Lost* finds herself not only "defac't" and "deflowrd" but "to Death devote" because she has "violate[d] / The sacred Fruit forbidd'n" (IX, 901–04), having become, as God says, "to destruction sacred and devote" (III, 208; Leviticus xxvii, 28–29: "every devoted thing *is* most holy unto the Lord. None devoted . . . shall be redeemed; *but* shall surely be put to death").

The foregoing should provide ample indication of what we have already seen to be true of the sacred tree. The ambivalence of the sacred is fundamental to the tabooed object. As Wilhelm Wundt states in *Elements of Folk Psychology*, "two opposing ideas are combined in the conception of the taboo: the idea of the sacred as something to be avoided because of its sanctity, and that of the impure or loathsome, which must be avoided because of its repulsive or harmful nature."[54] Thus, "there are two sorts of of sacredness, the propitious and the unpropitious, and not only is there no break of continuity between these two opposed forms, but also one object may pass from the one to the other without changing its nature. The pure is made out of the impure, and reciprocally. It is in the possibility of these transmutations that the ambiguity of the sacred exists."[55] That this idea was familiar to Renaissance thought may be seen in Edward Leigh's discourse on αϊιος in *Critica Sacra* (London, 1639): "αϊιος" or "*sanctus*," says Leigh, signifies not only "*purus*" but "*pollutus*," both that which is "*sacra*" and that which is "*scelus*" (p. 7). In his treatment of ancient Semitic religion, W. Robertson Smith portrays the idea graphically: "at the Canaanite shrines the name of 'holy' (masc. *cĕdeshīm*, from *cĕdeshōth*) was specifically appropriated to a class of wretches, whose life, apart from its connection with the sanctuary, would have been disgraceful even from the standpoint of heathenism."[56] These wretches became "holy" because they were set apart from common use.

Such is precisely the character that tabooed objects take on as the result of the Levitical injunctions. "Alongside of taboos that exactly correspond to rules of holiness, protecting the inviolability of idols and sanctuaries, priests and chiefs, and generally of all persons and things pertaining to the gods and their worship, we find another kind of taboo which in the Semitic field has its parallel in rules of uncleanness. Women after child-birth, men who have touched a dead body and so forth, are . . . taboo and separated from human society, just as the same persons are unclean in Semitic religion."[57] Milton's fondness for drawing upon restrictions of this kind for use in his poetry may be seen in poems ranging from Sonnet 23, which speaks of his "late espoused saint" "washt from spot of child-bed taint" through "purification in th' old law" (l, 5-6), to *Samson Agonistes*, which deals with the violation of the Nazarite vows of sacredness and the consequent "uncleanness" of the violation (321).

In accord with the laws of clean and unclean, certainly the most fundamental and pervasive taboo is that which concerns eating the interdicted object.[58] In *Taboo and Perils of the Soul*, Sir James Frazer has an entire section devoted to the matter. He proceeds to offer one example after the next: "The Flamen Dialis was forbidden to eat or even name several plants and animals, and . . . the flesh diet of Egyptian kings was restricted to veal and goose. In antiquity many priests and many kings of barbarous peoples abstained wholly from a flesh diet. The *Gangas* or fetish priests of the Loango Coast are forbidden to eat or even see a variety of animals and fish, in consequence of which their flesh diet is extremely limited; often they live only on herbs and roots."[59] The list of examples goes on for pages.

That the nature of the taboos provided by these examples was hardly foreign to Milton becomes discernible if we refer once again to his treatment of the Britons in *The History of Britain*. Their religion, Milton observes, may be characterized by their custom of "abstaining from a Hen, a Hare, and a Goose, from Fish also" (CM, X, 50–51). Taboo for the Britons, these foods are interdict, Milton would maintain, because of the unwritten laws regulating custom, whose force is as strong as that of a written law. As Milton says in *Tetrachordon*, "all who understand Law will consent, that a tolerated custom hath the force of a Law, and is indeed no other but an unwritt'n Law . . . and is as prevalent as any writt'n statute" (CM, IV, 111). Their most compelling characteristic is their irrationality, a characteristic that underlies the Levitical laws themselves. The "irrationality" of these laws is "so manifest that they must necessarily be looked on as having survived from an earlier form of faith and of society" and thus must be classed as "savage taboos."[60]

From the doctrinal point of view, of course, the Levitical laws represent the ceremonial counterpart of the moral law that forms the basis of the covenant of works.[61] As such, they form part of the Old Dispensation communicated by God himself to Moses on Sinai. This, of course, is how Milton understood them (*Christian Doctrine*, CM, XVI, 98–111). Nevertheless, their apparent irrationality proved perplexing right from the very beginning, so much so, in fact, that exegetes like Moses Maimonides felt compelled to set the record straight, to make sense of these laws, much in the manner that other exegetes felt called upon to make sense of the first prohibition.

Thus, in *Guide of the Perplexed*, Moses Maimonides states:

No question concerning the end need be asked with regard to . . . [moral] *commandments.* For no one was ever so perplexed for a day as to ask why we were commanded by the Law that God is one, or why we were forbidden to kill and steal, or why we were forbidden to exercise vengeance and retaliation, or why we were ordered to love each other. The matters about which people are perplexed and opinions disagree—so that some say there is no utility in them at all except the fact of mere command, whereas others say there is a utility in them that is hidden from us—are the *commandments* from whose external meaning it does not appear that they are useful [that is, rational]. Such, for instance, are the prohibitions of the *mingled stuff*, of the *mingling* [of diverse species], and of *meat in milk*, and the commandment *concerning the covering of blood*, the *heifer whose neck was broken*, and the *firstling of an ass*, and others of the same kind. However, you will hear my explanation for all of them and my exposition of the correct and demonstrated causes of them all.[62]

He then presumes to show us the truly rational basis of such injunctions and, in so doing, merely shows us how irrational they are.

It is this irrationality that Milton, in keeping with his attitude toward the first prohibition, attributes to ceremonial law in general and to dietary law in particular. Emphasizing the "unreasonable" nature of ceremonial law in *A Treatise of Civil Power* (CM, VI, 36),[63] he refers in *Christian Doctrine* to dietary law in the following terms: "Thus the eating of fat was forbidden by the law, . . . yet no one infers from hence that the use of fat is unlawful, this prohibition applying only to the sacrificial times" (CM, XVI, 161). That is, it represents a provisional or conditional prohibition.

The idea recalls none other than our initial discussion of Milton's view of the first prohibition not only as that which is extralegal but as that which is dispensational. For Milton's outlook regarding ceremonial law, as we have discovered, is perfectly in keeping with his outlook regarding the first prohibition. That outlook is one which views both laws as conditional, on the one hand, and irrational, on the other.[64] Although one would be loath to push the analogy too far, associating the first prohibition with dietary law does serve finally to suggest the way in which Milton's extralegal and dispensational views complement each other.[65] If one is to make the analogy, however, it is to be done not in the "doctrinal" sense but in the "cultic" sense. The distinction is one that we have already seen to operate in Milton's treatment of the Fall in *Christian Doctrine* and in his unwillingness to subscribe in any doctrinal way to the theory of the sacraments.

What results from this point of view is a perspective that can only be termed "mythic," a perspective that enhances its doctrinal viewpoints with nondoctrinal or, perhaps, extradoctrinal considerations. This approach, we have found, is particularly true of Milton's attitude toward the first prohibition, which is at once extralegal and dispensational, a combination that associates it not doctrinally but culturally with ceremonial law, as that which has no basis in reason (the foundation of moral and natural law) but which, at the same time, is essential to the covenant of works.

If Milton dismisses the covenant of works in his consideration of the first prohibition, he also imposes upon that prohibition a dispensational framework, one that has affinities with none other than that ceremonial dimension that he would presume to reject in his consideration of the first prohibition. If he rejects it doctrinally, he accepts it in terms that must be called "cultic," a view which Milton himself defines in his treatment of the Fall as that which characterizes "all nations and . . . all religions from the earliest period" (*Christian Doctrine*, CM, XV, 185). From this perspective, the ceremonial dimension forms part of the larger anthropological viewpoint that associates the first prohibition with the taboo. In doing so, it underlies what we have seen to be the "*cultum institutum*" that the Renaissance was so fond of associating with the Genesis story. That is, it inhabits the world of myth, a world, after all, that has its very roots in the Jahwistic account out of which the narrative of the Fall emerged in the first place.

University of Illinois at Chicago Circle

## NOTES

1. All references to Milton's poetry in my text are to *The Complete Poetry of John Milton*, ed. John T. Shawcross, 2d ed. rev. (Garden City, N. Y., 1971).

2. John M. Evans, *Paradise Lost and the Genesis Tradition* (London, 1968), pp. 9–20.

3. *Paradise Lost and the Genesis Tradition*, p. 20. For a discussion of the cultic dimension, see E. Basil Redlich, *The Early Traditions of Genesis* (London, 1950), p. 34.

4. *The Writings of Tertullianus*, vol. 18 of the *Ante-Nicene Christian Library*, ed. Alexander Roberts and James Donaldson (Edinburgh, 1870), vol. III, p. 204. The idea is likewise implicit in rabbinical commentary. See, for example, the *Pirkê de Rabbi Eliezer*, trans. Gerald Friedlander (New York, 1965), p. 84. According to *The Targum of Palestine* (*The Targum of Jonathan Ben Uzziel*), "God took the man [Adam] from the mountain of worship, where he had been created, and made him dwell in the garden of Eden, to do service in the law, and to keep its commandments" (*The Targums of Onkelos and Jonathan Ben Uzziel on the Pentateuch, with the Fragments of the Jerusalem Targum from the Chaldee*, trans. J. W. Etheridge [New York, 1968], p. 163.)

5. *The Works of John Milton*, ed. Frank Allen Patterson, 18 vols. in 21 (New York, 1931–38), vol. XVI, p. 109; cf. Romans iii, 19. All references to Milton's prose are to this edition, hereafter cited as CM.

6. In *The Works*, ed. John Keble, 3 vols., 6th ed. (London, 1874), vol. II, p. 543.

7. My analysis at this point owes much to Stanley Fish's *Surprised by Sin: The Reader in Paradise Lost* (New York, 1967), pp. 242–43: "The arbitrariness of God's command, that is to say, its unreasonableness, is necessary if compliance is to be regarded as an affirmation of loyalty springing from an act of the will." The arbitrariness of the command has long been recognized. See studies ranging from Basil Willey's *The Seventeenth-Century Background* (Garden City, N. Y., 1953), pp. 240–58, to C. S. Lewis' *A Preface to Paradise Lost* (New York, 1961), p. 71.

8. Evans, *Paradise Lost and the Genesis Tradition*, pp. 11–14.

9. Ibid., p. 14.

10. *A Rabbinic Anthology*, ed. C. G. Montefiore and H. Loewe (London, 1938), pp. 156–57.

11. Evans, *Paradise Lost and the Genesis Tradition*, pp. 48–49.

12. The *Archaeologiae Philosophicae* is attributed to Burnet.

13. *A Preface to Paradise Lost*, pp. 71–72. Such irrationality reflects the very processes of mythic reasoning, characterized not by the establishment of "an unequivocal relation between *specific* 'causes' and *specific* 'effects' " but by that which "has a free selection of causes at its disposal. Anything can *come from* anything" (Ernst Cassirer, *The Philosophy of Symbolic Forms*, trans. Ralph Manheim, 3 vols. [New Haven, 1955], vol. II, p. 46.)

14. *Unpremeditated Verse: Feeling and Perception in Paradise Lost* (Princeton, 1967), p. 6.

15. Ibid., p. 15.

16. For a full account of that tradition, see Don Cameron Allen's *Mysteriously Meant: The Rediscovery of Pagan Symbolism and Allegorical Interpretation in the Renaissance* (Baltimore, 1970), pp. 1–82.

17. In the same sense, Theophilus Gale (*The Court of the Gentiles: or A Discourse touching the Original of Human Literature*, 4 vols., 2d ed. [Oxford, 1672], vol. I, sig. N1ʳ) refers to the study of "θεολογια μυθικη, *Mythic or Fabulous Theologie*."

18. θεολογουμενα παντοδαπα, p. 158. See, for example, Gale, *Court of The Gentiles*, vol. I, sig. Qq3; and Bompart, *Parallela Sacra et Profana*, p. 17.

19. See James Cook, *A Voyage to the Pacific Ocean*, 3 vols., 2d ed. (London, 1785), vol. I, pp. 286, 338, 410; vol. II, p. 248; and Robert Henry Codrington, *The Melanesians* (Oxford, 1891), pp. 215–16.

20. Cook, *Voyage to the Pacific*, vol. I, p. 286.

21. Andrew Lang, *Magic and Religion* (New York, 1901), p. 257.

22. *Encyclopedia Britannica*, 11th ed., s. v. "Taboo."

23. See *Logic* (CM, XI, 20–70) for a full discussion of terminological distinctions.

24. Trans. Joseph Ward Swain (London, n. d.), p. 301.

25. *Encyclopedia Britannica*, 11th ed., s. v. "Taboo."

26. In *The Works of Aurelius Augustine*, ed. Rev. Marcus Dods, 15 vols. (Edinburgh, 1871–76), vol. IV, pp. 106–07. See also the *City of God*, vol. I, p. 545; and the commentary on Genesis (*De Genesi ad Litteram*), in *Patrologiae Cursus Completus*, ed. J.-P. Migne (Paris, 1845), vol. XXXIV, pp. 383–86.

27. *Milton's Earthly Paradise: A Historical Study of Eden* (Minneapolis, 1972),

p. 141. For a similar view, see Dennis Burden's *The Logical Epic: A Study of the Argument of Paradise Lost* (Cambridge, Mass., 1967), pp. 124–49.

28. F. R. Tennant, *The Sources of the Doctrines of the Fall and Original Sin* (New York, 1968), pp. 70–71.

29. Ibid., p. 38.

30. J. H. Philpot, *The Sacred Tree or the Tree in Religion and Myth* (New York, 1897), pp. 110–11. Compare Nebuchadnezzar's dream in Daniel iv, 10–11: "I saw, and behold, a tree in the midst of the earth, and the height thereof *was* great. The tree grew, and was strong, and the height thereof reached unto heaven, and the sight thereof to the end of all the earth."

31. The lines are those originally deleted from *Comus*. For commentary, see *A Variorum Commentary on the Poems of John Milton*, ed. A. S. P. Woodhouse and Douglas Bush (New York, 1972), vol. II, pp. 856–57.

32. Cited ibid., vol. II, p. 908.

33. *Lectures on the Religion of the Semites* (New York, 1889), pp. 125–26.

34. Ibid., pp. 423–24.

35. P. 95.

36. See Purchas, pp. 542–43. The phrase "sacred things" comes from Charles de Brosses' full study of "the holy" in *Du Culte des Dieux Fetiches* (Paris, 1760), p. 19. For another early and revealing study, see William Bosman, *Voyage de Guinée* (Utrecht, 1704).

37. Purchas, pp. 542–43.

38. Ibid., p. 432.

39. See, in particular, Sigmund Freud's own classic *Totem and Taboo*, trans. James Strachey (New York, 1950), pp. 34–35.

40. For a full commentary on the allusion, see *The Poetical Works of John Milton*, ed. Rev. H. J. Todd, 6 vols. (London, 1826), vol. III, pp. 287–88.

41. Freud, *Totem and Taboo*, p. 18.

42. Smith, *Lectures on the Religion of the Semites*, pp. 170–72.

43. In *Luther's Works*, ed. Jaroslav Pelikan (St. Louis, 1958), vol. I, p. 94.

44. In *Reformed Dogmatics*, ed. and trans. John W. Beardslee III (New York, 1965), pp. 64–65.

45. *The Confession of Faith Together with the Larger and Lesser Catechismes Composed by the Reverend Assembly of Divines, Sitting at Westminster*, 2d ed. (London, 1658), pp. 25–28.

46. Trans. Rabbi I. Epstein, 35 vols. (London, 1935–52), vol. V, pp. 382–83.

47. Trans. Rabbis H. Freedman and Maurice Simon, 10 vols. (London, 1939), vol. I, p. 131.

48. *A Letter of Novatian, the Roman Presbyter, On the Jewish Meats*, in *Ante-Nicene Christian Library*, vol. XIII, p. 385.

49. For commentary on the passage, see Michael Fixler, "The Unclean Meats of the Mosaic Law and the Banquet Scene in *Paradise Regained*," *MLN*, LXX (1955), 573–77.

50. The practice of reading the Genesis account in ceremonial terms is firmly rooted in Jewish practice. See, for example, the pseudepigraphic *Book of Jubilees* (*The Apocrypha and Pseudepigrapha of the Old Testament*, ed. R. H. Charles, 2 vols. [London, 1913], vol. II, p. 16), which envisions the birth of Eve entirely in Levitical terms: Eve must be "clean" of the impurity of natal blood before she may enter the sanctuary of Eden and "touch" the "hallowed thing[s]" that are there. "This is the

law and testimony which was written down for Israel, in order that they should observe (it) all the days."

51. Smith, *Lectures on the Religion of the Semites*, pp. 147–48.

52. *The Elementary Forms of the Religious Life*, p. 320.

53. Ibid., p. 318.

54. Trans. Edward Leroy Schaub (London, 1916), pp. 193–94.

55. Durkheim, *Elementary Forms of Religious Life*, p. 411.

56. *Lectures on the Religion of the Semites*, p. 134.

57. Ibid., p. 142.

58. Wundt, *Elements of Folk Psychology*, pp. 199–200.

59. 3rd ed. (London, 1911), pp. 291–93,

60. Smith, *Lectures on the Religion of the Semites*, p. 430.

61. See Wollebius, *Reformed Dogmatics*, p. 79; William Ames, *The Marrow of Theology*, trans. and ed. John Eusden (Boston, 1968), pp. 110–12.

62. Trans. Shlomo Pines (Chicago, 1963), p. 513.

63. In *A Treatise of Civil Power*, Milton maintains that, unlike the "*reasonable service*" required by Gospel law (Romans xii, 1), ceremonial or "Jewish law" requires "unreasonable service, that is to say, not only unwilling but unconscionable" (CM, VI, 36). Such an attitude is in keeping with Milton's view that the covenant of works is completely abrogated by the covenant of grace (*Christian Doctrine*, CM, XVI, 112–63).

64. From the conditional point of view, its ceremonial basis is not unlike that which binds Samson to God. As Milton suggests in *Samson Agonistes*, Samson, the "Select, and Sacred" Nazarite (363), was to have "preserv'd [his] locks unshorn / The pledge of [his] unviolated vow" (1143–44). Instead, he "profan'd / The mystery of God giv'n [him] under pledge / Of vow" (377–79) by betraying God's trust to a woman (379–80). That betrayal, of course, results in his fall. It is not without significance that Milton compares the fallen Adam in *Paradise Lost* to Samson: "So rose the *Danite strong / Herculean Samson* from the Harlot-lap / Of *Philistean Dalilah*, and wak'd / Shorn of his strength" (IX, 1059–62). Samson's response to his fall, like Adam's, is to question divine dispensation: "God, when he gave me strength, to shew withal / How slight the gift was, hung it in my Hair" (58–59). Although Samson's questioning of God's ways is wrong-headed, we are made to focus our attention upon the apparent arbitrariness of the dispensation, an arbitrariness, as we have seen, that underlies precisely the first prohibition.

65. Modern rabbinical thought would seem to accord with this view. Thus, in his commentary on *The Pentateuch* (5 vols., 2d ed. [London, 1963], vol. I, p. 60), Rabbi Samson Raphael Hirsch says that the prohibition is "not a so-called 'reasonable prohibition' . . . but rather one which all the human means of judgment would speak against." As such, it is "a dietary law."

# THE AESTHETICS
# OF SELF-DIMINUTION: CHRISTIAN
# ICONOGRAPHY AND *PARADISE LOST*

## Albert C. Labriola

A tree, a garden, and a tableau of figures make up the central setting for much of the action of *Paradise Lost*. In this setting God created and married Adam and Eve and commanded them to "Be fruitful." In this setting Adam and Eve yielded to temptation and committed sin. As these same events of the Old Testament are depicted in the iconography of the Middle Ages and the Renaissance, a similar visual context is used. Most importantly, these iconographic depictions tend to interrelate persons and events of the Old Testament with counterparts from the New Testament. In iconography the temptation of Eve, for example, is interrelated with the Annunciation, which is also depicted in a garden setting; and Eve's sinfulness is contrasted with Mary's purity. At times the tree of knowledge of good and evil is visually juxtaposed with the cross, which is often depicted to resemble a tree; and Satan's pride at the Fall of mankind is contrasted with Christ's humility at the Redemption of mankind. When adapted into the literary framework of *Paradise Lost*, this kind of iconographic conceptualization enables Milton to interrelate the causes and consequences of the Fall with the means and manner by which Redemption is achieved. To a very great extent iconographic conceptualization is reflected in the development of character and action in *Paradise Lost*, in the elaboration of central themes, and in the selection of imagery.

THE TREE of knowledge of good and evil is a dominant feature of the symbolic landscape of Book IX of *Paradise Lost*. Because it marks the scene of Satan's successful temptation of Eve, it is associated with the Fall of mankind not only in Milton's epic but throughout the Christian tradition. In Genesis, chapter iii, and in Book IX of *Paradise Lost*, Adam sins after he partakes of the forbidden fruit offered by

Eve; and Sin and Death, who appear as allegorical figures in Milton's epic, can enter the world. But the paradox of the *felix culpa* (or the Fortunate Fall) emphasizes that man's regeneration is accomplished through the intercession of Christ. In *Paradise Lost*, Adam exclaims "O goodness infinite, goodness immense! / That all this good of evil shall produce" (XII, 469–70) after he has learned through his vision into the future that Christ's death will redeem man.[1] As Adam also learns (XII, 386–435), Christ's death and Resurrection will be a triumph over Satan, Sin, and Death and will enable man to triumph over the onset of evil in the fallen world. Just as the tree of knowledge of good and evil suggests the Fall of mankind and the consequences thereof, so also the cross signifies the culmination of Christ's ministry, the availability of grace to mankind, and the offer of salvation. Typological correspondence between the tree of knowledge of good and evil and the cross was omnipresent in seventeenth-century devotional poetry. For Giles Fletcher, "A Tree was first the instrument of strife," whereas "A Tree is now the instrument of life."[2] In "Hymne to God my God, in my sicknesse," Donne fixes the site of the Crucifixion on the very spot in the midst of paradise where the tree of knowledge had grown: "*Christs* Crosse, and *Adams* tree, stood in one place" (22).[3] In addition to the two trees, Christian iconography depicts two Adams and two Eves. Christ is the second Adam or the New Man, and Mary is the second Eve, who remains undefiled by sin. Eve's sin is sometimes interpreted as an adulterous act consummated with Satan, whereas Mary's conception of Christ is viewed as the outcome of her chaste marriage to the Deity.

A humble heart is the necessary prerequisite for indwelling by God. Mary's humility is depicted in iconography of the Annunciation when she professes her unworthiness to be the mother of God, and Christ willingly divests himself of the glory of godhead in order to die for mankind. Humility is the essence of *imitatio Christi*, and in the aphoristic wisdom of the Gospels, the humble shall be exalted. The opposite of humility is pride, the sin that precipitates Satan's fall and that is engendered by him in the hearts of our first parents. In Book IX of *Paradise Lost*, Satan gains access to Eve's "heart" (550, 734); and only after Eve has become humble and repentant (X, 1086–1104) and has experienced an infusion of prevenient grace (XI, 1–8) can she have "th' upright heart and pure" (I, 18) in which the Lord will dwell. Satan is dispossessed of the human heart when man's desire to be exalted is replaced by the willingness to be humbled. Man "shalt possess / A paradise within" (XII, 586-87) when the cross, which Christian iconography often depicts as a tree of life, has supplanted the tree of knowledge of good and evil in the human heart.

These typological correspondences were developed in Scripture, in patristic commentary, and in the religious literature of the Middle Ages and the Renaissance. At the same time, they were depicted in iconography, a tradition of visual interpretation that greatly contributes to an understanding of seventeenth-century devotional poetry. Within a visual context often characterized by a tree, a garden, and a tableau of figures, iconography interrelates the Creation of mankind, the causes and consequences of the Fall, and the means and manner by which Redemption is achieved. A similar perspective is developed in *Paradise Lost,* and the *mise en scène* often described in the epic may be correlated with the visual context of Christian iconography. In accordance with the tradition of Christian iconography, Milton celebrates the theme of humility and gives literary embodiment to the aesthetics of self-diminution.

I

In Book IX of *Paradise Lost,* Eve refers to herself and Adam as gardeners:

> *Adam,* well may we labor still to dress
> This Garden, still to tend Plant, Herb and Flow'r,
> Our pleasant task enjoin'd. (205-07)

To *dress* means to cultivate, but the Latinate meaning (from *dirigere*) suggests direction and supervision. *Dress* is sometimes used in translations of Genesis iii, 15, when God enjoins man to "till," "keep," or "dress" the Garden of Eden. St. Augustine interprets Genesis iii, 15, as "a directive to man to care for his own soul or a promise that God will work in man as in a garden."[4] The sanctified soul as a garden implanted by God was a commonplace image in devotional literature and iconography. In the thirteenth-century *Somme le Roi,* written by Friar Lorens d'Orléans for King Philip of France, God is the "grete gardener" and "goode gardyner." In the "good erthe" of the sanctified heart "graffes of vertue" are planted, so that the heart "wexe al grene and bere flour and fruyght." Within man there is "a paradis right

delitable, ful of goode trees and precious."[5] Similarly, St. John of
the Cross and St. Teresa of Avila liken their souls to enclosed gardens
in which God walks; and trees, plants, and flowers signify virtues
and indicate a state of holiness.[6] Several of George Herbert's poems,
including "The Flower," "Paradise," "Grace," "Miserie," and "Man,"
elaborate this same image; and in George Wither's *A Collection of
Emblemes* (1635), God's arm extended from the heavens is cultivating
plants, which are supported by props and protected by enclosures
(figure 1). Sunlight, water, and God's personal attention are images
of his grace. In *Paradise Lost,* God is also "the sovran Planter" (IV,
691), and "Of God the Garden was, by him in the East / Of *Eden*
planted" (IV, 209–10). In "the fertile ground he caus'd to grow /
All Trees of noblest kind for sight, smell, taste" (IV, 216–17); this
is his "blissful Paradise" (IV, 208). *Paradise* (from Old Persian, Hebrew,
and Greek) means a royal garden or park often enclosed by thick
vegetation and walls. Milton situates Eden on the summit of a hill
within "enclosure green" (IV, 133) of many trees. But "higher than
their tops / The verdurous wall of Paradise up sprung"; moreover,
"higher than that Wall" was "a circling row / Of goodliest Trees loaden
with fairest Fruit" (IV, 142–47). Milton also views Eden as an image
of man's soul implanted by God, and luxuriant growth signifies the
efficacy of God's grace. Adam and Eve are described as plants in
the Garden of Eden, which is intended for God's glory, because they
are expected to nurture the potential for growth that God's grace
implanted in their souls at creation. They are entrusted with the care
and supervision of the Garden of Eden, and they are expected to
cultivate their own souls for indwelling by God. Images of gardening
describe Adam and Eve's relationship not only with God but also
with each other, and these images are applied to them at their creation
and marriage and during their mutual labor in the Garden of Eden.

Adam and Eve were created in the midst of trees, fruits, and
flowers. Adam (from *adamah*, Hebrew for earth) is described as soil
cultivated by God and vitalized by grace (VII, 524–26). In recalling
his creation, Adam uses images of moisture, sunlight, and ascent as
if he were a plant that had sprung from dormancy into growth:

> As new wak't from soundest sleep
> Soft on the flow'ry herb I found me laid
> In Balmy Sweat, which with his Beams the Sun

FIGURE 1. George Wither, *A Collection of Emblemes* (London, 1635), p. 107. STC 25900, HEH 79918. Reproduced by permission of the Huntington Library.

Soon dri'd, and on the reeking moisture fed.
Straight toward Heav'n my wond'ring Eyes I turn'd,
And gaz'd a while the ample Sky, till rais'd
By quick instinctive motion up I sprung.          (VIII, 253–59)

Eve, too, recalls having awakened "from sleep" while "Under a shade on flow'rs" (IV, 449–51). In iconography Adam's creation from the earth and Eve's creation from Adam's side are almost always depicted under a tree (or with trees nearby) and in the midst of plants and flowers. *The Visconti Hours* and *The Hours of Catherine of Cleves*, both of which are illuminated manuscripts of the late Middle Ages, show Eve's creation in the midst of the fertility of Eden. Adam and Eve are depicted to resemble the verdure of the garden. John Plummer observes that the border of the miniature of Eve's creation in *The Hours of Catherine of Cleves* is "composed of spreading leaves and fleshly buds," so that the decorative design "parallels the fullness of Eve's figure and the fertility of Eden."[7] In *The Visconti Hours*, the border of the miniature of Eve's creation is made up of ivy arabesques and clusters of fruit-bearing trees.[8] The creation of Adam is one of the illustrations on the title page of the second edition of Christopher Froschauer's large folio Bible (Zurich, 1536). God the Father is reaching down to Adam's outstretched arms in order to lift him upright from an opened mound of earth, as if he were a seedling that God had cultivated into sudden growth. In another illustration on the same page, Eve is lifted by God from an aperture in the side of the sleeping Adam, who appears as dormant earth stirred to life by God. Moreover, the first edition of Froschauer's large folio Bible (Zurich, 1531) has an illustration by Hans Springinklee in which God the Father is lifting Eve from the side of Adam, who is asleep at the base of a tree. The roots of the tree are partially exposed, and Adam is lying on them, as if he were the tree from which Eve was germinated. Her dependency indicates that she should not be separated from him. Other Bibles with similar illustrations of Eve's creation include Heinrich Quentel's Low German Bible (Cologne, 1478–1480), Lucantonio di Giunta's Italian Bible (Venice, 1490), and Martin Lempereur's French Bible (Antwerp, 1534). In Ludowick Dietz's Low German Bible (Lubeck, 1533) Adam and Eve are depicted near two trees in the Garden of Eden. Adam is sitting at the base of a thick and sturdy tree, and Eve is next to a slight tree. Adam's tree also appears more dominant because it is in the foreground. The trunks and roots of both trees are very close, and their upper branches are intertwined.[9]

The illustrations in many of the early vernacular Bibles were influenced by fifteenth-century block books, especially the *Ars Moriendi*, the *Speculum Humanae Salvationis*, and the *Biblia Pauperum*. The creation of Eve in the *Biblia Pauperum* is the first panel of an iconographic triptych that includes two scenes from the Old Testament and one scene (the middle panel) from the New Testament (figure 2). On the viewer's left, God the Father creates Eve by lifting her from the side of the sleeping Adam, who is recumbent on the fertile ground. Eve is upraised in the midst of a garden with a solitary fruit tree nearby. The other panels of the triptych also depict the emergence of life in a garden setting. On the viewer's right, Moses is shown against a background of trees while he strikes the rock to bring forth the waters of life. In the middle panel the crucifix, often described and visualized as the "tree of life to all,"[10] is emplaced near a rock; and when the centurion lances Christ's side, the water and blood that will restore life to mankind will begin to flow. Just as mankind is reliant on Christ, so also is Eve dependent on Adam, who is figuratively described as the "tree of life" from which she derived life, on which she is dependent, and to which she was conjoined. The commentary accompanying the triptych in the *Biblia Pauperum* interprets the sleeping Adam as an Old Testament prefiguration of Christ: "Adam, asleep, is a type of Christ already dead upon the cross, from whose side flowed for us the sacraments when the soldier, with a lance, pierced the side of Christ."[11] In *Paradise Lost* the manner in which Adam participates in Eve's creation suggests his resemblance to the godhead and establishes his primacy over Eve. Just as Adam assisted God with the creation of Eve, so also Eve is to assist Adam in the procreation of their children. Their relationship is explained by the epic narrator: "Hee for God only, shee for God in him" (IV, 299).

At Adam's request Raphael describes God's creation of mankind:

> Male he created thee, but thy consort
> Female for Race; then bless'd Mankind, and said,
> Be fruitful, multiply, and fill the Earth.          (VII, 529–31)

After having created man and woman, God marries them by blessing their union and enjoining them to propagate. The word *consort* means

FIGURE 2. *Biblia Pauperum* (Netherlands or Germany, ca. 1460-1470), leaf 9ʳ. HEH 92581. Reproduced by permission of the Huntington Library.

sharer, partner, spouse; it suggests the intimate, inseparable, and pro-creative ("Be fruitful") relationship of Adam and Eve. Their marriage and the command to procreate emphasize that their union is not simply desirable but actually necessary. In fact, Eve was created in response to Adam's need for "fellowship" that is "fit to participate / All rational delight" (VIII, 389–91). Adam recognizes that man alone lives in "single imperfection" (VIII, 423). His request for "Collateral love, and dearest amity" (VIII, 426) is met when God promises to provide him with "Thy likeness, thy fit help, thy other self" (VIII, 450). Adam first sees Eve when she is "Led by her Heav'nly Maker, though unseen, / And guided by his voice, nor uninform'd / Of nuptial Sanctity and marriage Rites" (VIII, 485–87). He responds to Eve's presence and expresses his desire to be united with her by participating in the rite of marriage and by recognizing that he must "to his Wife adhere" (VIII, 498). The botanical meaning of *adhere* (*OED*, def. 5) describes a process of adhesion between two plants or between two parts of a plant: to "be naturally united or soldered to what is normally an *unlike* part." This connotation of *adhere* appropriately describes the relationship between Adam and Eve. When Eve was created from one of his ribs, Adam recalls, God's "forming hands" shaped a creature that was "Man*like*, but *different* sex, so lovely fair" (VIII, 470–71, italics added). When Satan first sees Adam and Eve (IV, 288–311) and later as he plans to tempt them, he recognizes that they are similar but different. Indeed, they comprise a natural union between unlike parts. This connotation of *adhere* is elaborated in images that describe Adam and Eve as plants that are interdependent. When they were created and married, and as they perform their duties in the garden, Adam is described, for example, as a tree and Eve, a vine; he is the prop or stalk, she the rose.

In *De Doctrina Christiana*, Milton asserts that marriage "was in-stituted, if not commanded, at the creation."[12] As the context makes clear, Milton means that the marriage ritual of Genesis ii, 24, reflects what was accomplished earlier during the very process of Eve's creation from Adam (Genesis ii, 22). Milton uses "*adhaerebit*" in *De Doctrina Christiana* when he renders Genesis ii, 24, into Latin: "*adhaerebit uxori suae, eruntque in carnem unam*" ("[a man] shall cleave unto his wife, and they shall be one flesh") (CM, XV, 122–23). The *OED* explains that *adhere* (def.1) means to "stick fast, to cleave . . . *to* a substance, as by a glutinous surface." This connotation can be related to Eve's creation. When God removed Adam's rib, "cordial spirits warm, / And Life-blood streaming fresh" issued from Adam's side (VIII, 466-67). God then "form'd and fashion'd" the rib until "a Creature grew" (VIII, 469-70). The issuance from Adam, who is Eve's "tree of life," becomes the "glutinous" substance or adhesive that is spread by God across the rib from which Eve begins to emerge. In *De Doctrina Christiana*, Milton observes that God created Eve "without the necessity of infusing the breath of life a second time" (CM, XV, 44–45). Under God's hands, Adam's principle of life was *trans*fused into Eve when "cordial spirits" and "Life-blood" adhered throughout her growing form. From the time of her creation, Eve is "one Flesh, one Heart, one Soul" (VIII, 499) with Adam.

In *l'Hortus Deliciarum*, a fourteenth-century illuminated manuscript, God is depicted as a builder who is forming Eve from Adam's extracted rib.[13] In some translations of Genesis ii, 22, God is described as having "builded the rib, which he had taken from Adam, to a woman."[14] This is the translation that Henry Ainsworth uses, and he quotes several passages from Scripture (Job iv, 19; 2 Corinthians v, 1; 1 Chronicles xvii, 10; 2 Samuel vii, 11; Psalm cxxxix, 14) to emphasize that God is a builder and that man is God's "wondrous workmanship."[15] In his Latin rendering of Genesis ii, 22, Milton uses *fabricavit*, which suggests that God built or constructed Eve from one of Adam's ribs (*De Doctrina Christiana*, CM, XV, 44). In the creation of Adam, God is likewise viewed as a builder. Milton uses *formavit* to indicate that God molded man as the breath of life was being infused (*De Doctrina Christiana*, CM, XV, 38–39). Even Satan, after having viewed Adam and Eve, remarks "such grace / The hand that form'd them on thir shape hath pour'd" (*PL* IV, 364–65).

Throughout *Paradise Lost*, Eve periodically recalls her creation from Adam and her participation in the marriage rite in order to affirm her inseparability from Adam and her dependence on him. She remarks to him that she "was form'd flesh of thy flesh" (IV, 441). Shortly afterwards, she comments to Adam: "My Author and Disposer, what thou bidd'st / Unargu'd I obey; so God ordains, / God is thy Law, thou mine" (IV, 635–37). Eve's reliance on Adam is also indicated by the different instruction that each of them receives after having been created by God. Shortly after his creation, Adam experiences a dream-vision in which a "shape Divine" (VIII, 295), his "Guide" (VIII, 298), leads him up the mountain, through the enclosure of trees at the summit, and into the garden. The "Guide" vanishes but soon afterwards appears "among the Trees" (VIII, 313) in order to instruct Adam. After her creation, Eve does not see God but is led by his voice to her meeting and marriage with Adam:

> Whose image thou art, him thou shalt enjoy
> Inseparably thine, to him shalt bear
> Multitudes like thyself, and thence be call'd
> Mother of human Race.                    (IV, 472–75)

By acknowledging that Adam is her "Guide" and "Head" (IV, 442–43), Eve subordinates herself to him, and the relationship that she develops with Adam parallels his relationship with God. In *De Doctrina Christiana*, Milton explains the relationship between husband and wife by citing 1 Corinthians xi, 7–9: "for a man . . . is the image of the glory of God, but the woman is the glory of the man: for the man is not of the woman, but the woman of the man; neither was the man created for the woman, but the woman for the man" (CM, XV, 120–21).

When Eve had approached Adam after her creation, she viewed him "fair indeed and tall" under a tree (IV, 477). Adam's upright posture and his proximity to the tree suggest his near identification with it. The marriage ritual, also performed under a tree, pointedly recalls the manner of Eve's creation and emphasizes her relationship with Adam. Under the tree Eve stands next to Adam, who comments: "I lent / Out of my side to thee, nearest my heart / Substantial Life, to have thee by my side" (IV, 483–85). The repetition of *side* stresses that Eve, who was created from Adam's side, is to remain near him. As part of the marriage ritual, the joining of hands is accomplished when Adam's "gentle hand / Seiz'd" Eve's, and she "yielded" (IV, 488–89). This same dependency is evident as Eve "half imbracing lean'd / On our first Father" (IV, 494–95). Images that liken Adam and Eve to plants and that explain their duties as gardeners provide a continuous insight into the nature of their relationship, which was prescribed by the manner of their creation, by their marriage, and by God's enjoinder that they should "Be fruitful." The epic narrator, for instance, describes Eve's "golden tresses" (IV, 305):

> Dishevell'd, but in wanton ringlets wav'd
> As the Vine curls her tendrils, which impli'd

> Subjection, but requir'd with gentle sway,
> And by her yielded.                              (IV, 306–09)

Here Eve is likened to a vine that needs the support of a mainstay. The epic narrator also describes how Adam and Eve

> led the Vine
> To wed her Elm; she spous'd about him twines
> Her marriageable arms, and with her brings
> Her dow'r th' adopted Clusters, to adorn
> His barren leaves.                              (V, 215–19)

To "wed" the vine to the elm recalls Eve's marriage to Adam under God's supervision. Words like *wed, spous'd*, and *marriageable arms* underscore the parallelism. "Twines" calls attention to Adam's solitary state before the creation of Eve. The image of "barren leaves" refers to the elm's fruitless or nonproductive existence, which is overcome when it is conjoined to the vine. The creation of Eve and her marriage to Adam are depicted in *l'Hortus Deliciarum*. Adam is asleep under a tree while Eve is being created by God. Depicted in the branches of the tree are both fruits and human heads. For Gérard Cames this tree is an " 'Arbre de Vie' dont les fruits sont de surprenantes têtes d'enfants."[16] For Adam and Eve to "Be fruitful" they must beget progeny, who are visually identified as the "fruits" of their union. The depiction of human heads alongside the fruits in the tree provides an iconographic context for interpreting some of Milton's images. In saluting Eve, Raphael likens her progeny to fruits:

> Hail Mother of Mankind, whose fruitful Womb
> Shall fill the World more numerous with thy Sons
> Than with these various fruits the Trees of God
> Have heap'd this Table.                         (V, 388–91)

By begetting progeny, Adam and Eve will receive the assistance of "younger hands ere long" (IX, 246) in caring for the garden and in consuming its bounteous fruit.

## II

In *Paradise Lost*, God the Father announces that the Creation of the world and its inhabitants will be accomplished by "my Word, begotten Son, by thee / This I perform" (VII, 163–64), and the epic narrator emphasizes that the "Word, the Filial Godhead, gave effect" (VII, 175) to the Father's pronouncement. The Son embodies man from the "Dust of the ground" (VII, 525), infuses a soul into him, and creates Eve from Adam's side. Although Adam and Eve suffer spiritual death "at the very moment of the fall" (*De Doctrina Christiana*, CM, XV, 204–05), the process of regeneration, which is achieved through "the sprinkling of the blood of Christ" (CM, XIV, 124–25), causes mankind "to be 'born again,' and to be 'created afresh'" (CM, XV, 204–05). In *De Doctrina Christiana, Paradise Lost*, seventeenth-century devotional poetry, and Christian iconography, the Crucifixion is often associated with the re-creation of mankind. Throughout *De Doctrina Christiana*, Milton quotes and interprets scriptural passages (like 1 Peter i, 2; 1 John i, 7; Romans iii, 25; Romans v, 9; Acts xx, 28) that stress the importance of Christ's sacrifice and the efficacy of his blood in creating anew. In Donne's "Goodfriday, 1613. Riding Westward," Christ's "blood which is / The seat of all our Soules, if not of his, / Made durt of dust" (25–27). Thus the issuance from Christ causes an act of re-creation that parallels both the creation of Adam from the earth and the creation of Eve from Adam's side. Christ's issuance, like Adam's, may also be described as "cordial spirits" and "Life-blood," which embody "the Dust of the ground," adhere to mankind, and transfuse the principle of life. Mankind is re-created and upraised under "the tree of life to all." According to the legends of the cross, the Crucifixion occurred "in the very same place where God had fashioned Adam out of the dust of the ground"; and "Jesus died on the very spot where Adam was buried, so that His blood should flow over the bones of our first parent."[17] In stained-glass windows at Angers and Bourges, Adam and Eve are "receiving the blood which flows from the Cross."[18] In *Très Riches Heures*, Adam's skull and bones appear at the foot of the cross, and in the Dessau Psalter (ca. 1480) the blood of Christ flows on Adam's bones.[19] Louis Réau discusses iconography that shows Adam rising from the earth to receive Christ's blood at the Crucifixion.[20]

Like the Creation, the effect of the Crucifixion on mankind is described as a building process. In Herbert's "H. Baptisme" (I) the issuance from the Redeemer "spreads the plaister" (11) across man, who is not only re-created but also baptized in Christ's blood. Milton comments that man is God's "workmanship, created in Christ Jesus unto good works" (*De Doctrina Christiana*, CM, XVI, 40–41). Often the effect of the Crucifixion is related specifically to the human heart.

While discussing regeneration, Milton cites Psalm li, 10 (*De Doctrina Christiana*, CM, XV, 367–77) and Ezekiel xviii, 31 (CM, XVI, 13) to assert that the human heart in which Christ dwells is cleansed and re-created by his blood. *Imitatio Christi* involves man's willingness to undergo suffering after the manner of Christ and to emulate the love and charity shown by Christ. When man displays this willingness, he participates in the purification and re-creation of his own heart. In Herbert's "The Altar," man's broken heart is "cemented with teares" (2), and in "The Church-floore" love and charity are the "sweet cement" (10) causing the heart to adhere. Seventeenth-century devotional poetry emphasizes that the tears of man begin the processes of purification and adhesion that are completed when the issuance from Christ's side is received.

The parallelism between the Creation and the Crucifixion extends beyond the building process to include also the processes of implanting, ingrafting, and marriage. In Donne's *La Corona*, the sonnet entitled "Crucifying" ends with the speaker's plea for "*one drop*" of Christ's blood to "*Moyst*" his "dry soule." When likened to a garden that is intended as God's paradise, man's heart is implanted by the Word or Logos, nourished by grace, and illuminated by Christ. The image of the paradisiacal garden in the human heart is sometimes developed as an elaboration of the parable of the sower (Matthew xiii, 18–23), as it is by Milton (*De Doctrina Christiana*, CM, XIV, 130–31). It is an elaboration of 2 Corinthians iv, 6, in which the *fiat lux* decree is reenacted when God, through Christ, "hath shined in our hearts" (CM, XV, 6–7), and it is an elaboration of Ephesians iii, 17: "that Christ may dwell in your hearts by faith, that ye being rooted and grounded in love" (CM, XVI, 10–11). In addition to implanting and growth, ingrafting describes the effect of the Crucifixion on mankind. Milton comments that "believers are said to be ingrafted in Christ, when they are planted in Christ by God the Father, that is, are made partakers of Christ, and meet for becoming one with him" (CM, XVI, 2–3). There is a marriage between Christ and the sanctified soul, between the Logos and the human heart, which is consummated at the Redemption. One heart, one flesh, and one soul describe not only the conjugal relationship between Adam and Eve but also the loving interaction between the soul and Christ, who implants himself as the "tree of life" in the human heart to be ingrafted to mankind. Accordingly, the relationship between Christ and the soul is described as the interrelation between a vine and its fruit-bearing branches (John xv, 4-5), which is very similar to the conjugal union that Milton describes between Adam and Eve. While discussing Regeneration (*De Doctrina Christiana*, CM, XVI, 10-11), Milton cites John xv, 4-5, in which Christ enjoins the soul to abide in him as he does in it. This loving interaction, like the marriage of Adam and Eve, "bringeth forth much fruit." Donne explains this fruitful relationship briefly in "The Crosse." When the human heart loves the image of the cross, "Then doth the Crosse of Christ worke fruitfully / Within our hearts" (61-62). The significance of the cross in the marriage of Christ and the soul is dramatically explained by St. Augustine in *Sermo Suppositus* (CXX. viii): "Like a bridegroom Christ went forth from his chamber, he went out with a presage of his nuptials into the field of the world. He ran like a giant exulting on his way, and came to the marriage bed of the cross, and there, in mounting it, he consummated his marriage."[21]

Marital union describes Christ's relationship not only with the sanctified soul but also with the church. Milton comments that the "love of Christ towards his invisible and spotless Church is described by the appropriate figure of conjugal love" (*De Doctrina Christiana*, CM, XVI, 64-65). Milton cites Acts of the Apostles (xx, 28) to emphasize that the church, like the soul, was created from the issuance of Christ's blood (CM, XIV, 260-61). In describing the church in *De Doctrina Christiana*, Milton quotes extensively from St. Paul's epistles. The church, for example, is the "mystical body," which is characterized by the "union and fellowship" of all its "members"; and the bodily integrity that the church achieves is the result of an act of creation that enables the "members of that one body" to adhere, to receive "nourishment" from Christ, and to be vitalized by the "Spirit of Christ" (CM, XVI, 56-65). Christ and his church, which he created and then married, share "one body" and "one spirit" (CM, XVI, 60-61). As "the head" (CM, XVI, 60-61) of the church, Christ is likened to the husband. In iconography of the Crucifixion, the church is often visualized as a crowned woman (*Mater Ecclesia*) at the foot of the cross. In a stained-glass window at Bourges, for instance, and in *l'Hortus Deliciarum*, she holds a chalice (*aureus calix*) to receive the issuance of water and blood, which signify the sacraments of Baptism and the Holy Eucharist.[22] Some miniaturists even "represent the Church

emerging from the right side of Christ."[23] Thus the relationship between
Christ and the church parallels both the creation of Eve from Adam's
side and their marriage. Accordingly, images of building and procreation describe Christ's marriage to the church. The faithful are "framed
together," "builded together," and "fitly joined together"; furthermore,
they "increaseth" and "groweth" to become a "holy temple" for indwelling by Christ (CM, XVI, 60–63).

In *Paradise Lost*, the creation and marriage of Adam and Eve,
their relationship with God, and their participation in communal worship of God signify the inception of the Invisible Church or Mystical
Body, on the one hand, and the Visible Church, on the other.[24] After
having completed their gardening duties for the day, Adam and Eve
are attentive to the angels' "Singing thir great Creator" (IV, 684). Adam
and Eve "talking hand in hand" (IV, 689) move toward their dwelling.
Before entering, they "under op'n Sky ador'd / The God that made
both Sky, Air, Earth and Heav'n" (IV, 721–22). In Book IV of *Paradise
Lost*, as in "On the Morning of Christ's Nativity," mankind and the
angels harmonize in their praise of God, and the temple in which
God is praised extends from the human heart, through the cosmos,
and into heaven.

Both the Invisible Church, which encompasses the faithful "of
all ages from the foundation of the world" (*De Doctrina Christiana*,
CM, XVI, 62–63), and the Visible Church, which includes participants
in "the proper external worship of God" (CM, XVI, 220–21), are to
be increased by the marriage of Adam and Eve. In their evening
prayer of thanksgiving, Adam and Eve praise the fertility of the garden
and recall that God "hast promis'd from us two a Race / To fill the
Earth, who shall with us extol / Thy goodness infinite" (IV, 732–34).
Their evening prayer and the affirmation of the procreative purpose
of their marriage are described as "Rites" and as "adoration pure
/ Which God likes best" (IV, 736–38). After their prayer, Adam and
Eve "into thir inmost bower / Handed . . . went" (IV, 738–39). Their
bower is a holy "place / Chos'n by the sovran Planter" (IV, 690–91),
a veritable temple invested with the highest sanctity. The procreative
act, performed in their bower, is a perfect expression of their conjugal
union and is an act of worship because it fulfills God's injunction
to "Be fruitful." The bower is also an enclosed garden within the
more spacious Garden of Eden. Around the "blissful Bower" (IV,

690) various plants "Fenc'd up the verdant wall" (IV, 697); numerous flowers, like the iris, rose, and jessamin, "Rear'd high thir flourisht heads between" (IV, 699); and other flowers, like the violet, crocus, and hyacinth, inlaid the floor.

At the time of their creation and in the performance of their gardening duties, Adam and Eve are identified with trees, plants, and flowers. As God's chosen place, the bower epitomizes the fertility and verdant beauty with which Adam and Eve and their progeny are likened. Their conjugal union will procreate the faithful who will make up the church and who will join in a chorus of praise to God. As Adam and Eve "imbracing slept" (IV, 771), they are united with each other and with their fertile environment, and they are recipients of God's blessing: "on thir naked limbs the flow'ry roof / Show'r'd Roses" (IV, 772–73). A nuptial bed of roses within the privacy of a bed chamber is visualized in the *Canticum Canticorum*, a fifteenth-century block book that depicts scenes from the Song of Songs (figure 3). At the threshold of her bedroom, the bride has placed her hand on the shoulder of the bridegroom to invite him to the nuptial bed. Numerous commentators, including St. Augustine, St. Gregory the Great, Origen, St. Bernard of Clairvaux, St. John of the Cross, and St. Francis de Sales, have interpreted the Song of Songs. In their commentaries and in Christian iconography, the marriage of Solomon and his bride is interpreted as the relationships between Christ and the soul, Christ and the church, and also Christ and the Virgin Mary.[25] These loving relationships, like the marriage of Solomon and his bride, are often visualized in a garden setting; and iconographic depictions tend to highlight ironic resemblances between the Fall on the one hand and the Creation and the Crucifixion on the other. These relationships, as well as the visual context in which they are depicted, constitute a frame of reference in which to interpret the separation of Adam and Eve in Book IX, Satan's temptation of Eve, and the Fall of Adam and Eve.

### III

In Book IX of *Paradise Lost*, Adam and Eve emerge from their bower to begin their gardening for the day. The garden into which they enter is described as a temple in which nature is worshiping God. The flowers "breath'd / Thir morning incense," and "From th'

FIGURE 3.  *Canticum Canticorum* (Netherlands, ca. 1470), p. 14. HEH 144965.
Reproduced by permission of the Huntington Library.

Earth's great Altar send up silent praise / To the Creator" (IX, 193-96). Just outside their bower, Adam and Eve "join'd thir vocal Worship to the Choir / Of Creatures wanting voice" (IX, 198-99). Before the Fall, communal worship of God extended across the hierarchy of creation—from nature, to the animals in the Garden of Eden, to Adam and Eve (especially in the innermost garden of their bower), and to the angels in the cosmos. For the first time, however, Adam and Eve consider working separately. "Let us divide our labors" (IX, 214) is Eve's suggestion to Adam. But the irony of the proposal is underscored by the duties that each will perform. In the past their cooperation in gardening described how they themselves ought to be interrelated. Adam and Eve, for example, had "spous'd" the vine to the elm (V, 216), and this continuous adherence or fruitful embrace characterized their own united endeavor through the day, which culminated in the procreative function of their marriage. On the other hand, Eve now indicates that Adam himself should "wind / The Woodbine round this Arbor, or direct / The clasping Ivy where to climb" (IX, 215-17). When Adam later consents to "direct" the ivy and to dress the garden without Eve's assistance, his solitary activity will be an ironic commentary on his permissiveness, which is manifested in his failure to "direct" Eve to adhere to him. While Adam is gardening alone, Eve is to be working "In yonder Spring of Roses intermixt / With Myrtle" (IX, 218-19). The phrase "Spring of Roses" connotes lush beauty and fertility stimulated by the warmth and moisture of the growing season, and it recalls the embrace and kiss of Adam and Eve and their resemblance to Jupiter and Juno: "as *Jupiter* / On *Juno* smiles, when he impregns the Clouds / That shed *May* Flowers" (IV, 499-501). "Spring of Roses" also alludes to the conjugal union of Adam and Eve in their bower, which became a nuptial bed of roses. When "intermixt / With Myrtle," the roses are propped up by this other plant, which represents Adam's support and adherence to Eve. As Eve later works alone among the flowers, which "she upstays / Gently with Myrtle band" (IX, 430-31), the necessary union between husband and wife is underscored. The phrase "Spring of Roses" also anticipates Satan's later view of Eve working among the roses. She is "mindless the while, / Herself, though fairest unsupported Flow'r, / From her best prop so far" (IX, 431-33). Eve's diligent attention to the plants is contrasted with her negligence and irresponsibility toward herself and with her rashness in working

apart from Adam. In planning to "redress" (IX, 219) the roses and
the myrtle, Eve ought to be reminded of her own dependency on
Adam. In her assessment of the garden, Eve recognizes that trees,
plants, and flowers tend toward independent growth. By pruning and
propping up plants, Adam and Eve prevent the "wanton growth"
(IX, 211) that carries one plant away from its necessary adherence
to a kindred plant. Such outgrowth, which is "Tending to wild" (IX,
212), explains Eve's separation from Adam.

   Adam argues against Eve's intention to work independently by
reminding her of the paramount significance of mutual adherence,
which is the essence of their conjugal union. He paraphrases the view,
expressed earlier in his discourse with Raphael (VIII, 601–04), that
"this sweet intercourse / Of looks and smiles" (IX, 238–39) manifests
their communion of mind. Their rapport, especially their dialogue,
is "delight to Reason join'd" (IX, 243), and twice this loving relationship is described as the "food" (IX, 238–40) that sustains each of them.
Adam also advises Eve to "doubt not but our joint hands / Will keep
from Wilderness with ease . . . till younger hands ere long / Assist
us" (IX, 244–47). His reminder of their procreative function, which
was commanded by God, underscores the significance of their mutual
adherence. After having left Adam, Eve will establish with the serpent
a relationship that is an ironic counterpart to the mutual adherence
that she ought to have maintained with Adam. Eve's dialogue with
the serpent, her responsiveness to his guidance, her consent to his
suggestion, and her attempt to seek "food" (IX, 717) outside the relationship with her husband cause Eve "to withdraw / . . . fealty from
God" and enable Satan "to disturb / Conjugal Love" (IX, 261–63).
In the conversation with Eve, Adam's use of "sever'd" (IX, 252) and
"asunder" (IX, 258) anticipates conjugal disunion between himself and
Eve and between mankind and God. These words also suggest the
dismemberment of the church, which began with the mutual adherence
of Adam and Eve and was to have increased as they procreated.
When Adam finally enjoins Eve to remain with him, he likens himself
to a tree, and he alludes to Eve's creation from his side: "leave not the
faithful side / That gave thee being, still shades thee and protects"
(IX, 265–66). Like the triptych in the *Biblia Pauperum* (figure 2) that
parallels the creation of Eve with the Crucifixion, this literary image
highlights the resemblance between Adam and Christ as "trees of

life" and correlates the several loving relationships that are described as conjugal unions consummated in a garden setting: Adam and Eve, Christ and the soul, Christ and the church, Christ and the Virgin Mary.

In iconography of the Song of Songs, the biblical analogue for these loving relationships, the lover is often likened to the tree on which the beloved is dependent. In Quarles' *Emblemes* (1635), Canticles ii, 3, is illustrated with the lover, or Christ, crucified in an apple tree;[26] and his beloved, who reclines in the shade of the tree, is gazing upward at him (figure 4). The shadow mentioned in Canticles ii, 3, and visualized in Quarles' *Emblemes* may be correlated with Adam's assertion that he "shades . . . and protects" Eve. When the epic narrator laments the end of "sweet repast, or sound repose" (IX, 407) for Eve, he is alluding to her separation from Adam. Both Christ and Adam are the "trees of life" providing food, comfort, and protection to their spouses, who are to remain nearby. The verses composed by Quarles to accompany the illustration emphasize that the crucified Christ mercifully shields mankind from the "scorching beames" of the sun, which represents the "eye of vengeance" or divine retribution of God the Father (p. 237). In *Paradise Lost* the Son visits Adam and Eve after they have sinned, and his actions prefigure his later role as Savior incarnate. He covers "from his Father's sight" the "inward nakedness" of Adam and Eve "with his Robe of righteousness" (X, 221-23).

Quarles also indicates in his verses that the "wandring Soule," which leaves its sanctified relationship with Christ, becomes the "hourely prey" of sins (p. 237). The parallelism with Eve's separation from Adam is well defined, for she becomes the errant soul who has left her spouse. When she disrupts the conjugal union that obliged her to adhere in soul, mind, and body to Adam, "*Eve* separate" (IX, 422) clearly becomes Satan's "purpos'd prey" (IX, 416). Both Quarles and Milton elaborate the implications of this predatory relationship. Quarles likens "Sinnes" to "vultures" (p. 237), and in *Paradise Lost* Satan is likened to a vulture searching for prey (III, 431) and to a wolf (IV, 183). Furthermore, he assumes the shapes of a cormorant (IV, 196), a lion, and a tiger (IV, 402-03) as he stalks Adam and Eve and moves "Nearer to view his prey" (IV, 399). Sin and Death, like Satan, are also described as predators on mankind. When Satan converses with them at the gates of Hell, he promises Sin and Death that "all things

## XIV.

*I sat vnder the shadoue of him whom
I haue desired - Cane: 2   Will sim son
sculp:*

shall be your prey" (II, 844); and when they seek to follow him to Earth after the Fall of mankind, Death is directed by "a scent . . . / Of carnage, prey innumerable" (X, 267-68).

The intimacy between Sin and Death ironically parallels the relationship between Adam and Eve. Whereas Eve was created from Adam, is conjoined to him, and is urged to procreate with him, Death emerges from Sin, and "in embraces forcible and foul" (II, 793) copulates with his mother, who "of that rape begot" (II, 794) monstrous progeny. On the one hand, Adam and Eve are urged to gaze on each other, to converse, and to work together because this interaction is "of Love the food" (IX, 240); on the other hand, Sin remarks that Death "Before mine eyes in opposition sits" (II, 803), and "his Parent would full soon devour / For want of other prey" (II, 805-06). In Book X the relationship that is continuously maintained between Sin and Death is a demonic counterpart to the conjugal relationship that is forsaken by Adam and Eve and by every "wandring Soule" (in Quarles' phrase) that leaves Christ. In fact, Sin's relationship with Death may be interpreted in a context provided by Adam's assertion that he "shades" Eve and by Quarles' emblem that depicts Canticles ii, 3, in which Christ is inseparable from the soul while shading it (figure 4). Sin addresses Death as "my Shade / Inseparable must with mee along: / For Death from Sin no power can separate" (X, 249-51). In contrast to the separation of Adam and Eve, Death insists that he and Sin work together: "Nor shall I to the work thou enterprisest / Be wanting, but afford thee equal aid" (X, 270-71).

Quarles' various emblems interpreting the Song of Songs are remarkably analogous to Milton's interpretation of the conjugal union of Adam and Eve. Quarles' depictions show the lovers gazing at each other, holding hands, embracing, and kissing. In the illustration of Canticles iii, 3, for example, the lovers embrace at their reunion (p. 228); unlike Eve, the woman was very uneasy during her lover's absence. When she located him after a frantic search, her "Armes did twine, / And strongly twist, about his yeelding wast" (p. 230). They embrace near an elm that is encircled by a vine. Appropriately, she likens herself to the "branches of the Thespian vine" (p. 230) that clasp the elm, a metaphor also used in Quarles' verses on Canticles ii, 16. In seventeenth-century emblem books, illustrations of plants adhering to each other are often used to suggest mutual dependency and necessary interrelationship. In *Minerva Britanna* (London, 1612), Henry Peacham comments that the laurel and grapevine "In frendly league perpetually doe growe"; they have an "inviolate" union (p. 39). In another illustration, myrtle and a fruitful pomegranate tree are planted alongside each other, and their stalks incline toward each other while their upper branches are entwined. Peacham observes that their "armes embrac't" in "frendly league" and "mutuall amitie" (p. 41). In *A Choice of Emblemes* (Leyden, 1586), Geffrey Whitney interprets in a similar fashion an illustration of a grapevine clasping an elm (p. 62).

There are other parallels between Quarles' interpretation of Canticles ii, 16, and Milton's conception of the interrelationship of Adam and Eve. The beloved remarks that she and her lover "became entire" and that their "firm united soules did more than twine" (p. 253). The beloved likens herself to a "Holy Place" in which the lover is an "Altar" (p. 254). Like Adam and Eve conjoined in loving worship in their bower, Christ's indwelling makes the soul a temple. The lover is also described as "living Food" (p. 254), which recalls the illustration of Canticles ii, 3 (figure 4). The Eucharistic symbolism of Christ crucified in the apple tree, from which his beloved takes and eats fruit, may be likened to the "food" (IX, 238–40) provided Eve in her relationship with Adam and may be ironically paralleled with Death's instinct to devour Sin. The lover as "Altar," in short, refers to the crucifix as the tree of life implanted in the human heart, an enclosed garden. The loving relationship between Adam and Eve, which is consummated on their nuptial bed (IV, 772-73), corresponds to the amorous union between Christ and the soul and between Christ and the church. This union, as St. Augustine comments in *Sermo Suppositus*, is consummated on the bed of the cross. In Quarles' illustration of Canticles iii, 1, the lover has abandoned his bed in order to emplace himself on the cross, which is lying on the floor directly under the bed (figure 5). His beloved resolves to be united with him: "Wee'l never part, Ile share a Crosse with Thee" (p. 222).[27]

Adam continually emphasizes that he "protects" and "guards" Eve "where danger or dishonor lurks" (IX, 266-69), and his admonition anticipates Satan's "sly assault" against Eve (IX, 256). He argues that he and Eve are mutually dependent, since he becomes "More wise, more watchful, stronger" while she is "looking on" (IX, 311-12). Her

## X.

By night on my bed I sought him whom my
soule loueth; I sought him, but I found him not.
  Cant: 3·1.                    Will: simpson sculpsit.

FIGURE 5.  Francis Quarles, *Emblemes* (London, 1635), p. 220, STC 20540,
HEH 69011. Reproduced by permission of the Huntington Library.

presence enables Adam to develop increased strength against the force
of evil and intensified watchfulness against guile. Adam recognizes
that his increased strength is added physical resistance (IX, 312); more
importantly, however, it is a confirmed inner strength, which Milton
defines as fortitude in *De Doctrina Christiana*. Fortitude is a virtue
"exercised in the resistance to, or the endurance of evil" and "is chiefly
conspicuous in repelling evil" (CM, XVII, 246–47). The biblical proof-
texts cited by Milton describe fortitude as wisdom, strength, knowledge, courage, and watchfulness; it is, therefore, a composite of all
the virtues that are reinforced when Adam and Eve are together and
that will enable them to resist temptation. Adam reminds Eve that
he "with her the worst endures" (*PL* IX, 269); and she, in turn, is
instructed to remain alongside him: "thy trial choose / With me" (IX,
316–17). When Adam advises Eve to "Seek not temptation . . . which
to avoid / Were better" (IX, 364–65), he is cautioning her against
rashness, which Milton describes as a vice "opposed to fortitude."
Rashness "consists in exposing ourselves to danger unnecessarily" (*De
Doctrina Christiana*, CM, XVII, 250–51).

    When Eve is separated from the "tree of life" that gave her being
and that furnished protection, she becomes prey to the tempter, yields
to him, and undergoes spiritual death. Throughout Milton's description
of her fall, there are numerous typological correspondences that prefigure the means and manner by which Redemption will be achieved.
As Eve is working alone, Satan views her amidst the roses: "Veil'd
in a Cloud of Fragrance, where she stood, / Half spi'd, so thick the
Roses bushing round / About her glow'd" (IX, 425–27). Eve appears
clothed by the roses that surround her; but as Satan approaches her,
she is figuratively undressed and fully naked to his view:

> What pleasing seem'd, for her now pleases more,
> She most, and in her look sums all Delight.
> Such Pleasure took the Serpent to behold
> This Flow'ry Plat, the sweet recess of *Eve*.          (IX, 453–56)

The flower garden traditionally describes the Virgin Mary; and in
*Partheneia Sacra* (1633), an emblem book dedicated to the Virgin
Mary, she is viewed in relation to a garden setting and is identified
with particular plants and flowers. The entrance of the viewer into
the garden, his perspective inside it, and his conception of the Virgin
all contrast with Satan's access to Eden, his presence there, and his

relationship with Eve. In *Partheneia Sacra* the viewer is actually the reader who enters the garden of the Virgin "with the wings of Contemplation" in order to "secretly view, reflect, review, survey, delight, contemplate, and enjoy the hidden and sublime perfections therin."[28] The reader is to be led "into the Maze or Labyrinth of the beauties therin contained," which will "satisfy the Eye as wel as the Understanding" (p. 3). Henry Hawkins likens his emblem book to a "Tapestrie" (p. 3), for his intention is to provide visual perspective, to guide interpretation, and to help the viewer elicit meaning. Through the "Maze or Labyrinth" of iconographic detail, Hawkins leads his viewer to understand the virtues of Mary and the meaning of her relationship with God. By comparison, Satan's approach toward Eve through the labyrinth of trees and flowers (IX, 434–56) may be interpreted as the course of a well-directed viewer negotiating the details of landscape while heading toward the central figure. Satan's view of Eve, however, arouses his concupiscence and debases her.

The garden of the Virgin and the garden of Eve are similar because each is a *locus amoenus* in which the central figure is a woman. The *locus amoenus* is Venus' garden of classical antiquity that has been transmuted into the typical setting of the medieval romance, notably the *Roman de la Rose*.[29] Iconographic detail of the *locus amoenus* is basically the same, but an interpretation of its meaning depends on the nature of the presiding woman and her effect on the viewer or lover. The garden settings of the two parts of the *Roman de la Rose* are similar, but Guillaume's garden arouses concupiscence in the lover, whereas Jean de Meun's has a spiritualizing effect. Inhabited by the serpent, Eden may be likened to Venus' garden of sensuality and to Guillaume's garden, whereas the garden of the Virgin in *Partheneia Sacra*, though similar in iconographic detail, is the spiritual counterpart. When identified with Eve, for instance, the rose may be said "to typify the fading beauty of the flesh"; furthermore, the "use of the roses in Wisdom II. viii" indicates that "these flowers were also associated with *luxuria* and hence with Venus."[30] When identified with the Virgin Mary, however, the rose signifies "Shamfastnes and bashful Modestie."[31] Satan's view of Eve amidst the roses may be contrasted, for example, with the Virgin's appearance in Stefano da Zevio's *The Madonna in a Rosegarden*, in which the Virgin, like Eve, is to be interpreted as the "fairest" of the roses.[32] In the enclosed garden, which is tended and protected by numerous angels, two scenes are depicted. In the upper part of the painting, the Virgin is seated on the ground while holding the infant Jesus. In the lower part of the painting, there is a version of the Annunciation in which the Virgin, again seated on the ground, has two roses in her lap and an angel, who seems to be addressing her, points to them. The roses signify Mary and Christ, who are depicted together in the upper part of the painting. In the version of the Annunciation, Mary's left arm is extended outward (with the palm of the hand facing the angel) in a gesture of modesty and humility. Encircling her left forearm is a garland of roses; and she is wearing a crown. In both depictions the Virgin is fully clothed and veiled, a state which contrasts with Eve's naked appearance to Satan. This particular contrast is highlighted whenever the Virgin and Eve are visually juxtaposed—for example, in *The Hours of Catherine of Cleves* (Plate 89) or in the *Biblia Pauperum*, in which the temptation of Eve is depicted alongside the Annunciation. Eve's opposite is the Virgin Mary, for whom the veil and clothing, the garland of roses, and the crown signify her inaccessibility to evil, her chaste marriage to the deity, and her lasting spiritual beauty. Of course, Adam and Eve have been physically naked since their creation, but Milton has carefully suggested that they have been "clad" (IV, 289) in honor, righteousness, and innocence. Eve's nakedness to Satan in Book IX indicates that she is accessible to his approach; that she will be deprived of honor, righteousness, and innocence; that she will, in short, be "deflow'r'd" (IX, 901).

After the Fall the metaphor of nakedness is continually applied to Adam and Eve. Their "veil" of "innocence" (IX, 1054) has been removed; they are "naked" (IX, 1057); and they are "destitute and bare / Of all thir virtue" (IX, 1062-63). The contrast between Eve and the Virgin Mary is emphasized when Adam learns of Eve's "fatal Trespass" (IX, 889), and the garland or crown that he had prepared for her "Down dropp'd, and all the faded Roses shed" (IX, 893). Milton sometimes uses the garland or crown to indicate virtue and, in particular, resistance to temptation. At the end of *Comus*, the children win *"a crown of deathless Praise"* (973) for having overcome temptation; and in his discussion of temptation in *De Doctrina Christiana*, Milton quotes James i, 12: "Blessed is the man that endureth temptation; for when he is tried, he shall receive the crown of life"

(CM, XV, 88–89). Phrased differently, the crown is awarded whenever fortitude is displayed in the face of temptation. Adam had argued that his own fortitude, as well as Eve's, was strengthened by her presence, but with their separation the opportunity for mutual help was lost. Had they endured the trial together, the crown prepared by Adam would have been the appropriate reward for their success. Actually the image of the crown had been used earlier by Adam and Eve to signify their mutual dependency. Having completed a day's labor in the garden, they recognize that they "finisht happy" because of their "mutual help / And mutual love, the Crown of all our bliss" (IV, 727–28).

Another iconographic detail that characterizes the *locus amoenus* is the well or spring that serves as a glass. Narcissus is immediately recalled, and the folly of self-love that the myth suggests may be used to explain Eve's accessibility to Satan and to provide another contrast between Eve and the Virgin Mary. In *Partheneia Sacra*, Hawkins recognizes that the fountain, "the liquid Glasse or Mirrour" (p. 210), is associated with self-love. When applied to the Virgin, however, the fountain becomes a bountiful supply of grace that flows endlessly through her to the souls of the sanctified, which are likened to enclosed gardens (pp. 215–19). The Virgin is the "*Mirrour of puritie*" (p. 16), and "ful of love to God and her Neighbour" (p. 215). Eve, on the other hand, "pin'd with vain desire" (IV, 466) when she saw her image reflected from the water. Robertson comments that the well of Narcissus is transformed into "the mirror which medieval artists showed in the hand of *luxuria*, the mirror of Oiseuse, a mirror abused in a wide variety of ways, to the delight of medieval illustrators."[33] *Luxuria*, Oiseuse, or Idleness was "an invitation to the devil" and led "to a desire for fleshly delight" (p. 92). In Guillaume's *Roman*, she is the portress at the gate through which the lover, Aimant, enters the garden. In illuminated manuscripts of the *Roman*, she is depicted with a mirror and is preoccupied with her own image. Although Eve left Adam in order to work more assiduously in the garden, she converses with the serpent, is diverted from her work, and becomes idle. Like Oiseuse, who opens the gate while she is unduly preoccupied with herself, Eve does not maintain the "strictest watch" (IX, 363) necessary to ward off temptation; consequently, Satan breaches the *hortus conclusus* of her "heart" (IX, 550, 733–34) and corrupts the *hortus mentis* with evil temptation. Like Narcissus, who was transformed into a flower that perished, Eve is the flower cropped by Satan.

Allegorized interpretation of the myth of Narcissus explains Eve's downfall. George Sandys comments that those who are *"puft up with uncessant flattery, and strangly intoxicated with selfe admiration . . . contract such a wounderfull sloth, as stupifies their sences, and deprives them of all their vigour and alacrity."*[34] Sandys also relates the myth of Narcissus to the experience of the fallen angels: *"But a fearfull example we have of the danger of selfe-love in the fall of the Angells; who intermitting the beatificall vision, by reflecting upon themselves, and admiration of their owne excellency, forgot their dependance upon their creator"* (p. 106). Satan's temptation of Eve is successful because she becomes vainly preoccupied during her idleness with the lofty image of herself that he continues to describe. Under the influence of Satan, Eve enacts the manner of his fall, which involves the sins of pride and concupiscence. As he tempts Eve, Satan again indulges in pride and concupiscence and thus reenacts his own fall. The biblical text that interrelates pride and concupiscence is James i, 14–15, which Milton quotes in *De Doctrina Christiana* (CM, XV, 192–93) while explaining the nature of sin: "Every man is tempted, when he is drawn away by his own lust, and enticed"; and "when lust hath conceived, it bringeth forth sin; and sin, when it is finished, bringeth forth death." Lust is usually interpreted to mean pride and concupiscence, both of which are manifested in Satan's relationship with Sin. When God the Father "proclaim'd / *Messiah* King anointed," Satan "could not bear / Through pride that sight, and thought himself impair'd" (V, 663–65). While Satan is "conceiving" both "Deep malice" and "disdain" (V, 666), Sin emerges from "the left side op'ning wide" of his head (II, 755). Hesiod's account of Athene's birth from the head of Zeus (*Theogony*, 925–29) is fused with images from James i, 14–15. Milton is also alluding to Eve's birth from Adam's side and to the opening in Christ's side at the Crucifixion; and as the account of the birth of Sin continues, the myth of Narcissus is likewise suggested. Sin, who is "Likest to [him] in shape and count'nance bright, / . . . shining heav'nly fair" (*PL* II, 756–57), is a reflection of Satan's exalted image of himself. She comments that Satan saw in her his own "perfect image" and "Becam'st enamor'd" (II, 764–65). He manifests this perversion of self-love by desiring and copulating with his "perfect image," and ravenous Death is born from Sin. In Book IX of *Paradise Lost*, Satan seems to view Eve, like Sin, as a reflection of his own image. Her "Heav'nly form / Angelic" (IX, 457–58) reminds him of his former self, and she is "divinely fair, fit Love for Gods" (IX, 489), with whom he identifies himself. Possessing her is an act of pride, but also an act of concupiscence. With Sin, who is described as his daughter and paramour, Satan committed incest; with Eve his relationship is described as adulterous, for he violates the conjugal union between Adam and Eve. Satan's concupiscence was aroused when he witnessed the physical intimacy between Adam and Eve. As they embraced and kissed, "aside the Devil turn'd / For envy, yet with jealous leer malign / Ey'd them askance" (IV, 502–04). When he views Eve naked in the garden, "Such Pleasure took the Serpent to behold" (IX, 455). Eve alone, for whom it would have been "Safest and seemliest by her Husband" to stay, is now "opportune to all attempts" (IX, 481).

Commentary on Scripture and on the Old Testament Apocrypha often highlights the concupiscence in Satan's relationship with Eve. According to some rabbis, a passage (XXI. vi) in the Secrets of the Book of Enoch (ca. 30 B.C.–A.D. 70) describes Satan's sexual encounter with Eve: Satan "conceived thought against Adam, in such form he entered and seduced Eva, but did not touch Adam."[35] The ninth-century *Pirkê de Rabbi Eliezer* develops an explicitly sexual interpretation of Genesis iii, 3, which prohibits taking the "fruit of the tree in the midst of the garden." The prohibition is interpreted as a command against illicit sexual relationships. The "midst of the garden" is the "middle of the woman," and the tree is likened to a phallus implanted in the garden: "Just as with this garden whatever is sown therein, it produces and brings forth, so with this woman, what seed she receives, she conceives and bears through sexual intercourse."[36] In *Paradise Lost* the middle of Eve's body, when viewed by Satan, is likened to a garden: "This Flow'ry Plat, the sweet recess of *Eve*" (IX, 456). The serpent's "words" (IX, 550, 733) entering Eve's heart serve as a demonic opposite to the action of the Logos inseminating the heart. Eve alongside the tree of knowledge of good and evil is the illustration accompanying Quarles' interpretation of James i, 14; and in his verses that interpret James i, 15, Quarles mentions that the Fall has "Destroid . . . unborne seed" and that mankind will die "Like a new-cropt flowre" (p. 9). Eve thus enacts the experience of

Sin, who gave birth to Death, for her own sinful relationship with Satan has "Destroid . . . unborne seed" (to use Quarles' phrase) in her "fruitful Womb" that was to "fill the World more numerous with thy Sons / Than with these various fruits the Trees of God" (V, 388–90).[37] In her ravenous consumption of the fruits of the Tree of Knowledge, Eve is also likened to Death. Because of original sin, she and Adam impart death to posterity; and in engorging herself with the fruits of the tree, Eve is figuratively devouring her own offspring. In the "Arbre de Vie" depicted in l'Hortus Deliciarum, the human heads of the offspring of Adam and Eve appear with the fruits in the boughs of a tree. In the illustration accompanying his interpretation of James i, 15, Quarles depicts a womblike earth through which the heads of various animals are emerging (p. 8). Like Milton's Death, these animals are predatory. Before the Fall the earth, like Eve, possessed a "chast and pregnant wombe" (p. 10). After the Fall the earth, which has "become / A base adultress" (p. 10), enacts Eve's experience of giving birth to death.

Iconography of the tree of knowledge of good and evil continues to illustrate how pride and concupiscence characterize the relationship between Satan and Eve and how Eve's sins are contrasted with Mary's virtues. Before the Fall many of the epithets applied to Eve suggest her resemblance to the Virgin Mary. Raphael's salutation (V, 388) is nearly identical with Gabriel's address to Mary at the Annunciation. The narrator's description of Eve's "Virgin Majesty" (IX, 270) and Adam's assertion that she is "Daughter of God and Man . . . from sin and blame entire" (IX, 291–92) are typically applied to Mary. As he is tempting Eve, Satan employs similar epithets of royalty: "sovran Mistress" (IX, 532), "Heav'n of mildness" (IX, 534), "thy Celestial Beauty" (IX, 540), "Goddess" (IX, 547), "Empress" (IX, 568). These appellations are traditionally applied to the Virgin in litanies, books of hours, emblem books, and hymns. In fact, the ironic similarity between Eve and the Virgin Mary may be extended throughout Milton's description of Eve's countenance, her manner of speech, her gait, and her illusory ascent heavenward. Eve's experience with Satan becomes a virtual parody of the Virgin's life of humility, her Assumption into heaven, and her coronation. When applied to the Virgin, epithets of royalty paradoxically suggest her modesty and humility. When applied to Eve, they result in pride and self-love. In the Biblia Pauperum

printed in Bamberg in 1471, the serpent and Eve are on opposite
sides of the tree of knowledge of good and evil. The serpent, which
has Eve's face and long-flowing hair, is wearing a crown. This appearance of royalty is a visual counterpart to the exalted image of
Eve in *Paradise Lost* that Satan's flattery is developing. By adopting
Eve's countenance and elevating her to royal status, Satan in the *Biblia
Pauperum*, like Milton's Satan, is appealing to Eve's narcissism, because
she becomes vainly preoccupied with this image of herself that he
projects.

There are countless other representations of the serpent with a
woman's head and with a woman's torso.[38] In Jean, Duke of Berry's
*Très Riches Heures* (plate 20), Eve is accepting an apple from the
serpent entwined in the branches of the forbidden tree. The head
and torso of the serpent are identical to Eve's, including the long-
flowing golden hair. When Eve reaches up to accept the apple from
her mirror image high in the tree, she enacts the fall of Narcissus,
who attempted to grasp his reflected image. Satan's appearance as
woman and serpent combined indicates resemblance to Sin. At the
birth of Death, her offspring by Satan, Sin became serpentine from
the waist downward (II, 650-53, 782-85). After Eve has fallen to Satan,
Adam describes her as if she had been transmogrified: "thou Serpent,
that name best / Befits thee with him leagu'd" (X, 867-68).

A classical analogue for Sin's actual transformation and for Eve's
degradation is the myth of Scylla, which Sandys interprets in *Ovid's
Metamorphosis. Englished, Mythologiz'd, and Represented in Figures*:
Scylla "*represents a Virgin; who as long as chast in thought, and in
body unspotted, appeares of an excellent beauty, attracting all eyes
upon her, and wounding the Gods themselves with affection.*" On
the other hand, "*having rendred her maiden honour to bee deflowred
by bewitching pleasure, she is transformed to an horrid monster*" (p.
475). While consorting with Satan, Eve is described as having violated
her conjugal chastity. The cupidity aroused in her and in Satan is
described in iconography. In an ancient Egyptian line drawing an
upright serpent (on legs) is offering an apple to a woman opposite
him.[39] The genitals of the male are evident. Portrayals of the serpent
with the head and torso of a man include, for example, a painting
by the German artist Georg Penz (1500-1550) and a fresco (ca. 1560-
1565) by Girolamo Siciolante da Sermoneta in the church of Santa

Maria della Pace in Rome. In the painting by Penz the serpent has "the upper torso, arms, and bearded and horned head of a satyr."[40] In the fresco he is a man from head to thighs, which are joined into a serpent's tail encircling the tree. In the Huntington Kitto Bible (1850) Satan is depicted with the torso of a man and the head of a satyr (figure 6). Adam and Eve appear together at the base of the tree of knowledge. In the background appear two scenes: the creation of Eve from Adam's side and Cain's killing of Abel. According to some rabbinical commentary, Cain was Eve's son by the tempter, whereas Abel was her son by Adam. In giving birth to Cain, Eve thus gives birth to death, and the procreative function of her marriage to Adam is nullified by her relationship with Satan at the Fall.

Often the temptation of Eve is visually juxtaposed with the Annunciation because Mary's virginal conception of Christ is contrasted with Eve's adultery.[41] In addition, the Virgin's humility and purity are contrasted with Eve's pride and concupiscence. In iconography of the Annunciation, the Virgin is often glancing downward or away from Gabriel to indicate her unworthiness to be the mother of God. Her arms are sometimes crossed with the palms of her hands against her breast, or her arms are clasped in prayer, or an arm is extended outward in a gesture of modesty and humility. At the temptation Eve is often depicted with an outstretched arm and nearly lunging body because her "utmost reach" (IX, 591) is necessary in order to take the apple from the tree or to accept it from Satan. This attempt to elevate herself physically suggests ascent through pride and contrasts with the contemplative repose of the Virgin. Iconography of the Annunciation usually shows an enclosed garden with a locked gate or door, and in *Partheneia Sacra* this image of the *porta clausa* is contrasted with the accessibility of Eden to Satan's approach: "Wheras this Garden (our Ladie) was a Garden shut-up indeed from the beginning, and divinely preserved *Immaculate,* from Her first Conception, adorned with al those sorts of flowers and plants of Graces, Vertues, and Perfections I mentioned above; wherto no Serpent, nor Original sinne, much lesse Actual, could have acces, but was alwayes even from her first beginning, a most delicious Paradice and Garden *shut-up* from al invasions of Enemies" (pp. 12–13). The garden metaphor, which is applied to Eve's womb in *Paradise Lost,* is also applied to the Virgin's womb in iconography of the Annunciation. Gabriel's salutation announces

FIGURE 6. The Huntington Kitto Bible (London, 1850), II, Plate 299. HEH
49000. Reproduced by permission of the Huntington Library.

that Mary is "full of grace" and "blessed is the fruit" of her womb. Mary acknowledges conception when she replies "Be it done unto me according to thy Word." The action of the Word is an infusion of grace, a divine insemination that is sometimes visualized as the descent of beams of light onto the head, breast, or womb of Mary (figure 7). Within the visual context of the enclosed garden, the seed implanted in the virginal womb will become the "fruit" of Christ. In Quarles' *Emblemes*, Christ is the apple consumed Eucharistically in order to preserve or to restore life (figure 4). Garden imagery, therefore, is as closely associated with Mary as it is with Eve. Gabriel, for example, is sometimes presenting Mary with a lily, which signifies her own Immaculate Conception, the virginal conception of Christ, and the undefiled purity of Mary's life. In *Très Riches Heures* (plate 21), Gabriel is presenting three lilies, a symbol probably of Mary's consummated marriage with the Persons of the Trinity. This chaste marriage contrasts with Eve's relationship with the infernal trinity of Satan, Sin, and Death and with Adam after the Fall. At that time she and Adam consummate a lustful relationship near "a shady bank, / Thick overhead with verdant roof imbowr'd" (IX, 1037–38). The procreative act that was formerly performed as an act of worship in the templelike environment of their nuptial bower has become the means by which Adam and Eve will transmit sin and death to their offspring. A templelike atmosphere and sacred fertility characterize much of the iconography of the Annunciation. In *Très Riches Heures* (plate 21), the Annunciation takes place in a chapel; in Roger van der Weyden's *The Annunciation* Gabriel is wearing liturgical vestments; and in some representations Gabriel visits Mary in her bedchamber. In books of hours, missals, breviaries, and lectionaries, the miniatures of the Annunciation show foliage, trees, and flowers.

A graphic image of the sacred fertility associated with Mary is the tree of Jesse, which is a visualization of Isaiah's prophecy (xi, 1): "And there shall come forth a rod out of the stem of Jesse, and a Branch shall grow out of his roots."[42] The tree emerges from the sleeping Jesse, who is recumbent on the ground (figure 7). In the boughs of the tree are the heads of patriarchs and prophets described as Christ's ancestors in the Gospels. At the top of the tree are the Virgin and Christ. The recumbent Jesse resembles the sleeping Adam, from whom Eve emerged. As described in iconography and in *Paradise*

FIGURE 7. Book of Hours (Paris, 1511), C3ᵛ–C4ʳ. HEH 108798. Reproduced by permission of the Huntington Library.

*Lost*, the union and intergrafting of Adam and Eve were to have resulted in an "Arbre de Vie." After the Fall, sacred fertility becomes associated with the Virgin and Christ. In iconography of the tree of Jesse, the Virgin is variously described as the branch (*virga* in Latin), the stem, or the flower; Christ is either "bon fruit" or "fleur de fleurs."[43] Blossom and fruit sometimes appear together in depictions of the tree of Jesse.[44] Thus the Virgin, who is the radiant flower, contrasts with Eve, the flower cropped by Satan; and Christ, the fruit giving eternal life, contrasts with the forbidden fruit, the source of death. Didron observes that a fourteenth-century manuscript of the *Speculum Humanae Salvationis* depicts the tree of Jesse as a very large rosebush, at the top of which is a shining rose in which a dove is nesting.[45] This image of divine insemination and sacred fertility contrasts with the image of the cropped rose that describes Eve. In addition, the tree of Jesse suggests royalty because it is depicting Christ's lineage. In such representations the Virgin is wearing a crown and holding a scepter, and her appearance contrasts with the image of royalty that Satan depicts for Eve in *Paradise Lost*.[46] To describe the process of spiritualization and ascent heavenward, Raphael uses the image of the growing tree and flower, and his explanation accords with the central meaning of iconography of the tree of Jesse:

> So from the root
> Springs lighter the green stalk, from thence the leaves
> More aery, last the bright consummate flow'r
> Spirits odorous breathes.
>                                          (V, 479–82)

Visual interpretation of the virtues and vices developed concurrently with iconography of the tree of Jesse. Gregory the Great's sixth-century *Moralia*, an elaborate exposition of virtues and vices, was ingeniously illuminated by medieval miniaturists. In one manuscript of the mid-thirteenth century, a woman who is identified as Humility appears at the base of the tree of virtues.[47] At the top of the tree is Christ, who is identified as the "new Adam" (*Novus Adam*); and the stem of the tree between him and the woman is labeled *caritas*. Branches on both sides of the tree are labeled as the cardinal virtues, and heart-shaped leaves on the branches bear the names of other virtues. On the other hand, a fourteenth-century manuscript known as the *Speculum Virginum* (the maidens' mirror) depicts a tree with its roots in the Scarlet Woman, the whore of Babylon (Revelation xvii, 5), who is crowned and who is holding a golden cup.[48] Two serpents are entwined in the trunk, and two dragons sit in the branches. The heart-shaped leaves on the branches are inscribed with the names of vices. At the top of the tree is the "old Adam" (*Vetus Adam*). The concept of the two Adams and the two trees becomes very explicit in *Paradise Lost*. The epic narrator mentions Satan's plan "to confound the race / Of mankind in one root" (II, 382–83), and God the Father, while addressing the Son, comments that "As in [Adam] perish all men, so in thee / As from a second root shall be restor'd" (III, 287–88). The opposition between the Scarlet Woman and Lady Humility may also be related to the iconographic perspective in *Paradise Lost*. The Scarlet Woman is the demonic opposite of the traditional image of *Mater Ecclesia*, who is crowned and who holds a golden cup while she stands at the foot of the cross. In iconography of the Tree of Virtues, Lady Humility may be interpreted as the Virgin Mary, who also appears together with Christ in iconography of the tree of Jesse. In iconography of the Crucifixion, Mary appears at the foot of the cross, which is sometimes depicted, like the tree of virtues, with branches and heart-shaped leaves. Often the compliant boughs laden with fruit extend down to the woman below (whether it be Mary, *Mater Ecclesia*, or the personification of the sanctified soul).[49] A kiss, embrace, and conjugal union are suggested. Then, too, Christ crucified is sometimes depicted with wings, as he is, for instance, in Quarles' interpretation of Canticles ii, 3 (figure 4) and of Canticles iii, 1 (figure 5). The church fathers often liken the transverse beam of the cross to wings, and the metaphor of ascent is traditionally applied to the Crucifixion, Resurrection, and Ascension. Of course, Adam and Eve experienced an illusory ascent when they had eaten the forbidden fruit: they "fancy that they feel / Divinity within them breeding wings" (IX, 1009–10). But the true ascent heavenward is described by God the Father, who asserts that the Son's "Humiliation shall exalt" (III, 313). *Imitatio Christi* is the humility and suffering exemplified, for example, by Mary as she witnesses the death of Christ. As *Mater Dolorosa* she undergoes a symbolic death, for she is sometimes depicted with her heart pierced by the sword or lance that extends down and into her from the side of Christ. Christ's sighs and groans, often described as music in seventeenth-century devotional poetry, enter her heart, in contrast to the lyrical praise and flattery that Satan uses to

gain access to Eve's heart: "his Proem tun'd, / Into the Heart of *Eve*"
(IX, 549–50).[50]

The "glorious trial of exceeding Love" (IX, 961), which Adam
and Eve had mistakenly thought to be mutual disobedience of God,
appropriately describes the sacrifice of the Son and the mutual willingness of Adam and Eve to undergo the penitential experience. Much
as Adam cooperated with God in the creation of Eve, Adam and
Eve now participate with the Son in their re-creation. Images of implan-
tation, cultivation, and growth describe their spiritual renovation. Eve
falls before Adam as a "suppliant" (X, 917) to seek forgiveness. As
she reaches to "clasp" him (X, 918), Eve acknowledges that Adam
is her "only strength and stay" (X, 921). She is then "uprais'd" (X,
946) by Adam. Her submissive posture signifies humility toward Adam;
and "clasp," "strength and stay," and "uprais'd" recall the interrelation
of the vine and the elm, Eve's creation from Adam, and her marriage
to him. Adam proposes that they both seek God's forgiveness; and
"with tears / Watering the ground," with "sighs" coming "from hearts
contrite," and with "humiliation meek" (X, 1101–05), they elicit mercy
and prevenient grace from God. The Son recognizes the effects of
God's "implanted Grace in Man" and of the "seed / Sown with contrition
in [man's] heart" (XI, 23–27). The ingrafting of the Son to mankind
is mentioned (XI, 35), and God announces his intention to "intermix
/ My Cov'nant in the woman's seed renew'd" (XI, 115–16). When
Adam learns that God will be forgiving, he salutes Eve as the "Mother
of all Mankind" (XI, 159). The process of Redemption is thus described
by images of re-creation, remarriage, and procreation in order to
suggest a reunion between Adam and Eve and between God and
mankind. An appropriate iconographic context in which to interpret
these images includes scenes of the Crucifixion in which the cross
imagized as a tree of life is being cultivated by Adam and Eve. Christ
is outstretched on the boughs of the tree, and Adam sometimes has
a gardening tool that indicates "the labour that followed his expulsion
from Paradise." He and Eve are often depicted with nimbuses "showing
that they have been redeemed."[51] While explaining repentance and
Redemption in *De Doctrina Christiana*, Milton quotes Psalm cxxvi,
5: "they that sow in tears shall reap in joy" (CM, XV, 390–91). The
tree of life that Adam and Eve are cultivating is the image of the
cross within the enclosed garden of the heart. "Taught" by the "ex-

ample" (*PL*, XII, 572) of the Son, who is to become the Savior incarnate, Adam and Eve have learned the experience of humility, the consummate act of self-diminution.

Duquesne University

## NOTES

I am grateful to the Henry E. Huntington Library and Art Gallery, San Marino, California, for a research grant that enabled me to complete this essay.

1. Milton's poetry is quoted from *John Milton: Complete Poems and Major Prose*, ed. Merritt Y. Hughes (New York, 1957).

2. *Christ's Triumph Over and After Death*, in *Giles and Phineas Fletcher: Poetical Works*, ed. Frederick S. Boas (Cambridge, Eng., 1908), p. 61, stanza 13.

3. Donne's poetry is quoted from *The Poems of John Donne*, ed. Herbert J. C. Grierson (Oxford, 1912). I have modernized obsolete characters.

4. Barbara K. Lewalski, "Innocence and Experience in Milton's Eden," in *New Essays on Paradise Lost*, ed. Thomas Kranidas (Berkeley and Los Angeles, 1969), p. 89. Lewalski cites St. Augustine's *De Genesi ad Litteram*, VIII. 8-10, in *Patrologia Latina*, vol. XXXIV, cols. 379–82.

5. *The Book of Vices and Virtues: A Fourteenth Century English Translation of the Somme le Roi*, ed. W. Nelson Francis (London, 1942) p. 93. I have modernized obsolete characters.

6. See Stanley Stewart, *The Enclosed Garden: The Tradition and the Image in Seventeenth-Century Poetry* (Madison, Wis., 1969), p. 109 and passim, for relevant excerpts from *The Life of the Holy Mother Teresa of Jesus* and from St. John's *Spiritual Canticle*.

7. *The Hours of Catherine of Cleves*, ed. John Plummer (New York, n.d.), plate 88 and commentary. Hereafter plate numbers will be cited in parentheses. This book reproduces illustrations from two manuscripts: the one belongs to the Guennol Collection housed in the Pierpont Morgan Library, New York City, and the other is owned by the Pierpont Morgan Library. The manuscripts, which were prepared about 1440 for Catherine of Cleves, Duchess of Guelders, are masterpieces of Dutch miniature painting.

8. *The Visconti Hours*, ed. Millard Meiss and Edith W. Kirsch (New York, 1972), no pagination (see plate entitled "Creation of Eve"). This book reproduces illustrations from the manuscript in the National Library of Florence. The book of hours was commissioned by Giangaleazzo Visconti, Duke of Milan, toward the end of the fourteenth century; it was completed during the regime of his son, Filippo Maria, who became duke in 1412.

9. All the illustrations in the various bibles are reproduced in James Strachan, *Early Bible Illustrations* (Cambridge, Eng., 1957).

10. Herbert's "The Sacrifice," line 203. Herbert's poetry is quoted from *The Works of George Herbert*, ed. F. E. Hutchinson (Oxford, 1941).

11. I am quoting the translation that appears in Adolphe Napoleon Didron, *Christian Iconography*, trans. E. J. Millington (1886; reprint ed., New York, 1965), vol. II, p. 420.

12. In *The Works of John Milton*, ed. F. A. Patterson, et al. (New York, 1931–38), vol. XV, pp. 120–21; hereafter cited as CM.

13. Gérard Cames, *Allégories et Symboles dans l'Hortus Deliciarum* (Leiden, 1971), p. 13 and plate II. *L'Hortus Deliciarum* was prepared, in part, under the supervision of the Abbess Herrade de Landsberg, who resided at the convent of Saint Odile in Alsace. The manuscript was destroyed by fire in 1870, but many of its illustrations and some of its text had fortunately been copied.

14. Henry Ainsworth, *Annotations Upon the first book of Moses, called Genesis* (London, 1616), sig. B2ᵛ. I have modernized obsolete characters.

15. Ibid., sig C2ʳ. Genesis ii, 24, which describes the marriage of Adam and Eve, is often translated as follows: man "shal cleave to his wife," which is the translation used by Ainsworth, sig. B2ᵛ. Ainsworth notes that *cleave*, like *adhere*, connotes glutinous fusion: "for *shal cleav*, the Greek sayth *shalbe glewed*" (sig. C2ʳ).

16. ("A 'Tree of Life' whose fruits are astonishing children's heads"). Cames, *Allégories et Symboles*, p. 13. Plate II is entitled "Création d'Ève. Adam dort sous un arbre à têtes humaines" ("The Creation of Eve. Adam sleeps beneath a tree of human heads").

17. Emile Mâle, *The Gothic Image: Religious Art in France of the Thirteenth Century*, trans. from the 3rd ed. by Dora Nussey (1913; reprint ed., New York, 1958), pp. 186–87. The legends of the cross are a complex tradition not directly related to my purpose here. I do intend, however, to examine these legends and explain their relevance to an interpretation of *Paradise Lost* in an essay tentatively entitled "Rod, Ladder, and Tree: Milton and the Metamorphosis of an Image."

18. Ibid., p. 187, n. 1.

19. See *Très Riches Heures of Jean, Duke of Berry* (New York, 1969), plate 114. Hereafter plate numbers will be cited in parentheses. This book reproduces illustrations from the manuscript belonging to the Musée Condé, Chantilly, France. Jean, Duke of Berry (1340–1416), commissioned the Limbourg brothers to illuminate the manuscript with miniatures. For a reproduction of the illumination in the Dessau Psalter, see Edith Rothe, *Mediaeval Book Illumination in Europe* (New York, 1968), plate 81.

20. *Iconographie de l'Art Chrétien* (Paris, 1957), vol. II, pt. 2, pp. 490–91.

21. *Patrologia Latina*, vol. XXXIX, cols. 1984–85, as quoted and translated by C. G. Jung, *Mysterium Coniunctionis* (New York, 1963), pp. 396–97.

22. See the reproduction of this window at Bourges in Mâle, *Gothic Image*, p. 189; see the reproduction of this illumination from *l'Hortus Deliciarum* in Cames, *Allégories et Symboles*, plate XXVI.

23. Mâle, *Gothic Image*, p. 188, n. 2.

24. Milton's description of the Invisible Church appears in *De Doctrina Christiana*, CM, XVI, 56–65; his description of the Visible Church appears ibid., pp. 218–49.

25. For complete documentation see Stewart, *Enclosed Garden*, esp. chaps. 1 and 2.

26. Francis Quarles, *Emblemes* (London, 1635), p. 236. I have modernized obsolete characters.

27. This illustration and the illustration of the lover crucified in the apple tree appear also in Herman Hugo's *Pia Desideria* (1624), to which Quarles is greatly indebted. Quarles' *Emblemes* is representative of the tradition of Continental and British religio-erotic emblem books. For a discussion of this tradition, see Mario Praz, *Studies in*

*Seventeenth-Century Imagery* (London, 1939), chap. 3 ("Profane and Sacred Love");
see also Rosemary Freeman, *English Emblem Books* (London, 1948); and Jean Seznec,
*The Survival of the Pagan Gods*, trans. Barbara Sessions (1953; reprint ed., New York,
1961), esp. pp. 103–05.

28. Henry Hawkins, *Partheneia Sacra* (Rouen, 1633), p. 4.

29. For a discussion of the *locus amoenus* from classical antiquity through the
Renaissance, see A. Bartlett Giamatti, *The Earthly Paradise and the Renaissance Epic*
(Princeton, 1966).

30. D. W. Robertson, Jr., *A Preface to Chaucer: Studies in Medieval Perspectives*
(Princeton, 1962), pp. 95–96, n. 82.

31. *Partheneia Sacra*, p. 11.

32. For a reproduction of this painting, see Robert Hughes, *Heaven and Hell
in Western Art* (London, 1968), p. 25.

33. Robertson, *Preface to Chaucer*, p. 95 and figs. 15–16. Fourteenth- and fifteenth-
century manuscripts of the *Roman de la Rose* have many illuminations of the well
of Narcissus and of the mirror of Oiseuse. See John V. Fleming, *The Roman de la
Rose: A Study in Allegory and Iconography* (Princeton, 1969), figs. 3, 5, 8, 9, 17, 23–26.
See also Seznec, *Survival of the Pagan Gods*, p. 107.

34. *Ovid's Metamorphosis. Englished, Mythologiz'd, and Represented in Figures*
(Oxford, 1632), p. 106. I have modernized obsolete characters.

35. *The Apocrypha and Pseudepigrapha of the Old Testament*, ed. R. H. Charles
(Oxford, 1913), vol. II, p. 451.

36. *Pirkê de Rabbi Eliezer*, trans. Gerald Friedlander (London, 1916), p. 150. For
rabbinical commentary on the sexual encounter between Eve and the tempter, see
J. M. Evans, *Paradise Lost and the Genesis Tradition* (Oxford, 1968), pp. 36–55. Evans
includes commentary that identifies Cain as Eve's child by the tempter. For various
Christian interpretations of a sexual encounter, see Evans, pp. 59–104. Most Christian
and rabbinical commentators use *sexual metaphor* to describe the relationship between
Eve and the tempter; they do not assert that there was an actual sexual encounter.
Interestingly, Sir Thomas Browne in *Pseudodoxia Epidemica* (1646), after the manner
of the *Pirkê de Rabbi Eliezer*, speculates "whether the tree in the midst of the garden,
were not that part in the centre of the body, on which was afterward the appointment
of circumcision in males" (*The Prose of Sir Thomas Browne*, ed. Norman Endicott
[New York, 1968], p. 105).

37. Among Christian commentators Origen developed the theory of the *inquina-
mentum*, or the physical pollution of Eve, which is analogous to Quarles' interpretation
and to Milton's conception of Eve's relationship with the serpent: "The serpent had
beguiled Eve and by spreading the poison of sin in her with his inbreathed encourage-
ment had infected the whole of her posterity with the contagion of the Fall" (*The
Song of Songs: Commentary and Homilies*, trans. R. P. Lawson [Westminster, Md.
1957], p. 117).

38. See the illustrations and commentary, for example, in Hughes, *Heaven and
Hell*, pp. 78–85; J. B. Trapp, "The Iconography of the Fall of Man," in *Approaches
to Paradise Lost*, ed. C. A. Patrides (London, 1968), pp. 223–65; J. K. Bonnell, "The
Serpent with a Human Head in Art and in Mystery Play," *American Journal of Archae-
ology*, XXI (1917), 244–91; and Henry Ansgar Kelly, "The Metamorphoses of the Eden
Serpent During the Middle Ages and Renaissance," in *Viator: Medieval and Renaissance
Studies*, vol. II (1971), 301–28. See also John M. Steadman, "'Sin' and the Serpent

of Genesis 3: *Paradise Lost*, II, 650–653," *MP*, LIV (1957), 217–20; and John M. Patrick, *Milton's Conception of Sin as Developed in Paradise Lost* (Logan, Utah, 1960), esp. pp. 32–51.

39. Reproduced in Hughes, *Heaven and Hell*, p. 82. For other examples of the serpent with a man's head or torso, see the references in n. 38.

40. Kelly, "Metamorphoses of the Eden Serpent," p. 325. Kelly reproduces both the painting and the fresco.

41. For examples of iconography of the Annunciation, see Stewart, *Enclosed Garden*, figs. 5, 17, 25; Hughes, *Heaven and Hell*, pp. 116, 145; Cames, *Allégories et Symboles*, plate XXVIII; *The Hours of Catherine of Cleves*, plate 10; Rothe, *Mediaeval Book Illumination*, plate 127; Mâle, *Gothic Image*, pp. 242–43; *The Visconti Hours*, plate entitled "Annunciation"; André Grabar, *Christian Iconography: A Study of Its Origins* (Princeton, 1968), figs. 247, 249, 306; Erwin Panofsky, *Early Netherlandish Painting* (Cambridge, Mass., 1953), vol. II, passim; Gertrud Schiller, *Iconography of Christian Art*, trans. Janet Seligman (Greenwich, Conn., 1971–72), vol. I, pp. 33–52 and figs. 66–129; Réau, *Iconographie de l'Art Chrétien*, vol. II, pt. II, pp. 174–94.

42. For a discussion of the tree of Jesse and examples of its iconography, including Christ crucified in the tree of Jesse, see Stewart, *Enclosed Garden*, pp. 80–86 and figs. 25–26; Mâle, *Gothic Image*, pp. 165–70; Rothe, *Mediaeval Book Illumination*, plate 53; Schiller, *Iconography of Christian Art*, vol. I, pp. 15–22 and figs. 22–45; Réau, *Iconographie de l'Art Chrétien*, vol. II, pt. II, pp. 129–51; Cames, *Allégories et Symboles*, plates XVIII and XIX; Jonathan Goldberg, "*Virga Iesse*: Analogy, Typology, and Anagogy in a Miltonic Simile," *Milton Studies*, V, ed. James D. Simmonds (Pittsburgh, 1973), pp. 177–90.

43. Cames, *Allégories et Symboles*, p. 39.

44. "Towards the close of the Middle Ages the Virgin appeared in the calyx of a flower at the summit of the tree, carrying the infant Jesus in her arms" (Mâle, *Gothic Image*, p. 166, n. 1).

45. Didron, *Christian Iconography*, vol. I, p. 474 and note.

46. Mâle, *Gothic Image*, pp. 167–68.

47. See Rothe, *Mediaeval Book Illumination*, plate 39.

48. Ibid., plate 70. For a discussion of the tree of the old Adam contrasted with the tree of the new Adam, see Mâle, *Gothic Image*, pp. 106–08. For a discussion of the tree of virtues and the tree of vices, see Adolf Katzenellenbogen, *Allegories of the Virtues and Vices in Mediaeval Art* (1939; reprint ed., New York, 1964), pp. 57–74.

49. For discussion of the branch-cross, tree-cross, and flowering cross, see Schiller, *Iconography of Christian Art*, vol. II, pp. 133–36; Réau, *Iconographie de l'Art Chrétien*, vol. II, pt. II, pp. 483–85.

50. F. P. Pickering asserts "that music-making is perhaps a dominant idea among all the principal similes, metaphors and symbols of the Crucifixion" (*Literature and Art in the Middle Ages* [New York, 1970], p. 272). Pickering explains how the church fathers used the metaphor of music to describe the Crucifixion (pp. 285–312), and Rosemond Tuve explains that the metaphor of music was a commonplace in seventeenth-century devotional poetry that celebrated the Crucifixion (*A Reading of George Herbert* [Chicago, 1952], pp. 144–48). In Herbert's "Easter," for example, "[Christ's] stretched sinews taught all strings, what key / Is best to celebrate this most high day" (11–12). This image of the lyre, lute, or harp is also associated with iconography of the tree of Jesse, which is often said to depict the house or stock of David, from which Christ derived his ancestry (see Stewart, *Enclosed Garden*, pp. 80–86). Figure 26 in *The*

*Enclosed Garden* shows David playing a harp in the tree of Jesse, and in *The Hours of Catherine of Cleves* (plate 90), David is seated under the tree of Jesse while playing the harp. In Book XII of *Paradise Lost*, the angel Michael comments that "of the Royal Stock / Of *David* (so I name this King) shall rise / A Son, the Woman's Seed to thee foretold" (325-27).

51. Schiller, *Iconography of Christian Art*, vol. II, p. 132.

## DATE DUE